Manufacturing Engineering

AUTHOR

Dr. Santosh Kumar

Professor,

Department of Mechanical Engineering,

IIT (BHU) Varanasi, Varanasi, Uttar Pradesh

REVIEWER

Dr. Benu Madhab Gedam

Associate Professor,

Department of WILP (Work Integrated Learning Programme)

Birla Institute of Technology and Science, Pilani, Rajasthan

KHANNA BOOK PUBLISHING CO. (P) Ltd.

4C/4344, Ansari Road, Darya Ganj, New Delhi, India

All India Council for Technical Education

Nelson Mandela Marg, Vasant Kunj, New Delhi, India

Dear Readers,

To prevent the piracy, this book is secured with HIGH SECURITY HOLOGRAM on the front title cover. In case you don't find the hologram on the front cover title, please write us to at contact@khannabooks.com or whatsapp us at +91-99109 09320 and avail special gift voucher for yourself.

Specimen of Hologram on front Cover title:

Moreover, there is a SPECIAL DISCOUNT COUPON for you with EVERY HOLOGRAM.

How to avail this SPECIAL DISCOUNT:

Step 1: Scratch the hologram
Step 2: Under the scratch area, your "coupon code" is available
Step 3: Logon to www.khannabooks.com
Step 4: Use your "coupon code" in the shopping cart and get your copy at a special discount
Step 5: Enjoy your reading!

ISBN: 9789355388148
CODE: DIP445EN

Manufacturing Engineering
by Dr. Santosh Kumar

First Edition: 2025

Originally Published by:
All India Council for Technical Education, Ministry of Education, GOI

Exclusively Published & Distributed by:
Khanna Book Publishing Co. (P) Ltd.
4C/4344, Ansari Road, Daryaganj,
New Delhi (INDIA)

Visit us at: **www.khannabooks.com**
Write us at: **contact@khannabooks.com**

To view complete list of books, Please scan the QR Code:

KPH

Printed in Bharat.

प्रो. टी. जी. सीताराम
अध्यक्ष
Prof. T. G. Sitharam
Chairman

सत्यमेव जयते

आज़ादी का अमृत महोत्सव

अखिल भारतीय तकनीकी शिक्षा परिषद्
(भारत सरकार का एक सांविधिक निकाय)
(शिक्षा मंत्रालय, भारत सरकार)
नेल्सन मंडेला मार्ग, वसंत कुंज, नई दिल्ली-110070
दूरभाष : 011-26131498
ई-मेल : chairman@aicte-india.org

ALL INDIA COUNCIL FOR TECHNICAL EDUCATION
(A STATUTORY BODY OF THE GOVT. OF INDIA)
(Ministry of Education, Govt. of India)
Nelson Mandela Marg, Vasant Kunj, New Delhi-110070
Phone : 011-26131498
E-mail : chairman@aicte-india.org

FOREWORD

Engineers are the backbone of any modern society. They are the ones responsible for the marvels as well as the improved quality of life across the world. Engineers have driven humanity towards greater heights in a more evolved and unprecedented manner.

The All India Council for Technical Education (AICTE), have spared no efforts towards the strengthening of the technical education in the country. AICTE is always committed towards promoting quality Technical Education to make India a modern developed nation emphasizing on the overall welfare of mankind.

An array of initiatives has been taken by AICTE in last decade which have been accelerated now by the National Education Policy (NEP) 2020. The implementation of NEP under the visionary leadership of Hon'ble Prime Minister of India envisages the provision for education in regional languages to all, thereby ensuring that every graduate becomes competent enough and is in a position to contribute towards the national growth and development through innovation & entrepreneurship.

One of the spheres where AICTE had been relentlessly working since past couple of years is providing high quality original technical contents at Under Graduate & Diploma level prepared and translated by eminent educators in various Indian languages to its aspirants. For students pursuing 2nd year of their Engineering education, AICTE has identified 87 books, which shall be translated into 12 Indian languages - Hindi, Tamil, Gujarati, Odia, Bengali, Kannada, Urdu, Punjabi, Telugu, Marathi, Assamese & Malayalam. In addition to the English medium, books in different Indian Languages are going to support the students to understand the concepts in their respective mother tongue.

On behalf of AICTE, I express sincere gratitude to all distinguished authors, reviewers and translators from the renowned institutions of high repute for their admirable contribution in a record span of time.

AICTE is confident that these outcomes based original contents shall help aspirants to master the subject with comprehension and greater ease.

(Prof. T. G. Sitharam)

ACKNOWLEDGEMENT

The authors are grateful to the authorities of AICTE, particularly Prof. T. G. Sitharam, Chairman; Dr. Abhay Jere, Vice-Chairman; Prof. Rajive Kumar, Member-Secretary and Dr Amit Kumar Srivastava, Director, Faculty Development Cell for their planning to publish the books on Manufacturing Engineering. We sincerely acknowledge the valuable contributions of the reviewer of the book **Dr. Benu Madhab Gedam**, Department of Work Integrated Learning Programme, BITS, Pilani. Authors wishes to acknowledge the assistance of Mr. Ashish, Mr. Pankaj Kr. Singh, Mr. Md. Meraz, Mr. Ravi Prakash Singh, Mr. Govind Kr. Verma, and Mr. Sankatha Kr. Tiwari in compiling technical contents and figures of different units.

This book is an outcome of various suggestions of AICTE members, experts and authors who shared their opinion and thought to further develop the engineering education in India. I also acknowledge the contributors by different workers in this field whose published books, review articles, research papers, photographs, footnotes, web pages, references and other valuable material information have been taken at the time of writing the book.

Dr. Santosh Kumar

PREFACE

The book titled "Manufacturing Engineering" is an outcome of the teaching and manufacturing practice experiences in field of manufacturing processes and engineering. The main motive behind writing this book is to expose the basic fundamental of practice part of manufacturing, including basics of metal machining, finishing and forming using various machines like Lathe, drilling, broaching, milling, grinding, polishing and press working etc. and their applications, and to develop understanding on how to use these processes and machines in relation and ways to utilize it for different applications on using metallic and non-metallic parts manufacturing. Keeping this in mind for the purpose of wider coverage as well as to provide essential supplementary information, topics as recommended by AICTE, the effort has been made to make it systematic and orderly manner of units throughout the book. Efforts has also been made to explain the fundamental concepts of the subject using suitable schematic diagrams where ever it is possible.

The content of the manuscript has been prepared considering international standard textbooks, handbooks besides with manufacturing practices and development experience of the author. Additionally, each unit is supported with few sections like questions for self-assessment, and activities for further information, references for further reading etc. Apart from illustrations and examples as required, the book has been enriched with numerous short questions in every unit for proper understanding of the related topics.

The book entitled "Manufacturing Engineering" is largely based on model curriculum of AICTE for second year diploma level students, which is also suitable for under-graduate programs on mechanical, production, manufacturing engineering of other University and Institutions for subjects related to manufacturing engineering. The book comprises five units in following sequence (a) Cutting Fluids & Lubricants and Lathe operations (b) Broaching and drilling Machines (c) Welding processes and milling machines (d) Gear making and press working and (e) Grinding and finishing processes. It is important to note that in all units, the relevant laboratory practicals and videos have also been included.

The present book "Manufacturing Engineering" is meant to provide a thorough grounding on presented topic related to manufacturing engineering which will enable future diploma and graduate engineers understand the basic machining processes using fundamental machines and equipment for various material machining and forming operations and to help how to select the sequence of operations on machines in light of engineering applications. The subject matters are presented in a constructive and smooth manner so that graduate engineers could better understand the work while operating at real shop floor at the very forefront of manufacturing.

I am sure that the book will inspire the students to learn and discuss the ideas behind basic principles of manufacturing engineering and will surely contribute to the development of a practice based foundation of the subject. I would be thankful to all beneficial comments and suggestions which will contribute to the improvement of the future editions of the book. It gives me immense pleasure to forward this book in the hands of the teachers and students. It was indeed a great pleasure for me to work on different aspects of the book for the benefit of student's community.

Dr. Santosh Kumar

OUTCOME BASED EDUCATION

For the implementation of an outcome based education the first requirement is to develop an outcome based curriculum and incorporate an outcome based assessment in the education system. By going through outcome based assessments, evaluators will be able to evaluate whether the students have achieved the outlined standard, specific and measurable outcomes. With the proper incorporation of outcome based education there will be a definite commitment to achieve a minimum standard for all learners without giving up at any level. At the end of the programme running with the aid of outcome based education, a student will be able to arrive at the following outcomes:

Programme Outcomes (POs) are statements that describe what students are expected to know and be able to do upon graduating from the program. These relate to the skills, knowledge, analytical ability attitude and behavior that students acquire through the program. The POs essentially indicate what the students can do from subject-wise knowledge acquired by them during the program. As such, POs define the professional profile of an engineering diploma graduate.

National Board of Accreditation (NBA) has defined the following seven POs for an Engineering diploma graduate:

PO1: Basic and Discipline specific knowledge: Apply knowledge of basic mathematics, science and engineering fundamentals and engineering specialization to solve the engineering problems.

PO2: Problem analysis: Identify and analyses well-defined engineering problems using codified standard methods.

PO3: Design/development of solutions: Design solutions for well-defined technical problems and assist with the design of systems components or processes to meet specified needs.

PO4: Engineering Tools, Experimentation and Testing: Apply modern engineering tools and appropriate technique to conduct standard tests and measurements.

PO5: Engineering practices for society, sustainability and environment: Apply appropriate technology in context of society, sustainability, environment and ethical practices.

PO6: Project Management: Use engineering management principles individually, as a team member or a leader to manage projects and effectively communicate about well-defined engineering activities.

PO7: Life-long learning: Ability to analyse individual needs and engage in updating in the context of technological changes.

COURSE OUTCOMES (CO)

After completion of the course the students will be able to

CO -1: To identify manufacturing processes for various component making and to choose suitable machines and cutting fluid and lubrication for machining operations

CO - 2: Ability to choose suitable machine tool for machining operations and parameters

CO - 3: Ability to choose suitable cutting/ forming operations and cutting tools

Course Outcomes	EXPECTED MAPPING WITH PROGRAMME OUTCOMES (1- Weak Correlation; 2- Medium correlation; 3- Strong Correlation)						
	PO-1	PO-2	PO-3	PO-4	PO-5	PO-6	PO-7
CO-1	1	2	3	1	3	3	1
CO-2	1	2	3	1	3	2	1
CO-3	1	2	3	1	3	3	1

GUIDELINES FOR TEACHERS

To implement Outcome Based Education (OBE) knowledge level and skill set of the students should be enhanced. Teachers should take a major responsibility for the proper implementation of OBE. Some of the responsibilities (not limited to) for the teachers in OBE system may be as follows:

- Within reasonable constraint, they should manoeuvre time to the best advantage of all students.
- They should assess the students only upon certain defined criterion without considering any other potential ineligibility to discriminate them.
- They should try to grow the learning abilities of the students to a certain level before they leave the institute.
- They should try to ensure that all the students are equipped with the quality knowledge as well as competence after they finish their education.
- They should always encourage the students to develop their ultimate performance capabilities.
- They should facilitate and encourage group work and team work to consolidate newer approach.
- They should follow Blooms taxonomy in every part of the assessment.

Bloom's Taxonomy

Level	Teacher should Check	Student should be able to	Possible Mode of Assessment
Creating	Students ability to create	Design or Create	Mini project
Evaluating	Students ability to Justify	Argue or Defend	Assignment
Analysing	Students ability to distinguish	Differentiate or Distinguish	Project/Lab Methodology
Applying	Students ability to use information	Operate or Demonstrate	Technical Presentation/ Demonstration
Understanding	Students ability to explain the ideas	Explain or Classify	Presentation/Seminar
Remembering	Students ability to recall (or remember)	Define or Recall	Quiz

GUIDELINES FOR STUDENTS

Students should take equal responsibility for implementing the OBE. Some of the responsibilities (not limited to) for the students in OBE system are as follows:

- Students should be well aware of each UO before the start of a unit in each and every course.
- Students should be well aware of each CO before the start of the course.
- Students should be well aware of each PO before the start of the programme.
- Students should think critically and reasonably with proper reflection and action.
- Learning of the students should be connected and integrated with practical and real life consequences.
- Students should be well aware of their competency at every level of OBE.

LIST OF FIGURES

LIST OF TABLES

CONTENTS

1 Cutting Fluids, Lubricants and Lathe Machine Operations

Introduction; Types of cutting fluids, Fluids and coolants required in turning, drilling, shaping, sawing & broaching; Selection of cutting fluids, methods of application of cutting fluid; Classification of lubricants (solid, liquid, gaseous), Properties and applications of lubricants.

Lathe Operations: Types of lathes- light duty, Medium duty and heavy duty geared lathe, CNC lathe; Specifications; Basic parts and their functions; Operations and tools- Turning, parting off, Knurling, facing, Boring, drilling, threading, step turning, taper turning.

UNIT SPECIFIC / LEARNING OBJECTIVES

- To introduce significance, advantages, properties and applications of cutting fluids, coolants and lubricants in machining
- To introduce the machines for machining such as lathe for different operations
- To understand the significance of various types of lathe operations and parts of a lathe machine

Additionally, few fundamental questions for self-assessment based on the unit contents are also included in this unit in form of recall, application, comprehension, analysis, synthesis and videos. There are further suggested readings and reference for reader's assistance.

RATIONALE

Essence of Engineering and Technology is to make human life more comfortable on the earth. Various needs of individual are fulfilled by converting natural resources into useful products. These transformation of natural resources into products require machines and manufacturing processes like conventional and unconventional in optimal ways at economical cost. Few commonly used conventional method of shaping are casting, machining, welding, forming etc. Popular unconventional methods are electrocheemical machining (ECM), ultrasonic machining (USM), electrical discharge machining (EDM), 3D printing (give full form of all these) etc. Conventional methods (as well as unconventional methods) are used based on subtractive manufacturing methods while Additive manufacturing process or 3D printing works on deposition of materials to build shapes. Various machine tools like Lathe, Drilling, Milling, Planning, Shaping etc. are used in subtractive processes where the materials are removed by machining work-pieces. Machining methods are used to do job work on a machine tool with proper cutting fluids and lubricants. The essential application of a machine tool, like Lathe is for product development and assembly of components.

PRE-REQUISITES

Basic mechanical engineering and mechanics

LEARNING OUTCOMES

U1-O1: Ability to choose suitable cutting fluid and lubrication for machining operations

U1-O2: Ability to choose suitable machine tool for machining operations

U1-O3: Ability to choose suitable cutting operations and tools

U1-O4: Ability to choose suitable cutting conditions and parameters (revolution per minute (RPM), depth of cut, and feed rate)

U1-O5: Ability to predict the behavior of machined work piece and its dimensions

COURSE OBJECTIVES

- To understand the importance of cutting fluids & lubricants in machining process.
- To study and recognise various types of Lathe machine, their parts the operations.
- To be able to select, operate and control the appropriate lathe operations for specific applications

Mapping of learning outcomes and course objectives

Unit-1 Outcomes	EXPECTED MAPPING WITH COURSE OUTCOMES (1- Weak Correlation; 2- Medium correlation; 3- Strong Correlation)					
	CO-1	CO-2	CO-3	CO-4	CO-5	CO-6
U1-O1	1	2	3			
U1-O2	1	2	3			
U1-O3	1	2	3			
U1-O4	1	2	3			
U1-O5	1	2	3			

1.1 INTRODUCTION

Cutting fluids are liquid emulsion mixtures used in cutting operations during metal-working and machining procedures. Cutting fluids can be either gaseous or liquid in nature. It's possible to machine metals or non-metals via milling, turning, drilling processes etc. A cutting fluid may occasionally serve as a coolant when it cools the machinery, the cutting tool, and the work piece. The primary function of cutting fluid is to remove heat generated during metal cutting and other machining operations. It also acts as a lubricant to improve cutting conditions and lengthen the life of the cutting tool. A cutting fluid lessens resistance between the tool and the chip and the work piece. Heat can be eliminated as soon as it is produced if the proper amount of cutting fluid is used. Therefore, reducing fluid usage is required to boost production effectiveness. Cutting fluids can be applied in a variety of ways, including floods, fluid jets, mist spraying, etc. The key difference between cutting fluid and lubricant is that cutting fluids can lubricate the interface between the cutting tool's cutting edge and the chip, whereas lubricants can lubricate between hard materials by reducing the friction between the objects. Cutting fluids are substances that can act as both coolants and lubricants.

Table 1.1: Types of cutting fluids

Cutting fluids	Descriptions
Straight Oil	Straight oils are non-emulsifying and are used without diluting them with water. The compositions of such type of oil have base minerals or petroleum oil. For examples, paraffin oil, Naphthlenic oil, vegetable oil are straight oils. In cases where environmentally friendly oil is required, vegetable oil is used because it is biodegradable. Straight oils are best for lubricating, but they cannot serve as a good coolant because they have very cool properties.
Cutting Oil	Cutting oil is made by mixing minerals oil and fatty oil. It is used as both as a coolant and as a lubricant.
Soluble Oil	These are made by mixing mineral oil, water, & coupling agents to provide good lubrication between water-inaccurate liquids. Soluble oils are used in the machining of both ferrous and non-ferrous metals when high cooling quality is required & chip bearing capacity is not very high. Soluble oils are the most widely used and they are very cheap.
Mineral Oil	These oils are typically found in high production machines that have high metal removal rates and cutting operations. A disadvantage of these oils is that they are corrosives and therefore are not used for copper or its alloys.
Synthetic liquids	Synthetic liquids, do not contain mineral oil or petroleum, these are water-based liquids, and water provides very good cooling properties. Corrosion can be prevented by adding corrosion inhibitors to synthetic liquids. Typically, synthetic fluids are used in grinding operation.
Semi-synthetic fluids	Synthetic fluid and soluble oils are combined to create semi-synthetic fluid. About 5 to 20 percent of mineral oil is released with water in semi-synthetic liquids to cause micro abrasion. Microalgae particles, which range in size from 0.01 to 0.1 mm, are easily able to transmit all light. Semi-synthetic fluids are particularly effective in cooling and are priced halfway between synthetic and soluble fluids. Molybdenum disulfides, graphite, wax sticks, etc. are a few examples.
Solid and paste lubricants	These lubricants come in paste or solid form. Direct application of these lubricants to the tool or workpiece is required. Examples of this include wax sticks, graphite, and molybdenum disulphide.

1.1.1 Types of Cutting Fluids

Cutting fluids may be classified as oil, oil-water emission, pastes, gels, etc. The cutting fluid may be referred to as the cutting fluid, cutting oil, coolant, or lubricant, depending on the type of cutting fluid and its application. Cutting fluids is beneficial for most metal and machining processes. Table 1.1 lists such cutting fluids with descriptions.

1.1.2 Uses of Cutting Fluids

The cutting fluid can be used for different purposes. Some of its uses are listed below in Table 1.2.

Table 1.2: Usages of cutting fluids

Application as	Escriptions
Coolant	The main task for which the fluid was discovered is to cool the equipment and work piece. By cooling the equipment and work piece, we can reduce tool wear, thermal expansion of the tool, and a good surface finish.

Application as	Escriptions
Lubricant	Cutting fluids are also used for lubrication for reducing friction between tool chip interface, which keeps the cutting forces down and also reduces heat generation. By cutting fluid flow, chips and other contaminants can be easily removed from the work piece.
Cleaning the machining area	Cutting fluids are also used as a cleansing agent and remove chips, dust near and inside the cutting area. This is important because chips, dust can cause uneven bites.
Others	By shielding the freshly created surface from oxidation and corrosion, it is utilized to enhance the surface's polish. It serves to stop rust. Higher cutting speeds and greater rates of metal removal are now possible. It stops built-up edges (BUE) from forming.

1.1.3 Selection of Cutting Fluid

The choice of cutting fluid in machining processes depends on various factors such as:

1.1.3.1 Types of Machining Process

Typically, more difficult machining processes utilizes more cutting fluids. Heavy cutting oil is required for heavy machining processes such as broaching or screwing with a tap. Heavy cutting oils should be used in horizontal broaching, but in the vertical broaching process, emulsions and solutions may be used. For the threading and drilling process, the cooling characteristics of cuttings fluids are more important.

1.1.3.2 Type of Workpiece Material

The next factor for the selection of cuttings fluids is the workpiece material. The cast iron and cast group of materials are brittle during machining, and therefore small chips are produced that do not cause too much friction. Therefore, emulsion should be used as it increases the surface finish, and the concentration should be kept between 10 and 15 percent. For steel and stainless-steel work piece materials, high-pressure cutting oils should be used. For machining of steel alloys, water-based cutting fluids are used because they are heat resistant & difficult to cut.

1.1.3.3 Type of Cutting Tool Material

Another factor for the selection of cutting tool materials is cutting tool material. High-speed steel cuttings tools can be used with any type of cutting tool, but when the material is difficult to cut, the waterless cutting liquid is used with the HSS cutting tool. For tungsten carbides, the cooling characteristics of cutting fluids are more important because higher heat is produced when it is used as a cutting tool material.

1.1.4 Quality of a Good Cutting Fluids

Cutting fluid should have good chemical properties. It should be chemically neutral and should not harm the machine and operator. It must have high specific heat or high heat-absorbing ability to disperse the heat generated during machining. It should be transparent so that the operators can easily go through it in the cutting area. It should have good lubricating properties so that it reduces friction during machining. It should be nontoxic when it comes in contact with heating and should not create any toxic fumes. It should be odorless and should not cause any odor at high temperatures. It should have low viscosity so that it can flow easily over the work piece. It should be non-corrosive for work pieces and machines. It should not glue parts of the machine. It should have small molecular sizes to allow it to penetrate the chip tool interface and spread rapidly. It should have a high flash point & should not burn due to heat generated during machining.

1.2 LATHE OPERATIONS

Lathe is the oldest machine tool, stemming from the early tree lathe (Figure 1.1), which was turned by a rope passing around the work-piece a few times and attaching to springy branch overhead. The work was supported by two dowels stuck in adjacent trees. Operator foot supplied the motion, which was fluctuating. The tool was held in the operator's hand. From this crude lathe over a period of more than two centuries, the modern engine lathe has evolved. Until about 1770, lathes were useless for metal cutting because it lacked power and a holding torque enough for accurately guide the tool and later Henery Mauldsley, developed the sliding carriage and in 1800 build a true cutting lathe. Later (Fig. 1.2) early manually operated wheel lathe was developed and motorised Lathe (Fig. 1.3) became base for next generation of Lathe. Now Lathe has become general purpose machine tool, employed in production and repair work permitting large variety of operations to be performed on it. Work piece material from a rotating work is removed in the form of chips with help of a single point cutting tool which can be fed deep (meaning is not clear). The cutting tool is harder than the work piece and it is held securely and rigidly on the machine that may be given any direction.

Figure 1.1: Early tree lathe [8]

Figure 1.2: The early manual wheel lathe [9]

Figure 1.3: The early motorised lathe [10]

1.2.1 Types of Lathe Machines

There are basically five types of Lathes as: Light duty, medium duty, Heavy duty, Geared lathe and CNC lathe. The differences may be seen as given below in Table 1.3.

Table 1.3: Types of lathes

Types	Description
Light duty Lathe	A light duty lathe machine is designed for small scale jobs at workshops and tool rooms. One can easily turn, drill, groove, shape, cut, knurl and create threads on the harder metal or wooden surfaces by using a light duty lathe at a workshop.
Heavy duty lathe	A heavy-duty lathe is an efficient tool for crafting different objects. The machine is designed to handle the toughest shaping jobs in numerous industries and several workshops. It is primarily a user-friendly machine that helps to cast a variety of shapes from wood or metal using easy to use controls.
Medium duty lathe	The medium duty lathe machine is typically used for very accurate and superior grade machining. This multipurpose equipment is highly durable and can deliver optimum output using limited resources. It can effectively process high end solid materials in bulk quantities.
Geared lathe	The all-geared lathe machine is mainly used for executing various metal shaping tasks in different industries. They basically have a gear box with lead screw and feed shaft that increases its machining capacity.
CNC lathe	A CNC lathe machine is a Computer Numerically Controlled machine that can produce a range of products, from larger items such as automobile frames and airplane engines to smaller items, such as surgical instruments, gears and garden tools Operated with Computer Numerical Control (CNC) systems and provided with precise design instructions. CNC Lathes are machine tools where the material or part is clamped and rotated by the main spindle, while the cutting tool that work on the material, is mounted and moved in various axis with help of digital motors (stepper and servo motor).

1.2.2 Specification of Lathe

In order to specify a lathe completely, following specifications should be included such as:

- Height of the centers, Type of bed (strait, semi-gap, gap type), centre distance.
- Swing over bed, swing over cross slide, swing in gap, Gap in front of face plate, width of bed.
- Spindle speeds range, spindle nose type, spindle bore, taper in nose.
- Metric thread pitches, Lead screw pitch, longitudinal feeds, cross feeds.
- Motor horse power and RPM, Shipping dimension (length, width, height, weight), accessories if any.

1.2.3 Parts of a Lathe and their Functions

The lathe machine (Figure 1.4) is an assembly of several parts having different functions. These parts are: bed, guide ways, head stock, spindle, and carriage, saddle, cross slide, compound rest, compound slide, tool post, apron, tail stock, chuck, face plate, center, feed shaft, lead screw, legs, chips pan, hand wheel, speed controller, bull gear and sleeve.

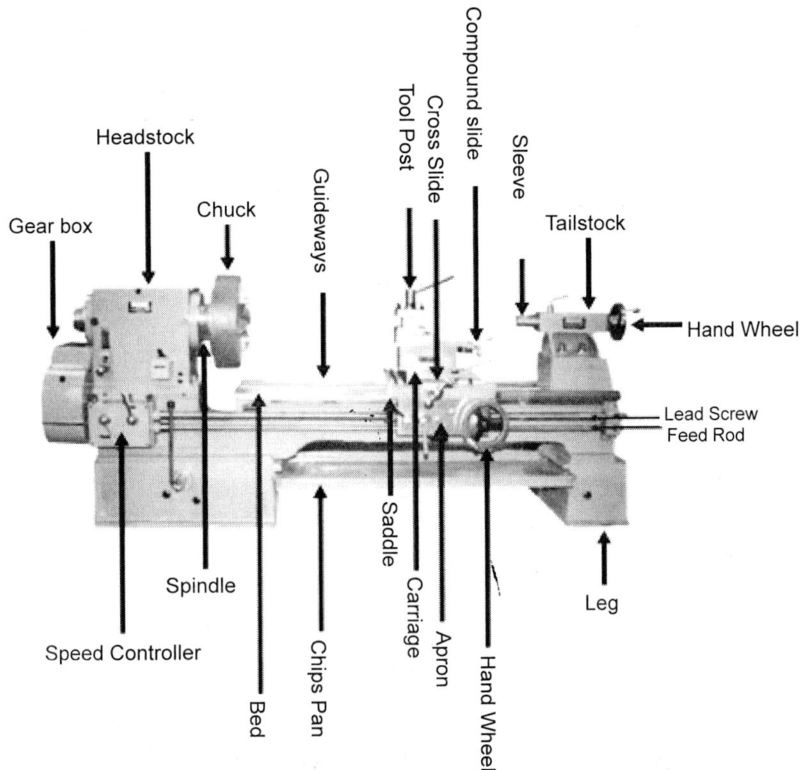

Figure 1.4: Basic parts of a lathe machine [11]

While there are different types of lathes as mentioned above, the function of these parts is listed below in Table 1.4 to facilitate their operations.

Table 1.4. Parts of a lathe and their functions

Parts	Function
Bed	The bed is a large horizontal structure or beam that's used to support other parts of a lathe machine tool like the head stock and tail stock. .
Guideways	The main function of the guideway is to make sure that the cutting tool or machine tool operative element moves along a predetermined path. There are two guide ways provided, inner ways and outer ways, which are accurately machined to make them parallel to the axis. The lathe should take up the various vibrations, which are causing due to different types of force. The guide ways provide sliding surfaces to the carriage and the tail stock.
Headstock	The head stock is clamped on left-hand end of bed. It houses the spindle, speed change mechanism, and change gears. The head stock supports one end of the work piece and imparts rotational motion to the work. The tail stock merely supports the other end of the work piece as it rotates.

Parts	Function
Spindle	The head-core stock's is its spindle. "Business end" of a lathe is a lathe spindle. From the perspective of the operator, the spindle is often found near the left-hand end of the lathe bed. There are many different configurations and sizes available for lathe spindles, which are used to cut, shape, and mill metal or wood. The sole function of the spindle is to support and rotate the material being worked on while preventing excessive vibration or flutter. The bits, or cutting tools, can be hand-held, attached as an accessory, or built into the lathe itself. Therefore, the component of the machine that distinguishes it as a lathe is the lathe spindle.
Carriage	The carriage is the part of the lathe which slides over the bed-ways between the head stock and the tail stock and contains apron, saddle, compound rest, cross slide and tool post. The lead screw is used to move the carriage automatically during threading. It is used to move the carriage from left to right and vice versa.
Saddle	The saddle is technically part of the carriage featuring an H shape. It is responsible for supporting cross slide movements. It comprised of the cross slide, compound rest and took post, as well as the apron, which houses the gear box that controls feed direction and mode.
Cross slide	A lathe cross slide serves as a mobile platform for a static tool bit when performing facing operations. Cross-slide is situated on the saddle and slides on the dovetail guide ways at right angles to the bed guide ways. It carries compound rest, compound slide and tool post. Cross slide hand wheel is rotated to move it at right angles to the lathe axis. It can also be power driven. The cross-slide hand wheel is graduated on its rim to enable to give known amount of feed as accurate as 0.05mm.
Compound rest	Compound rest is a part which connects cross slide and compound slide. It is mounted on the cross slide by tongue and groove joint. It has a circular base on which angular graduations are marked. The compound rest can be swiveled to the required angle while turning tapers. A top slide known as compound slide is attached to the compound rest by dove tail joint. The tool post is situated on the compound slide.
Compound slide	The compound slide offers a way to turn tapers and cut angles on a lathe without rotating the head stock. Four mounting holes are in the base for solid positioning on the cross slide. The base has a red anodized finish with laser engraved angle scales to make setting an angle easily readable.
Tool post	This can be found atop the compound slide. It serves to firmly hold the tools in place. Tools are chosen based on the type of operation, mounted on the tool post, and then set up in a comfortable working position. Tool posts come in a variety of varieties, including Single way, Four way, and Quick change. The tool is secured in a single way tool post by a screw. It is made out of a round bar with a slotted hole in the middle for attaching the tool with a setscrew. The height of the tool point is fixed at the ideal height using a concave ring and a convex rocker. The tool fits on the rocker's smooth top surface. Because there is just one clamping screw used to secure the tool, the tool post is not sturdy enough for hard operations. The four open sides of the Four Way Tool Post allow for the simultaneous use of four tools. Separate screws hold the tools in place, and the Center also has a locking bolt. By rotating the tool post, the necessary tool can be set up for machining. Because the necessary tools are already set, machining can be finished more quickly.

Parts	Function
Apron	Apron is attached to the carriage and hangs over the front side of the lathe bed. It is useful in providing power and hand feed to both carriage and cross-slide. It is also used to provide power feed to the carriage during thread cutting through two half nuts.
Tail stock	On the inner guide ways at the right side of the bed, across from the head stock, is where you'll find the tail stock. The tail stock spindle is housed in the drilled body of the tail stock. Inside the hole, the spindle goes forward and backward. The dead Centre or the shanks of tools like drills or reamers can be inserted into the spindle's taper hole. The spindle moves forward when the tail stock hand wheel is turned clockwise. If the hand wheel is turned counterclockwise, the spindle will be withdrawn into the hole. When a long work piece is machined between the centers and, the tail stock supports the other end. It is handy for holding tools like drills, reamers, and taps.
Chuck	The body of the tail stock is bored and houses the tail stock spindle. The spindle moves front and back inside the hole.
Face plate	A lathe face plate is a basic work holding accessory for a wood or metal turning lathe. It is a circular metal (usually cast iron) plate which fixes to the end of the lathe spindle.
Center	It is used for accurate positioning of a work piece about its point or axis between a lathe chuck or head stock spindle and tail stock spindle. Lathe centers ensure concentricity of work by enabling the work piece to rotate/revolve.
Feed shaft	The feed shaft (rod) is a power transmission mechanism used for precise linear movement of the carriage along the longitudinal axis of the lathe. The lead screw transmits power from the head stock to the carriage for screw thread cutting operations.
Lead screw	A lengthy threaded shaft known as a lead screw serves as a master screw. During thread cutting, it is activated to move the carriage a predetermined distance. Lead screw are typically Acme threaded. Two bearings on the beds face support the lead screw. The phrase "gear on lead screw" refers to a gear that is fastened to the lead screw. To engage half nuts with the lead screw, a half nut lever is included in the apron.
Legs	This component sends the machine tool's entire weight to the ground while supporting it, and the foundation bolt firmly fastens it to the floor. Legs on a lathe are the vertical components that create an elevated working surface. However, lathes don't use any old legs. Commercial-grade lathes typically have legs that bolt onto the floor on which they are placed because of their enormous weight.
Chips pan	Chip pan is used to collect the chips that are produced during the lathe operation. It is the wheel that is operated by hand to move a cross slide, carriage, tail stock and other parts that have hand wheel.
Hand wheel	A hand wheel allows an operator you to control the lathe machine's linear movements as it cuts through threaded stock, metal, and other materials. Hand wheels have different designs and specifications, which determines how an operator use them on their lathe machine.
Speed controller	This device controls the speed of the motor by directly changing the frequency or the amplitude. By using the system to that end, there are hardly any heat losses and the speed control provides numerous programs that allow an operator to operate the machines.

Parts	Function
Bull gear	Bull gear (inside the gearbox) is used to refer to the larger of two spur gears that are in engagement in any machine. The smaller gear is usually referred to as a pinion. On a lathe a "bull gear" is a gear which allows one to connect the spindle to the drive shaft.
Sleeve	The Morse Taper Sleeve is mainly used in lathe machine. Morse taper shank allows the tool to be inserted directly into the machine spindle to facilitate high-torque applications such as large cut diameters.

1.2.4 Operations and Tools

In order to carry out tasks like cutting, facing, knurling, deformation, and more, a lathe rotates the object on its axis. Other frequent tasks carried out with a lathe machine include metal working, thermal spraying, wood turning, and metal spinning. Turning, facing, grooving, parting off, facing, threading, drilling, boring, knurling, step turning, taper turning, and tapping are among the most popular lathe operations. The frequently used common lathe operations are shown in Figure 1.5. Table 1.5 shows descriptions the operations with their schematic diagrams.

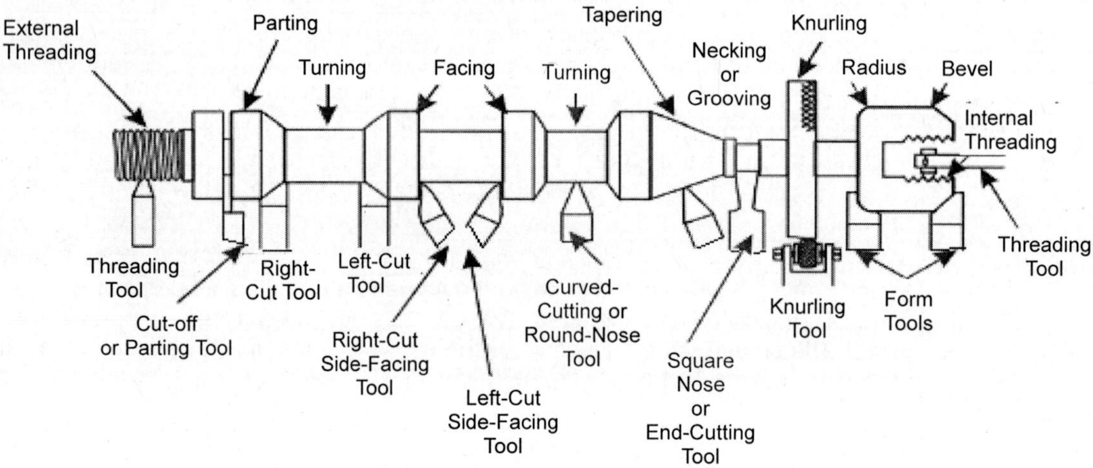

Figure 1.5: Common lathe operations [12]

Table 1.5: Descriptions of lathe operations and their schematic figures

Operations	Descriptions	Schematic Figures [13]
Turning	Is a type of machining where a cutting tool, typically a non-rotary tool bit -moves roughly linearly as the work piece rotates, describing a helix tool path.	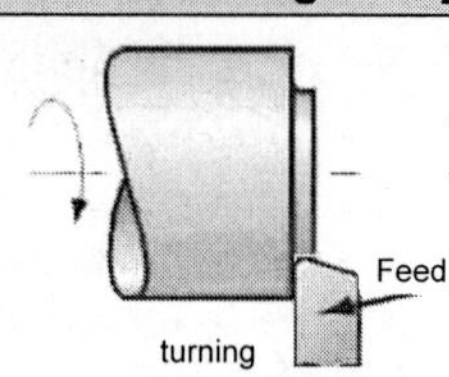

Operations	Descriptions	Schematic Figures [13]
Parting off	Is a technique that involves employing a unique cutting tool to split metal into two parts.	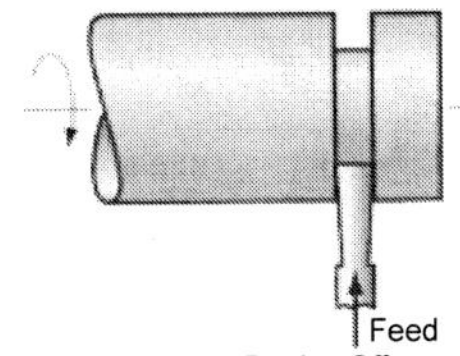 Parting Off
Knurling	Is a manufacturing process in which a design made of straight, angled, or crossed lines is rolled into the material. Usually, a lathe machine is used for this.	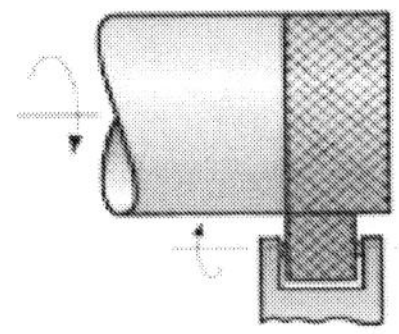 Knurling
Facing	The face tool is rotated counterclockwise to remove the material as the table feeds the work piece across the cutter.	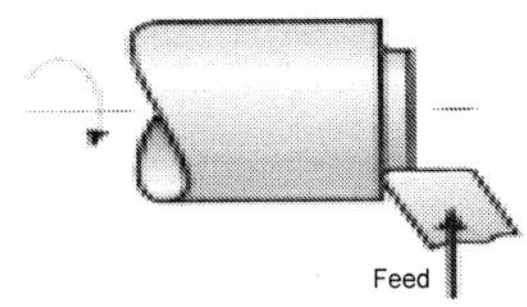 Facing
Boring	To make a hole, a boring bar, a specialized tool holder, is used. It is capable of making deep cuts in the metal. By counter boring, the hole's end is extended through a predetermined distance.	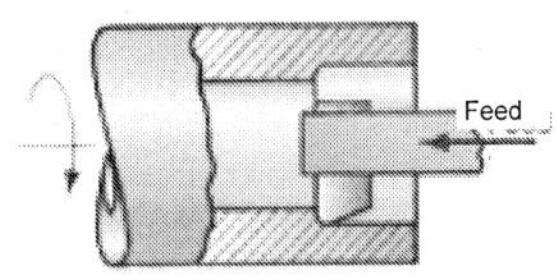 Boring
Drilling	The lathe can be carried out in one of two ways: by turning the task while guiding the drill into it. By feeding it work while turning the drill. The drill bit tool is utilized in this operation to drill the work piece. Following drilling, a lathe machine performs other tasks including tapping, boring, internal threading, etc.	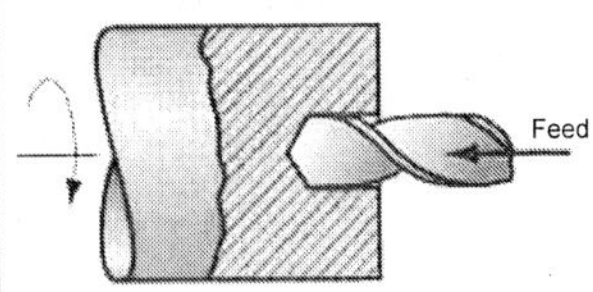 Drilling
Threading	The process of creating a thread form on a cylinder or cone with a single-point instrument is also known as single-pointing (or merely thread cutting when the context is implicit). The tool advances linearly, but the lead of the thread is determined by the precise rotation of the work piece.	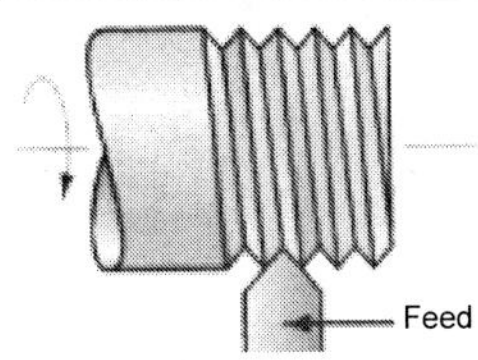 Threading
Step turning	Is a turning procedure that uses a lathe to generate a series of steps with various diameters. It incorporate the cylindrical work piece and securely fasten it into the chuck.	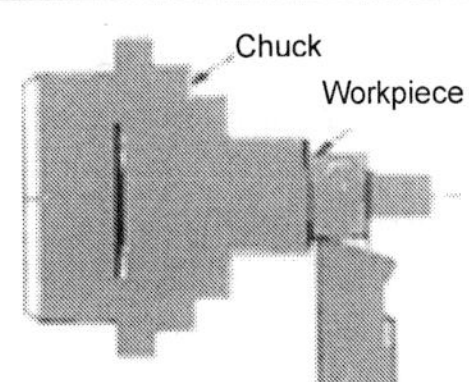 Step Turning

Operations	Descriptions	Schematic Figures [13]
Taper Turning	Is a turning procedure where the cutting tool rotates at an angle to the work piece's axis to produce a tapered surface in the work piece. A tapered component surface has a uniformly changing diameter from one end to the other. The work piece may have an internal or external taper surface.	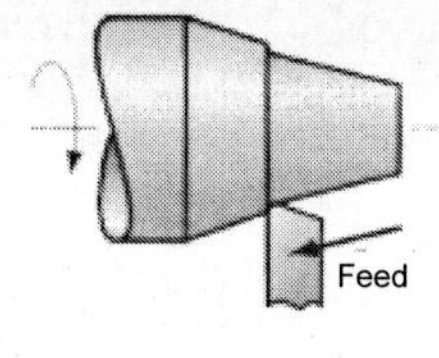 Taper Turning

1.2.5 Common Tools Used on Lathe

A lathe tool is a tool or piece of equipment used on a lathe machine for various operation of shaping. Following (Figure 1.6) are the types of lathes cutting tools used in lathe machine namely Turning tool, Chamfering tool, Thread cutting tool, Internal thread cutting tool, facing tool, grooving tool, Forming tool, Boring tool etc. These are all single point cutting tools.

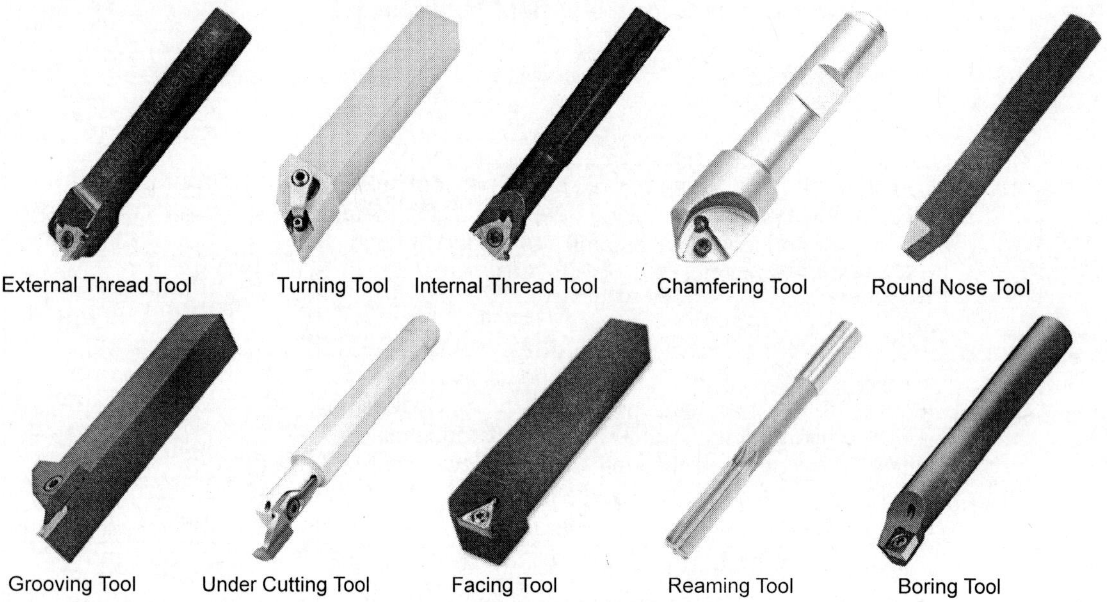

Figure 1.6: Common single point cutting tools for lathe [14]

1.2.6 SAFETY ON LATHE

All lathe operators must be continually aware of the safety risks connected to lathe use and must be familiar with all safety measures to prevent mishaps and injuries. Two major threats to human safety are carelessness and ignorance. Working with the lathe can provide additional risks that are mechanical in nature, such as safe machine setup and maintenance. When operating lathes, it's crucial to take the following safety precautions: It's crucial to dress appropriately; take off jewelry and watch, and roll up one's sleeves.

To make adjustments, the lathe must always be stopped. Till the lathe has come to a complete stop, do not modify the spindle speed. Use caution when handling drills, centres, and sharp cutters. Chuck keys and wrenches must be taken out before using. Wear safety glasses at all times. When installing a chuck, use caution when handling heavy chucks and cover the lathe ways with a block of wood. Before using the lathe, be aware of the location of the emergency stop.

Never remove chips and swarf with your hands; instead, use pliers or a brush. Tools should never be placed directly on the lathe ways. Use a large board with cleats on both sides to lay on the ways if a separate table is not readily accessible. Maintain the shortest tool overhang possible. Never try to measure a turning piece of work. Never use a file on a lathe without a handle. File if at all possible left-handed. When filing or grinding, keep the lathe ways safe. When sanding the work piece, use two hands. Avoid covering the work piece with emery cloth or sandpaper.

UNIT SUMMARY

Cutting fluids and lubricants are lifesaving ingredients for a machine tool. Cutting fluids work as friction reducer, as coolant and as head remover during machining process. Whereas lubricants as coating on the matting surfaces of a machine tool for easy smooth motion and flow between relative moving bodies. All machine tools like Lathe, milling, shaper, planner etc. require lubrication time to time for various parts of a machine tool. Cutting fluids as mixture of water, emulsion and oil is necessary for smooth cutting of chips under single point or multipoint cutting tools. A Lathe machine tool is oldest and versatile machine tool on which all operations can be done using single point or multipoint cutting tools. Many forming operations like sheet metal forming, grinding etc. can also be performed on it. Tool life plays an important role in machining and therefore optimal cutting conditions (depth of cut, feed rate and RPM) is needed with proper cutting fluids and lubricated slides. A well experience operator of a Lathe machine knows about how to cut materials on Lathe with proper conditions so that production of components from the machine tool is higher.

EXERCISE

Multiple choice questions for self-assessment

1. Which of the following properties should a cutting fluid possess?
   (a) It should have a low flash point.
   (b) It should have high viscosity.
   (c) It should have a non-foaming tendency.
   (d) It should be stable at low temperature.
2. Soluble oil is the mixture of _____.
   (a) water (b) mineral oil
   (c) coupling agents (d) All of the above.
3. Which of the following is a solid lubricant?
   (a) graphite (b) wax
   (c) soap bar (d) all of the above

4. When you will perform machining operation on copper materials, the preferable cutting fluid you should use is
   (a) kerosene (b) turpentine
   (c) mineral oil (d) dry fluid
5. Which of the following purposes, cutting fluid is used
   (a) for cooling the tool (b) for lubrication
   (c) for decreasing friction (d) all of the above
6. Which of the following is not true?
   (a) cutting fluid helps in lubrication
   (b) cutting fluid acts as a cleaner
   (c) Cutting fluid helps in thermal distortion.
   (d) Cutting fluid reduces the tool wear.
7. Which machine tool is known as the mother machine tool?
   (a) Drill (b) Milling
   (c) Lathe (d) none of mentioned
8. Which type of surface is produced by turning operation in lathe machine?
   (a) flat (b) cylindrical
   (c) taper (d) none of the mentioned
9. What is the necessary condition for turning?
   (a) material of work piece should be harder than the cutting tool
   (b) cutting tool should be harder than the material of work piece
   (c) hardness of the cutting tool and material of piece should be same
   (d) none of the mentioned
10. Which type of feed is needed in facing operation?
    (a) Longitudinal (b) cross
    (c) both cross and longitudinal (d) none of the mentioned
11. In taper operation, which type of surface is produced?
    (a) Flat (b) curve
    (c) circular (d) none of the mentioned
12. Which type of surface can be produced by lathe?
    (a) Flat (b) cylindrical
    (c) curvilinear (d) all of the mentioned
13. In lathe machine, in order to produce cylindrical surface, the cutting tool must '-------'
    (a) Move perpendicular to the axis of rotation
    (b) Move parallel to the axis of rotation
    (c) Move along the circumference of the surface
    (d) Be stationary
14. In lathe machine, the tool has
    (a) one type of motion (b) two types of motions
    (c) three types of motion (d) no motion

15. The angle between lathe centre is _______
    (a) 15°
    (b) 30°
    (c) 45°
    (d) 60°

ANSWERS															
1.	(c)	2.	(d)	3.	(d)	4.	(b)	5.	(d)	6.	(c)	7.	(c)	8.	(b)
9.	(b)	10.	(b)	11.	(d)	12.	(d)	13.	(b)	14.	(b)	15.	(d)		

Short and Long Answer Type Questions

1. What is a cutting fluid?
2. State the usage of different cutting fluids?
3. What are functions of cutting fluids and a lubricant?
4. What is difference between cutting fluid and lubricants?
5. What is a Lathe?
6. What is the working principle of a Lathe machine?
7. What are the different parts of the Lathe machine?
8. What are the different types of lathe operations?
9. Mention variety of uses of a lathe machinery?
10. What factors determine the price of a lathe?
11. Write brief historical description of lathe machine and early components.
12. State the various parts mounted on the carriage?
13. State safety features on a Lathe machine.

PRACTICALS

1. Perform different operation like turning facing and knurling.
2. Draw top view, side view and clearly depict the angle of SPCT.
3. Perform Turning and facing on ductile material (e.g., mild steel) to observe types of different chip formation by machining on lathe.
4. Perform turning and facing operation on brittle material to observe chips formation during operation.
5. Observe the formation of built-up edges on cutting tool during machining on lathe.

KNOW MORE

Explore the historical machining work for objects making like in wood and try to find how it is evolved with time as one could see the modern lathe machine and the operations today.

SUGGESTED RESOURCES FOR FURTHER READING/ LEARNING

Reference books & websites referred

1. Manufacturing technology – P N Rao, Tata McGraw-Hill Publications.
2. Elements of workshop Technology (Volume I & II) – S. K. Hajra Chaudary, Bose & Roy, Media Promoters and Publishers Limited.
3. Production Technology (Volume I & II) – O. P. Khanna & Lal, Dhanpat Rai Publications.
4. Fundamental of metal cutting and machine tools– B. L. Juneja, New age international limited.
5. Manufacturing Technology, Metal Cutting & Machine tools– P. N. Rao, Tata McGraw- Hill Publications.
6. Production Technology – R.B. Gupta, Satya Prakashan, New Delhi Publication.
7. Fundamentals of Design & Manufacturing- G K Lal, Vijay Gupta, N. V. Readdy, Narosa Publication. House, New Delhi
8. https://i.pinimg.com/originals/ee/e2/72/eee27268a8177548393ecc191207413d.jpg
9. https://thumbs.dreamstime.com/b/vintage-old-turning-lathe-machine-isolated-over-white-background-vintage-old-turning-wooden-lathe-machine-isolated-over-white-129436016.jpg
10. https://encrypted-tbn0.gstatic.com/images?q=tbn:ANd9GcSXpH07HPT_iOrqX6E2HEzpxOZjNT1oZxosr9JSr8jRA02dOZn9wZ_Kro6KwRpnW53qtfc&usqp=CAU
11. https://qph.cf2.quoracdn.net/main-qimg-b5e8f537b59ab900b158c3c35e3f7491-pjlq
12. https://engineeringlearn.com/wp-content/uploads/2021/11/Lathe-Cutting-Tools.jpg
13. https://3.bp.blogspot.com/-mF03WVfYNs/VxderXbLKsI/AAAAAAAAAck/NKY4VkB53P4a7fGd06Rf-LH4iJorKTLXwCLcB/s1600/center-lathe-machine.png
14. https://learnmech.com/wp-content/uploads/2019/05/lathe-operation.jpg
15. https://www.google.com/search?q=lathe+machine

VIDEOS

Cutting fluids

https://www.youtube.com/watch?v=-o5luQ5Tw80

https://www.youtube.com/watch?v=owDNvZj4VYw

Lathe work

https://www.youtube.com/results?search_query=Lathe+work

https://www.youtube.com/watch?v=MCHznzJHff4

2 Broaching and Drilling Machines

Broaching Machines: Introduction to broaching; Types of broaching machines- Horizontal type (Single ram & duplex ram), Vertical type, Pull up, Pull down, and Push down; Elements of broach tool; Broach teeth details; Nomenclature; Tool materials.

Drilling: Classification; Basic parts and their functions; Radial drilling machine; Types of operations; Specifications of drilling machine; Types of drills and reamers.

UNIT SPECIFIC / LEARNING OBJECTIVE

Objective of this unit in to talk about following aspects

- To introduce significance of Broaching and Drilling function
- To learning about the importance of Broaching and Drilling tools and their operations
- To introduce the underlying advantages and applications of Broaching and Drilling machines
- To introduce the Broaching and Reaming operations
- To understand the significance of various types of Broaching, Drilling and Reaming operations
- To learn about Broaching, Drilling and Reaming operations and specifications

Additionally, few fundamental questions for self-assessment based on the unit contents are also included in this unit in form of recall, application, comprehension, analysis, synthesis and videos. There are further suggested readings and reference for reader's assistance.

RATIONALE

Machining methods are used to convert jobs (raw work pieces) into given shape and sizes on a machine tool like Lathe, Milling, Broaching, Drilling, Boring, Planning, Grinding, Shaper etc. Proper tooling and cutting fluids are also selected along with holding and supporting the job on the machine. Each machine tool performs variety of operations according to the choice of cutting tools and vision of the mechanic who operates the machine. In this unit, essential part of a machine tools, like broaching and drilling are discussed for making various types and the operations that can be made on it including their details and materials used for machining components on these machines. Basics classifications of broaching and drilling machines also discussed with exercises.

PRE-REQUISITES

A course on basic Mechanical Engineering and mechanics

COURSE OBJECTIVES

- To understand the importance of broaching and drilling machining process.
- To study and recognise various types of broaching and drilling machines, their parts and operations.
- To be able to select, operate and control the appropriate broaching, drilling and reaming operations for specific applications

LEARNING OUTCOMES

U2-O1: Ability to choose suitable work-piece for machining jobs on broaching, drilling machines

U2-O2: Ability to choose suitable broaching, drilling machine tools and their cutting tools for machining operation

U2-O3: Ability to choose suitable operations and proper cutting tools for broaching and drilling

U2-O4: Choose suitable cutting conditions and parameters (RPM, depth of cut and feed rate) for broaching, drilling and reaming operations

U2-O5: Ability to predict the behavior of machined work piece and its dimensions after broaching, drilling and reaming

Mapping of learning outcomes and course objectives

Unit-2 Outcomes	EXPECTED MAPPING WITH COURSE OUTCOMES (1- Weak Correlation; 2- Medium correlation; 3- Strong Correlation)					
	CO-1	CO-2	CO-3	CO-4	CO-5	CO-6
U2-O1	1	2	3			
U2-O2	2	2	3			
U2-O3	1	2	3			
U2-O4	1	2	3			
U2-O5	1	2	3			

2.1 INTRODUCTION TO BROACHING

A particular instrument having many, progressively higher cutting blades is called a "broach," and it is used to remove metal using the technique called as broaching. A broaching tool's teeth (Fig. 2.1a) remove the whole machining allowance in a single motion. Early in the 1850s, crucial ways in pulleys and gears were first cut using the broaching technique, which dates back to that time. Gun barrels were rifled by broaching following World War I. The history of Broaching Machine Specialties (BMS) in the machine tool industry is quite extensive. The company was founded in the 1920s under the name Machinery and Equipment Exchange (MEE), and it became a legal entity in 1946.

The method of broaching is distinct from other machining procedures in that the tool's primary cutting action is the sole motion involved. By progressively embedding the teeth deeper inside the tool, the feed is obtained, and each tool edge removes a layer of material (refer Fig 2.1 b). Along the broach axis, translational cutting is used most frequently. Any cross-sectional shape of through hole, straight and helical slot, external surface, external and internal toothed gear, spline, key way, and rifling may be machined with broaching.

Surface broaching refers to removing material from exterior surfaces, whereas internal or hole broaching refers to removing material from interior surfaces. Figure 2.2 illustrates common broaching designs used for various tasks. A The size of holes, cutting of serrations, key ways, straight or helical splines, cannon rifling, etc. are examples of common internal broaching operations (Fig. 2.3).

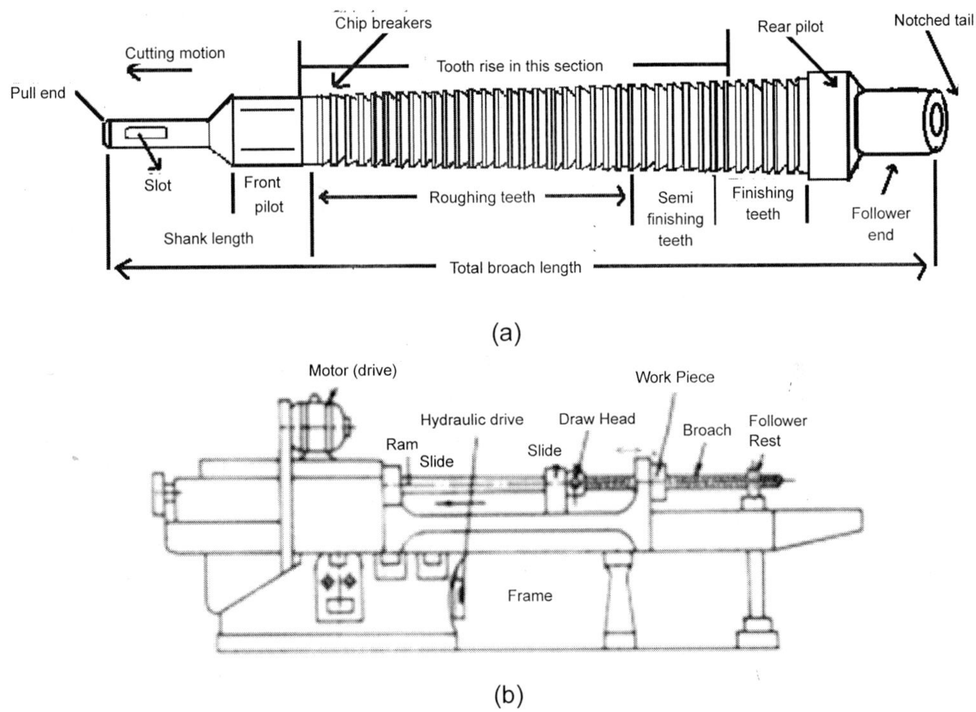

Figure 2.1: (a) A broaching tool (b) A broaching Machine with a broaching tool [6]

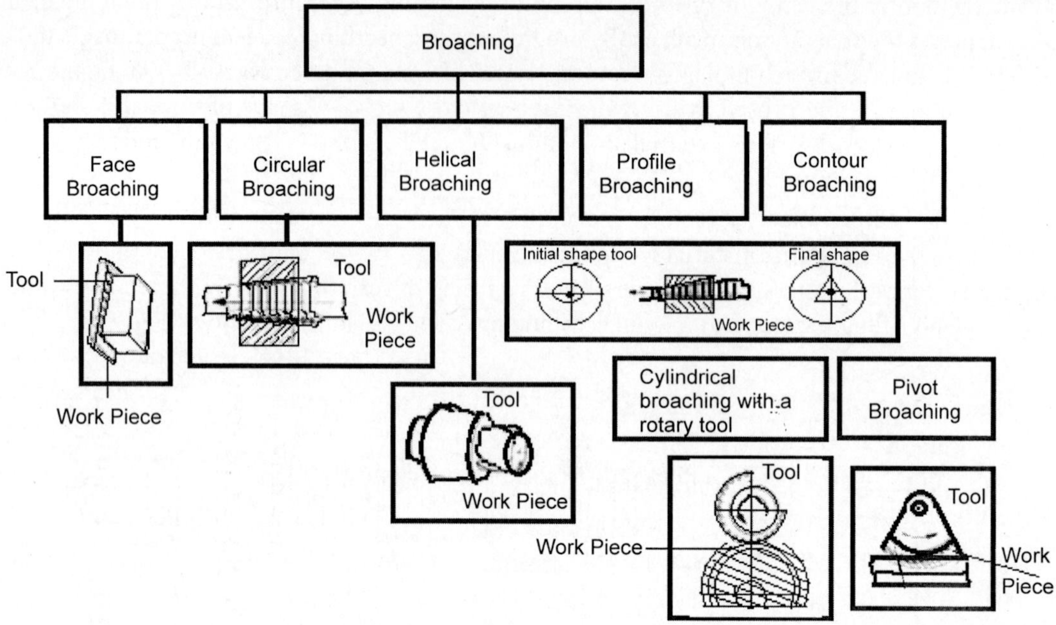

Figure 2.2: Broaching operation types [9]

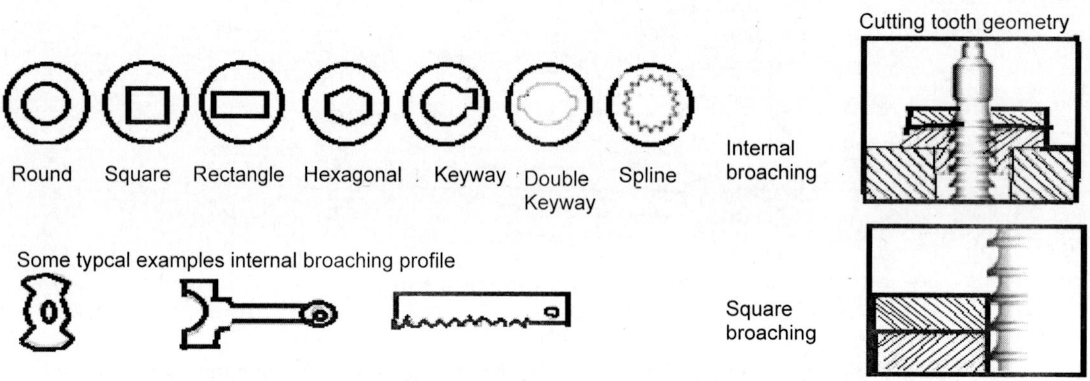

Figure 2.3: Internal & External shapes produced by broaching [6]

Despite the relatively moderate cutting rates (2 to 15 m per min), utilized in broaching, the total length of the cutting blades that are operating concurrently is rather long, resulting in a very high output capacity. If broaching machines with continuous working motion are employed, together with automated work piece loading and unloading, the output in broaching may be increased even further. Broaching is becoming more and more popular in the engineering and metal-working sectors because to its high production, machining precision, and good surface finish. However, broaches are pricey tools, and their usage is typically only justified in large-scale and mass manufacturing.

2.1.1 Advantages and Limitations of Broaching Process

Due to its exceptional qualities and benefits, broaching has become a popular metal cutting technique for tasks requiring mass production. With the right broaches, fittings, and machinery, production rates are quite high. High precision and good surface finish (tolerance of 0.0075mm, 0.8 micron surface finish is feasible), both roughing and finishing cuts are carried out in a single tool pass. Any profile might be machined by providing the tools various forms, and the process is appropriate for both internal and exterior surface finishing.

Despite the foregoing benefits, it has certain drawbacks, such as the high cost of tooling, which makes it uneconomical for small-scale work. It is not appropriate for the removal of huge amounts of stock because it necessitates sturdy machinery to handle the high forces generated during cutting. It is suitable for extremely big workpieces that cannot be broached without any obstructions since a tapered hole cannot be produced with a broach.

2.2 Types of Broaching Machines

A broaching machine is made up of an appropriate frame, a driving mechanism, a work-holding device (fixture), and a broaching tool. The main slide of the broaching machine is typically where the broach is fixed and moves together with the slide. In accordance with their intended uses, these devices come in many varieties. Hydraulic or elector-mechanical options are both possible. Pull-up, pull-down, and push-down types, for example, as well as horizontal (single ram and duplex ram) and vertical types. A general categorization might be provided as shown in Figure 2.4.

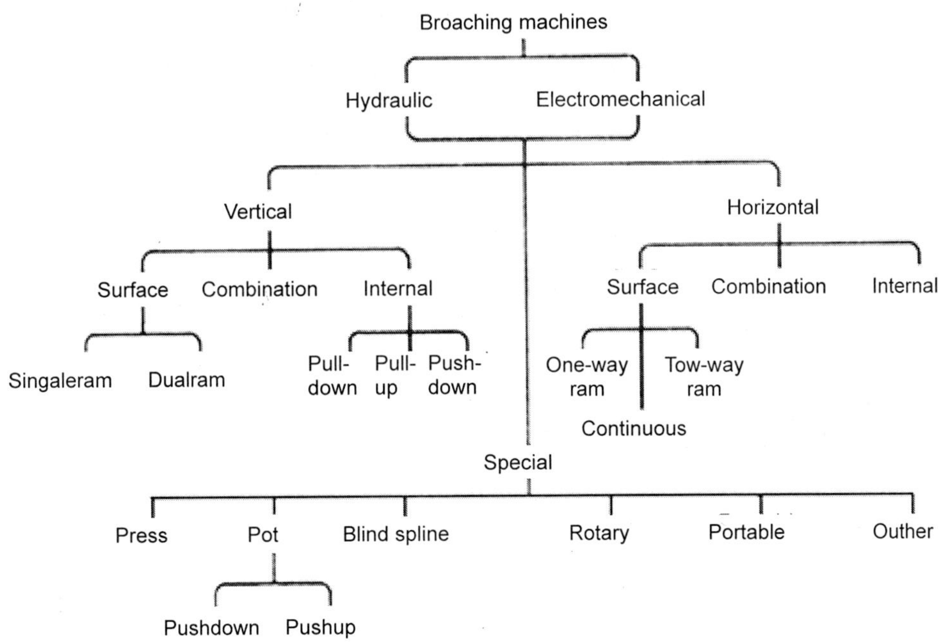

Figure 2.4: Types of Broaching machines [10]

Depending on whether the slide moves in the horizontal or vertical planes, a broaching machine (see Fig. 2.5) may be either horizontal or vertical. The qualities of a horizontal machine are as follows: Any area of it is easily accessible from the floor, particularly the work station. (ii) A lengthy slide can be levelled and supported at several spots to maintain it in place.

One can identify a vertical machine by its features as (i) It takes up less space on the floor, (ii) A pit or a platform for the operator to access the workstation should be sunk for a machine with a long stroke. There are push and pull internal broaching machines, which may be either horizontally or vertically oriented.

In pull broaching machines, the shank receives the force while the body of the broach is under strain (Fig. 2.5 a, b). It is a "push broach" and is in compression if the force is applied to the back of the broach (Fig. 2.5 c). A push broach should be shorter than a pull broach and typically does not expand in length by more than 15 times of diameters in order to prevent buckling. Internal broaching, such as hole sizing and key-way cutting, is typically done on a vertical push broaching machine. The cutting force in the horizontal pull broaching machine (Fig. 2.5 a) securely clamps the work against the platen during the broaching process.

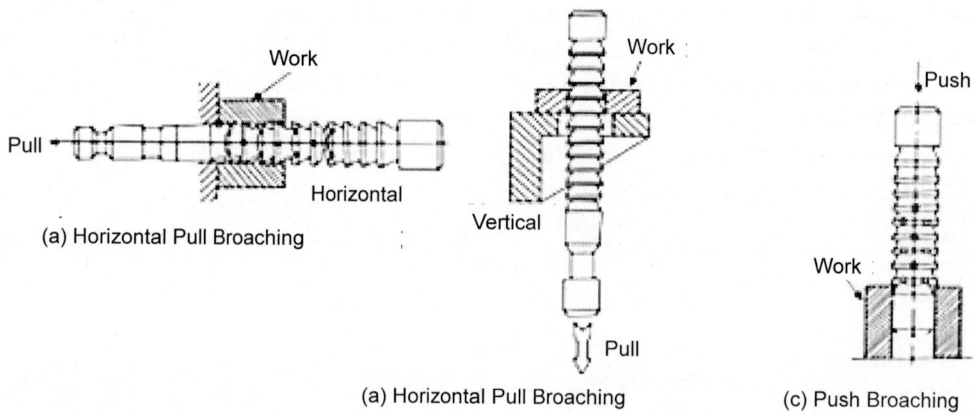

Figure 2.5: Internal Broaching [6]

Vertical pull-down machines or vertical pull-up machines are both examples of vertical pull broaching machines. In vertical pull down broaching machines, the broach is dragged through the work rather of being pushed (Fig. 2.5 b). The machine's base houses the pulling mechanism. An upper carriage suspends the broach above the work surface. The broach is lowered through the workpiece that is being held in a fixture on the worktable to begin the broaching operation. The pulling mechanism automatically engages the broach, which is then drawn downward throughout the task. The broach then reverses direction to return to its initial location. The pulling mechanism for a vertical pull up broaching machine is located above the worktable, while the broach is located at the machine's base. The broach is dragged upward as it enters the work while being held up against the table's underside. The work is released at the conclusion of the process and drops into a container.

2.2.1 Surface Broaching Machines

According to the surface they cut through, external surface broaches may be divided into three categories: flat (slab), peripheral, and contour. The most often used surface broaching devices are:

2.2.1.1 Vertical Broaching Machine

Figure 2.6 (a) features a column in the shape of a box that holds the hydraulic and electric driving components. Tools for broaching are mounted on a slide that is hydraulically propelled and precisely directed along the column ways. The hydraulic drive regulates the different speeds at which the slide with the broaches moves. Its stroke is modified to fit the intended broaching operation. There is a quick return stroke on the slide. In front of the column, the base of the worktable 1 is mounted. It may be advanced to a predetermined broaching position and retracted to load and unload the broaching fixture. The broaching device holding workpiece 2 is fixed to the table. The workpiece is machined once the table has been moved to the broaching position, clamped, and the slide carrying the broach moves downward. A fresh workpiece is subsequently loaded onto the table, and the slide moves back up to its top position. After then, the cycle is repeated in the same manner. "Single slide machine" is the name given to such a device. There are two slides that operate in opposition to one another in a vertical "double slide" surface broaching machine. The work is kept on shuttle worktables, which swivel out for loading and unloading while the slide slides back to its starting position. The other slide is working while this is going on.

2.2.1.2 Horizontal Surface Broaching Machine:

The work piece is held in the fixture on the worktable as the broach is moved over its top surface in this instance. Cutting speeds range from 3 to 12 mpm, while returning speeds can reach 30 mpm.

2.2.1.3 Continuous Surface Broaching Machine:

Figure 2.6 (b) depicts a continuous chain type surface broaching machine. A continuous chain 4 moves over sprockets positioned in a box-shaped base in a horizontal plane. 2 locating and holding tools for work pieces on the chain, 3 are mounted at various intervals. Under bracket 7 that is attached on the base, broach 5 is fastened horizontally above the chain. In the area where the work pieces pass under the broach, a rigid guiding member 6 is positioned under the chain to allow for horizontal movement of the chain and a certain amount of stock removal from the work pieces. At station A, the work pieces are put into the fixtures and either manually or mechanically clamped. The work pieces are located and clamped on the travailing chain, which moves the work pieces between the broach and the guiding plate. At station B, the work pieces are automatically unclamped and discharged, where they fall into the machine's hopper 8. Machine for continuous surface broaching boosts output. surface broaching boosts output.

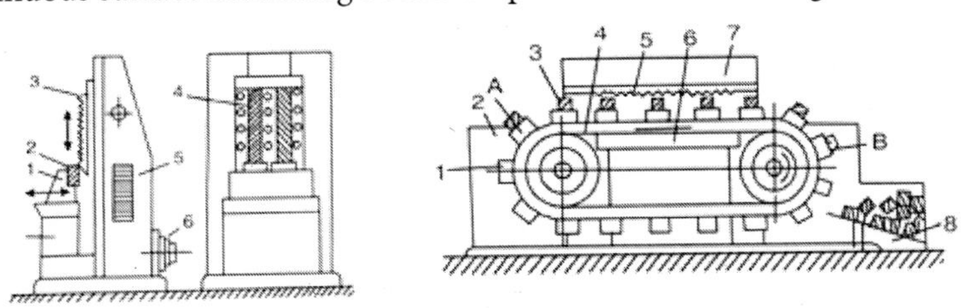

(a) (b)

Figure 2.6: (a) Vertical Surface broaching (b) Continuous Surface broaching [6]

2.3 ELEMENTS OF A BROACH TOOL

Figure 2.7 shows the various elements of a broach tool, including the front pilot, length, rear pilot, cutting teeth, tooth land, pitch and gullet, chip load, and chip-breakers. The pull end is used to engage the broach in the machine and places it centrally with the hole that has to be broached. Front pilot neck is close to the pull end. Where the broach is permitted to fail when overloaded is at a lesser diameter and length neck. The purpose of the front pilot is to first locate the broach in the hole. Metal removal is accomplished by the roughing and finishing teeth. For lighter cuts, finish and burnish the teeth. After the final tooth has exited the work-piece, the rear pilot and follower rest or retriever is used for support.

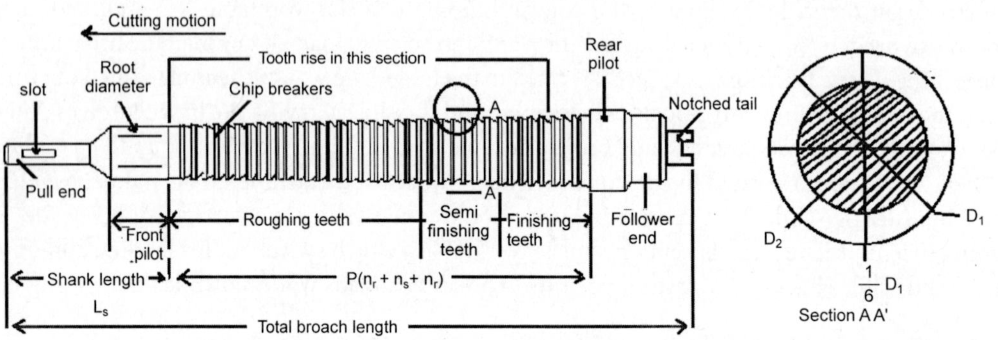

Figure 2.7: Elements of a broach tool [6]

2.4 NOMENCLATURE AND BROACHING TOOL MATERIALS

The nomenclature of Teeth details of a common broach tool is shown in Figure 2.8 as given below. The important elements of broaching tool are:

Pich of teeth, P
Depth of teeth,D(0.4P)
Land behind cutting edge (2.25P),L
Radius of gullet (0.25P), R
Hook anggle or rake angle, αα
Backoff angle or clearence angle, ¥ Rise per tooth (chip load), RPT/

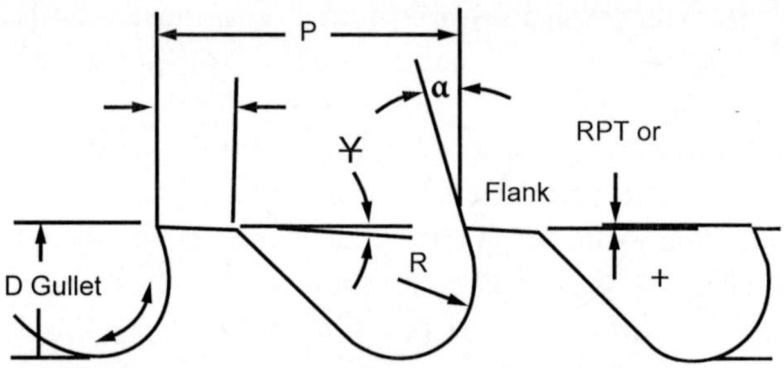

Figure 2.8: Teeth details of a broach tool [11]

Broaching machine can be specified in terms of length of the stroke, driving force (rated pulling force–10 /12 ton), broaching speed (cutting stroke speed), return stroke speed, type of drive, maximum size of cut and the machine power (HP).

High speed steel (HSS) or an alloy steel is the material used most frequently for broaches, and titanium nitride (TiN) coatings are frequently used to extend the life of HSS. However, because the cutting edge would shatter on the first pass when used to broach materials like cast iron, tungsten carbide is rarely employed as a tooth material. Some popular work materials used in broaching include cast or malleable iron, brass, aluminium, titanium, stainless steel, and alloy steel. The broaching process, similar to shaping with multiple teeth, is used to machine internal and external surfaces such as holes of circular, square, or irregular shapes, key-ways and teeth of internal gears.

2.5 INTRODUCTION TO DRILLING

Drilling is the process of creating a hole for a job. This is a sizeable portion of the machining operations carried out by the multi-point drilling tool's rotary and axial feed movements (Fig 3.1).

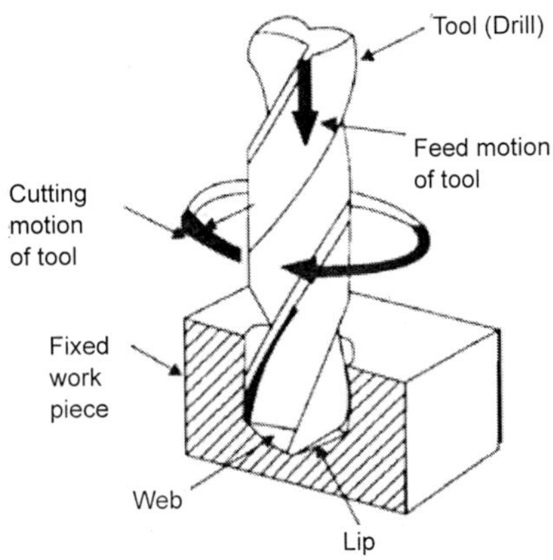

Figure 2.9: Drilling tool and the operation [12]

Homo sapiens first utilised rotational tools, which were pointed rocks spun between their hands to pierce other materials, some 35,000 years ago. This discovery gave rise to the hand drill, which was employed by numerous ancient civilizations, including the Mayans. Since they transform a back-and-forth action to a rotating motion, bow drills (also known as strap-drills) are the first machine drills. They date to about 10,000 years ago. By 3000 BC, Egypt had invented the core drill. In ancient Rome, the pump drill was developed. As early as 221 BC, under the Chinese Qin Dynasty, churn drills were created in the East. These drills could go 1500 meters beneath the earth's surface. The advent of the electric drill was a result of the next significant development in drilling technology. The inventors of the electric drill are credited as being *William Blanch Brain* and *Arthur James Arnott* of Melbourne, Australia. The brothers Wilhem and Carl Fein of Stuttgart, Germany invented the first portable hand-held drill in 1895. The electric drill has been produced in several forms and sizes throughout the past century.

Round holes are machined in drilling machines, boring machines, engine lathes, vertical boring mills, turret lathes, semi-automatic and automatic lathes, broaching machines and grinders. Whereas, drilling machines and lathe machines are used to originate or cut a hole in none previously existed one. The boring machines, broaching machines and grinders are mainly used to enlarge/ finish the existing holes. Of course, holes are also being enlarged and finished on drilling machines and lathe type machine tools. Holes up to 75 mm in diameter can be machined on drilling machines and lathe type machine tools, holes over 75 mm in diameter are usually cut by special drilling heads and, this operation is performed in boring machines. Generally, holes should meet the following requirements:

i. The diameter size must be restricted to the predetermined range.
ii. The hole's axis or cylindrical surface must be straight and meet the requirements.
iii. The hole needs to have a true cylindrical shape, meaning there must be no taper, ovality, or lobed edges.
iv. The part's faces and the hole must be square to one another.

When compared to milling an external surface of a revolution of the same size and accuracy, drilling correct holes always takes more time on the machine and costs more in cutting tools. The reason is because, in comparison to turning tools, hole-making equipment lacks the same rigidity, particularly in the design of its mounting components and clamping mechanisms.

2.6 BASIC NOMENCLATURE OF DRILL TOOL AND THEIR FUNCTIONS

The body of the drill is made somewhat smaller in diameter, leaving a narrow "margin" at full nominal diameter along the edge of each flute. As a result, there is less friction between the drill and the hole wall, which enables the cutting fluid to reach the drill point. The two margins make it easier to remove the heat produced while drilling and correctly position and guide the drill. To facilitate Tang Taper Shank, Shank Axis, Neck Flutes, Helix, or Rake Body Length, Point Margin, Web, Flute Length, Overall Length, Cutting Lips Spaces Land Dead in the Center Flute (a) Principal parts: Diameter Tool Land Machine Drill bodies are given a modest back taper (about 0.0075 mm per cm of length) in order to further reduce the rubbing motion.

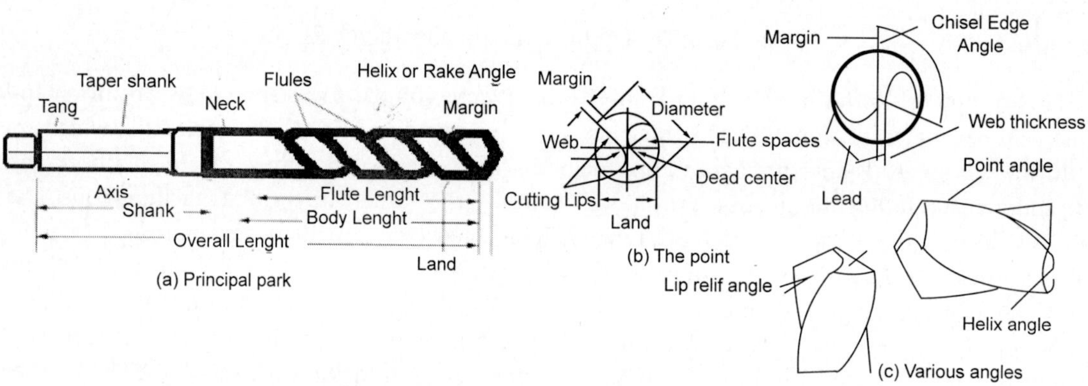

Figure 2.10: Nomenclature of a Drilling tool & details [13]

The twist drill with two cutting edges or lips is the most used drilling equipment (Fig. 2.10 (a) & (b). The point, body, neck, and shank are the four primary components of a twist drill. While the body steers the drill while it is operating, the point contains the cutting components. Due to the drill's web thickness, the cutting edges are straight and spaced apart. The web gets thicker as it gets closer to the shank, which helps give the drill enough strength and rigidity. Various angles are present on other portions of the drill, as shown in Fig. 2.10 c.

2.6.1 Lip Relief (Clearance) Angle

To provide relief behind the cutting lips, the heel of the drill point is backed off when ground. The cutting edges will be able to cut freely as a result. This is equivalent to the single point cutting tool's end relief angle. It is maintained between 12 and 15 degrees as shown in Fig. 2.10 c.

2.6.2 Point Angle

The tip angle is chosen to complement the material's hardness and brittleness. Cast iron and medium hard steel are 116° to 118°, hardened steel is 125°, and brass and bronze are 130° to 140°. Only 60 degrees apply to wood and fibre. The side cutting edge angle of a single point tool is indicated by this angle (half) as shown in Fig. 2.10 c.

2.6.3 Helix Angle

The rear rake angle of a single point cutting tool is the same as this helix angle and most drills operate between 24° and 30°.

2.6.4 Dead Centre

The "dead centre" or "chisel edge" is a sharp elevated line that is created at the drill's centre by the intersection of the two ground surfaces of the point and the web.

The "chisel-edge angle" is the angle formed by the elevated line at dead centre and the cutting edges. The clearance on the cutting edge close to the chisel edge is shown by this angle. Typically, this angle ranges from 120° to 135°. The chisel edge doesn't actually cut anything. It only shifts the material so that the cutting edges may remove it later. When beginning a hole, the chisel edge frequently wanders or walks over the surface. By making an indentation where the hole will begin on the work piece with a centre punch or a centre drill, the drill must be held in place.

Drill bushings can be used to guide the drill, which will help keep it in position. When using a twist drill, two cutting blades are occasionally offered for further cutting, which increases efficiency. Cutting pressures are evenly distributed, helical flutes allow cutting fluid access and aid in chip disposal, and small margins left on the cylinder's surface offer further guidance. Core Drill has three or four flutes with helical ribs. These drills are used to widen already-drilled holes as well as holes that have been punched, cast, or forged because they cannot create new holes.

The range of the helix angle is 10° to 30°. The advantages of these drills over a typical twist drill are as follows: The three or four margins (finding and guiding components of the drill) enable superior machining precision by avoiding tool swerving to one side during use, and (ii) having more cutting edges allows for higher feed per revolution, increasing productivity. These drills are often referred to as spiral or core reamers. Standard drills come in four size series, with the size reflecting the drill body's diameter: Fractional Size (i) Sizes are available in increments of 1/64 inch and 1/ 4 inch. Millimeter Size (ii) Sizes are available in increments of 0.1 mm from 0.5 to 10 mm. Numbered Size (iii) (80 to 10). Sizes are available in very small increments between 0.0135 and 0.228 inches and Lettered Size (iv) (A to Z). Sizes range from 0.234 to 0.413 in really small steps.

A drill's shank is used to hold and rotate it, as stated above. Both straight and tapered drill shanks are available. For smaller drills, a straight or cylindrical shank is offered (up to 12.7 mm diameter). Drills with a taper shank are placed right into the drilling spindle's taper hole (the taper is standard Morse taper, 1:20). The tang at the end of the tapered shank engages a slot at the end of the tapered hole to prevent any potential slippage. Adapting mechanisms, such as tapered sockets or sleeves, are used when the diameters of the tool shank and spindle hole tapers do not match. A drift in the shape of a wedge that fits into the spindle hole is used to withdraw the drill from the hole. Depending on the chuck's construction, straight shank drills are held in drill chucks and clamped either by hand or with a chuck key. These chucks may fit inside the drilling machine spindle's tapered hole because of their taper shanks.

2.6.5 MATERIALS OF DRILL

Although drills made of carbon tool steel have a cheap initial cost, they should only be used infrequently and at medium speeds. The most widely used and strong drills are made of high speed steel. While pricey and needing cautious handling to prevent breakage, drills with cemented carbide tips are inexpensive for high production. These are mostly used for drilling malleable iron castings as well as nonferrous metals and alloys including copper, brass, aluminum, magnesium, and zinc as well as plastics and hard rubber, etc. Due to the possibility of breaking from high tip pressure, these should not be used for steel components.

2.7 CLASSIFICATION OF DRILLING MACHINES

Drilling machines are classified as: General-purpose, single purpose and sspecialized drilling.

General purpose machines

Here, any hole making operation can be performed This class includes: bench type drill press, single and multiple-spindle upright drill presses, radial drilling machines and others. *Single Purpose Machines:* This class includes centre-drilling and deep hole drilling machines (horizontal and vertical types); semi-automatic and automatic drilling machines.

2.7.1 General Purpose Drilling Machines

The block diagram of a single-spindle general purpose machine (drill press) is shown in Fig. 2.11, wherein various parts of it are: Head Spindle, Column, Table, Base Distance, Throat, Pulley, Bearing Housing, Pinion, Bearing, Spindle, Sleeve Bearing, Key, Key-way, drill etc. Its main parts are: the base, column, table and head. The upright column is supported by a heavy base. The table is suspended from the column and may be moved up and down and clamped at the desired height. The drill head is mounted on the top of the column and consists of the main operating parts. The cutting tools (held in spindle) are power driven from the motor by a pair of cone pulleys-V belt drive or through a speed gear box to obtain various speeds. The axial feed of the tool is controlled by hand (on small machines) but larger machines provide power feed for the drill spindle. The spindle has a key way or spline, so that it may be moved up and down along its axis for feeding, but, still retains its drive at any point (Fig. 2.12).

2.7.2 Specialized Machines

Special unit-built multiple-spindle drilling machines, intended for performing a single definite operation, are used in mass production.

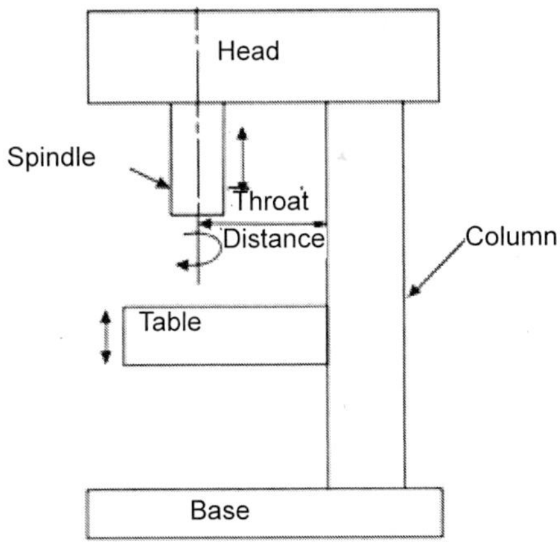

Figure 2.11: Block diagram of a drill press

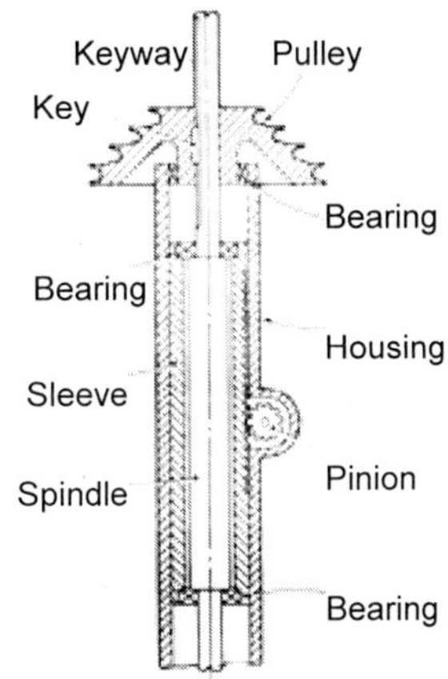

Figure 2.12: Feeding arrangement of a drill press [6]

The rack pinion is rotated through a worm gearing (in power feeding) and hand feed lever (in manual feeding). The pinion meshes with a rack secured to a non-revolving sleeve or quill in which the spindle freely rotates. The spindle is fed in the axial (vertical) direction together with the sleeve. Tables and often bases, are provided with T slots for clamping work or work-holding devices.

The size of a drill press is expressed in one or more of the following ways: (i) by the "swing" which is twice the distance from the nearest face of the column to the centre of the spindle. This indirectly refers to the diameter of the largest disc that can be drilled through the centre. (ii) by the maximum diameter of the drill that can be used on steel. (iii) by the maximum distance between the spindle and the table, that is, the maximum height of the job that can be accommodated with the table in its lowest position. (iv) by the distance the spindle moves up and down, that is, by the length of the spindle feed.

2.8 TYPES OF DRILL PRESSES

The drill press, often known as the drilling machine, is a tool for making holes in hard materials. The work piece, which is typically secured in a vice resting on a table, is fed into and the drill is held in a rotating spindle. Such presses come in several varieties, and some machines can automatically feed the drill into the workpiece while others may provide changing spindle speeds.

2.8.1 Bench Type

This is the simplest type used in industry. They are also called "sensitive" drill presses because the feed lever is operated by hand. This allows the operator to "feel" how the force is operating. If the drill gets into trouble, the pressure on it can be released. With little drills, this style is utilized for light labour (upto about 9.5 mm to 12.5 mm diameter drills). 800 to 9000 rev/min is a normal range, and the controls are delicate and light.

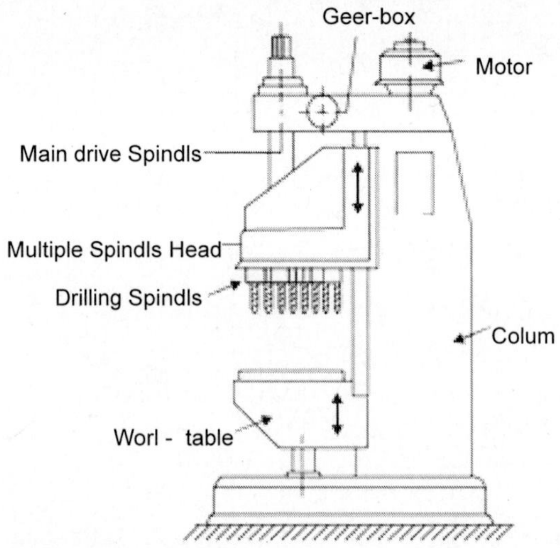

Figure 2.13: Non-adjustable multi-spindle machine of a drill press [6].

2.8.2 Upright Drill Presses

These are medium heavy duty machines and stand on floor. This machine usually has a gear-driven mechanism for different spindle speeds and an automatic or power feed device. This machine will take larger drills and cutting tools than the standard bench type machines. Single- spindle upright drilling machines can drill holes up to 75 mm in diameter and up to 350 mm deep. These machines have a wide range of spindle speeds and feeds and are employed, therefore, not only for drilling from the solid, but also for core drilling, reaming and tapping operations.

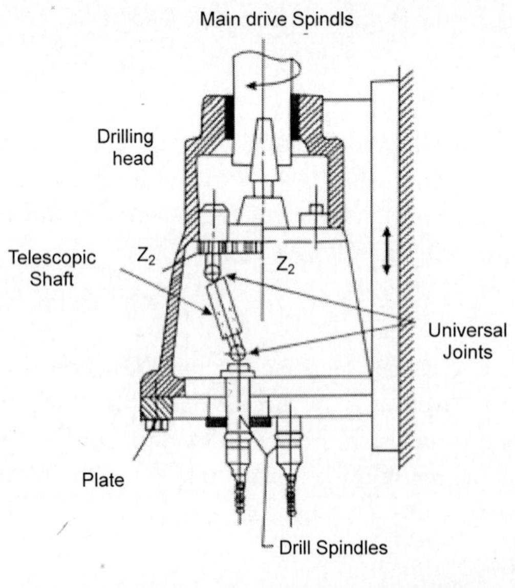

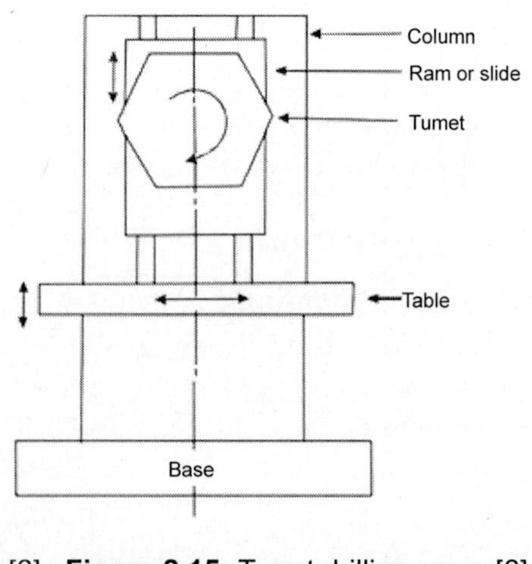

Figure 2.14: Adjustable multi-spindle machine drill press [6] **Figure 2.15:** Turret drilling press [6]

There are two constructions of the column: (i) Box-Column arrangement (Upright Machine). The column is of box section. The box column is bolted to the base. The work table is incorporated with a bracket which slides on ways at the front of the machine. Support and elevating movement of the table is provided by a telescopic screw underneath its centre. The table on these machines can be swung. (ii) Round-Column type (Pillar Machine). Here, the table instead of being carried on vertical slides is carried on the round pillar. This helps in swinging the table to one side so that tall work pieces can be mounted on the base. Here, the table support is less rigid than the upright machine and places a restriction on its width. A box-column machine being more rigid than a round column machine, is adopted for heavier work.

2.8.3 Multiple-Spindle Drilling Press

These machines also called as 'cluster drilling machines' are mass production machines with the several spindles (from 4 to 48 or more) driven by a single power head and fed simultaneously into the work. These machines are very useful when a number of parallel holes must be drilled in a part. These machines are subdivided into two group (according to the design of their spindles): those with nonadjustable (fixed position) spindles and those with adjustable spindles. (i) Non-adjustable Spindle Machine. (Fig. 2.13). The main drive spindle is rotated by an electric motor through a change speed gearbox. From the main drive spindle, the motion is transmitted to the drilling spindles, through appropriate gearing. The multiple-spindle head is moved up and down by the feed drive which has facilities for rapid traverse and feed motions. The worktable can be raised or lowered along the ways on the column.

The drilling spindles have a fixed position in the head designed for drilling the holes in a definite work piece. Their arrangement may be either symmetrical or asymmetrical, as the case may be. The spindle head can be replaced by another head designed for some other work piece or to perform some other operations. Different spindles in such a head may run at different speeds but they all have the same feed. (ii) Adjustable Spindle Machine. The drilling head of a multiple- spindle machine with adjustable spindles is shown in Fig. 2.14. Here, the main drive spindle travels up and down the column ways with the drilling head, being actuated by the feed drive. The drill spindles are driven from the main drive spindle through gears and through the universal joints and telescopic shaft. This arrangement enables the offset spindles to be driven. The drill spindles are mounted in a plate which has slots in various directions along which the spindles can be adjusted. Consequently, drill spindles can be positioned in the plate as required for a certain work piece. They can be readjusted to other positions for drilling some other work piece.

2.8.4 Gang Drilling Press

A gang drilling press is equivalent to 2, 3, or 4 or more (upto 8 or 10) upright drill presses in a row with a single common long table or base. Because of its small size, this machine is particularly practical for mass production. It is possible to configure the machine such that work can be transferred between spindles to complete two or more processes that may be related (drilling holes of various diameters) or distinct (drilling, reaming, counter- boring etc.). The identical processes could be carried out over all spindles in another configuration. With automatic feed control, two or more operations may be going on simultaneously attended only by one operator.

2.8.5 Turret Drilling Press

A turret drilling press, (Fig. 2.15), overcomes the floor space restriction caused by a gang drill press. Numerical control is also available. Two fixtures can be located on the worktable. This enables loading and unloading of one part while the other part is being machined. This reduces the cycle time.

2.8.6 Radial Drilling Machine

These machines (Fig. 2.16), are used for drilling holes at different locations on heavy and bulky work pieces which are either inconvenient or impossible to mount on the table of an upright drilling machine and cannot be moved easily. A large arm extends out from the column. It can be raised or lowered along the column with the help of an elevating screw and it also swings in a complete circle around the column. The drilling head moves back and forth on this arm. On most radial drilling machines, the movements of the arm, the drill head, and the spindle are controlled by power feeds. Due to the back and forth movement of the drilling head along the arm and the swinging motion of the arm around the column, holes can be drilled in many different locations without moving the work-piece

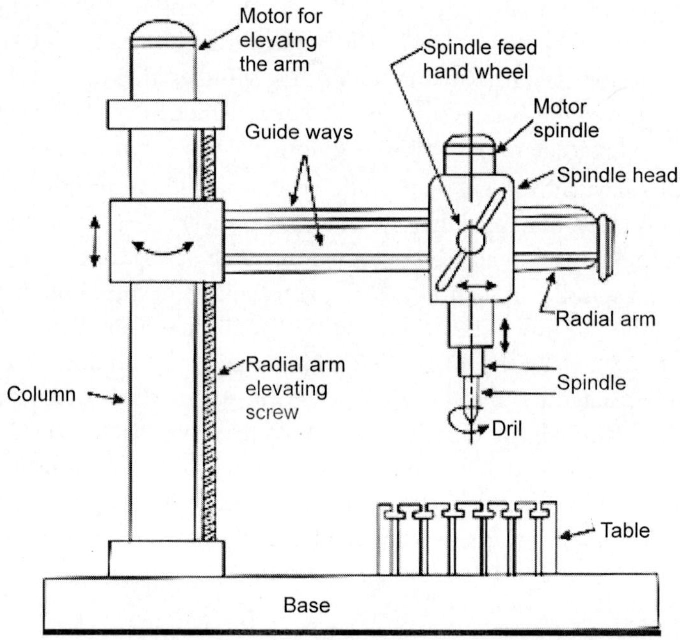

Figure 2.16: Radial drilling machine [6]

Three different designs are offered for radial drilling machines: (i) Simple one, the only spindle motion in this design is vertical, Semi-universal (ii) this machine allows for the drilling of holes at an angle in a vertical plane by allowing the spindle head to be swung about a horizontal axis normal to the arm, Universal is (iii). Additionally, the radial arm can be turned around a horizontal axis. This enables holes to be drilled at any desired angle. Radial drilling machine size. A radial drilling machine's dimensions are as follows: (i) The column's diameter in centimeters (ii) The diameter of the greatest disc into which a centre hole can be bored while the drilling head is at the farthest end of the arm.

2.8.7 Specialized Drilling Machines

In mass production, special unit-built multiple-spindle drilling machines are employed for drilling housing-type and other parts. These machines are assembled from standard units and mechanisms. Such machines perform drilling, reaming, tapping and other operations that are commonly done in drill presses. In many cases, such multiple-spindle machines are built into an automatic transfer line. As a rule, the only special units of these machines are the spindle head and the jig or fixture for holding the work piece. To changeover to the production of a new part, it is usually necessary to design, manufacture and install these two special units only. Various arrangements of the standard units to obtain different designs of unit built machines are illustrated as shown in Fig. 3.9 (*a-f*).

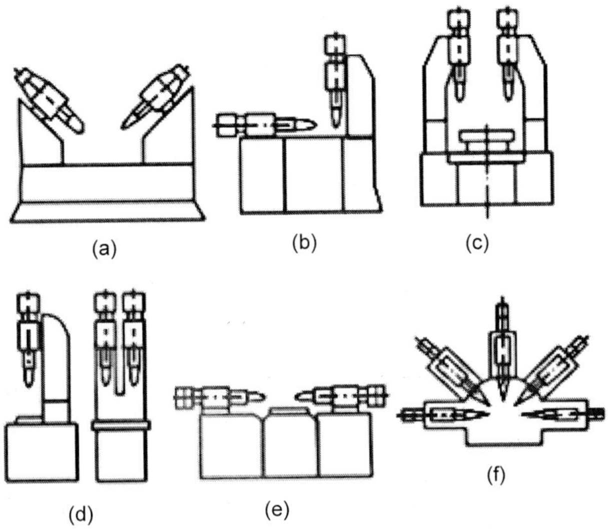

Figure 2.17: Unit build drilling machines [6].

2.9 SPECIFICATIONS OF DRILLING MACHINE

Varied drilling machines have different specifications, such as the work piece surface, drilling size, hole diameter, number of holes, maximum drill diameter that might be coupled to it, etc. The arm length and column diameter of radial drill machines can be used to identify them. The drilling area, hole size, and number that the tool may create serve as indicators of a multiple spindle drill.

2.10 TYPES OF OPERATIONS

There are numerous linked drilling operations. In order to make seats for a bolt head and nut, a screw or rivet head, a washer, etc., further machining is done to holes that have already been drilled from a solid with one drill. Figure 2.1 shows these allied efforts that are described later.

1. **Core drilling** - A core drill is used to drill holes in order to increase their size and enhance their geometric form.
2. **Step drilling** -The "Step drill" or "combination drill" is an operation that involves creating a hole of two or more diameters with a single drill.

3. **Boring**-Boring is the process of completely completing and widening the hole using a single point cutting instrument. Although the lathe group of machine tools can also be used, boring machines are often used for this activity. By boring, the hole's location is adjusted and brought into alignment with the spindle's axis of rotation.
4. **Reaming** - Reaming, which often comes after drilling or core drilling, uses a multipoint cutting tool called a "reamer" to eliminate all coarse remnants of earlier machining processes. A hole that has been reamed is precise in size and has a smooth surface. Since the reamer only follows the previously drilled hole, reaming cannot change the location of the hole.
5. **Counter boring** - Consists of making the surface at the bottom of a bigger diameter hole level and square and extending a section of an existing hole to a larger diameter. This is done to allow space for a screw head, bolt head, or nut beneath the hole's top surface. Using a "Counter bore," a specialized tool, or a standard boring tool, the procedure is carried out.
6. **Countersunk** - is carried out after a hole has been drilled in order to chamfer the entry or to create a conical recess or seat for a flat-headed screw or rivet so that the heads are flush or below the main surface. Standard countersinks have an incorporated angle of 60, 82, or 90°. A countersink is a small instrument that resembles a reamer.
7. **Spot facing** - spot facing is the process of milling a boss or pad onto a hole's face. The goal is often to provide a square bearing surface for a washer and nut or the bolt head. Pilot guidance is used for both spot facers and counter-borers.

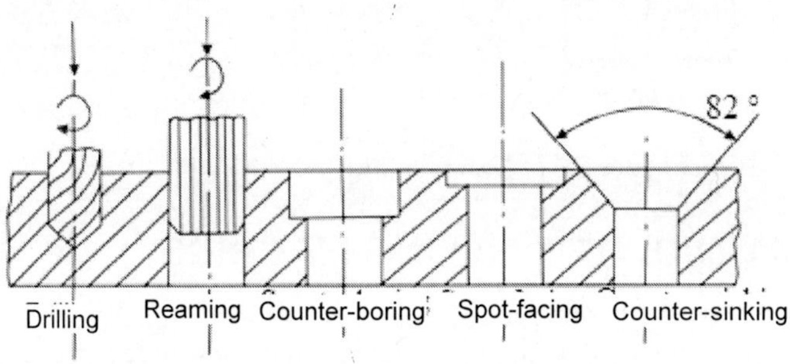

Figure 2.18: Drilling and allied operations [6].

2.11 TYPES OF DRILLS

Drills are an essential part of every person's toolbox for the garage. When drilling is required, it can be utilized for commercial operations, do-it-oneself-projects, and household maintenance. In the history of human creation, the first drill was the primordial awl. However, a variety of drill types are used nowadays. Drills come in two primary categories: electric and manual. They are all equipped with the same features, such as multi-function power, a selection of driving bits, and various drilling powers. By being informed of the many types of drills, one may get the precise drilling equipment they desire. Table 3.1 list the best drill type options for such situations:

Table 2.1: List of drill type options for different applications [14]

Drill types	Descriptions	Figure
Hand drill	Gear-driven manual tools include the hand drill and eggbeater drill. In order to drill a hole, a handle must be turned. The pinion and chuck both move in tandem with the rotating wheel. The connected bit or shank spins as a consequence. Soft metal, plastic, and softwood can all be drilled through with this kind of drill.	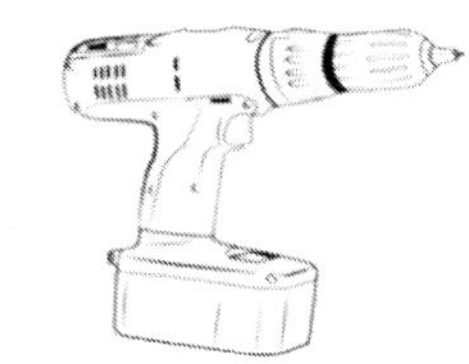
Brace drill	The invention of this manual drilling instrument dates back to the 1420s. The U-shaped spindle distinguishes this drill from others. More torque is produced by cranking the spindle's grip. The top spindle makes it simpler to hold and adjust the manual tool. In order to drill and countersink holes in timber materials, brace drills are employed.	
Corded drill	The corded drill type is an excellent option when it comes to electric drills. For best performance, it needs a power source. The pistol grip is the most widely used style. Projects involving drilling become more pleasant and easy. In contrast to cordless drills, this kind of drill has higher power since it has more torque. This may be used to drill into wood, fibreglass, plastic, and metal.	
Hammer drill	The hammer drill, which combines rotary and hammer movements, is a great instrument for drilling into concrete, metal, and stone blocks. Depending on needs, one may choose between corded and cordless hammer drills. The hammer drill can cut through thick concrete, yet it may also be used as a regular drill. Because of its strong hammering action, it is very different from other varieties.	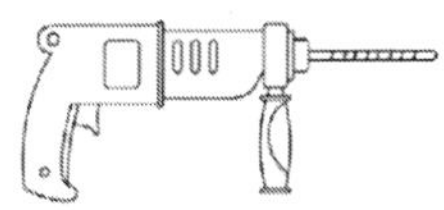
Cordless drill	Cordless drills are nearly identical to their corded counterparts in terms of design. However, their weight makes the distinction clear. This type is lighter than other drills due to the fact that it is cordless. A greater voltage can provide a more powerful drilling function. Drills that run on batteries, such as the Cordless Drill batteries, are not designed for heavy drilling in concrete. As an alternative, one may use it on wood, plastic, fibreglass, and thin metal sheets.	
Drill press	The drill press, a stationary form of drill, is constructed using both stationary and motor bits. With specified width and depth, they quickly and repeatedly drill holes. The angles from which you wish to drill holes can be changed. You may easily apply this to both softer and harder materials, depending on your use.	

2.12 TYPES OF DRILL BITS

The drill bits are designed to create holes in a variety of materials. This uses a variety of materials, including concrete, ceramic tile, porcelain, metal, plastic, and wood. Additionally, drill bits for sheet metal, fiberglass, brick, cast iron, steel, aluminum, copper, and other materials are available. Drill bits are made in a variety of designs depending on their diameter to help with particular jobs. According to Table 2.2, there are 22 different types of drill bits.

Table 2.2: Different types of drill bits in use [15]

Drill bits	Descriptions	Figure
Flat Drill	Typically, thin sticks of high carbon steel are pounded into this sort of drill. They are tempered and toughened after grinding their cutting edge. Any size or form may be manufactured with ease. Upon forging, they are then produced in various sizes. They are relatively affordable drills. For drilling holes in iron, it is not employed. It is typically used to bore holes in soft metals for carpentry work. Keep the cutting point at a 90° angle. After being suitably hardened and heated, this drill may be used on those solid metals where conventional drills break.	
Straight Fluted Drill	A straight fluted drill has grooves or flutes that are perpendicular to the drill axis. A straight fluted drill is comparable to a cutting tool without rakes. Soft metals like brass or copper are frequently drilled with the help of these drills. The conventional twist drill has a propensity to grind or gouge into soft metal. The head, neck, and shank make up a straight or flat drill. The sides of the skull might be parallel or have a little backward taper. To lower the friction during drilling, a rear taper of 2° to 3° may be offered. The operation accuracy and tool life of drills with parallel sides are both better. A flat drill's tip angle spans from 90° to 120°.	
Twist Drill Bit	Today, twist and thick drills are utilized to swiftly bore holes that are clean and the right size. High-speed steel and thin alloy steel rods are typically used to make them. The bottom end is then formed with a cutting edge, and the body is then cut with a flute, which is a twisting groove running from top to bottom. It is referred to as a twist drill because to the twisted flute. Tang, shank, body, point, and neck are some of its primary components.	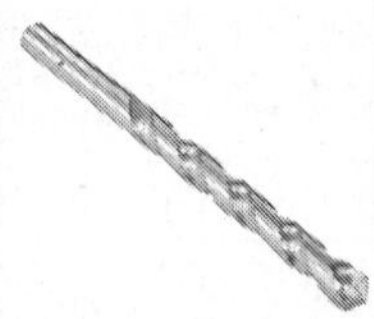
Double Fluted Drill	This kind of drill is the finest and most powerful. In this drill, two flutes are cut in opposition to one another. Nearly every form of employment uses it.	
Multi-fluted drill	This drill is utilised for very specialised tasks. In this drill, there are more than two flutes. Its standout characteristic is how swiftly and cleanly the hole is bored because to its larger cutting edge.	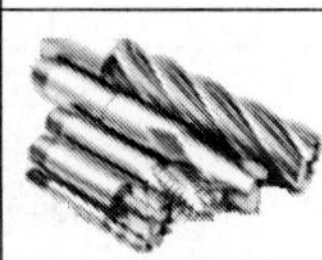
Centre Drill	It is sometimes referred to as a combination drill. It has a cutting edge on both of its ends, and its midsection is plain. With this drill, countersinking and drilling may be done concurrently. It is used to drill the centre of a rod when lathe machines are turning long jobs from centre to centre.	

Drill bits	Descriptions	Figure
Counter Sinking Drill	In order to countersink, holes must be drilled where counter head screws are to be placed. In this manner, the screw's head work fits well. This drill has four flutes and is multi-fluted. At 60° or 82°, the cutting point is ground. This kind of drill is seen in the illustration together with a screw that is placed within the hole that it creates.	
Counter Boring Drill	With this drill, counter boring is done when Allen screws are installed. On the surface of the project, these kinds of screws are likewise installed like countersunk screws. The task surface stays comparable to the plain surface for the purpose of fitting this type of screw. There is no functional difficulty caused by the screw heads. One interesting difference between counter boring and countersinking is that with counter boring, the hole is drilled deeper and larger, up to the height of the screw head. A counter boring cutter is another name for the drill used for counter boring.	
Oil Hole or Tube Drill	When drilling holes, a coolant or lubricant is required to keep the drill tip from losing its cutting ability as it gets heated. A hole is constructed from the shank to the cutting point of some drills, in addition to standard drills, to allow lubrication up until the cutting point.	
Spirec Drill	These drills are extremely fine. These are used to drill very small holes in items like the spray pump nozzle and storage nipple. They are between 0.0086" to 0.0984" in size.	
Shell Drill	Unlike other drills, this one is unique. When milling, a face cutter with a shape akin to a side is employed. It is formed into four flutes. 1/3" per foot is the taper of its top portion. Mandrels are needed in order to use it. For expanding a hole, they are frequently employed.	
Step Drill	A step drill is required if you wish to drill holes in sheet metal. Its appearance resembles a ladder that is falling. Even so, if one works with sheet metal frequently, this is what one needs even if their working method is slightly more expensive than other drill bits. The step bit's construction makes it possible to firmly drill holes of various sizes. Deburring holes are another great feature these bits produce, allowing one to remove superfluous materials.	
Installer Bit	These drill bits are specialized twist drill bits that are employed to drill holes for the installation of cables for security and entertainment systems. These drill bits, which may reach a length of 18 inches, resemble auger bits. They work well for drilling through masonry, wood, and some plaster. In the bit's tip, there is a little hole. After drilling a hole in the surface, one must force the wire through the hole by inserting it into the tip's hole. Pull it while assuming the opposing side.	
Masonry Bit	Wherever brick, stone, and concrete work is being done, these drill bits are employed. Despite how durable these parts are, you must repair them frequently as they wear out. The tip will melt if you drill into the concrete for an extended period of time. By frequently taking the drill out of the concrete, you can lessen this issue.	

Drill bits	Descriptions	Figure
Rivet Drill	The usage of these rivet bits is probably not possible unless one works in professional construction. These particular drill bits are made for drilling small rivets into thin sheets of metal.	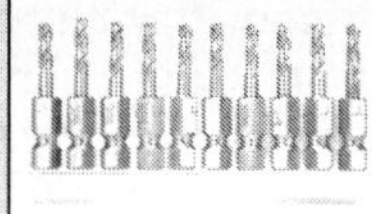
Auger Bit	A drill bit called an auger can be used to create a hole in thick, dry wood. One doesn't need to exert as much pressure since a hole may be made in the trees relatively quickly. These have a screw tip that both drills the hole and aids in pulling out the bit to produce a tidy hole. Since several of these bits are up to 18 inches in length, they may be used on thicker wood. Its big flute, which allows dust to enter the opening, supports the channel. Some varieties allow for even greater chip removal since the centres are hollow.	
Tile Bit	To drill into specific tile and lessen the possibility of chips and cracks, these drill bits include a carbide tip. According to the different sorts of tiles, different tile bits are designed.	
Hammer Bit	In order to accurately and completely measure relative humidity, a precise hole must be drilled in a concrete slab using a hammer bit.	
Glass Bit	With this sort of drill bit, holes may be made through glass, plastic, composite materials, brick, marble, and hollow bricks. It offers a greater endurance to high temperatures, speeds up dust clearing, and is perfect for drilling into dense material.	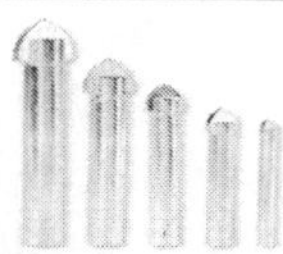
Forstner Bit	This kind of drill bit is ideal if one want to drill neat, smooth holes in wood. With this bit, precise holes may be made. It features a sharp tip that aids in keeping the bit in the desired location. It doesn't have a flute, and you have to routinely remove it to dust and chip the flute. A drill press with this kind of drill bit is necessary for a number of applications.	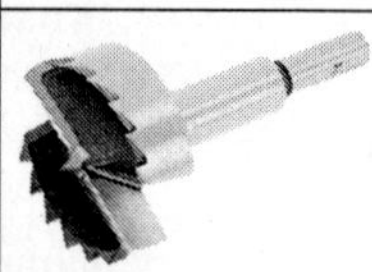
Hole Saw	If installing door hardware or creating a wire pass-through is required, this kind of drill bit can be used. A side cutout in the saw cylinder forces the worthless plug that the hole saw produces out of the way. To centre the hole and steady the blade, one can also use an attachment and a pilot bit. A built-in shank is used instead of a pilot bit by small hole saws. You can cut holes in both wood and metal with a bi-metal hole saw.	
Plug Cutter	This kind of drill bit is required if one wish to create a hole in the wood or cut a wooden plug together. Having woodworking that is on par with expert work is advantageous using this kind of bit.	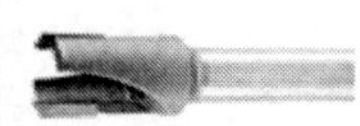

2.13 REAMING AND TYPES OF REAMERS

Reaming is a continuous cutting activity using a multi-edged cutting instrument. To finish drilled holes precisely to size and with a fine surface quality, reaming is used. Reaming has the benefit of allowing for the production of a higher quantity of holes of consistently high quality. This calls for a hole that has been exactly pre-machined (good true-running accuracy and sufficient machining allowance). Some of the common reamer types are listed in Fig. 2.19. Lubricants can be used to increase the reamer's lifespan. Fitting and taper holes both require reaming. For finishing morse taper holes or sleeves, use morse taper reamers. Car parts including steering arms, ball joints, and tie rod ends are reamed from steel using automotive reamers.

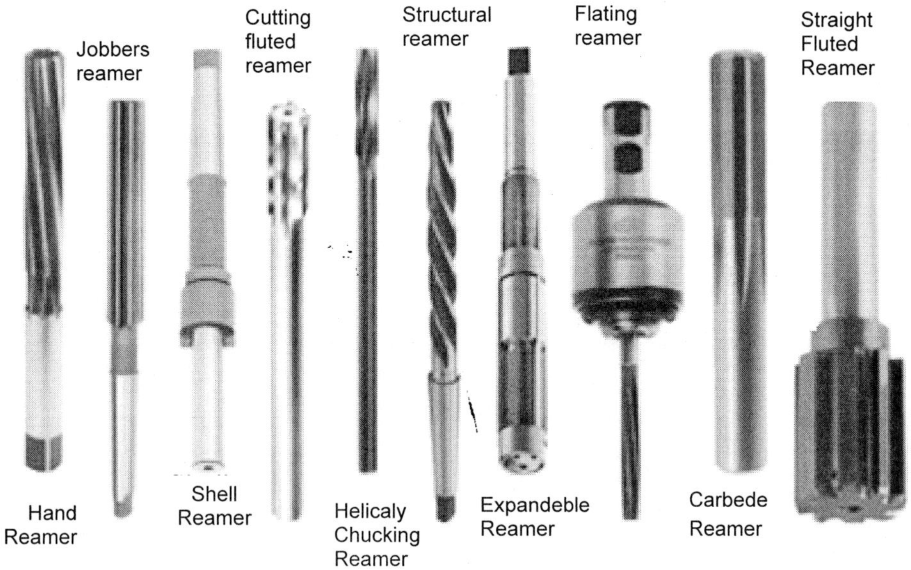

Figure 2.19: Common Reamer Types in use [16].

For diverse machining purposes, numerous types of reamers made from various materials exist. Reamers are also divided into groups according on how they are held or driven and how they are built. The common types and classes that machinists could encounter are listed above in Fig 2.19. When viewed from either end of the reamer, the flutes of the reamer exhibit a right hand helix, which twists away from the viewer in a clockwise motion. Alternatively, when they twist in a counterclockwise manner, they have a Left hand helix.

Reamers can be grouped according to how they were made:

i. Solid Reamers are ones that are crafted from a single piece of tool metal.
ii. Tipped Solid Reamers have a body made of one material with cutting blades that are brazed or attached to the body of the tool.
iii. Inserted Blade Reamers feature replaceable, mechanically held, solid or tippable, and typically adjustable, blades.
iv. Expansion Reamers can have their size enlarged by bending or deflecting certain reamer body parts.
v. Adjustable reamers have movable blades that may be slid or moved in relation to the reamer axis to vary the size of the reamer.

Reamers can also be categorized according to how they are held or operated:

i. The left and right hands. Reamers are used to characterize the rotational axis and flute helix direction of reamers.

ii. Hand of Cut (or Hand of Rotation):

iii. Right Hand Rotation, also known as Right Hand Cut, is the counterclockwise rotation of a reamer that, when viewed from the cutting end, rotates to form a cut.

iv. A left hand rotation, also known as a left hand cut, is the clockwise rotation of a reamer so that, when viewed from the cutting end, it makes a cut.

v Pull reamers are said to be right-hand cut if, when seen from the cutting end, cutting requires a clockwise rotation.

vi. The Hand of the flute helix

vii. Reamers with straight flutes have cutting blades that are parallel to the reamer axis.

viii. Alternate helix reamers are those with every other flute having a different (left and right hand) helix.

ix. Right hand or Left hand helix reamer only have one orientation for the flute helix.

UNIT SUMMARY

Broaching, drilling machining operations are integral part of machining operation system for such processes. In this section, types of broaching and drilling processes and operations are explained including the machines on which various operations of broaching and drilling can be done. Common cutting tool materials used for broaching, drilling and reaming is also clarified. It is wise decision of the designer and application engineers to select a proper machine and tooling as per the application and material to be cut. It also important to select proper steps of operations and the optimal machining conditions for a tool-work piece combination for economical machining. Generally, specialized operators are needed to carry our broaching and drilling operations.

EXERCISES

Multiple Choice Questions

Questions for self-assessment

1. Which of the following cutting tools is used in broaching?

   (a) Single point tool (b) Multi point tool
   (c) both (A) and (B) (d) No cutting tool is used

2. In broaching, the whole machining allowance is removed in

   (a) Multiple strokes
   (b) Two strokes
   (c) One stroke
   (d) It depends upon the amount of material to be removed

3. Which of the following shapes can be machined by broaching?

   (a) the shaft of gears (b) grooved components
   (c) flat surfaces (d) all of the above

4. Broaching is used for machining of
   (a) external surfaces
   (b) internal surfaces
   (c) internal and external surfaces
   (d) none of the above
5. Following is true for broaching operation
   (a) very high tool cost
   (b) production rate is high
   (c) single reciprocating motion is required for cutting
   (d) all of the above
6. Following type of teeth are part of broaching tool
   (a) roughing teeth
   (b) semi-finishing teeth
   (c) finishing teeth
   (d) all of the above
7. In broaching tool, the rake angle (face angle) of tooth depends ___ of the material.
   (a) ductility
   (b) hardness
   (c) toughness
   (d) all of the above
8. In broaching tool, the land of the tooth determines its
   (a) strength
   (b) surface area
   (c) thickness
   (d) all of the above
9. The pitch determines the ____ which a broach can handle.
   (a) length of cut
   (b) chip thickness
   (c) both (A) and (B)
   (d) none of the above
10. During broaching operation the broach is
    (a) pushed
    (b) pulled
    (c) either pushed or pulled
    (d) rotated
11. Following is (are) the broach material (s).
    (a) High Speed Steel
    (b) Carbide
    (c) both (A) and (B)
    (d) Aluminium oxide
12. Broaching machines are specified by
    (a) Driving forces
    (b) Length of stroke
    (c) both (A) and (B)
    (d) Height from base
13. In drilling operation, the work piece remains____________in position.
    (a) Horizontal
    (b) Vertical
    (c) Stationary
    (d) Rotating
14. Drilling machine can also be used for_____________.
    (a) Turning
    (b) Thread cutting
    (c) Knurling
    (d) Tapping
15. The rotating drill is made to__________into the job.
    (a) Speed
    (b) Feed
    (c) Parallel
    (d) Perpendicular

16. Drilling removes solid metal from the job to produce a__________.
    (a) Circular hole (b) Taper hole
    (c) Step turning (d) Reaming
17. The__________machine can be easily taken to required place.
    (a) Sensitive drilling (b) Portable drilling
    (c) Gang drilling (d) Radial drilling
18. The sensitive drilling machine is a________machine widely used in workshops.
    (a) Heavy duty (b) Light duty
    (c) Hand drilling (d) None of them
19. Power from the driving unit is transmitted to__________through the belt drives.
    (a) Spindle (b) Headstock
    (c) Tailstock (d) None of them
20. In sensitive drilling machine the holes up to__________can be drilled in these machine.
    (a) 10 mm (b) 15 mm
    (c) 20 mm (d) 25 mm
21. Spindle is mounted on________shaft which fixed vertically on the radial arm.
    (a) Drive (b) Arm
    (c) Electric motor (d) None of them
22. The__________is attached with the chuck to hold the drill.
    (a) Radial arm (b) Spindle
    (c) Motor (d) None of them

ANSWERS															
1.	(b)	2.	(c)	3.	(d)	4.	(c)	5.	(d)	6.	(d)	7.	(d)	8.	(a)
9.	(c)	10.	(c)	11.	(c)	12.	(c)	13.	(c)	14.	(d)	15.	(b)	16.	(a)
17.	(b)	18.	(b)	19.	(a)	20.	(b)	21.	(c)	22.	(b)				

Short and Long Answer Type Questions

1. Draw a typical internal broach and explain it.
2. Describe the vertical push broaching operation and the horizontal pull broaching operation using clear illustrations.
3. Explain the operation of a continuous surface broaching machine using a clean drawing.
4. Outline the benefits and drawbacks of the broaching method.
5. Describe in a schematic diagram the broaching, drilling, and reaming operations.
6. Draw a twist drill. List all of its components along with what they do.
7. Why is the drill's body manufactured with a little smaller diameter than its entire nominal diameter?
8. Describe the components of broaches, drills, and reamers.

9. What are the four drill size classification systems?
10. What is a core drill, exactly? When is it utilized? Describe what makes it superior to a "regular twist drill."
11. Draw a diagram and describe the allied processes of reaming, counter boring, countersinking, and spot facing.
12. How are various drilling machines categorized?
13. Sketch the structural layout of a broaching machine. Identify its four main components.
14. How is a drill press's capacity or size determined?
15. Draw a diagram and explain the two different kinds of multiple-spindle drill presses.
16. What exactly is a radial drilling device? Draw it out and explain it.
17. How is a radial drilling machine's size or capacity specified?
18. Draw a Reamer and describe how each component works.
19. Compose a brief remark about the reaming process.
20. What are left- and right-handed reamers, and what do they do?

PRACTICAL

1. Perform vehicle push and horizontal pull broaching operation on broaching machine.
2. Understand and write the different components used for drilling operation.
3. Perform and create a hole of 30 mm diameter in metallic plate by selecting a proper drill bit on drilling machine.
4. Perform and understand the remaining operation run in question number 3.
5. Draw a neat sketch of a drill bit consisting of different parts.

KNOW MORE

Explore the historical machining work for objects making like in wood using drilling and broaching machines and try to find how it is evolved with time as one could see the modern drilling and broaching machines and the operations today. One can study it carefully.

SUGGESTED RESOURCES FOR FURTHER READING/ LEARNING

Reference books & websites referred

1. Elements of workshop Technology (Volume I & II) – S. K. Hajra Chaudary, Bose & Roy, Media Promoters and Publishers Limited.
2. Production Technology (Volume I & II) – O. P. Khanna & Lal, Dhanpat Rai Publications.
3. Fundamental of metal cutting and machine tools– B. L. Juneja, New age international limited.

4. Manufacturing Technology, Metal Cutting & Machine tools– P. N. Rao, Tata McGraw- Hill Publications
5. A Text book of Production Technology: Manufacturing processes –P.C. Sharma, S. Chand & Com. Pvt. Ltd., New Delhi
6. Production Technology – R.B. Gupta, Satya Prakashan, New Delhi
7. Fundamentals of Design & Manufacturing- G K Lal, Vijay Gupta, N. V. Readdy, NarosaPub. House, ND
8. https://link.springer.com/referenceworkentry/10.1007/978-3-642-20617-7_6686
9. http://learnmech.com/wp-content/uploads/2018/09/types-of-broaching-process.gif
10. http://upload.wikimedia.org/wikipedia/commons/thumb/f/fa/Broach_tooth_geometry.svg/400px-Broach_tooth_geometry.svg.png
11. https://www.researchgate.net/publication/332458830/figure/fig1/AS:892980021968896@1589914436335/Twist-Drill-Motion-8.jpg
13. https://m.media-amazon.com/images/I/
14. https://www.theengineerspost.com/wp-content/uploads/2021/07/Types-of-sprockets-2-e1625638418915.jpg
15. https://engineeringlearn.com/wp-content/uploads/2021/04/Types-of-Reamers.jpg

VIDEOS

Broaching

https://www.youtube.com/watch?v=rAJx-6SLdP0

https://www.youtube.com/watch?v=S1njLLL0Rg0

Drilling

https://www.youtube.com/watch?v=aJC75tJwuwg

https://www.youtube.com/watch?v=peQkk25q3r8

3 Welding-Brazing-Soldering and Milling Machines

Classification; Gas welding techniques; Types of welding flames; Arc Welding- Principle, Equipment, Applications; Shielded metal arc welding; Submerged arc welding; TIG / MIG welding; Resistance welding-Spot welding, Seam welding, Projection welding; Welding defects; Brazing and soldering: Types, Principles, Applications.

Introduction; Types of milling machines: plain, Universal, vertical; constructional details- specifications; Milling operations: simple, compound and differential indexing; Milling cutters - types; Nomenclature of teeth; Teeth materials; Tool signature of milling cutter; Tool & work holding devices.

UNIT SPECIFIC / LEARNING OBJECTIVE

Objective of this unit in to talk about following aspects

- To introduce significance of Welding and Milling functions
- To learn about the importance of Welding and Milling processes & their working principles
- To introduce the underlying advantages and applications of Welding and Milling machines
- To introduce the welding and milling toolings, their operations and materials
- To understand the significance of various types of welding, and Milling operations
- To learn about Welding, and Milling machine equipment and their specifications

Additionally, few fundamental questions for self-assessment based on fundamentals are also included in this Unit in form of recall, application, comprehension, analysis and synthesis. There are further suggested readings and reference for reader's assistance.

RATIONALE

Welding and Milling processes are very versatile processes and are being used since 3000 BC. Various types of welding exists like Gas welding with different flames as per their applications. Other welding methods are Arc Welding for joining similar metals together. Shielded metal arc welding, Submerged arc welding, TIG / MIG welding, Resistance welding, Spot welding, Seam welding, and Projection welding are some more types of arc welding. Any welding process must control defects. The common welding defects and their remedies are important precautions during welding of various welding methods. Brazing and soldering methods are popular for joining dissimilar metals, their applications are chosen wisely for safe joints. Milling is also an important machining process using milling cutters. The details of milling machines are needed to understand their constructional details. Specifications of milling machine require many parameters for deciding proper machine applications. Various milling operations gives an idea to choose proper one for better sequence. Therefore, different differential indexing methods used for holding the workpiece is also important before cutting. Different milling cutters & their types with their nomenclature of teeth are also equally important in gear cutting. There are different milling cutter materials available for machining different work materials.

PRE-REQUISITES

A course on Engineering mechanics, basics of mechanical elements & mechanisms

Learning outcomes

U3-O1: Ability to choose suitable work-piece for joining and machining job on welding and milling machines

U3-O2: Ability to choose suitable welding process and their joining tool for welding, milling machines & tools for machining operation

U3-O3: Ability to choose suitable operations and proper tools for welding and milling

U3-O4: Ability to choose suitable working conditions and parameters (welding process & milling process) for welding and milling operations

U3-O5: Ability to predict the behavior of welded/ milled part workpieces and its dimensions after welding, and milling.

COURSE OBJECTIVES

- To understand the importance of welding and milling machines and the process equipments.
- To study and recognise various types of welding and milling machines, their parts and operations.
- To be able to select, operate and control the appropriate welding and milling operations for specific applications.

Mapping of learning outcomes and course objectives

Unit-3 Outcomes	EXPECTED MAPPING WITH COURSE OUTCOMES (1- Weak Correlation; 2- Medium correlation; 3- Strong Correlation)					
	CO-1	CO-2	CO-3	CO-4	CO-5	CO-6
U3-O1	1	3	3			
U3-O2	2	2	2			
U3-O3	1	2	3			
U3-O4	1	3	3			
U3-O5	1	2	3			

3.1 INTRODUCTION TO WELDING

Welding is the process of permanently connecting two metallic parts together using heat and/or pressure. It is a localised metal coalescence in which coalescence is accomplished by heating to an appropriate temperature, with or without pressure, and with or without the use of filler metal. The melting point of the filler metal is similar to that of the base metals. The welding process is used to metallurgically combine two metal parts to create what is basically a single piece of metal. The procedure produces a 'permanent joint.' A well-welded junction is as durable as the parent metal. The product is called 'Weldment.'

During the late nineteenth century, Le Chatelier and Joule, among others, used developments in electricity to heat and/or combine metals, and before to World War I, welding was not trusted as a means to join two metals due to crack concerns. However, from the 1930s to the 1940s, industrial welding gained favour and was widely employed during the war effort to construct tanks, aircraft, and ships, among other things. Modern welding during the nuclear and space ages contributed to the advancement of welding from an art to a science, as seen in Fig 3.1.

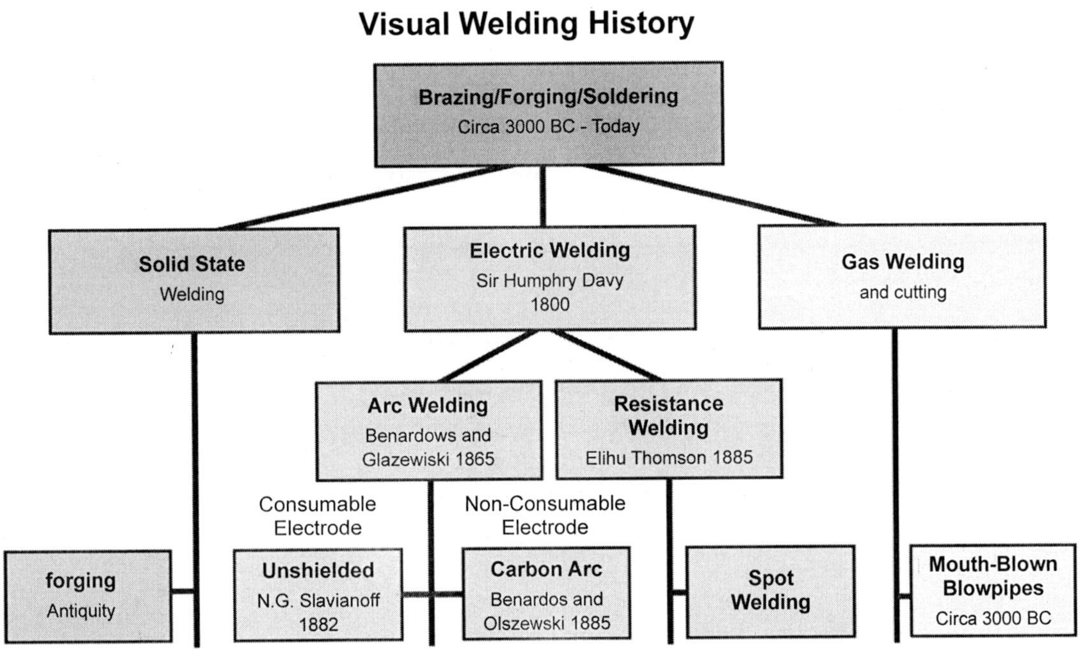

Figure 3.1: History of Welding

The welding process is widely used in almost all branches of industry and construction, and it is extensively used in the fabrication and erection of steel structures in industrial construction and civil engineering, such as structural members of bridges and buildings, for example; vessels of welded-plate construction (steel reservoirs, boilers, pressure vessel tanks, and pipelines, for example); and concrete reinforcement. It is the primary method of connecting panels and members together in vehicle bodies, as well as in the aviation industry. For a considerable part of machine, jig, and fixture bases, bodies, and frames, it has replaced castings. The procedure is also widely employed in the repair of broken parts, the construction of warning surfaces, and the restoration of defective castings. In fact, the destiny of every metal may be determined by how well it lends itself to manufacture via welding.

3.2 ADVANTAGES AND LIMITATIONS OF WELDING

Welding is becoming increasingly popular due to the following benefits:

1. Welding results in material savings and a lower labour component of production.
2. Welded joints are inexpensive to produce.
3. Welded constructions are often lighter in weight than riveted or bolted structures.
4. Welding joints provide optimal efficiency, which other types of joints do not.
5. Additional and alternative structures can be readily added to the existing structure. A welded joint provides very rigid joint and has a great strength.
6. The welding procedure is faster than other types of joints.
7. The medium's dependability, that is, the weldments are safer.
8. It allows the designer a lot of freedom in terms of planning and creating.
9. Welding can also be used to repair cracked, worn, or defective metal parts. As a result, the cost of reinvestment can be avoided.
10. Lightweight fabrication technologies, which are critical to the automotive and aerospace industries, would be unimaginable without welding procedures.

The welding procedure is easily adaptable to streamline structures, and the welded joints are extremely tight and sturdy, even under static strain. However, because to stress concentration, residual stresses, and numerous weld flaws such as cracks, incomplete fusion, slag inclusions, and so on, they have low fatigue resistance. However, all of these disadvantages can be mitigated to a great extent.

3.2.1 Advantages of Welded Joints Over Riveted Joints

1. *Economy of material and lighter weight of structure owing to:*

   (a) improved usage of metal elements (plates, angles) since their working sections are not weakened by rivet holes; as a result, the sections of welded parts can be made smaller than the sections of riveted elements for the same acting forces. (b) the ability to use butt-jointed seams widely without the need for extra elements such as cover straps, and (c) reduced weight of the connecting elements (rivets weight more than the welds). Welds account for roughly 1 to 1.5 percent of total work weight, while rivets account for about 3.5 to 4%. Welding, rather than riveting, saves between 10% and 20% of the weight.
2. *Greater joint strength due to the absence of riveting holes.*
3. *There is less labor required* because there is no need to mark out and drill or punch holes. Riveting requires far more labor and is a lot more intricate and time-consuming task than welding, which can frequently be entirely automated.
4. *The ability to combine curved pieces.*
5. *The joint's tightness and impermeability.*
6. *Noiselessness, riveting is inevitably accompanied by noise.*

3.2.2 Advantages Welded Joints Over Casting Process

1. Lighter weight and material savings due to: (a) lower machining allowances and (b) the ability to use smaller sections, because the wall thickness of cast parts, which is often defined by the casting process, is 2 to 3 times more, and often even more, than that of welded components.

Metal savings in welded machine components may amount to 40% when compared to cast ones.

2. Lower the cost.
3. Greater strength.
4. Maximum homogeneity.

Design and economic considerations determine whether machine parts should be welded in each scenario. The disadvantages of welding include: not all metals are suitably weldable, and weldments are less easily machinable than castings.

3.3 TYPES OF WELDED JOINTS

The relative positions of the two pieces being welded determine the type of joint. Welded structures are assembled by five basic types of joints such as: Butt, Lap, Corner, T and Edge joints, as shown in Fig. 3.2. All other possible joints are variations of these basic joints.

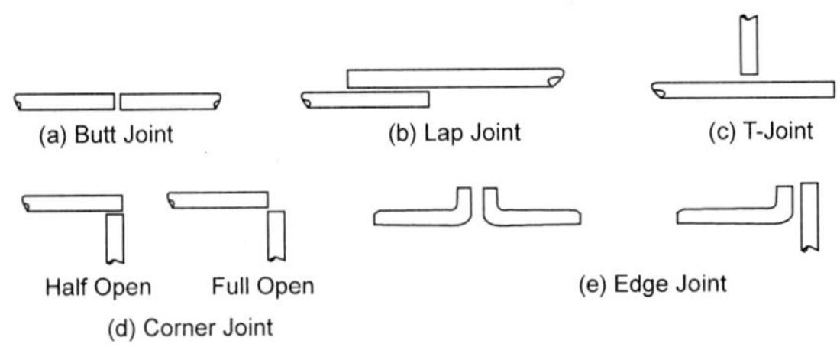

Figure 3.2: Basic welded joints.

The two pieces to be linked are located and clamped or held in the precise position to perform a weld. Butt joints are created by welding the components’ end surfaces or edges together. The two elements being welded should overlap by 3 to 5 times their thickness in lap joints. Each piece’s edge is soldered to the surface of the other. T-joints are used to link two parts with surfaces that are roughly at right angles to each other. Butt Joint (a) Halfway Open (d) Edge Joint (e) Full Open (d) Lap Joint (b) Corner Joint (d) T-Joint as the basic Welded Joints shown in Fig. 3.2. Corner joints are used to connect the edges of two parts whose surfaces are roughly perpendicular to one another. Fig. 3.3 shewn below is various types of welds used in making a joint.

Types	Descriptions
Bead’ weld	A 'bead' weld is one in which the filler metal is placed at a joint when the two adjacent surfaces are in the same plane. A 'bead' is a single run of welded metal.
Fillet’ weld	A ‹fillet› weld is one that has the filler metal deposited at the intersection of two intersecting surfaces, such as a T or Lap joint.
Groove’ weld	A ‹groove› weld is one in which the filler material is deposited in a groove created by the edge preparation of one or both components.
Plug’ or ‘Slot’ weld	A ‹plug› or›slot› weld is one in which a hole is made through one of the to-be-welded pieces, and the filler material is then placed into this hole and fused with the matching part.

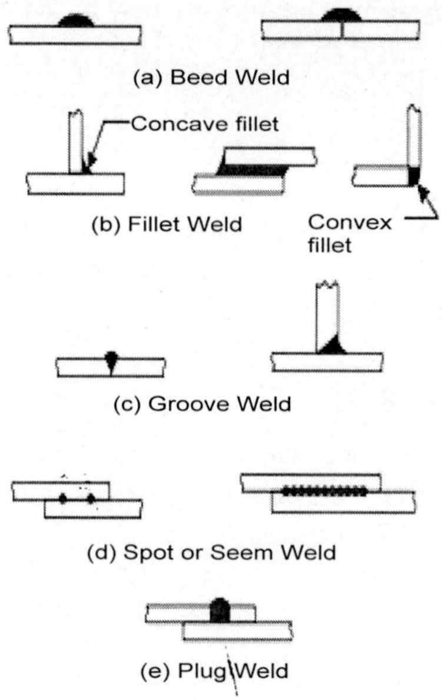

Figure 3.3: Types of welds

3.4 METHODS OF WELDING

Welding techniques are categorised based on the source of energy used to heat the metals and the state of the metal at the welded location. Welding procedures are characterised based on the source of heat as follows:

1. Chemical (oxygen + flammable fuel gas, such as acetylene, propane, butane, natural gas, hydrogen, and so on).
2. Mechanical - Chemical (Pressure gas welding, Thermit welding)
3. Electro chemistry (Atomic hydrogen welding)
4. Electro-Mechanical (Electric resistance welding) (Electric resistance welding)
5. Arc welding with an electric current.

These may be divided further into two groups as follows:

(a) Pressure Processes The parts to be joined are heated to a plastic state (fusion may occur to a limited amount) and then pressed together with external pressure to form the junction. Some of the most prevalent processes in this category are listed below: 1. Forge welding 2. Thermit Pressure Welding 3. Pressure Gas Welding 4. Electric Resistance Welding

(b) Fusion Procedures Without the use of pressure, the material at the junction is heated to a molten condition and allowed to solidify to form the joint. Some joints can be produced without the use of a filler metal in this case, but in general, a filler metal must be added to the weld to fill the space between the pieces being welded. Normally, the filler metal deposited should be of the same composition as the base metal. The following are some of the most frequent welding methods in this category: 1. welding with gas 2. welding with an electric arc 3. fusion welding with Thermit.

There are three types of welding processes: Autogeneous, Homogeneous, and Heterogeneous. In 'autogeneous' procedures, such as cold and hot pressure welding and electric resistance welding, no filler metal is injected to the joint interface. In 'Homogeneous' methods, filler metal of the same type as the parent metal is applied, for example, welding plain low- C steel with a low- C welding rod and welding 70 - 30 brass with a 70 - 30 brass welding rod. In 'Hetrogeneous' techniques, such as brazing and soldering, a filler metal of a different kind than the parent metal is utilised.

According to the definition of welding process given above, brazing and soldering are not precisely welding procedures. These methods, however, are also part of the welding process family. The two most common welding techniques are gas welding and arc welding. Because an electric arc has a far higher temperature than a gas flame, the joint zone melts almost instantly in arc welding. Gas welding requires a lengthy preheating period during which the metal close to the junction is heated to a high temperature. This has an adverse effect on the crystalline structure, resulting in significant stresses being created. As a result of this difficulty and the time required for preheating, gas welding is inappropriate for relatively large cross-sections. Plates in excess of 20 mm thick are, therefore, best welded by arc welding. However, as illustrated in Fig. 3.4, the basic welding methods can also be categorised as:

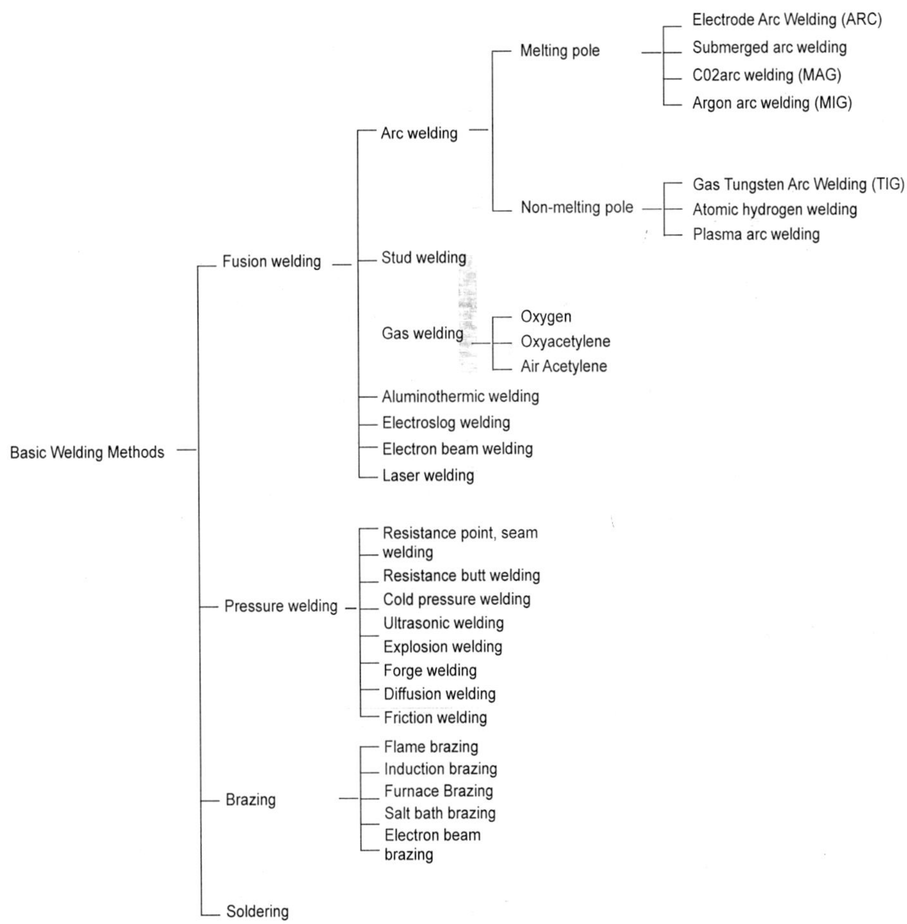

Figure 3.4: Basic welding methods

3.5 TYPES OF WELDING FLAMES

Different flames (Fig. 3.5) are employed to heat and cool metals or thermoplastics. The majority of gas welding procedures employ oxyfuel welding. It is one of the oldest welding methods, having been invented in 1903. A liquid fuel or gas, such as acetylene, is required for oxyfuel welding, also known as oxyacetylene welding. To raise the temperature of the flame, the gas is mixed with oxygen. The torch utilised in this operation is made up of hoses that connect to gas tanks. When ready to begin welding, open the valve and ignite the gas as it escapes the flashlight. The valves must then be adjusted to modify the flow of each gas with proper gas ratio. Each flame has numerous regions.

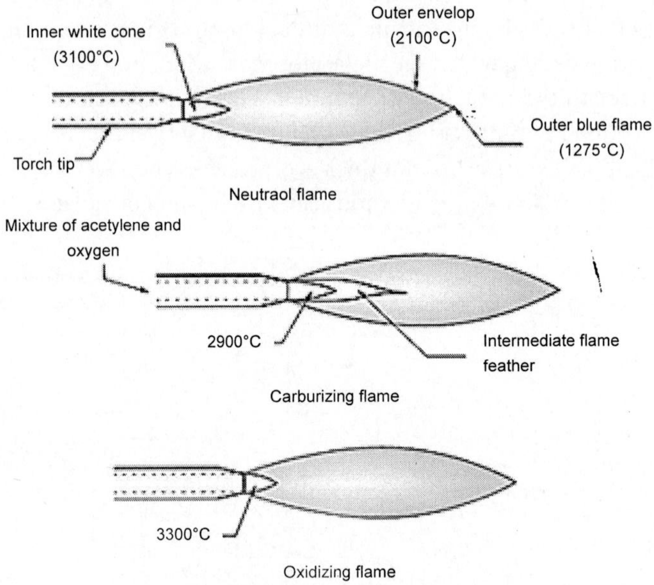

Figure 3.5: Types of flames used in welding

Natural flame, carburizing flame, and oxidising flame are the three types of flames utilised in welding. Natural flames have a synchronised mixing of fuel and oxygen, whereas carburizing flames contain more fuel and oxidising flames contain more oxygen. Depending on the weld situation, different materials used different flames.

(a) ***Natural flame.*** In this gas welding flame, oxygen and acetylene are released in a one-to-one ratio. That is, an equal amount of oxygen and acetylene is emitted. It collects additional oxygen from the air while providing complete combustion. A neutral flame is fine, clear, and well-defined. It is often preferred for welding. It generates a light cone that indicates the completion of the flame. Neutral flames are used to weld both ferrous and nonferrous metals such as mild steel, cast iron, copper, stainless steel, aluminium, and so on. Welders are expected to adjust to neutral before using any other flame. The flame is identified by its inner cone, which consists of a brilliant cone that is bluish-white. It is also noted for its surroundings, which have a bright blue flame coating. A flame with feather extension of inner cone is produced by raising the oxygen valve. The acetylene flame feather vanishes, and only the neutral flame remains. The temperature of the inner core tip is roughly 585 degrees Fahrenheit, whereas the temperature of the outside sheath or envelope is approximately 2300 degrees Fahrenheit.

Carburizing flame. Excess acetylene is supplied in this oxyacetylene flame. This white feather, also called as acetylene feather, has a feather edge that extends beyond its inner core. This acetylene is 2x if it is twice as long as the inner cone, which assists in determining the amount of acetylene supply. Carbon may be added to one volume of welded metal by a carburizing flame. It is accomplished by first adjusting to a neutral flame and then increasing the acetylene valve. The inner core will undergo a transformation, revealing an acetylene streamer or "feather" at its tip. The length of the streamer determines the level of carburization flame. The length of the streamer should not exceed half the length of the inner core. Three distinct flame zones distinguish the carburizing flame:

1. A distinct bluish-white inner cone
2. A white cone indicates the amount of excess acetylene.
3. A bright blue flare envelope on the outside.

This flare emits a coarse rushing sound when it burns. The temperature at the inner cone tip is around 3700 degrees Fahrenheit. When welding with a carburizing flame, carbon absorbs from the flame, causing metals to boil. When this metal boils, it transforms into high carbon steel, becomes brittle, and cracks.

(b) ***Oxidizing flame.*** This is the third and last oxyacetylene flame. It is formed when slightly more than one volume of oxygen is combined with one volume of acetylene. The torch is set to a neutral flame, just as it is in a carburizing flame. The oxygen valve will then be opened until the inner core is one-tenth of its original length. If the flame is appropriately set, it will be slightly purple with a pointed inner cone. This flame is also distinguished by a distinct hissing sound. The temperature of the oxidising flame at its inner core tip is roughly 6300 degrees Fahrenheit. Metals such as zinc, copper, manganese steel, and cast iron are welded with it. When this flame is applied to steel, molten metal forms and sparks off, suggesting that the steel is receiving an excess of oxygen. It is not utilised to weld steel because it makes it porous, oxidised, and brittle.

3.6 ELECTRIC ARC WELDING

The first arc welding technology was created in the nineteenth century, and it became commercially relevant in shipbuilding during WWII. It is still an important process for automotive and steel structure manufacturing today. This is one of the most well-known welding processes for combining metals in industries. The joint can be made in this method of welding by melting the metal with the help of electricity. As a result, it is known as an electric arc. The fundamental advantage of this welding is that a high temperature may be easily created for welding. The temperature range for arc welding will be 6k degrees Celsius to 7k degrees Celsius.

The definition of arc welding is a welding procedure that uses electricity to generate enough heat to soften the metal, and then the metals are welded once the softened metal is cooled. This type of welding (Fig. 3.6) employs a power supply to create an arc between a metal stick and the base material, softening the metals at the point of contact. These welders can use either DC or AC power, as well as consumable or non-consumable electrodes. In general, the welding region can be protected with a shielding gas, slag, or vapour. This welding procedure could be entirely or partially automated.

Heat can be generated in the Arc welding process by striking an electric arc between an electrode and the workpiece. The electric arc is a bright electrical discharge between two electrodes created by the use of ionised gas. Any form of arc welding process is dependent on an electric circuit, which consists of several components such as a power supply, a workpiece, a welding electrode, and electric cables that connect the electrode and the workpiece to the power supply.

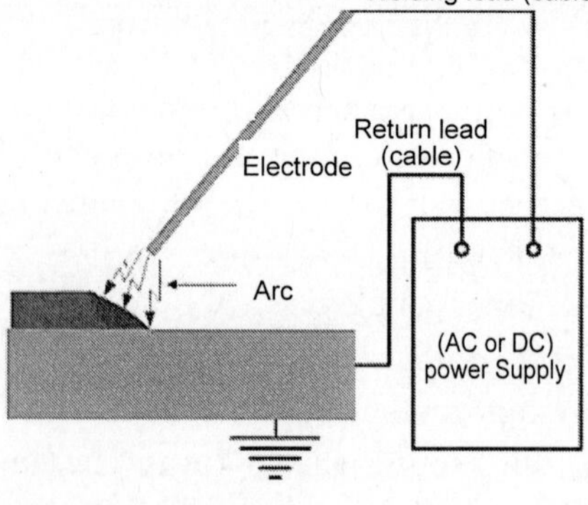

Figure 3.6: Circuit used in electric arc welding

3.6.1 Principle Electric Arc Welding

The operating idea of arc winding is that during a welding operation, heat can be generated by an electric arc strike between the workpiece and an electrode. This is a blazing electrical discharge between two electrodes in an ionised gas. An electric arc between the electrode and the work piece can produce the arc winding circuit. The temperature of the arc may reach 6500°C, which is sufficient to join the work piece's edges. When a long join is required, the arc can be shifted through the joint line. Once the back edge of the pool hardens to form the connection, the weld pool of the front edge dissolves the welded surface whenever a filler metal is required.

The chemical composition of a filler metal is connected to that of the work piece. The molten metal in the weld pool is chemically active and responds to the surrounding atmosphere. As a result, the weld may become infected by oxide and nitride inclusion, weakening its mechanical qualities. As a result, the weld pool can be shielded against contamination using neutral shielding gases such as helium, argon, and shielding fluxes. Shields are supplied in the form of a flux coating (Fig. 3.7) for the weld zone and in different forms for the electrode. Arc welding equipment primarily consists of an AC or DC machine, an electrode, a holder for the electrode, cables, cable connectors, earthing clamps, a chipping hammer, a helmet, a wire brush, hand gloves, safety goggles, sleeves, aprons, and so on.

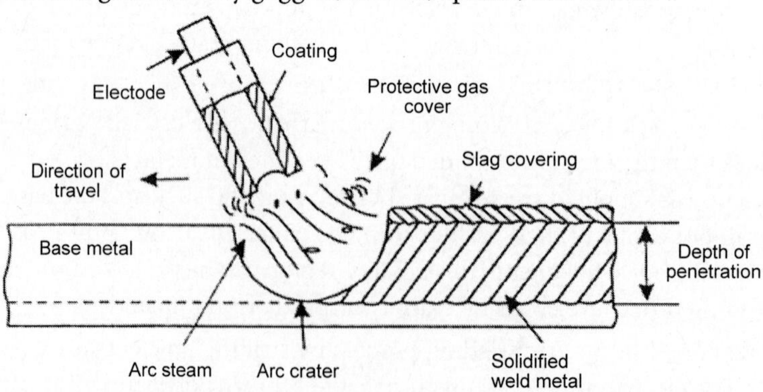

Figure 3.7: View of the arc welding with a coated electrode

3.6.2 Types of Arc Welding

Arc welding is categorised into several categories, which are listed in Table 3.1 below.

Table 3.1: Types of welding

Type of Welding	Working details	Representative Figures
Plasma arc welding	Plasma arc welding (PAW) is analogous to gas tungsten welding (GTAW). In this type of welding operation, an arc will form between the work piece and the tungsten electrode. The main difference between plasma arc welding and gas tungsten welding is that the electrode in plasma arc welding is positioned within the torch. It is possible to heat the gas to 30koF and convert it to plasma in order to attack the welding region.	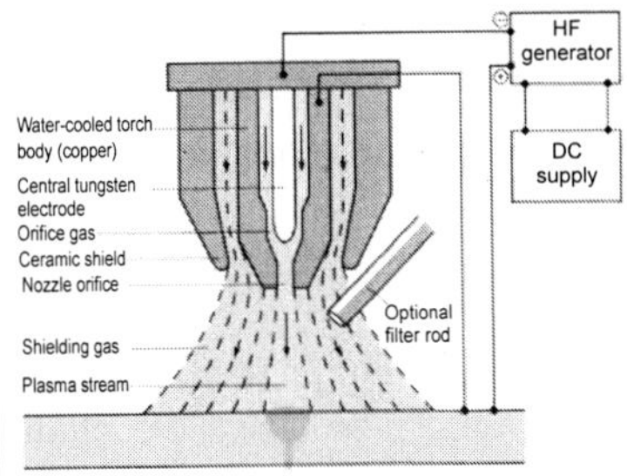
Metal arc welding	Metal arc welding (MAW) is a welding procedure that primarily employs a metal electrode. Depending on the application, this metal electrode might be consumable or non-consumable. The majority of the spent consumable electrode can be covered by flux, and the main advantage of this type of welding technique is that it requires less heat than others.	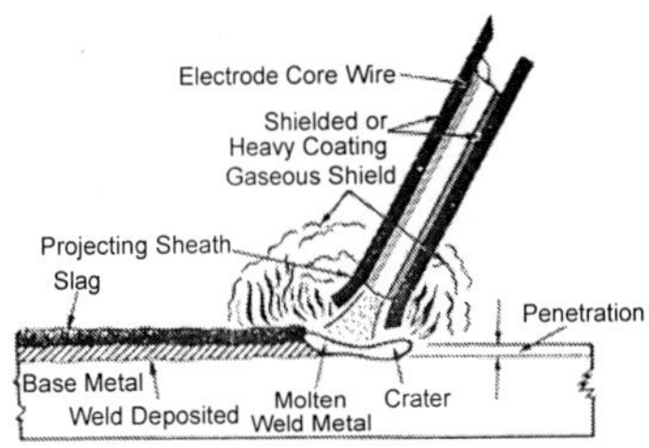
Carbon arc welding	For welding the metal joint, the carbon arc welding procedure primarily employs a carbon rod as an electrode. This is the earliest arc welding process and requires a high current, low voltage to generate the arc. In some situations, an arc can be created between two carbon electrodes, a process known as twin carbon arc welding.	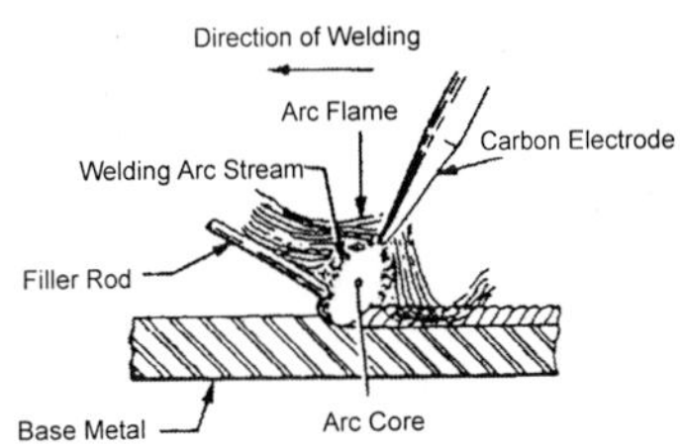
Gas tungsten arc welding	Tungsten inert gas welding is another name for gas tungsten arc welding (TIGW). A non-consumable tungsten electrode can be used to weld the material in this type of welding procedure. The electrode used in this welding can be surrounded by gases like as argon, helium, and others. These gases will protect the weld area from oxidation. This type of welding is suitable for joining thin sheets.	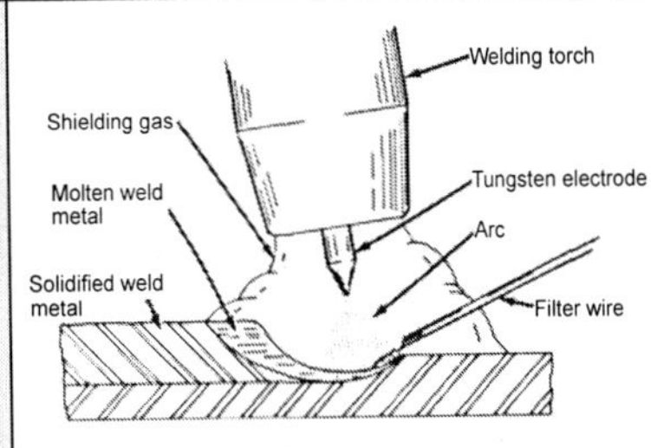

Type of Welding	Working details	Representative Figures
Gas Metal Arc Welding	Metal inert gas welding (GMAW) is another name for gas metal arc welding (GMAW) (MIGW). It employs a new metal electrode that is shielded by a gas such as helium or argon. These gases shield the join region from oxidation and create numerous layers of welding material. In this sort of arc welding procedure, a filler wire can be fed continuously while welding the metal with a non-consumable metal electrode.	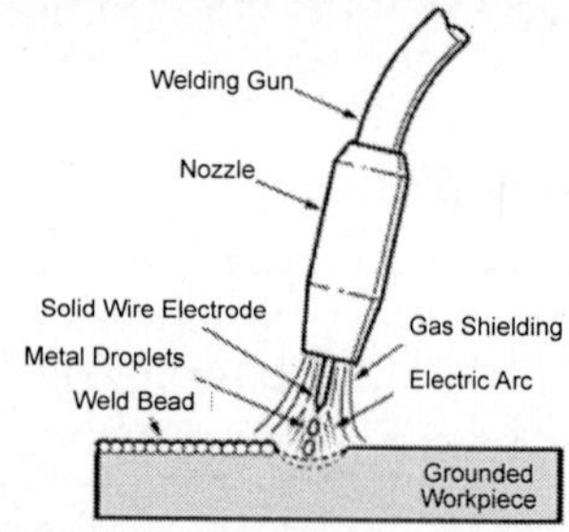
Flux Cored Arc Welding	Shield metal arc welding is an alternative to this type of welding. This flux-cored arc welding uses an electrode and a stable voltage power supply to generate a stable arc length. This approach protects against contagion by using a shielding gas or the gas created by the flux.	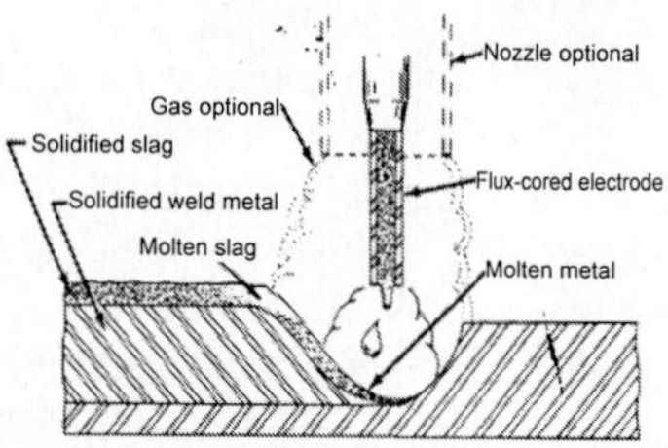
Electroslag Welding	This faster welding process was invented in the 1950s. This type of welding joins hefty metals for use in industrial equipment and machineries. It is derived from the copper water holders encased in the instrument used for electroslag welding, as the name implies. Throughout a welding process, the water prevents liquid slag from spreading into other areas.	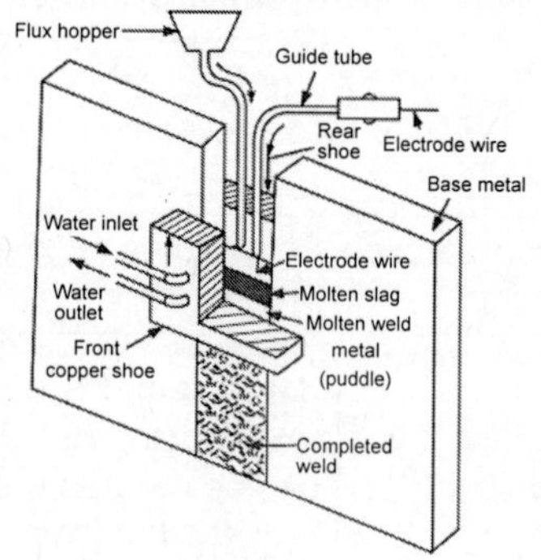
Arc Stud Welding	This technique of welding is incredibly dependable and can weld any size metal to a workpiece with the greatest weld penetration. This technique of welding may produce robust welds on a single side over base metals with a thickness of 0.048-inch. A DC power supply, metal fasteners, ferrules, and a stud welding gun can be used to create this arc. There are three typical welding processes utilised in this welding: drawn arc, short arc stud, and gas arc stud welding. During arcing, the flux is vaporised and responds to contaminating components in the environment to keep the weld zone clean. The gas arc stud method uses static shielding gas rather of a ferrule or flux, making it easier to automate.	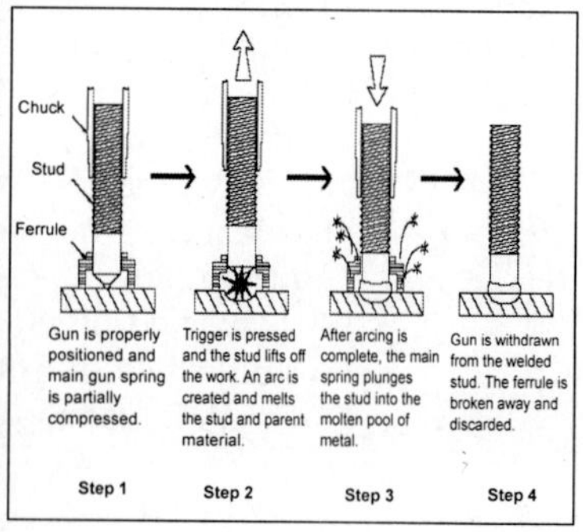

3.6.3 Other Types of Arc Welding

Most industries employ metal design, and the most often used welding has already been described. However, various additional processes, such as the ones listed below, can also be used to join two or more metals.

Type of Welding	Working details	Figure
Electronic Beam Welding	EBM, or electronic beam welding, is a method of joining metals in which electron waves are discharged at high speeds to join one metal surface to another. When the electron wave hits its target, the afflicted area melts just enough to merge the neighbouring component into place. This type of welding is particularly common in the industrial sector. The technology is especially beneficial for aerospace and automotive firms, who utilise it to join several metal elements within trucks, vehicles, planes, and spacecraft. Because of the nature of vacuum-based electronic beam welding, the approach is safe for crisis work in vacant houses and buildings.	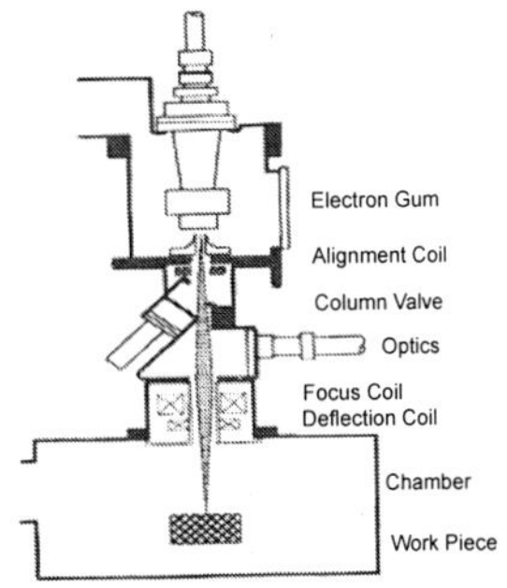
Atomic Hydrogen Welding	AHW, or atomic hydrogen welding, is an old technique for joining metals that has frequently given way to more efficient processes such as gas metal arc welding. Tungsten welding is one application where automated hydrogen welding is still used. Because tungsten is exceptionally heat resistant, this welding procedure is safe.	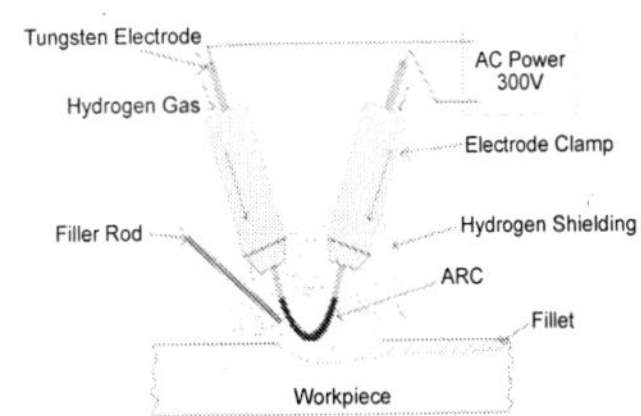
Oxy-Fuel Welding	This type of welding employs oxygen and liquid fuel to fuse metal into shape. The 20th century saw the invention of French engineers Charles Picard and Edmond Fouché. The oxygen-generated temperature is utilised in metal surface regions in this process. This welding takes performed in an enclosed environment.	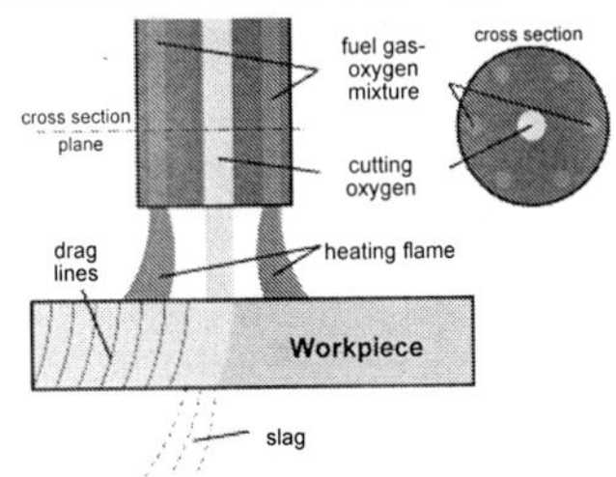
Cold Welding	Contact welding is another name for this type of welding. This technique of welding is used to join metal surfaces without melting them by heat.	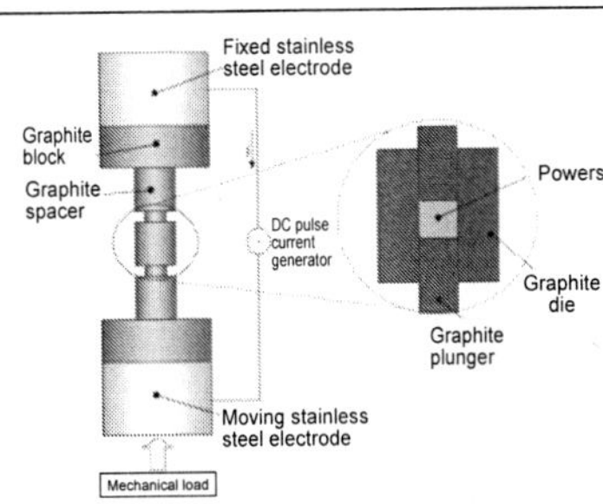

3.6.4 Advantages of Arc Welding

The advantages of Arc welding mainly include the following.

i. Arc welding offers a high welding efficiency and speed.
ii. It comes with a basic welding setup.
iii. It can simply be moved.
iv. Arc welding creates a physically strong link between the welded metals.
v. It ensures consistent welding quality.
vi. Arc welding provides a superior welding environment.
vii. This welding's power source is not expensive.
viii. This welding method is quick and consistent.
ix. The welder can work with standard household current.

3.6.5 Disadvantages of Arc Welding

The disadvantages of Arc welding include the following.

i. Arc welding necessitates the use of a highly skilled operator.
ii. As the electrode covering burns and decreases in thickness, the rate of deposition may be insufficient.
iii. The electrode length is 35mm, and the electrode must be changed for the complete production rate.
iv. These are not suitable for reactive metals like titanium and aluminium.

3.6.6 Applications of Arc Welding

Arc Welding applications include the following:

i. Used in sheet metal welding
ii. For welding thin, ferrous, and non-ferrous metals
iii. Used to design pressure and pressure vessels
iv. Industrial piping developments
v. Used in the automobile and home furnishing industries
vi. Shipbuilding industries
vii. Aircraft and aerospace manufacturers
viii. Auto body restorations Railroads
ix. Construction, automotive, mechanical, and other industries
x. In the aerospace industry, gas tungsten arc welding is utilised to link several locations such as sheet metals.
xi. These weldings are usually utilised for repairing dies, tools, and metals made of magnesium and aluminium.
xii. GTAW is widely used in the fabrication industry to weld thin workpieces, particularly nonferrous metals.

xiii. GTAW weldings are employed where extreme corrosion and cracking resistance over a long length of time is required.
xiv. It is utilised in the production of space vehicles.
xv. It is used to weld small-diameter parts and thin wall tubing, making it useful in the bicycle industry.

As a result, electric arc welding is the most adaptable welding technology. Because of advantages such as convenience of use and high welding efficiency, electric arc welding applications are used in manufacturing industries all over the world to create strong joints. It is widely employed in a variety of industries for the protection of otherwise deteriorating works, including automotive, construction, shipbuilding, and aerospace. Here's a question for you: what is the temperature range of arc welding?

3.6.7 Equipments for Electric Arc Welding

The various pieces of equipment necessary for electric arc welding (AC and DC) are seen in the image (Fig. 3.8) and detailed further below. The welding machine used for electric arc welding can either be a DC or AC welding machine.

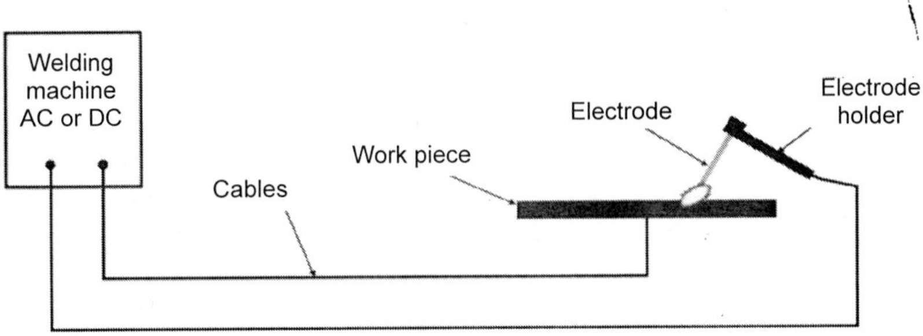

Figure 3.8: Requirements for electric arc welding

AC Welding Machine:

The step-down transformer on the AC arc welding machine reduces the input supply voltage from 220 V to 80 V. The AC arc welding machine is powered by a 50 Hz or 60 Hz power supply. The efficiency of the AC welding transformer ranges from 80% to 85%, with around 3 to 4 kWh spent per kg of deposit. Despite the fact that the AC welding equipment has a low power factor of 0.3 to 0.4.

DC Welding Machine:

A motor-generator set is often used in DC arc welding machines. To provide drooping characteristics, the motor is a squirrel cage induction motor and the generator is a differential compound DC generator. An engine-driven generator or transformer-rectifier welding system can also provide DC electricity. The energy spent per kg of deposit by a DC arc welding machine is around 6 to 10 kWh, and the output voltage of the DC arc welding machine can be changed between 40 and 80 Volts and the current from 30 to 300 A. The DC arc welding motor has a power factor of 0.6 to 0.7.

Electrode Holder:

The electrode holder is the piece of equipment used to keep the electrode at the proper angle. Arc welding electrode holders range in size from 50 A to 500 A, depending on the current rating.

Leads or Cables:

The electric current is carried by the cables or leads from the welding machine to the work-piece. The cables used in the welding process are flexible and constructed of copper or aluminium. Electric arc welding cables are constructed of 1000 to 2000 very small wires that are twisted together to give the cables flexibility and mechanical strength. A rubber coating protects the cable cables.

Lugs or Cable Connectors:

The cable connections are used to connect machine switches to the welding electrode holder. Mechanical connectors are commonly utilised because they are easily assembled and disassembled. The cable connectors used in welding procedures are developed based on the current rating of the cable.

3.7 SHIELDED METAL ARC WELDING

Shielded metal arc welding (Fig. 3.9), also known as manual metal arc welding, flux shielded arc welding, or stick welding informally, is a manual arc welding procedure that uses a consumable electrode covered in flux to lay the weld. An electric current from a welding power supply, either alternating current or direct current, is utilised to generate an electric arc between the electrode and the metals to be connected. The workpiece and electrode melt, creating a pool of molten metal that cools to form a junction. As the weld is formed, the flux coating of the electrode disintegrates, releasing vapours that act as a shielding gas and forming a layer of slag that protects the weld region from ambient contamination.

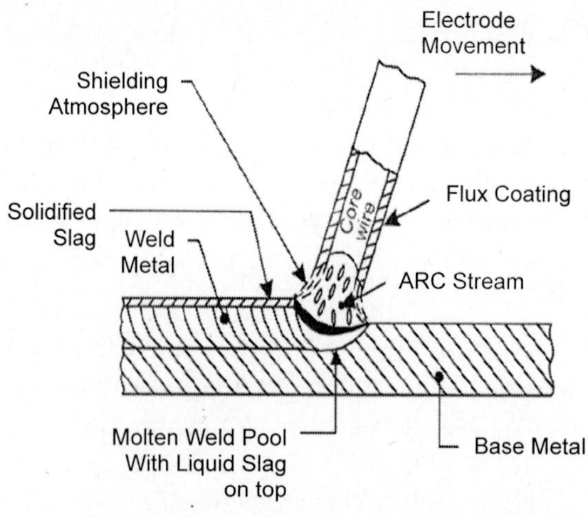

Figure 3.9: Shielded metal arc welding

Shielded metal arc welding is one of the world's first and most common welding procedures due to its versatility and simplicity of equipment and operation. It dominates other welding methods in the maintenance and repair business, and while flux-cored arc welding is gaining popularity, SMAW is still widely utilised in the construction of big steel structures and industrial fabrication. The process is typically used to weld iron and steels (including stainless steel), but it can also be used to weld aluminium, nickel, and copper alloys.

The procedure is adaptable and suited for field use, although it needs great skill. If the metal and slag harden quickly enough, welding in all positions, including overhead welding, is achievable. The method is almost entirely used for job-shop (non-production and general maintenance and repair) work, but it is also used in many high-volume operations, such as the manufacture of machinery, transportation equipment, piping systems, and various structures (on-site erection) such as buildings, trusses, machine bases, and so on. To avoid flux corrosion, the slag or molten flux must be removed after welding. As previously stated, coated stick electrodes are only appropriate for manual arc welding. "Stick Welding" is another name for this technique. After establishing the arc, the welder feeds the electrode uniformly to the job while preserving a short-arc. To create a weld bead, the electrode is kept at an angle of 15° to 20° from the vertical on a flat weld. The welder can control the depth to which the parent metal is melted and the rate at which the welding pool cools by adjusting the angle of inclination of the electrode.

The electrode is moved three times during the welding operation. To maintain the arc length, the electrode is continuously fed downward along its axis. It is gradually fed along the weld, and finally, the electrode tip is oscillated across the weld. The electrode tip's sideways oscillating movement is used to: (i) obtain and maintain correct bead width. (ii) Float slag out. (iii) Ensure enough penetration at the weld's margins and (iv) allow gases to escape, avoiding porosities. Transverse oscillating movements of the electrode tip promote heating of the joint edges, delay cooling of the molten pool of deposited metal, allow for a more homogenous, sound efficient, and robust weld.

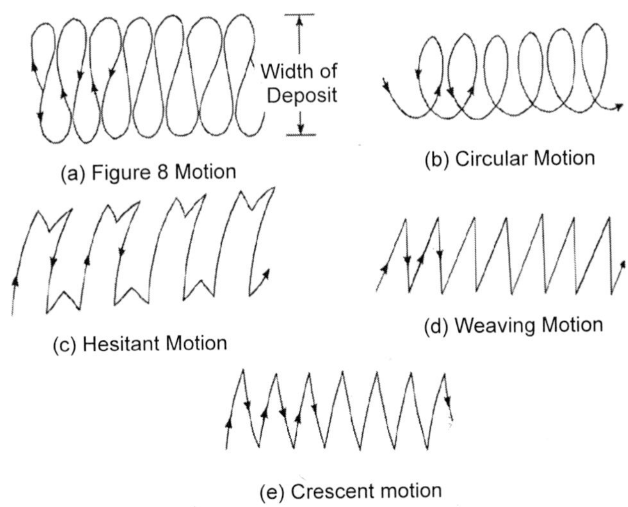

Figure 3.10: Various oscillating motions of electrode tip

The numerous oscillating motions of the electrode tip are depicted in Fig. 3.10. Various Oscillating Motions of Electrode Tip could be (a) Width of Deposit Figure 8 Motion (b) Circular Motion (c) Hesitant Motion (d) Weaving Motion and (e) Crescent motion). The type of oscillating motion and the pace of oscillations are determined by the following factors: the thickness of the work, the duration of the run, and the type of electrode and current level used. However, these are primarily determined by experience. Figure 4.11 shows multiple-pass welding. The brittle slag coating on the bead after the first pass (root pass) is chipped off and cleaned with a wire brush before starting the second pass, and similarly for the subsequent passes.

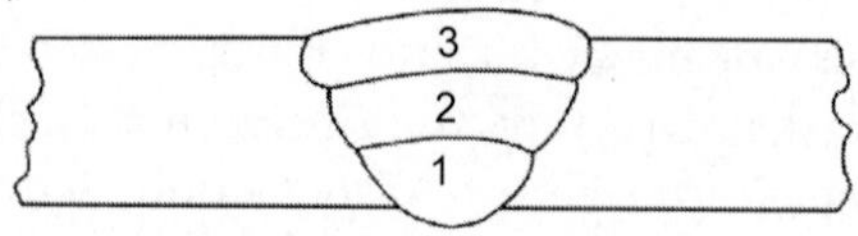

Figure 3.11: Multipass arc welding

The thermal action of the arc melts the end of the electrode and the edges of the work in metal arc welding. It has been determined that molten metal drops travel through the arc at a rate of 40 m/s and that the number of drops fluctuates between 10 and 30 per sec. The essential factor in high-quality hand arc welding is the selection of welding conditions, which are governed by the electrode diameter, welding current, and voltage as

(a) **Electrode diameter.** the diameter of the electrode will depend upon the thickness of the metal being welded and the type of the joint. Electrode diameter, according to the thickness of the metal to be welded, is given below:

Metal thickness, mm	Upto 2	2 to 4	4 to 6	6 to 8	over 8
Electrode diameter, mm	2	3	4	5	5-6

(b) **Welding current.** the amplitude of the welding current is determined by the following factors: the thickness of the welded metal, the type of joint, the welding speed, the position of the weld, the thickness and type of coating on the electrode, and the electrode's working length. However, for practical reasons, the welding current is governed by the electrode diameter chosen, as shown below:

Welding current, $I = k.\ d$, amperes; d is in mm,

where k = a constant = 45 to 60 for ordinary steel electrodes

= 18 to 22 for graphic

= 5 to 8 for carbon electrodes

In general practice, welding is performed with currents over 50 A.

(c) **Voltage**: The arc voltage depends only upon the arc length.

It is given by the relation: $V = k1 + k2\, l$, volts,

Where l is the arc length in mm and $k1$ and $k2$ are constants,

$k1 = 10$ to 12 and

$k2 = 2$ to 3

The minimum Arc voltage is given by $Vmin = (20 + 0.04\ I)$, Volt

(d) **Arc length:** It is the distance between the end of the electrode and the surface of the molten metal on the work, as previously specified. A short arc length is required for good welding because:

1. That permits the heat to be concentrated on the joint.
2. It is more stable due to the reduced arc blow effect.
3. The molten weld pool is protected from atmosphere due to the vapours surrounding the electrode metal and molten weld pool.

A long arc, on the other hand, causes: (i) significant heat loss into the atmosphere, resulting in poor penetration and fusion; (ii) an unstable arc due to the increasing effect of the magnetic arc below; and (iii) the weld pool is not protected from the atmosphere. As a result of the absorption of O2 and N2, the weld becomes polluted, and (iii) the weld has low strength (due to large porosity), poorer ductility, poor fusion, and extensive spatter.

The arc length is determined by the following factors: I the type of electrode used, (ii) its coating, (iii) its diameter, (iv) the current employed, and (v) the position of welding. Vertical, horizontal, and overhead welding often require shorter arc lengths than flat welding. As previously stated, an arc length of 0.6 to 0.8 times the electrode diameter can be used to provide the stable arc required for high quality welding. Except for pure copper, aluminium, and several low melting point and reactive metals, SMAW is applicable to practically all metals and alloys.

3.8 SUBMERGED ARC WELDING

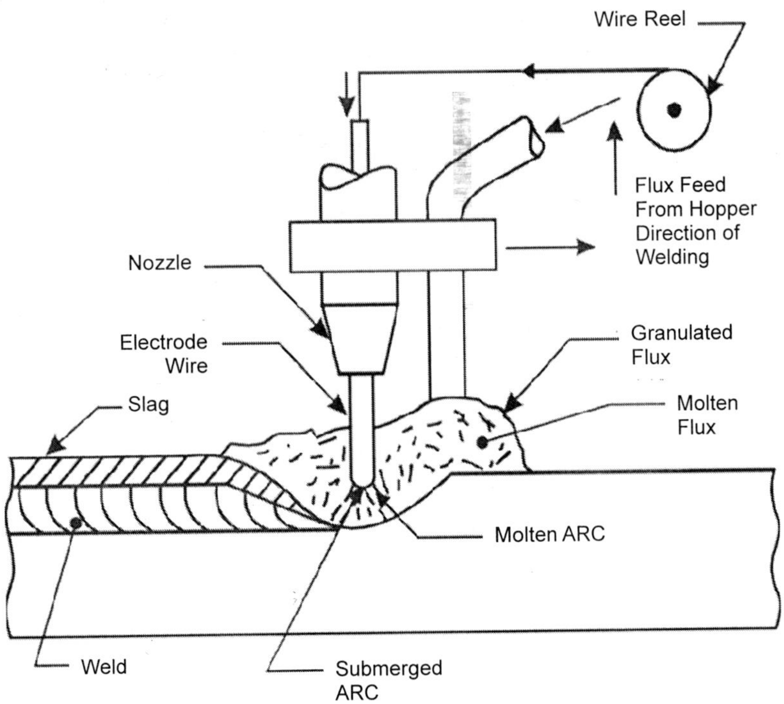

Figure 3.12: Submerged Arc Welding

In this, coalescence is produced by heating with an arc between a bare wire electrode and the work. The weld zone is shielded by a blanket of fusible granular flux material supplied directly on the weld seam ahead of the electrode to shield the arc. Pressure is not used and molten filler metal is obtained from the electrode. The flux also acts as a deoxidizer and scavenger and may contain powder metal alloying elements. The method can be used in fully automatic equipment where the feeds of both the electrode and granular flux are controlled, Fig. 3.12. The method is also adaptable for semiautomatic equipment where the feed of the electrode and granular flux are controlled manually. This method is characterised by good appearing welds, high welding speeds and high welding currents up to several thousand amperes. Because of the large diameter electrodes which can be used, rather large welds can be made in one single pass in plates over 25 mm thick. Deep penetration is also obtained.

Since the granular flux must cover the joint to be welded, this method is restricted to making straight welds in the flat position. Thus it is suitable for steel line pipes, boiler pressure vessels, railroad tank cars, structural shapes and cylinders etc. and also for circular welds if the workpiece is rotated under the welding head. Double submerged arc welding (with one weld from the inside, the other from the outside) is used in making spiral- welded pipelines. It can also be used with welding robots, with the workpiece manipulated into appropriate positions. Submerged arc welding can be used to weld low C- steels, high strength low alloy steels, chromium steels, and austenitic chromium-nickel steels. With special methods, it is also possible to weld high-alloy air hardening steels.

Advantages: 1. Joints can be prepared with a shallow V-groove, resulting in lesser electrode consumption. 2. Wire electrodes are inexpensive. 3. Weld spatters are eliminated. 4. Nearly 100% deposition efficiency is achieved.

Limitations: 1. It cannot be used for plates less than 5 mm thick. 2. It cannot cut C.I. because of high heat input. 3. Slag has to be removed continuously after it has melted in order to avoid entrapment between passes.

3.9 TIG WELDING

TIG (Tungsten Inert Gas) welding (Fig. 3.13) uses an inert gas for welding where in arc does not throw sparks and can be used to weld various metals, including stainless steel, aluminum, and iron. Non-consumable tungsten is used for the discharging electrode and an inert gas such as argon or helium is used as the shielding gas.

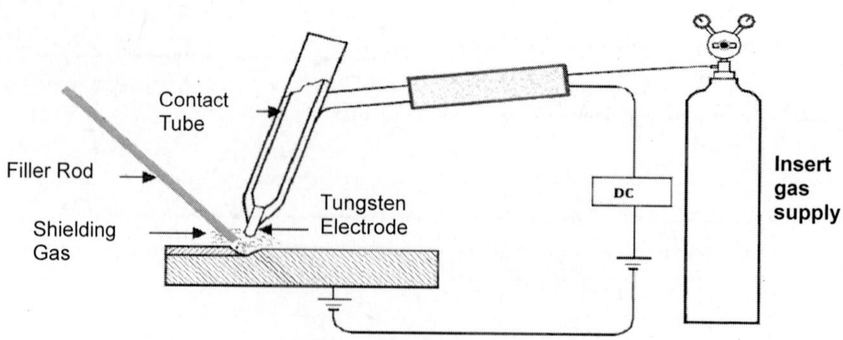

Figure 3.13: TIG Welding

The process strikes an arc in an inert gas and uses the arc heat to melt and weld the base material. Although a filler material is used, spatter is rare because the weld area is covered with the inert gas and the arc is stable. The unique aspects of TIG welding are the absence of physical contact between the electrode and the metal pieces and that the electrode is not consumed in the process. As a result, the arc is stable and clean and produces aesthetically pleasing welds. A semi-automatic TIG welding machine mainly consists of: Welding power supply, Welding torch and Gas cylinder and gas flow controller. Some other instruments are added when the torch is a water-cooled type or the filler material is a wire. The polarity of the electric current (positive or negative) should be selected depending on the base material. Consequently, the welding power supply requires a controller for selecting the polarity according to the base material.

There are various types of TIG welding that can be classified according to the use of AC or DC power, the use of pulse or non-pulse current, and whether a filler wire is used or not. AC or DC is selected depending on the base material. A pulse or non-pulse current can be selected. The method using a pulse current is called pulse TIG welding. In pulse TIG welding, the welding current is changed alternately at a constant frequency between a pulse current and a base current. The base material melts while the pulse current flows, and cools while the base current flows. This creates weld spots periodically, resulting in a bead looks like a string of beads. There are two types of TIG welding that use a filler wire: cold wire welding and hot wire welding. Cold wire welding uses a normal filler wire. Hot wire welding heats up the wire beforehand by passing a current through it. This can increase the amount of deposition per unit time. Since about three times the amount of filler material can be melted compared with cold wire welding, welding can be completed more quickly. Hot wire welding makes up for the weakness of TIG welding where it can provide high-quality welding but takes time to melt the necessary amount of filler material. Shielding gas in TIG is selected according to the material being welded like:

- Argon - the most commonly-used shielding gas which can be used for welding a wide range of materials including steels, stainless steel, aluminium and titanium.
- Argon + 2 to 5% H2 - the addition of hydrogen to argon will make the gas slightly reducing, assisting the production of cleaner-looking welds without surface oxidation. As the arc is hotter and more constricted, itpermits higher welding speeds. Disadvantages include risk of hydrogen cracking in carbon steels and weld metal porosity in aluminium alloys.
- Helium and helium/argon mixtures - adding helium to argon will raise the temperature of the arc. This promotes higher welding speeds and deeper weld penetration. Disadvantages of using helium or a helium/argon mixtureis the high cost of gas and difficulty in starting the arc.

TIG welding equipment is more expensive than MIG or stick welding gear. There are affordable TIG welders on the market, but they don't offer all of the previously discussed functions for arc control. Other necessary equipment for TIG welding includes as given below in Table 3.2:

Table 3.2: Equipment for TIG welding

Equipment	Usages
TIG welder	This is most expensive piece of the setup. The TIG welding machine must support AC TIG output to weld aluminum.
Tungsten electrode	Lanthanum, cerium, thorium, and pure tungsten rods are most commonly used. Thoriated tungsten is radioactive, but lanthanum is an excellent, safe substitute.

Equipment	Usages
Filler rods	Use ER70S-6 for general mild steel, ER308 for standard 200 and 300-series stainless steels, and ER4043 for most aluminum applications.
Shielding gas tank	Buy and refill, don't rent. It's cheaper that way. Read our guide on shielding gas tank sizes here, or just get an 80CF argon gas bottle that works great for most jobs and workloads
Welding helmet	The hood should be rated for low TIG amperage if welding thin materials that require a low amp start.
Gloves	Don't use heavy-duty gloves for MIG or stick welding. Use light, flexible goatskin gloves designed for TIG.
Foot pedal	It allows you to moderate the amperage output in real-time, but not all welding machines support foot pedal connection.

3.9.1 Advantages of TIG Welding

Maximum joint quality, Welds almost all materials, Perfect for thin stock, Low chance of weld contamination, Weld with or without filler metal, No spatter or smoke, It doesn't require flux or slag, Allows welding in all positions, Maximum control over arc and heat input, Provides excellent visibility of arc and weld pool and TIG makes the best-looking welds.

3.9.2 Disadvantages of TIG Welding

It's a challenging process to learn, TIG welding is a slow process, which reduces productivity, Small mistakes in travel speed, amperage output, pulse settings, or tungsten preparation can significantly impair weld quality, Welding outdoors blows away the shielding gas and Expensive equipment.

3.9.3 Applications of TIG Welding

TIG welding is applied in all industrial sectors but is especially suitable for high quality welding. In manual welding, the relatively small arc is ideal for thin sheet material or controlled penetration (in the root run of pipe welds). Because deposition rate can be quite low (using a separate filler rod) MMA or MIG may be preferable for thicker material and for fill passes in thick-wall pipe welds.

TIG welding is also widely applied in mechanised systems either autogenously or with filler wire. However, several 'off the shelf' systems are available for orbital welding of pipes, used in the manufacture of chemical plant or boilers. The systems require no manipulative skill, but the operator must be well trained. Because the welder has less control over arc and weldpool behaviour, careful attention must be paid to edge preparation (machined rather than hand-prepared), joint fit-up and control of welding parameters.

3.10 MIG Welding

MIG (Metal Inert Gas) welding (Fig. 3.14) is another method of arc welding. As with TIG welding, an inert gas is used for the shielding gas, but MIG welding is a consumable electrode type of welding that uses a discharge electrode that melts during welding. Metal Inert Gas (MIG) welding was first patented in the USA in 1949 for welding aluminium. The arc and weld pool formed using a bare wire electrode was protected by helium gas, readily available at that time. From about 1952, the process became popular in the UK for welding aluminium using argon as the shielding gas, and for carbon steels using CO_2. CO_2 and argon-CO_2 mixtures are known as metal active gas (MAG) processes. MIG is an attractive alternative to MMA, offering high deposition rates and high productivity. The process is generally used for joining stainless steel or aluminum alloy workpieces. For iron and steel, the shielding gas made of argon and a small amount of CO_2 or oxygen is used.

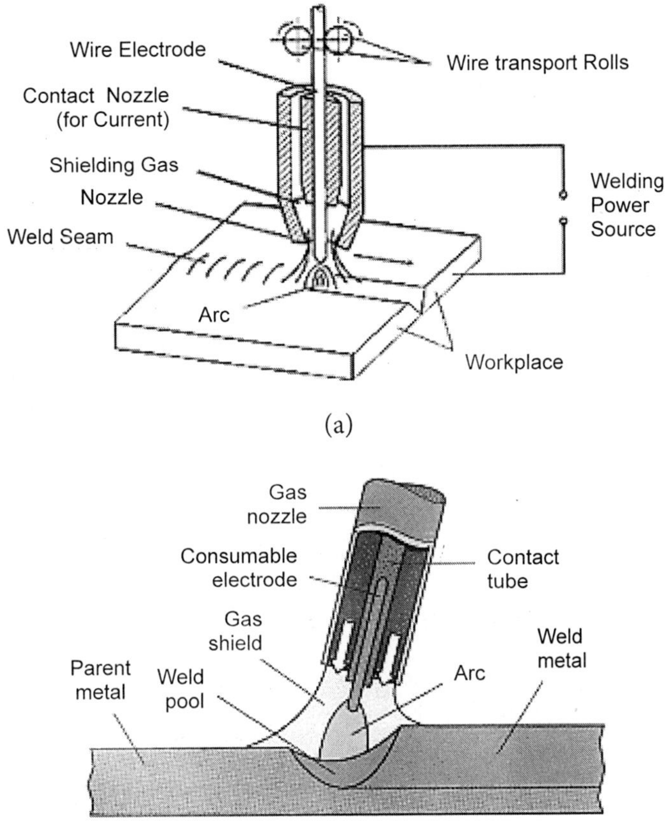

(a)

(b)

Figure 3.14: MIG welding.

An appropriate type of shielding gas must be used depending on the metal to be welded. A coiled welding wire is used for the electrode. The coiled wire is attached to the wire feed unit and is sent automatically to the torch tip by a feed roller that is driven by an electric motor. The wire is energized when it passes through the contact tip. An arc is struck between the wire and base material, which melts the wire and base material simultaneously to weld them. During the process, the shielding gas is supplied through a nozzle into the weld area and its surroundings to shield the arc and weld pool from the atmosphere. A semi-automatic MIG welding machine mainly consists of: Welding power supply, Wire feed unit, Welding torch and Gas cylinder.

Since MIG welding is often used for welding aluminum, the wire feed unit has to be improved to allow stable feeding of soft aluminum wire (four-roll system).

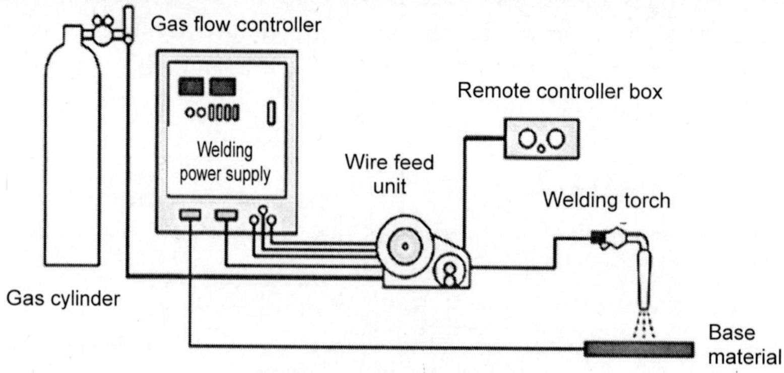

Figure 3.15: MIG setup

MIG welding can be classified according to its use of AC or DC, or a pulse or non-pulse current as described below:

	Pulse	Welding method
Direct current (DC)	No	Short-arc MIG Welding
		Spray MIG welding
		Large-current MIG welding
	Yes	Pulse MIG welding
		Low-frequency superimposed pulse MIG welding
Alternate current (AC)	Yes	AC pulse MIG welding
		Low-frequency superimposed AC pulse MIG welding
DC+AC	Yes	AC/DC composite pulse MIG welding

Short-arc MIG welding is a welding method that uses the short-circuit transfer (short arc) phenomenon. It is often used in semi-automatic systems intended for thin plates due to the low heat input to the base material. In case of MIG welding, such workpieces are often welded with pulse MIG welding.

Spray MIG welding is a process that sets the welding current higher than the critical current to set a higher arc voltage. It uses the spray transfer phenomenon where the molten filler material vaporizes. When an aluminum workpiece is welded such that no spatter is generated, lack of fusion or other welding defects may result. To prevent this problem, the arc voltage must be decreased a little to allow welding in small spray transfer mode. Spray MIG welding is no longer commonly used because pulse MIG welding that can handle workpieces with low to medium thickness has become common.

Large-current MIG welding uses welding wires with thick diameters (approx. 3.2 to 5.6 mm 0.13" to 0.22"). The welding system includes a welding torch with double-shielded gas nozzle and a constant-current characteristic power supply with a rated output current of about 1,000 A.

MIG welding using DC and pulse current is also called conventional pulse MIG welding. The basic principle is the same as that of pulse MAG welding. This welding method passes a small base current to maintain an arc and a pulse current exceeding the critical current alternately to allow spray droplets to transfer from the wire even when the average current drops below the critical current. They ensure effective and high quality welding of thin to thick plates.

Low-frequency superimposed pulse MIG welding is a method developed based on pulse MIG welding to achieve high-value added welding of aluminum workpieces. Since the process can create beautiful scale-like beads, it is used to weld thin aluminum plates for automobiles or motorbikes.

3.10.1 Application of MIG Welding

Used for most types of sheet metal welding, Fabrication of pressure vessels and steel structures and Automotive industry and home improvement industry.

3.10.2 Advantages of MIG Welding

Creates high-quality welds, Minor weld splatter, can be used to join dissimilar metals, and can be fully or semi-automatic and good weld speed.

3.10.3 Disadvantages of MIG Welding

Unsuitable for outside welding, Unsuitable for thick metals and Needs metal preparation.

3.10.4 Similarity of Principle with MIG and TIG Welding

MIG and TIG welding operate under a similar principle; heat generated by an electrical current melt the base materials and/or bonding materials, which, when cooled, form a solid joint. Despite similarities between the two processes, they remain distinct in their benefits and best use cases. Both MIG and TIG welding can be used on a wide range of metals, with MIG welding more suitable for thick materials and TIG more appropriate for thin materials. Typical weld materials include aluminum, carbon steel, and stainless steel.

3.11 RESISTANCE WELDING

Resistance welding is the joining of metals by applying pressure and passing current for a length of time through the metal area which is to be joined. The key advantage of resistance welding is that no other materials are needed to create the bond, which makes this process extremely cost effective.

The amount of heat generated at the contacting area of the elements to be welded, is determined from Joule's law:

$Q = I^2 .R. t.k$ joules,

Where I = current in amperes, R = resistance of the circuit at the contacting area of the elements in ohms, t = time during which the current flows, in seconds, k = a constant to account for losses due to radiation and conduction. k is usually < 1.

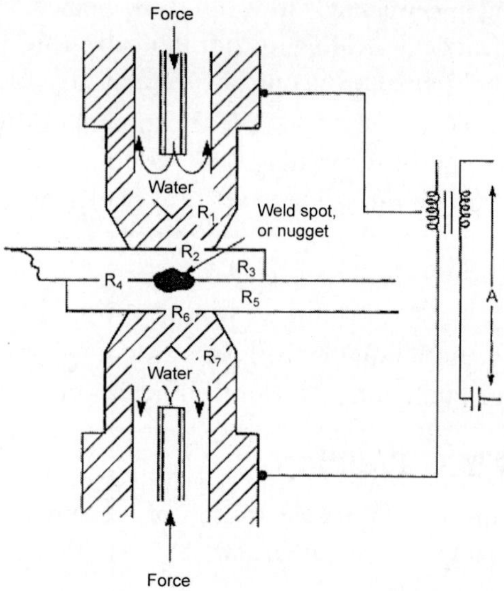

Figure 3.16: Resistance Welding

The voltage can be low, typically 0.5 to 10V, but currents are very high (thousands of amperes). Metals can be joined by this process using both alternating and direct current. However, heavy currents (upto 10k A) can be easier and more efficiently applied through transformers, and therefore, in practice only alternating current is used in resistance welding. Materials of high heat conductivity and specific heat (Al and Cu) call for very high currents to prevent dissipation of heat.

A special feature of resistance welding is the rapid heating of the surface being welded (in hundredths of a second) due to the application of currents of high amperage. The advantages of the resistance welding are: The heat is localised, action is rapid, no filler metal is needed, the operation requires little skill and can be easily mechanised and automated, suitable for large quantity production, all the common metal and dissimilar metals can be resistance welded, the parent metal is normally not harmed and none is lost, many difficult shapes and sections can be processed, and a high degree of reliability and reproductibility can be achieved.

The main disadvantage is high cost of equipment, and there are limitations to the types of joints made. The resistance welding process finds extensive application in construction and the engineering industries. There are six types of resistance welding processes: (1) resistance spot welding (2) resistance seam welding (3) projection welding (4) flash welding (5) upset welding, and (6) percussion welding, which differ primarily by the types and shapes of weld electrodes that are used to apply the pressure and conduct the current. The electrodes, typically manufactured from copper based alloys due to superior conductive properties, are cooled by water flowing through cavities inside the electrode and the other conductive tooling of the resistance welding machine.

Resistance welding machines are designed and built for a wide range of automotive, aerospace and industrial applications. Through automation, the action of these machines is highly controlled and repeatable allowing manufacturers to staff production readily.

3.11.1 Resistance Spot Welding (RSW)

In resistance spot welding (Fig. 3.17), the overlapping metal parts are held between two bar type metal electrodes which apply pressure, while an electric current is passed through them, Fig. 3.17 When the current is switched on and applied for a predetermined number of cycles (in the automotive industry 20 - 30 cycles), the lapped pieces of metal are heated in a restricted area.

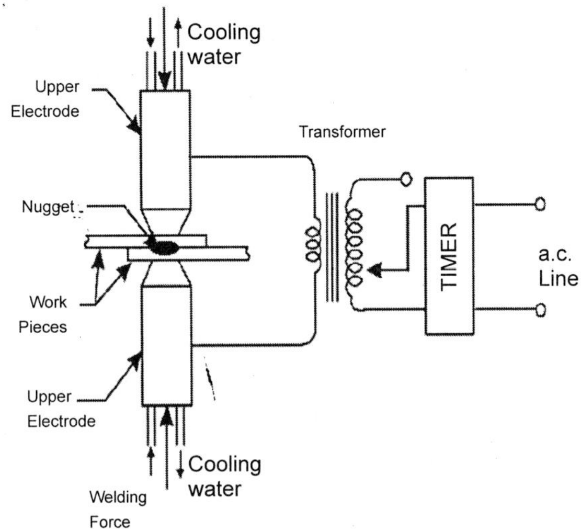

Figure 3.17: Resistance spot welding

The generated heat melts the surface layer of the metal in the central, more highly heated, area of contact with the electrodes, and the adjacent layers of metal are softened to a plastic state. Then the current is switched off and the electrodes are pressed and the pressure is released only after the weld stop (nugget) has solidified. The spot weld (nugget) is approximately the same size as the electrode tip, usually between 3 or 6 mm in diameter. Electrode tip diameter Thickness of plate to be welded. Distance between the nearest edge of the plate and centre of weld = 1.5 × electrode tip diameter. The sheet surface shows a slight depression and decolouration. The welding cycle to produce one spot can be written as:

(i) Position the workpieces and squeeze between the electrodes.

(ii) Apply a low voltage current to the electrodes.

(iii) Hold until the proper temperature is attained.

(iv) Release current, continue pressure.

(v) Release pressure and remove work.

The electrode pressure can be in the range of upto 2 kN The electrodes used must possess high electrical and thermal conductivity and retain the required strength at temperatures upto 400°C. Electrodes are made of cold-rolled electrolytic copper with some *Cd, Cr,* or *Be* additions, or copper - tungsten or molybdenum alloys. Electrodes are usually of hollow construction and are cooled with water during operation to prevent their overheating.

Because of the widespread application of sheet metal parts, resistance spot welding finds extensive application in the aircraft and automobile industries for manufacturing air frames and bodies (there are some 8000 to 10,000 spot welds per car), attaching handles of cookware, as well as in railway car building and the instrument industry and for making reinforcement in concrete construction etc.

Spot welding is primarily restricted to thin metals (for example 0.025 to 3.2 mm thick for steel and magnesium and 4 mm thick for aluminium), namely steels, stainless steels, aluminium, magnesium, nickel, nickel alloys, bronze and brass. Some dissimilar metals can be spot welded, but with difficulty.

The method is also difficult to use for highly conducting materials like Al and Mg. (a) The diameter of spot welds, $d = 1.4\,t + 4$ mm, for $t < 3$ mm $= 1.5\,t + 5$ mm, for $t > 3$ mm where t = Thickness of parts being welded. (b) Spacing of spot welds = $3d$.

3.11.1.1 Resistance Spot welding machines.

There are three types of spot welding machines which are in use:

I. Standard machines.
II. Special multiple-electrode machines
III. Portable welders

I. Standard Machines.

These machines have an upper and lower horn (arm) carrying the electrodes and extending from an upright frame. The upper horn is movable (up and down) while the lower horn is fixed. There are two designs of standard machines: (i) Rocker arm type (ii) Press type spot or projection welders.

(i) **Rocker Arm Type Machine.** In this machine (Fig. 3.18), the movable horn is mounted on a rocker arm which is pivoted in the frame. It is tilted upward to open the gap and downward to apply the pressure, by the rocking action of the upper arm (the lower electrode arm being stationary). This design is adaptable to a wide range of work, usually for light production work with lighter gauges. The throat depth (distance from the face of the upright frame to the end of the horn) is about 1.2 m for these machines. These machines are of two types :

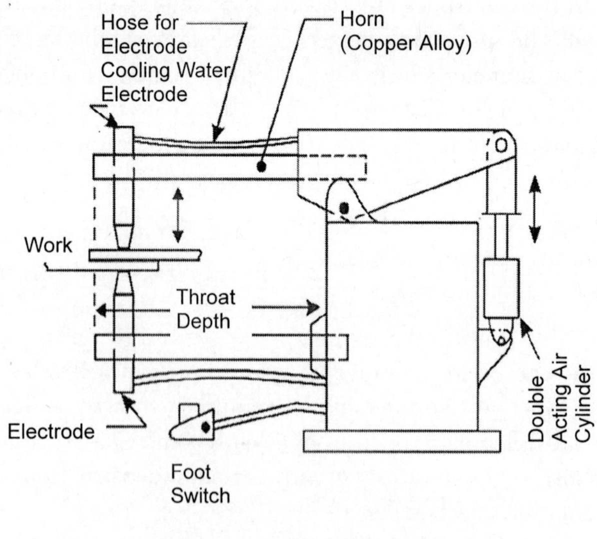

Figure 3.18: Rocker-arm spot welding machine

(a) **Foot Type.** When the foot treadle is pressed down, the two electrodes are brought together. The welding pressure is then transmitted to the work through a compression spring on the rear rod (see Fig. 3.18, where an air cylinder is shown in place of a rod, the other construction of the machine is same). After a suitable amount of compression is obtained, the welding circuit is closed by means of a mechanical switch. As the compression movement of the rear rod follows through, the switch trip opens and welding current ceases to flow. Releasing the pressure on the foot treadle opens the electrodes and resets the trip switch.

(b) **Air Operated Machines.** In this design, a double acting air cylinder replaces the rear rod and compression spring, (Fig. 3.18).

Press Type Machine. The name comes from straight line vertical stroke of the upper welding head. The straight line motion is provided by an air or hydraulic cylinder, (Fig. 3.19). These machines are used for mass production. The throat depth for these machines is about 1.5m.

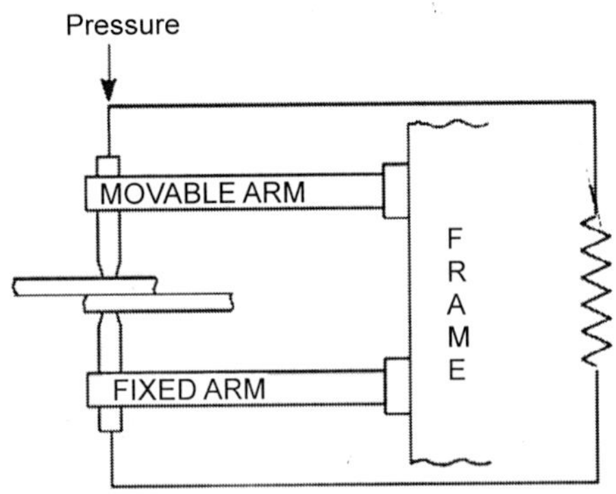

Figure 3.19: Press type spot welding machine

II. Special Multiple Electrode Machines.

These machines are employed for high-production jobs. (i) In one system, there is one common welding transformer and a hydraulic cylinder for each electrode pair. The electrodes are brought in contact with the work one pair at a time. (ii) In another system, all electrode pairs are pressed together against the work at one time, and the current from the transformer secondary is commutated to one electrode pair at a time. Some machines have a separate transfer and controls for each electrode pair.

III. Portable Spot Welding Guns.

These welders are used when the work is too large to be moved to a welding machine, for example, trucks and railroad cars. The gun consists of a transformer and controls in a case, usually hung from the ceiling, with leads and an air line to a pair of jaws. This permits bringing the welding unit and the operator to work. The jaws carry the electrodes and can be moved about in the work area. The jaws are closed by an air cylinder and the electrodes bite like teeth on the work and pass current to make the weld. These guns ca make 200 spots/minute.

3.11.2 Resistance Seam Welding (RSW)

To obtain a series of spot welds along a line by the RSW method, an interrupted work movement will be necessary. The same result can be achieved much more conveniently and rapidly in the resistance seam welding where the electrodes are in the form of rotating disc electrodes, with the working being welded moving continuously by the electrodes, (Fig. 3.20).

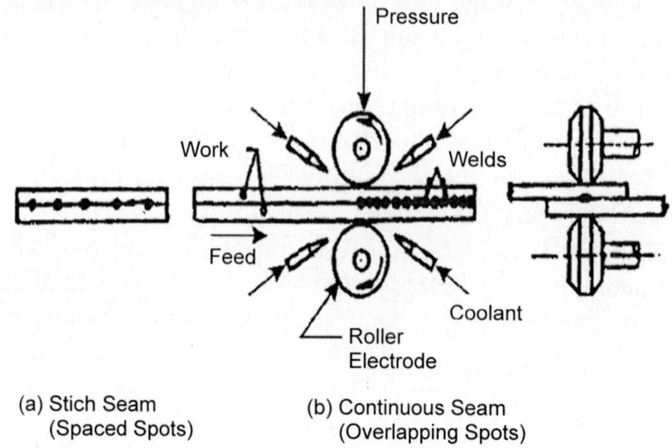

Figure 3.20: Resistance seam welding

Seam welding may be either intermittent (stitch seam or spaced spots) or continuous seam (over lapping seam). In the former case, a current interrupter is employed. When the a.c. is left on, a spot weld is made every time the current reaches its peak, and the welds are spaced close enough to give a gas and liquid- tight joint. The rollers are made of the same materials as the electrodes for sport welding.

Rollers may vary in diameter from 40 to 350 mm. Welding currents range from 2000 to 5000A while the force applied to the rollers may be as high as 5 to 6 kN. Welding speeds range is commonly from 0.5 to 3.5 m/min. In most cases of seam welding, a stream of water is directed over the disc electrodes and the area of the work pieces being welded to keep everything cool except the joint interface.

Seam welding is used in the manufacture of tanks, tubes and other articles of steel and nonferrous metals which must have airtight joints. Seam welding is primarily used for quantity production but is restricted to joining metal gauges that are thinner than those which can be joined by spot welding. The normal range of thickness compatible with seam welding is 0.25 to 3.2 mm.

3.11.3 Resistance Projection Welding (RPW)

The projection welding process is similar to spot welding except that the current is concentrated at the spots to be welded, when small dimples or projections are embossed or coined on one of the sheets, (Fig. 3.21). When the current is applied, the projections soften and are pushed back in place by the electrode pressure as the weld nuggets form. Electrodes are relatively large and several welds can be made simultaneously with a single electrode, resulting in a lower cost of operation. Also, because larger diameter electrodes can be used with a greater heat capacity, the need for water cooling is often eliminated. The projections tend to localize the heat, permitting thicker materials to be welded resulting in a stronger weld structure than that obtained with spot welding. Unlike spot welding, the method leaves no depression on the free surface.

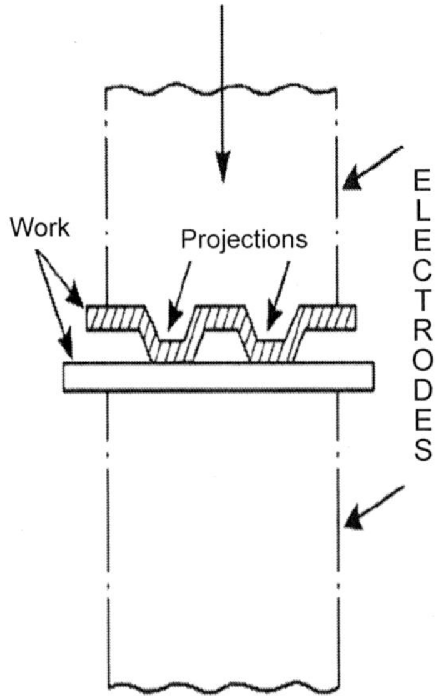

Figure 3.21: Resistance projection welding

Projection welding is used extensively by Automobile industry for joining nuts, bolts and studs to steel plates in car bodies. Because of their higher thermal conductivity, the method is especially suitable for copper, aluminium, brass etc.

Projections at the point of contact should be approximately = 10 to 80% of the sheet thickness. If pieces of unequal thickness are to be welded, jobs of bigger thickness should have the projections to develop uniform heating of the two pieces.

3.12 WELDING DEFECTS

When a weld is completed, the parent (base) metal is hottest at the point of fusion. The temperature of the base metal progressively decreases further away from the center of fusion zone. Due to this temperature gradient, a fusion weld and the metal adjacent to it contain various zones having distinctly different grain structures and hence different properties. Various zones of a typical weld are shown in Fig. 3.22. These are:

(i) Fusion Zone. It is the portion of weld in which the base (parent) metal has been fused (melted).

(ii) Heat Affectel Zone (HAZ). This is the zone wherein the base metal is metallurgically affected by the heat of welding, but is not melted.

(iii) Weld Metal Zone (WMZ). This is the portion of the weld which consists of weld metal. This zone includes any base metal which is melted and re-solidified, as well as any filler metal which did likewise.

(iv) Weld Zone. Weld Zone = WMZ + HAZ

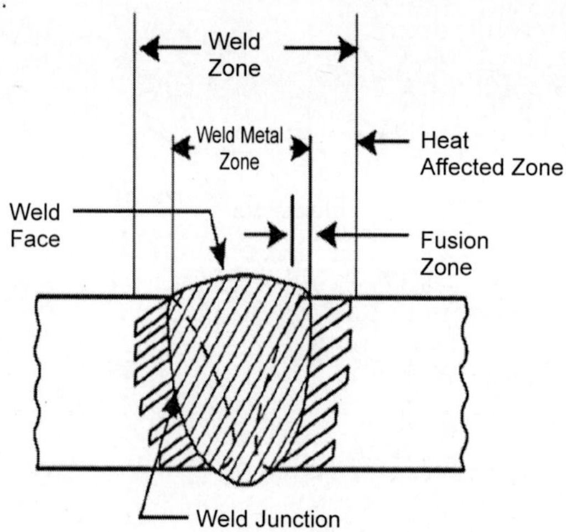

Figure 3.22: Welding zones

The welded joint should be free from any defect that would make it unsuitable for its intended purpose. The principal defects to be found in welded joints are shown in Fig. 3.23.

1. **Cracks.** Cracks that occur in or near a weld act as stress raisers which make the service life of the weldment very unreliable. Welding cracks are of the following types: (a) Micro-cracks. They are very small and are revealed only under a microscope. (b) Macro-cracks. These cracks can be seen by the unaided eye or by the use of a low power (5 to 10 X) magnifier. (c) Fissures. These are wide cracks which emerge to the surface of the metal.

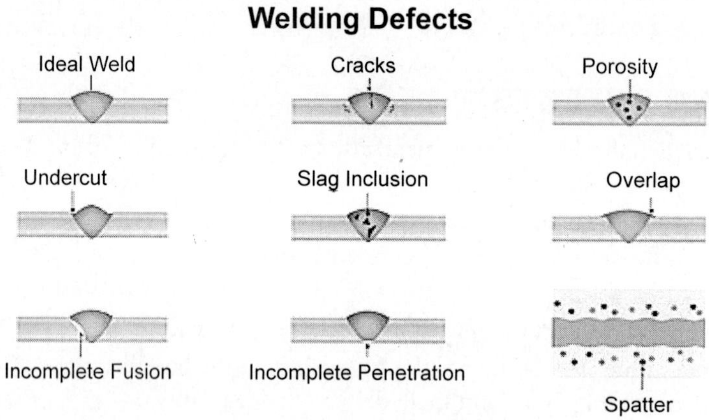

Figure 3.23: Welding defects

Cracks may occur at the following locations: (i) In the weld (Fuse) Metal Zone (ii) In the Base metal zone and (iii) Sometimes, the cracks originate in one Zone and then spread to the other Zone.

Cracks in the base metal usually occur at low temperatures (around 200°C) and are known as Cold cracks, On the other hand, the cracks in the weld metal zone occur while the metal is still very hot. Such cracks are called hot cracks. Cracks in the weld may be due to structural stresses in the metal (for example, the formation of martensite), heavy shrinkage, extra high amount of sulphur, phosphorous or carbon in the metal, excessively rigid clamping of the parts being welded or the presence of gases in the weld metal.

Cold cracking can occur due any to the following several factors: improper welding conditions, the presence of gas and other impurities in the weld, wrong choice of filler rod and metallurgical factors such as excessive cooling rate resulting in the formation of martensite and formation of brittle phases in the weld when cold or the formation of phases which are brittle at high temperatures [Allotropic transformations]. Cracks in the base metal can occur due to the following reasons: Corrosion, Base metal defects, Base metal composition variations, hydrogen embrittlement and internal stresses set up due to restrained shrinking after welding.

The phenomenon of cracks can be explained as below:

With thick parts, the weld zone is normally a small spot within a large mass of cooler metal. Heat flows off rapidly into the surrounding metal. When the welding is completed, what is called a "mass quench" results. This causes hard martensite to form in hardenable steel in part or all of the zone heated above the critical temperature. The martensite is brittle and does not yield but breaks when the stresses in the weld becomes high enough. Formation of martensite must be avoided. The more hardenable the steel, the slower must be the rate of cooling. The parts should also be preheated to retard the cooling rate.

Heating and cooling cause expansion and contraction in the weld. The metal in the joint is hotter and tends to shrink more on cooling than the bulk of the metal on either side. If the members being welded are restrained in a fixture or by a structure to which they are attached, high stresses are induced across the weld and thus cause cracking. Even if cracking does not occur, residual welding zones. The stresses may impair fatigue strength and cause warpage or distortion when they are unbalanced by later machining. These can be prevented by: using as thin material and as little filler metal as possible, preheating to minimize temperature difference between the weld and the base metal, and welding from the inside or confined portion of a structure to the outside or points of most freedom, a minimum number of welds and the maximum use of intermittent welds.

Gases such as O_2, N_2 and H_2 are readily absorbed by the molten weld metal. As the molten metal cools, its solubility for these gases diminishes and the gases try to escape. If they are not able to escape and remain within the weld, they will cause porosity and gas pockets in the weld. If they are able to reach just under the outer surface and are not able to escape (if the metal has cooled), they exert pressure and crack the metal. H_2 is a major cause of cracking in steel. Cracking due to gases can be avoided by preventing the evolution of these gases during welding (by thoroughly cleaning the joint from moisture, oil, grease, paint etc.) and absorbing of these gases from the atmosphere (by proper shielding). Slow cooling also eliminates cracking as the gases are able to escape.

2. **Undercut.** An undercut is a groove melted into the base metal adjacent to the toe of the weld, Fig. 3.24. The reasons for this can be: non-uniform feed of the filler rod, improper position of the electrode or torch tip or excessive heating. Undercutting can sometimes be corrected by adding additional metal to fill the groove.

3. **Porosity or voids.** Blowholes and gas pockets weaken welds appreciably and act as stress raisers from which cracks spread. The causes of these defects and the remedies have already been discussed above under cracking defect.

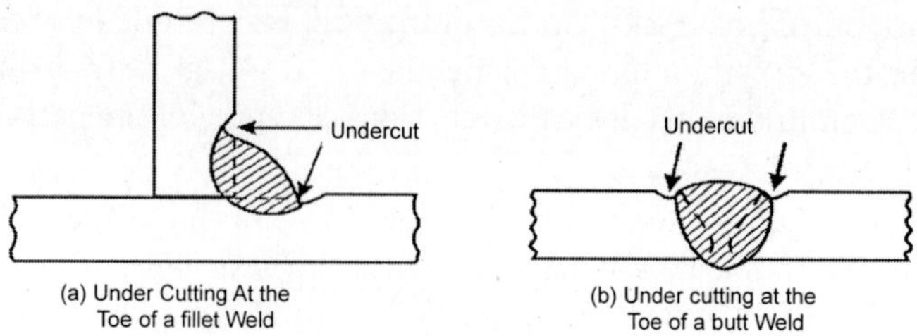

Figure 3.24: Undercut

4. Inclusions. Inclusions usually refer to slag but may be scale or dirt entrapped in the weld deposit during welding. The inclusions are due to the contamination of the base metal and the deposited metal by oxides, non-uniform melting of the electrode coating, high melting point and high viscosity of the slag or insufficient deoxidising of the metal in the weld.

5. Lack of fusion. It is the lack of coalescence between the deposited and the base metal or incomplete penetration of the weld metal into the base metal. The usual cause is in ability to raise the temperature of the base metal to its melting point, and faulty welding conditions and/or techniques.

6. Burning. It is oxidation of the metal in the weld and adjacent base metal. It is caused by a strong oxidising medium, an arc of excessive length or excessively high welding current.

7. Internal residual stresses and distortion. Internal residual stresses and distortion or warping have already been discussed under 'cracking'

3.13 BRAZING AND SOLDERING

Brazing/ soldering (Fig. 3.25) is a method of connecting that does not involve the melting of the base materials. It instead employs a filler substance (brazing paste or soft filler material, such as solder) that melts at a lower temperature than the base materials. Flux is used in filler materials to facilitate appropriate connecting with the base material. Pipes, connectors, and valves requiring leak tightness; pressure vessels requiring pressure resistance and leak tightness; and car parts requiring corrosion and heat resistance are all applications for brazing/soldering. Electronic circuits, electrical connectors, and precision electronic components are all commonly soldered using a soft filler material (solder).

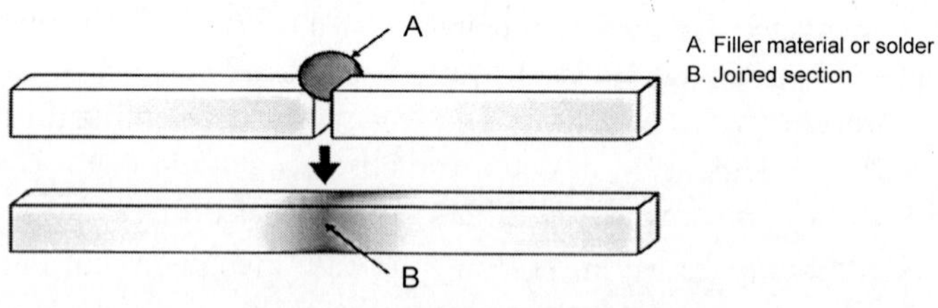

Figure 3.25: Brazing / soldering

The brazing process is described as the joining of two metal components heated to acceptable temperatures using a filler metal with a liquidus greater than 427°C and less than the solidus of the base metals. Capillary attraction distributes the filler metal between the closely fitting surfaces of the joint.

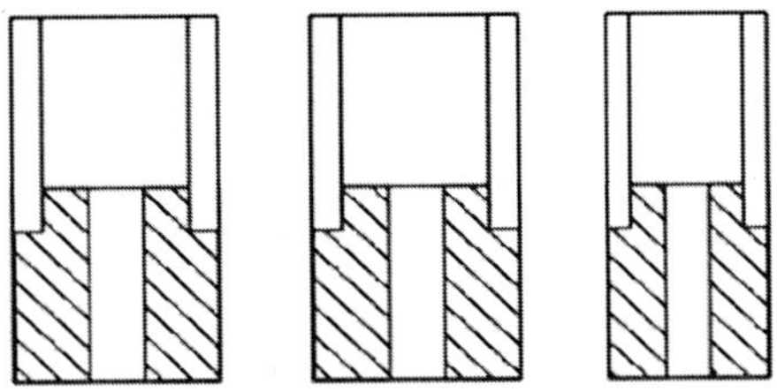

Figure 3.26: Brazing joints

The base metal of the two components to be connected is not melted during brazing. Even though the base metal does not reach its solidus temperature, some diffusion or alloying of the filler metal with it occurs. The stronger the mechanical strength of the joint, the greater the degree of adhesion and inter-diffusion between the molten filler metal and the base metals. The primary prerequisite for achieving this and obtaining a strong bond is that the filler metal thoroughly wet the base metal surfaces. As a result, the surfaces must be clean and devoid of impurities that would interfere with adhesion.

Thus, scale is removed mechanically (with a steel wire brush or emery cloth) or chemically (by pickling in acids), while heavy oily residues (oil, grease, paint, and so on) are removed by degreasing with hot alkaline solutions or organic solvents. Again, when the assembly is heated to melt the filler metal, oxides may develop, preventing the molten filler metal from contacting the surfaces. This can be overcome by I performing brazing in a vacuum or an appropriate (neutral or reducing) environment, and (ii) applying fluxes to assure wetting of the surfaces.

3.13.1 Steps in Brazing

(i) The surfaces to be joined are cleaned (and subsequently rinsed and dried) and fitted closely together. (ii) A flux is applied to all surfaces where the filler metal is to flow. (iii) After that, the joint is heated to the proper brazing temperature.

Solid filler metal may be preplaced on the metal pieces and thus melted as the metal pieces are heated, or it may be applied to the metal pieces after the brazing temperature is reached. Only a small amount of filler metal is needed to fill the joint completely, (Fig. 3.26), which shows the various ways of placing the filler metal at the joint. Some other commonly used joints in brazing are shown in Fig. 3.27.

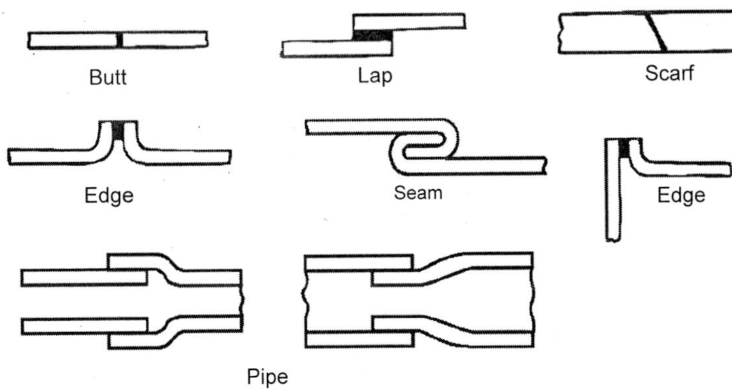

Figure 3.27: Brazing Joints Types

3.13.2 Fluxes

Fluxes are used to keep the base metal and filler metal from oxidising during brazing, to generate a fusible slag of any oxides that may be present or formed, and to encourage the free flow of the filler metal by capillary attraction. The following are the prerequisites for a good flux:

(a) It melts at a low enough temperature to keep the base metals and filler components from oxidising.
(b) Because of its low viscosity, it is replaced by the molten filler metal.
(c) It may react with surfaces to make wetting easier.
(d) It protects the joint while the filler is still wet.
(e) It is reasonably simple to remove after the filler has solidified.
(f) It reduces the surface tension of the molten filler metal, allowing it to flow into the joint.

Common fluxes are compounds of borates, fluorides, chlorides, borax, and boric acid in varied amounts based on specific requirements Fluxes are employed in the form of powder, paste, or slurry. Borax is utilised as fused borax because water in it causes bubbling during heating. A paste can be made by combining alcohol and fused borax. Most fluxes are corrosive, therefore the residue should be removed from the work when the brazing is finished.

3.13.3 Filler Materials

The filler metal or the braze metal must:

i. wet the base metal surfaces at the junction.
ii. be fluid enough to penetrate crevices. Capillary attraction requires a very small clearance between the parts being joined (0.03 to 0.05 mm), else the filler metal will run out of the joint. A joint's strength decreases as its clearance increases.
iii. have a restricted melting range.
iv. do not cause galvanic corrosion during service.

The filler metal is added to the joint region in the form of wire, strip, preforms, powder, or paste, as described above in step (iii) under "steps in brazing." Alternatively, the filler metal is pre-applied as a coating or cladding to the surface of one of the contacting parts, often by rolling, electrolytic deposition, or hot dipping. Table 4.3 lists typical filler metals for various base metal classes. Because the base metals are not melted, the composition of the brazing metal is always different from that of the base metals. Higher melting point brazing metals will generally provide greater strength, however this may have an effect on the strength of the base metals. These brazing metals, sometimes known as 'hard solders,' are based on Ag, Cu, and Ni.

Table 3.3: Brazing materials

Braze metal	**Composition %**	**Brazing** *process*	**Base metal**	**Brazing** *Temp. °C*
Brazing Brass	Cu : 60, Zn : 40	Torch, Dip Furnace	Steel, Cu, High Cu alloys, Ni alloys, Stainless steel	900

Braze metal	Composition %	Brazing *process*	Base metal	Brazing *Temp. °C*
Manganese Bronze	Cu : 58 : 5, Sn : 1, Fe : 1, Mn : 0.25, Zn : 39.5	Torch	-do-	-do-
Nickel Silver	Ni : 18, Cu : 55 to 65, Zn : 27 to 17	Torch Induction	Steel, Ni, Ni alloys	-do-
Copper	Si : 1.5, Mn : 0.25, Cu : 98.25, or Si : 1.5,	Torch	Steel	-do-
Silicon	Zn : 1, Cu : 97.5			
Silver alloys	Ag : 5 to 80, Cu = 15 to 52 balance : Zn + Sn + Cd	Torch, Furnace Induction Registance, Dip	Steel, Cu, Cu alloys, Ni, Ni alloys, Stainless Steel	700
Silver alloys with P	Ag : 15, P : 5, Cu = 80	-do-	Cu, Cu alloys	-do-
Copper phosphorus	Cu : 93, P : 7	-do-	-do-	-do-

3.13.4 Brazing Methods

The numerous brazing procedures are listed below, depending on the heat source used to melt the brazing metal.

(a) *Torch Brazing.* A joining method that uses acetylene, natural gas, butane, or propane in combination with air or oxygen to provide the heat needed to melt the filler rod and diffuse it into the base metal's surface. This method is not often employed in continuous mass production. The flux used is either a paste or a powder.

(b) *Furnace Brazing.* This is a high-volume manufacturing technique in which heat is supplied by gas or electric heating coils. The furnaces are either box (batch) or continuous. The latter uses a wire mesh belt to convey the brazed components. Prior to entering the furnace, prefabricated shapes of filler metal are placed on the components to be connected. The method lends itself well to large output. If an inert environment is maintained in the furnace, the need of flux can be avoided. The flux is applied as a paste.

(c) *Induction Brazing.* The filler metal is likewise employed in the premade shape here. Heat is applied to the parts by placing them in the field of a high frequency induction coil. Because the pieces to be linked give electric-magnetic resistance to the changing induction field, eddy currents are used to heat them. Heating is very fast, and heat can be applied in the local area of the brazed joint by properly structuring the induction coils. The procedure can be automated. The flux is applied as a paste.

(d) *Dip Brazing.* dip brazing is of two kinds : (i) In chemical dip brazing, pieces containing prepared filler metal are immersed in a molten flux bath. (ii) The completed pieces are prefluxed before being immersed in a molten bath of filler metal in the molten metal bath process. The first method is more suited for combining large pieces, whilst the latter is limited to small parts.

(e) *Resistance Brazing.* These costly processes are only justified for precise work on high-value, high-temperature materials. In industry, only the first four brazing procedures are used. Traditional brazing and soldering techniques can be performed in an inert gas (such as Ar) atmosphere or in a vacuum to avoid the need of flux (As in EB brazing).

(f) *Laser Brazing and Electron Beam Brazing.* These expensive procedures are only warranted for precise work on high-value, rather high-temperature materials. Only the first four brazing processes are used in industry. The use of flux in traditional brazing and soldering processes can be avoided by performing the process in an inert gas (such as Ar) atmosphere or in a vacuum (As in EB brazing).

3.13.5 Braze Welding

It differs from traditional brazing in that a significantly larger gap is filled with brazing brass using a torch. Capillary motion has no role in the formation of the joint here. The method is also used to repair iron and steel castings. Bronze rods can also be used to fill grooves and fillets, and the procedure is known as "Bronze welding." The technique is very beneficial for mending cast iron castings. Straight welding needs complete preheating of the casting, which is not always desirable or practicable. Brasses and bronzes are stronger and more ductile than cast iron, and they form a strong and satisfying bond with the base metal. Because the base metal is neither fused nor strongly heated, internal tensions are maintained to a minimum, and cooling cracking is unlikely. *Silver Brazing.* When silver alloys are used for brazing, the process is known as "Silver brazing," which is also known as "Silver Soldering" or "Hard soldering." Because the filler metal is more expensive, the process is more expensive than plain brazing. The approach is preferred when a superior joint is desired and a modest amount of filler metal is required. It is commonly employed in the electrical and refrigeration industries and is particularly popular in small area repair work.

3.13.6 Advantages of Brazing

1. Brazing involves lower temperatures than fusion welding. This reduces distortion and enables for joining at lower preheat temperatures than fusion welding. As a result, medium and high carbon steels and C.I. that harden in the heat affected zone and may break can be brazed or braze welded with little or no significant hardening.
2. Almost all typical engineering materials can be brazed or braze welded successfully.
3. Brazing can generate inaccessible joint locations that could not be formed by MIG or TIG techniques, as well as spot or seam welding.
4. Brazing can be used to join thin-walled tubes and light-gauge sheet metal components that cannot be bonded by welding.
5. Brazing can be used to unite different metals such as brass to stainless steels and carbon steels to stainless steels.
6. As in furnace brazing, several joints can be created at the same time.
7. Can be used for joints that will need to be disassembled later.
8. A neat-looking joint that requires little cleaning.
9. The procedure can be completed more swiftly and cheaply.

10. Many brazing operations can be automated.
11. Metallurgical damage to the base metal may be avoided due to the lower temperatures involved when compared to fusion welding.

3.13.7 Limitations of Brazing

(a) Parts are of limited size. Due to the cost and availability of large equipment such as brazing furnaces, very large assemblies, while brazable, can be fabricated more affordably via welding.
(b) It is expensive to machine the joint edges to get the necessary fit.
(c) A high level of skill is necessary to accomplish the brazing operations.

3.13.8 Uses of Brazing

For pipe fitting assembly, carbide tip tooling, radiators, heat exchangers, electrical parts, and casting repair Brazing is a simple way to link leak-tight joints in pressured and vacuum systems. High-temperature service is provided by copper-brazed steel joints and nickel-alloy-brazed stainless steel joints. Corrosion resistance can be offered for food-service equipment that uses silver-brazing alloys to link stainless steels. Nickel alloy brazing is used in the chemical sector to join corrosive stainless steels.

3.14 SOLDERING

Soldering is the joining of two pieces with the use of a molten filler metal whose melting point is lower than the solidus (melting point of the base metals) and, in all situations, lower than 427°C. Brazed joints are stronger than soldered connections. Because of the lower working temperatures, wetting is more important than brazing. The soldering procedure follows the same phases as the brazing procedure, namely, (i) Surface preparation which involves fitting the surfaces to each other, cleaning them mechanically and chemically and covering the cleaned surfaces with a flux. The clearance in a joint is about 0.05 to 0.20 mm (for steel) and (ii) After this, soldering proper is done.

Commonly used soldering joints are: Lap, butt, seam and pipe joints. There are two types of flux used in soldering as corrosive and non-corrosive. Zinc chloride and combinations of zinc chloride and ammonium chloride are common corrosive fluxes. To prevent corrosion, the flux must be removed after soldering. Rosin and rosin with alcohol are two common non-corrosive fluxes. These are required for electrical connections where corrosion might result in localised high resistance and even loss of conduction. Tin and lead alloys in varying amounts are the most often used solders. Other metals in trace amounts may be added. These soldering filler metals are known as "Soft solders."

I. 63/37 Tin-lead solder has the lowest melting point and solidifies at a constant temperature. It is most suitable for electrical connections.
II. 70/30 Tin lead : Good pretinning alloy
III. 60/40 Tin lead : Good electric grade solder
IV. 50/50 Tin lead : General purpose solder
V. 32/68 Tin lead: Plumber's solder.
VI. Tin-lead-silver solder: High temperature electrical solder for instruments.
VII. 96.5/3.5 Tin-silver: High temperature electrical instrument solder.

VIII. A low (<5%) tin content gives higher strength and is suitable for automotive radiators and lock seam cans, and tubes made of tin plate.

IX. 35/65 Tin Lead: Its wide freezing range makes it ideal as a wiping solder for the joining of copper tubes.

X. Lead silver solders are used for higher temperature service. Ag: 1.5 to 3.5%. Certain other metals such as cadmium, bismuth and indium may be added for some specific purposes.

Because lead is poisonous, it has a negative impact on the environment. As a result, lead-free solders are being developed and are becoming more widely used. They are employed in the delivery of drinking water as well as other purposes. Typical examples of it are:

(a) Tin-silver (given above) for electronics.
(b) Tin-Bismuth (42%, 58%) : for electronics.
(c) Tin-zinc alloys with 9 to 100%. Zinc for soldering of aluminium in conjunction with special fluxes.
(d) Zinc-aluminium: for corrosion resistance, soldering of aluminium.
(e) Cadmium-silver: for strength at high temperatures.

3.14.1 Soldering Techniques

The various brazing procedures can also be utilised for soldering (flame, hot dip, resistance, induction). Fluxless soldering of aluminium and various nonferrous metals such as silicon and germanium is accomplished using ultrasonic soldering (similar to ultrasonic welding).

In 'Radiant heating (infrared heating),' special quartz-iodine incandescent tubular lamps that can be easily focussed to concentrate the heat at the region to be soldered are utilised. Radiant heating can also be utilised for brazing. In "wave soldering," new, hot solder is pushed to the connections by one or more standing waves of molten solder. The wave is created by constantly pushing solder through a tiny hole to the surface. As the assembly goes over the waves, all of the joints are produced. The operation is continuous and only restricted in speed by time and heat needs. This approach is appropriate for items such as transformer terminals and container lips. The technology is extremely useful in the assembly of printed-circuit boards.

Because the temperatures involved are lower, a hand-type heated copper or iron-plated copper bit (soldering iron) is commonly utilised. Before applying the iron to the job, the tip is tinned. The most popular type of iron is electric, and it is utilised in numerous industries such as radio and electronics. To solder, the iron is heated to 250 - 300°C, the tip is soaked in flux, tinned with solder, and then applied to the soldered pieces to heat them at the junction. Simultaneously, solder is applied to the junction, where it is melted by the iron as it travels along the joint and enters the clearing. The solder cools and produces the seam here.

3.15 INTRODUCTION TO MILLING

Milling is a machining operation that uses a revolving cutting tool to remove superfluous material from a work item. The revolving cutting tool known as a "Milling cutter" is a multiple-point tool with the shape of a solid of revolution with cutting teeth organised (equally spaced) on the periphery, end face, or both. The work could be held in a vice, a three-jaw chuck, an index head, a rotary table, between centres, in a customised fixture, or attached to the machine table. Milling is a process that includes simultaneous rotating cutter and linear (occasionally rotary) work motion, with the work fed against the cutter. The milling process is used to create flat, curved, or helical surfaces, threads, toothed gears, and helical grooves. In general, all milling processes can be classified into two types:

3.15.1 Peripheral Milling or Horizontal Milling

Here, the finished surface is parallel to the axis of the cutter and is machined by cutter teeth located on the periphery of the cutter as shown in Fig. 3.28 (a).

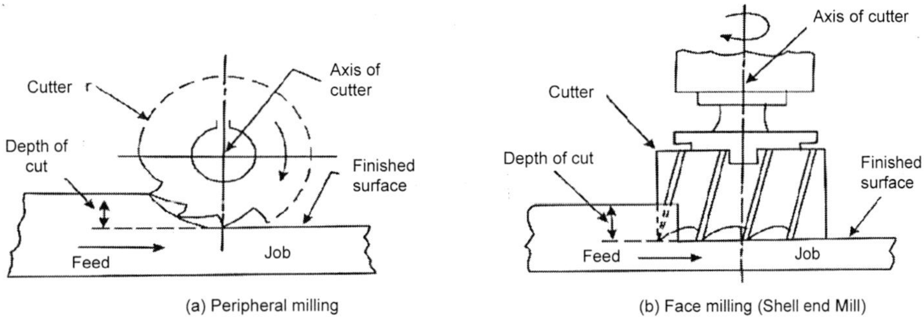

Figure 3.28: Types of Milling Operations

3.15.2 Face Milling or Vertical Milling

The final surface in face milling is at right angles to the cutter axis and is obtained by the teeth on the cutter's periphery and the flat end as shown in Fig. 3.28 (b). Methods for Creating Surfaces Depending on the relative direction of feed of the worktable and the rotation of the cutter, there are two ways for milling flat surfaces with plain milling cutters (these cutters have teeth just on the cutter's periphery).

3.15.2.1 Conventional (up) Milling

Here, the direction of feed of the worktable is opposite to the direction of rotation of the cutter as shown in Fig. 3.29 (a).

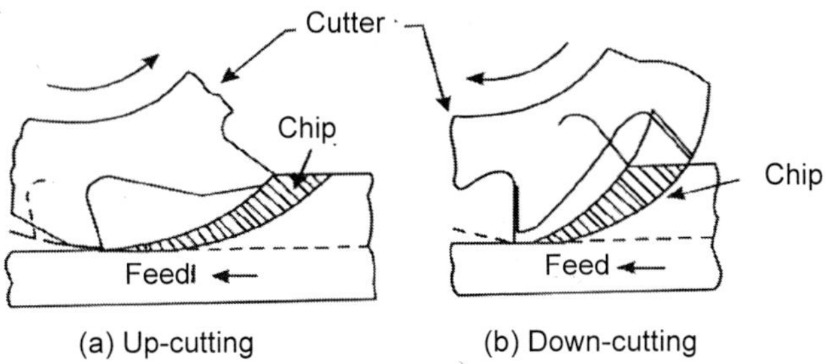

Figure 3.29: Up and down milling

3.15.2.2 Climb (down) milling

The rotation of the cutter and the direction of the worktable feed are the same in this case, as shown in Fig. 3.28 (b). In either instance, the individual milling chips have a varied thickness and a cross section resembling a comma. The thickness progressively grows during the cut in traditional milling; in climb milling, the cutter tooth takes a chip of maximum thickness at the start of the cut and zero thickness at the finish. The advantages of conventional milling are that the pressure on each cutter tooth is gradually increased and the teeth begin cutting beneath the workpiece's metal skin. The initial tooth contact is normally in clean metal and concludes with the rough surface scale being lifted or peeled off. As a result, this kind of milling is suited for machining sand castings, forgings, and metals with a rough or hard abrasive surface scale.

The downsides are that the cutter tends to lift the workpiece from the worktable, and because the teeth tend to dull, each tooth glides across the workpiece surface a minute distance before beginning to cut, resulting in a distinctive wavy surface. There is a propensity to lift the work table as well as the job off the table or fixture (since the cutting forces are directed upwards). This increases the amount of space between the table and the bed or saddle ways. When making large cuts, such clearances cause vibrations that degrade the job's surface polish. Chips build again ahead of the cutting zone, where they can be picked up by the teeth and moved around, causing the finish to deteriorate. Furthermore, where clamping is insufficient, it is difficult to process thin sheets and workpieces. Because the table must be fed against the cutting force, the feed motor and main motor power consumption are higher.

The work must be rigidly held to offset the tendency of the cutting forces to raise or drag the piece out of the vise or fixture, which is advantageous for conventional milling. The advantages of climb milling are as follows: the task is driven against the table, and the table is forced against the ways. Excess clearance in jointing surfaces and the resulting vibrations are eliminated. Furthermore, the chips are deposited behind the cutter, out of the way. These characteristics result in a superior surface polish than traditional milling. Again, less power is required in climb milling because the feed action consumes less power. Cutting speeds and feed rates can be increased. Thin sheets can also be easily machined. The following criteria are favourable for climb milling: the workpiece has no hard skin, the milling machine is in good working order, and there is no excessive backlash in the table screw and nut, as any looseness will allow the cutter to draw the workpiece ahead and take too large bites. The technique is typically utilised for milling operations on thin and complicated objects.

3.16 TYPES OF MILLING MACHINES

Milling machines were basically develop-ed to machine flat surfaces. But, the present milling machines can machine flat, contoured and helical surfaces, cut gears and do various other jobs. Due to all this, a milling machine is one of the most useful and necessary machine tools found in the shop and it ranks next to the lathe in importance.

Milling machines are designed to hold and rotate milling cutter or cutters, hold the workpiece and feed the workpiece to the milling cutter in one of several directions. Milling machines can be classified in different ways:

(a) According to the axis of the spindle of the machine, we have: Horizontal milling machines with horizontal spindle.

(b) Vertical milling machines with vertical spindle. According to their purpose, the milling machines may be classified as: (i) General purpose milling machines (ii) Production milling machines and (iii) Special purpose milling machines.

3.16.1 General Purpose Milling Machines

The most common kinds of milling machines in this category are the column and knee type models which are all single spindle machines. The various models under this category are:

(a) Plain (Horizontal spindle)

(b) Universal (Horizontal spindle with swivel table)

(c) Omniversal (Horizontal spindle with swivel table and swivel knee).

(d) Vertical spindle.

3.16.1.1 Plain column and knee type milling machines

This machine is called by this name because the spindle (the part that rotates) is fixed in the column. A block diagram of the machine is shown in Fig. 3.30 (a). The structure of the machine is mounted on the base or bed of the machine

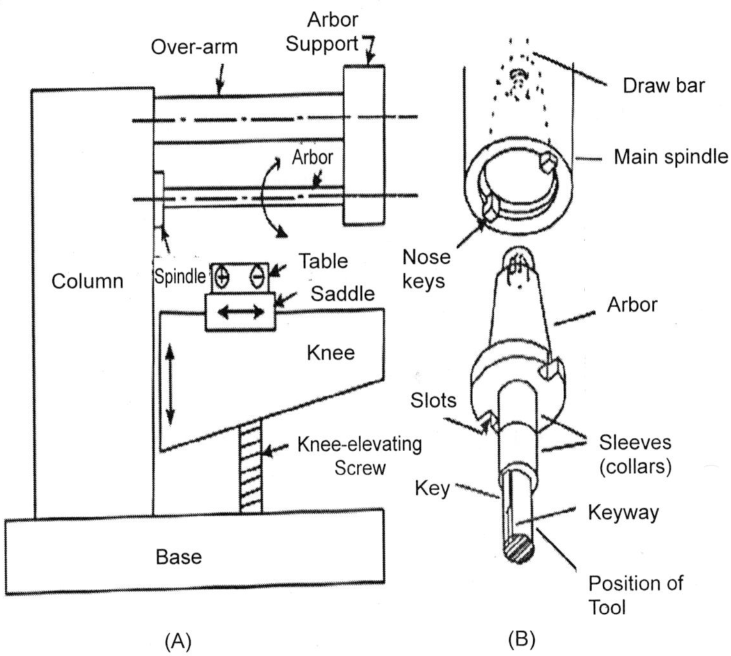

Figure 3.30: Plain column and knee type milling machine

It provides rigidity and strength to the machine. It may also serve as a reservoir for cutting fluid. The column is the main supporting frame. It is a heavy box like structure. Inside this is space for motor and much of the driving mechanism. The face of the column is a very accurate slide. The "knee" slides vertically (up and down) on the column face. A feed, or elevating screw extends from the base to the knee. On top of the knee is a "saddle". The saddle can move transversely (cross Machine Tools 511 movement toward and away from the column). On top of the saddle is the "table". The table moves longitudinally (back and forth) in front of the column. The surface of the table is cut with T slots to which work holding devices such as the vise can be clamped.

The machine provides for three movements of the workpiece: (i) Vertical (up and down) movement of the knee (ii) Transverse or cross (in-and-out) movement of the saddle (iii) Longitudinal movement (back-and-forth) movement of the table. Along any one of these coordinate directions, feeding may be accomplished. Movements along the other two coordinate directions are then used for locating the cut, which includes obtaining the depth of cut. The driving power for all the cutting tools comes from the rotation of the spindle. This is a hollow shaft that rotates in bearings. The front (end near the table) has a tapered hole. The arbor is an accurately machined shaft for holding and driving the arbor-type cutter (Fig. 4.30 (b)). It is tapered at one end to fit the spindle nose and also has two slots to fit the nose keys for locating and driving it. When it is in place, a draw in- bar goes through the spindle and is threaded on one end to screw into the threaded taper end of the arbor, holding the arbor tightly in place. The outer end of the arbor is supported by an overarm support in a proper bearing. The overarm extends out from the top of the column above the spindle. It can be moved in or out and clamped at different distances from the column.

(a) **Universal milling machine.** The universal horizontal milling machine varies from the plain horizontal milling machine in that its table may be swivelled through a 45-degree angle in the horizontal plane to mill helical grooves (e.g. the helical flutes of twist drills or the teeth of helical gears). The saddle is divided into two pieces so that the table can be rotated horizontally.

(b) **Omniversal milling machine.** When compared to a universal milling machine, an omniversal milling machine features an additional movement. On an axis perpendicular to the column face, the knee can be rotated. This allows for the creation of tapered spiral grooves in reamers, teeth on bevel gears, and angular holes, among other things.

(c) **Vertical milling machines.** The vertical milling machine is very similar to the plain horizontal milling machine except that the spindle is held in a vertical position instead of horizontal. Vertical milling machines are of two types: Fixed bed type, and column - and - knee type, (Fig. 3.31).

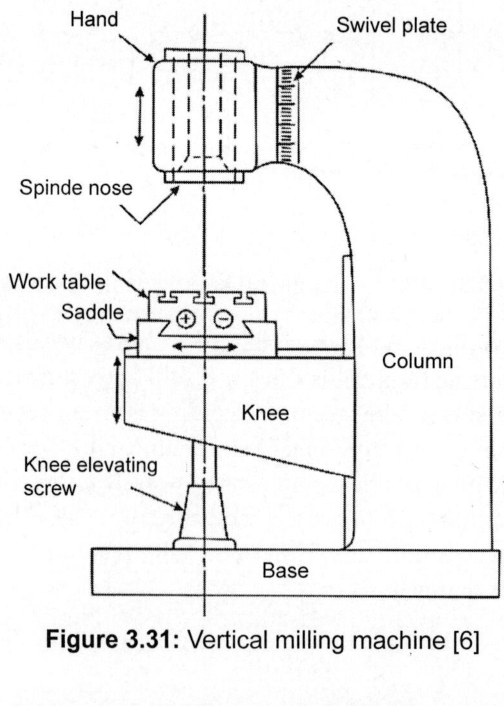

Figure 3.31: Vertical milling machine [6]

The column-and-knee type vertical machine has a vertical head and spindle, but the same feeds and adjustments as the plain horizontal machine. The overarm provides a strong support to the spindle. On some models, the head can be moved up and down to perform operations like grooving, slotting, die forming, facing, drilling and boring of accurate holes, with their exact locations. The machine can be with a fixed head and of swiveling head type with the head swiveling around a horizontal axis.

3.16.2 Size of Milling Machines

The sizes of column-and-knee milling machines are given in terms of the following parameters: (a) Table Travel. This indicates the distance the table will move longitudinally. It can be up to the range of 1.5 m. (b) In terms of the power of the machine. (c) In terms of the type of the machine: plain, universal, omniversal, vertical etc.

3.16.2.1 Production milling machines

Production or Manufacturing milling machines are designed to remove metal rapidly and to require a minimum amount of attention from the operator. The various models in this category are discussed below:

(i) *Planer Type Milling Machines.* A planer milling machine resembles a double column planer, but it has milling heads mounted in different planes, such as vertical milling heads on the cross rail and horizontal heads on the sides (on columns). This enables it to mill a workpiece on many sides at the same time. Planer milling machines are designed primarily for generating lengthy straight surfaces on massive and heavy machine parts.

(ii) *Bed Type Milling Machines.* Simplex and Duplex fixed bed milling machines are smaller variants of planer type milling machines with one horizontal spindle on one side or two spindles, one on each side as shown in Fig. 3.32. These machines are larger, heavier, and stiffer than column-and-knee machines, and they are not suitable for tool room operations. Because the spindle is fixed in a quill, the cutter can be adjusted in and out. The fixed bed only allows for regulated longitudinal travel.

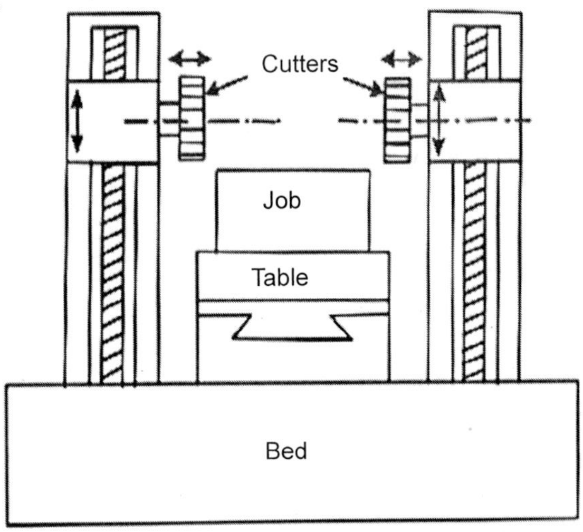

Figure 3.32: Duplex bed type milling machine

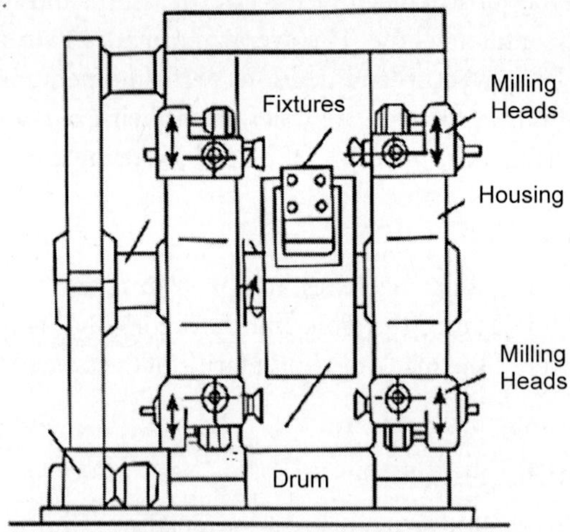

Figure 3.33: Drum type milling machine

(iii) *Drum Type Milling Machines.* These continuous-operation machines are commonly found in large-lot and mass production plants for the manufacture of big parts such as motor blocks, gear boxes, and clutch housings. Figure 3.33 depicts a drum milling machine. A square drum (or a regular pentagon or hexagon) is fixed on a shaft that runs through the frame. Parts are stored in fixtures that are installed on the drum faces. The drum continuously rotates, transporting the pieces between face mills. The milling heads can be changed and clamped along the housing as needed for the setup. The milling spindles have axial adjustment in addition to rotation to tune the cutters to the depth of cut. The output of such machines is determined by the quantity of components being machined at the same time as well as the speed at which the drum rotates (rate of feed).

(iv) *Hand Operated Millers.* These machines are typically column-and-knee in design and are common among smaller production equipment. Hand wheels or levers control table movements (which rotate a pinion that engages a rack on the underside of the table), offering high sensitivity and making them excellent for delicate operations (light cuts) on small parts, such as slotting screw heads. A motor powers the cutter.

(v) *Continuous or Rotary Millers.* These machines are usually of the vertical spindle type and have a rotary table for feeding jobs under the cutter continuously and are normally used for facing operations. It is used for facing automobile cylinder heads and crank pins etc. An unusual departure from the conventional rotary machines is the rotary-head machine. Suited primarily for tool, die, and small- quantity production, this miller adds a bit to the versatility of the rotary-table machine but is designed for much smaller work. Intricate radial cam work can be produced readily from drawings without the use of templates or patterns.

(vi) *Tracer Controlled Production Milling Machines.* The vertical spindle rotary-head machine discussed above eliminates the need for templates or patterns in the production of small quantities of complicated forms, cams etc. However, when mass production is required an automatic tracer controlled miller is indicated. A variety of vertical and horizontal tracers are available and represent the ideal machine for the production milling of odd shaped parts such as connecting rods, complicated gear housings, and extremely large or small cam tracks of intricate shape. Intricate machine parts can be profiled in stacks or groups where high accuracy for interchangeability is necessary but quantity does not warrant expensive tooling. A roller on a tracer control valve rides on a template bolted to the rear of the table and causes the cutter to cut in a path corresponding to that of the template.

3.16.2.2 Special purpose milling machines

The number and design of special purpose millers is probably unlimited as the design of machine parts themselves. Where quantity is sufficiently large, a special machine can offset its cost by virtue of increased output and automaticity. Thus one has: die sinking machines, cam millers, thread millers and keyway millers etc. Die-sinking machines are duplicating machines used to make forging dies, molds, forming dies etc. "Profilers" are capable of reproducing external and internal profiles from templates in two dimensions, "Duplicators" do the job in three dimensions. Some machines are hand operated, others are power fed. "Cam millers" produce disk cams. The profile of the cam is cut on a slowly revolving workpiece by an end mill positioned by a master cam revolving in unison with the workpiece.

3.17 CONSTRUCTIONAL DETAILS OF MILLING CUTTERS

As already written, the milling cutters can be solid, carbide-tipped solid cutters and inserted blade cutters with H.S.S. or carbide tipped blades, the body being of constructional steel. The advantages of carbide-tipped cutters (either solid or inserted-blade type) are:

(i) Their high production capacity.
(ii) The high quality of the surfaces they produce.
(iii) Elimination of grinding operation in some cases, the possibility of machining hardened steels and the reduction in machining costs that their use leads to.

Due to these advantages, they have been successfully applied in metal cutting industry where they have replaced many solid cutters of tool steels. Along with the especially popular carbide tipped face milling cutters, carbide-tipped side and form milling cutters and various end mills are used in industry

3.17.1 Specifications of a Milling Cutter

Milling cutter specifications are required to evaluate the machine's details, such as the number of working surfaces, the width and pitch of T-slots used, the maximum distance from the spindle centre to the underside of the over support, movements (longitudinal movement of the table by lower/screw, cross movement of the table by screw, vertical movement of the table by screw), spindle (bore, inside taper, arbour), motor type and capacity used, front space, height, weight, and coolant tank capacity.

3.18 MILLING OPERATIONS

Milling machines can be employed to produce a large variety of surfaces.

3.18.1 Milling Flat Surfaces

Horizontal Flat surfaces may be milled on: (i) Plain horizontal and Universal horizontal machines with plain milling cutters as shown in Fig. 3.34 (c). (ii) Vertical-spindle milling machines with face milling cutters, as shown in Fig. 3.35 (a).

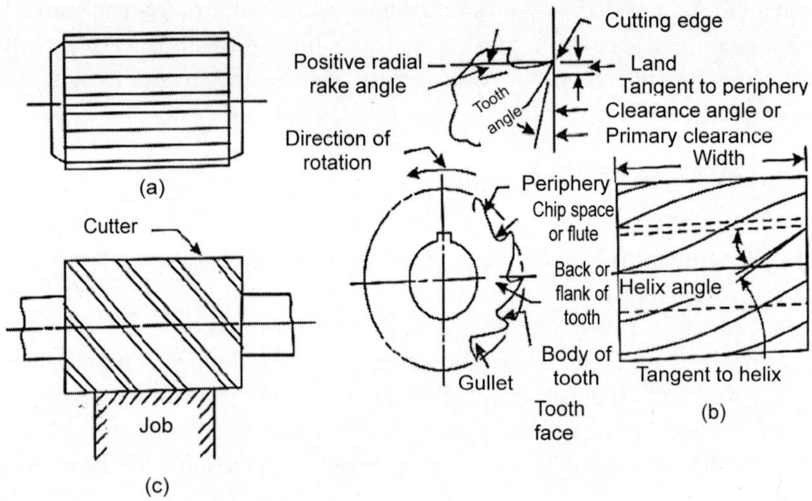

Figure 3.34: Plain milling cutters [6]

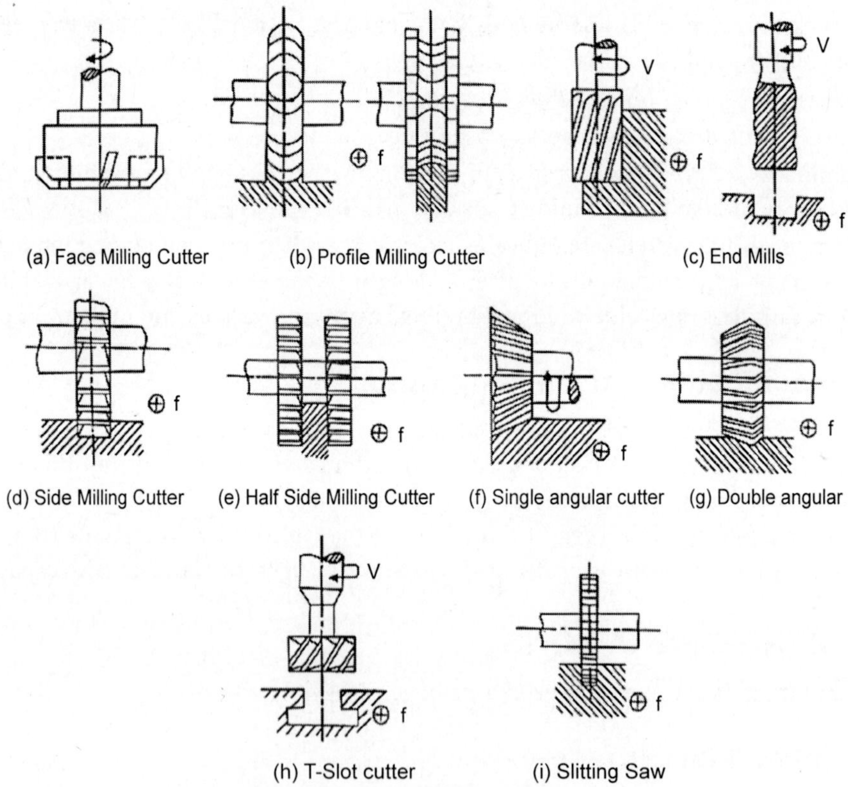

Figure 3.35: Milling cutters [6]

Vertical flat surface are milled on: (i) Plain horizontal and Universal horizontal machines by using side milling cutters. (ii) Vertical-spindle milling machines using end mills. (iii) Vertical flat surfaces may also be milled on planer-type machines with face milling cutters, (Fig. 3.36 (a))

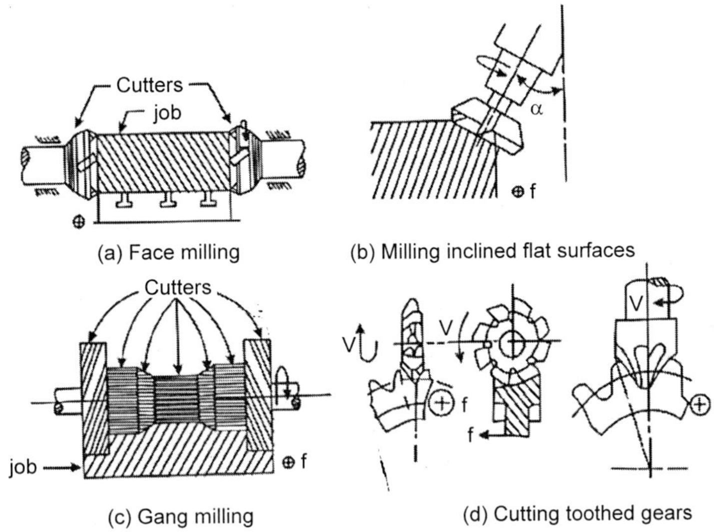

Figure 3.36: Milling operations [6]

Inclined flat surfaces are milled on: (i) Plain milling machines with single angle cutters (See Fig. 3.35 (a)) (ii) On vertical spindle machines with the spindle swiveled to the required angle as shown in Fig. 3.36 (b).

This arrangement is possible only on swivel-head vertical spindle milling machine in which the head can be swiveled in a vertical plane parallel to the column face. "Recesses" are milled on vertical spindle machines with end mills (See Fig. 3.35 (c)). In this case, the two perpendicular surfaces are machined simultaneously.

3.18.2 Milling Slots, Grooves and Splines

Rectangular, T-and dovetail slots are milled, as a rule, on vertical-spindle machines by means of suitable shank-type milling cutters, (see Fig. 3.35 (h)). Rectangular slots can also be machined on plain horizontal spindle milling machines with side milling cutters. Key ways of rectangular cross section are milled on vertical- spindle machines or on key way milling machines by using end mills and special cutters. Keyways can also be milled on horizontal spindle machines by using side milling cutters. Splines may be milled on horizontal spindle machines by using single-and double-angle cutters.

3.18.3 Milling Contoured Surfaces

Contoured surfaces of relatively small width are milled on plain milling machines, using formed milling cutters. The profile of the cutter coincides with that of the workpiece. Surfaces of more complex shape are milled by a gang of simple cutters, (Fig. 3.36 (c)). The operation is called as "Gang milling". Complex shaped surfaces can also be milled using a template on a tracer-controlled machine. Three dimensional contoured surfaces (for example on dies etc.) are milled on tracer-controlled contouring machines.

3.18.4 Cutting toothed gears and helical grooves

Spur and helical gears are cut by form milling cutters on plain milling machines or by end-mill type cutters on vertical-spindle machines, (Fig. 3.36 (d)). The cutter profile must exactly coincide with the tooth space of the gear. Dividing head is used to index the gear blank through the required angle from one tooth space to the next. Helical groves are milled on a universal milling machine. Here, the table is swivelled to the helix and the work is rotated by the dividing head which is linked by gearing to the lead screw of the table.

3.18.5 Gang Milling, Straddle Milling, String Milling

When two or more milling cutters are mounted on an arbor so that each cutter will produce its own distinctive surface as the workpiece is fed to it, the operation is called "Gang milling", (Fig. 3.36 (c)). "Straddle milling" is a special form of gang milling in which side milling cutters are used to machine both sides of a workpiece simultaneously (see Fig. 3.35 (e)). In "String milling", two or more workpieces are mounted on the milling machine table in a line, so that they are successively fed to one or more milling cutters. String milling results in a substantial reduction in handling time, as it is overlapped by the machining time. Depending upon the job set-up and tool set-up, the other milling methods are given below:

3.18.5.1 Abreast Milling

This is the simultaneous milling of several workpieces, placed in a row, parallel to cutter axis or of several surfaces of the same workpiece. It can be accomplished by (i) Mounting the required number of plain, side and form cutters on an arbor, or (ii) Mounting the required number of face milling cutters on different spindles (iii) Using a face milling cutter of sufficiently large diameter, or (iv) Using a plain milling cutter of sufficient length. Abreast milling leads to a sharp reduction in labour input, as a result of combination of several operation elements and less handling time. Same or different operations can be performed on each piece.

3.18.5.2 Combined abreast-and-string milling

The simultaneous milling of several workpieces (or several surfaces of a single workpiece), placed in a single or several rows on the machine table, is combined with consecutive milling. This method, in addition to the reduction in labour input, enables the machine time to be considerably reduced, due to, the reduction in handling time.

3.18.5.3 Transfer-base milling

Here, two fixtures are mounted on opposite ends of a two-station index base, which is secured at one end of the machine table. After one workpiece has been milled, the table is returned to the initial position, the second fixture is indexed through and the second work-piece is milled, while the first fixture is being unloaded and loaded. Economy is due to the combining of machine and handling times.

3.18.5.4 Index milling

Here identical multiple operations are done on one or more pieces, which are indexed (rotated through required angle) each time to present a new position and repeating the same operation, for example, milling of splines on a shaft or cutting gear teeth.

3.18.5.5 Reciprocal milling

Fixtures are mounted on the left and right-hand ends of the machine table. While milling the workpiece in one fixture, the other fixture is being unloaded and loaded. Thus, the machine is performing the productive work during the handling time.

3.18.5.6 Progressive milling

Here, two or more similar or different operations are performed either simultaneously/ successively, on separate workpieces on the same machine and are progressively moved from one fixture station to the next, until all the desired operations are performed [Fig. 3.37].

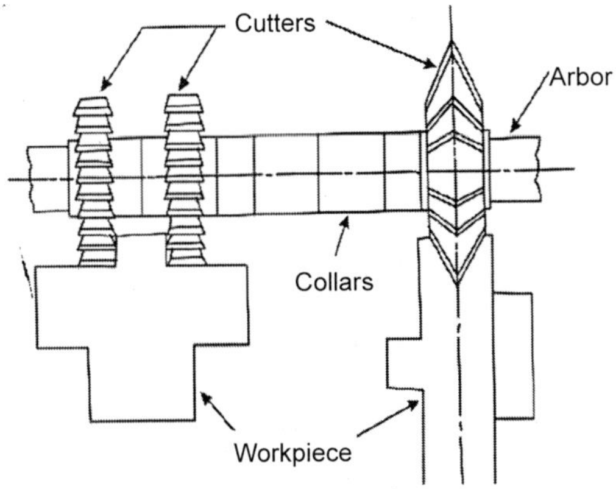

Figure 3.37: Progressive milling [6]

3.19 DIVIDING HEADS

The general design and operation of a dividing head have already been discussed under work holding devices. Milling machines are used to cut slots, grooves, and other patterns that must be evenly spaced around the perimeter of a blank, such as gear cutting, ratchet wheels, milling cutter blanks, reamers, and so on. This requires holding the blank (workpiece) and rotating it precisely for each groove or slot to be cut. This is referred to as "Indexing." The instrument used for this is the dividing head. It is aligned and attached to the machine table so that the axis passing between the head stock centre and tail stock centre is perpendicular to the machine's spindle axis.

The dividing head's head stock is essentially a spindle to which a 40-tooth worm wheel is keyed. This wheel is meshing with a single threaded worm. The worm spindle protrudes from the front of the head and is equipped with a crank and handle. The head spindle has a taper hole punched into it and is also screwed on one end. The workpiece is held between two centres, one of which is placed into the splitting head spindle and the other into the head's tailstock. Between these centres, the workpiece can alternatively be mounted on a mandrel.

For holding short work parts with no centre holes, a chuck can be installed on the spindle nose. By twisting the index crank with the handle, the workpiece is turned. Because the worm and worm wheel gear ratio is 40:1, it takes 40 crank turns to rotate the spindle and hence the workpiece through one complete revolution. Thus, one crank turn spins the work 1/40th of a turn. "Index plates" are used when divisions other than factors of 40 are necessary. An index plate is fixed on the worm shaft and has many circles of holes (each circle with a different number of holes) as shown in Fig. 3.38. The radius of a pin on the crank can be modified to fit in any desired circle of holes. Any fractional part of a turn of the index crank can be obtained by employing different circles of holes and index plates. The angle through which the index crank is cranked for indexing is determined by the two sector arms visible on the front of the plate.

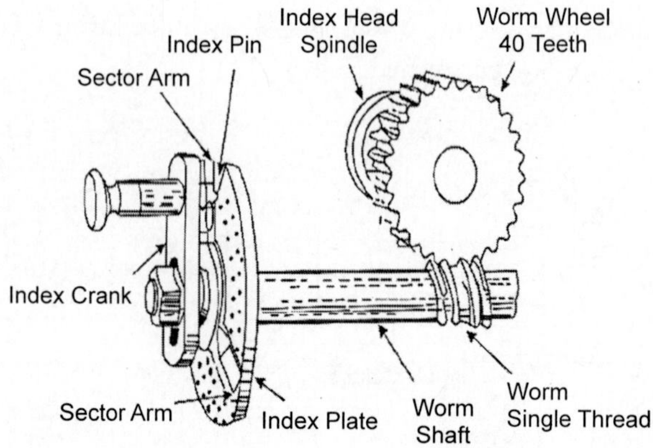

Figure 3.38: Indexing mechanism of dividing head [6]

3.19.1 Types of Dividing Heads

There are various dividing heads used with milling machines.

3.19.1.1 Plain

A plain dividing head has a fixed spindle axis and the spindle rotates only about a horizontal axis.

3.19.1.2 Universal

The spindle in these types can be rotated at various angles in the vertical plane from horizontal to vertical. A universal division head indexes the workpiece, imparts a continuous rotational motion to the workpiece for milling helical grooves (flutes of drills, reamers, milling cutters, and so on), and sets the workpiece in a given inclined position in reference to the table.

3.19.1.3 Optical

These models are utilised for highly accurate angular positioning of the work piece with regard to the cutter. An optical system is placed within the dividing head to read the angles.

3.20 METHODS OF INDEXING

The various methods of indexing are discussed as given below.

3.20.1 Direct Indexing

In direct indexing (Fig. 3.39), the index plate is directly mounted on the dividing head spindle. The intermediate use of worm and worm wheel is avoided.

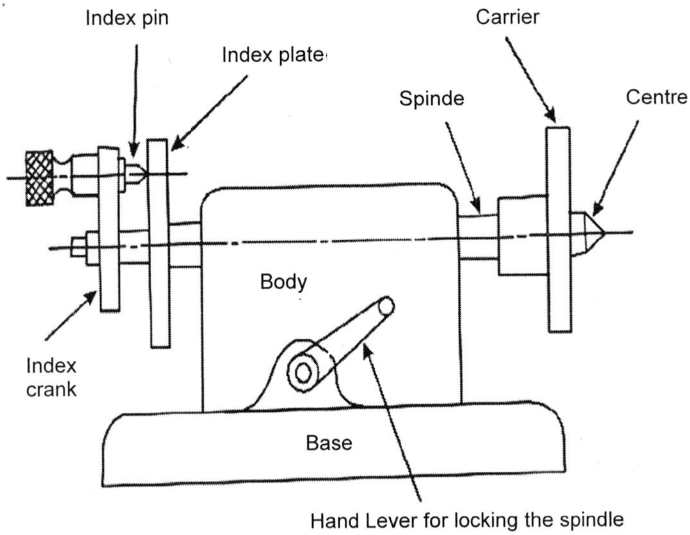

Figure 3.39: Direct indexing

To index, remove the index pin out of a hole, spin the work and index plate the necessary number of holes, and engage the pin. This method works with both plain and universal heads. Direct indexing is the quickest technique of indexing, although fractions of a full spindle turn are limited to those available with the index plate. All factors of 24 can be indexed using a conventional indexing plate with 24 holes, i.e. the job can be divided into 2, 3, 4, 6, 8, 12, and 24 pieces.

3.20.2 Simple Indexing

In simple or plain indexing (Fig.3.38), an index plate tailored to the application is inserted to the worm shaft and secured with a locking pin. The index crank pin is removed from a hole in the index plate to index the work through any desired angle. By rotating the index crank through a calculated number of entire rotations and holes on one of the hole circles, the spindle and therefore the work are indexed through the needed angle, and the index pin is repositioned in the required hole. If the number of divisions on the task circumference required is z, then the number of turns the crank to be rotated for each indexing may be calculated using the formula $n = 40/z$. Dividing heads are typically equipped with three index plates that have six concentric hole circles with varying numbers of equally spaced holes on each hole circle. A typical set has the following hole count:

I - 15, 16, 17, 18, 19, 20

II - 21, 23, 27, 29, 31, 33

III - 37, 39, 41, 43, 47, 49

Example. Let z = 16, i.e., $n = \frac{40}{16} = 2\frac{8}{16}$; That is, for each indexing we need two complete rotations of the crank plus 8 more holes on the 16 hole circle of plate I.

Example. Let z = 45, $n = \frac{40}{45} = \frac{8}{9} = \frac{8}{9} x \frac{2}{2} = \frac{16}{18}$

We will employ index plate I and use hole circle with 18 holes. For each indexing, the crank will rotate through 16 holes.

3.20.3 Compound Indexing

When none of the index plates has a hole circle which would enable the work to be divided by simple indexing method, more involved methods are employed. One method is "compound indexing". The compound indexing is achieved in two stages, by using two different hole circles of one index plate : (i) By a movement of the crank in the usual way as in simple indexing, say, n1 holes in hole circle N1, with the lock pin engaged in circle N2 of the index plate. (ii) By adding or subtracting a further movement by rotating the crank and the index plate together forward or back ward, through n2 spaces in the N2 circle. (by disengaging the locking pin of the index plate so that it is free to turn). The procedure is explained below:

Let z = number of divisions needed on the work.

Since Crank rotations for each indexing = $40/z$

Since this cannot be obtained by simple indexing, it is achieved by compound indexing. Therefore, addition or subtraction of the two movements given above should be equal to 40/z. This is done as explained below:

(i) Write z above and 40 below a straight line and factorise them.
(ii) Select two numbers representing two hole circles in the same plate.
(iii) Write these numbers below 40 and factorise them.
(iv) Write their difference above z and factorise it. These hole numbers are to be chosen in such a manner that all the factors above the line get cancelled out with factors below the line. Let these hole numbers be N_1 and N_2.
(v) Let *n1* be the number of holes to be indexed in N_1 hole circle and *n2* the number of holes to be indexed in N_2 hole circle.

Then, $\frac{n1}{N1} \pm \frac{n2}{N2} = \frac{40}{z}$

From here, n1 and n2 are found out by trial and error. Then the total indexing will be, holes in N1 hole circle by rotation of the crank $\pm n2$ holes in *N2* hole circle by rotating the crank and index plate together.

Example.

Let z = 87

Steps. (i) $\dfrac{87 = 29x3}{40 = 2x2x2x5}$

(ii) Let $N_1 = 29$ and $N_2 = 33$

$$\therefore \quad \frac{\begin{array}{l} 4 = 2 \times 2 \\ 87 = 29 \times 3 \end{array}}{\begin{array}{l} 40 = 2 \times 2 \times 2 \times 5 \\ 29 = 29 \times 1 \\ 33 = 11 \times 3 \end{array}}$$

Since all the factors above the line get cancelled out, therefore, selection of N_1 and N_2 is correct.

(iii) Now, indexing equation is :

$\frac{n1}{29} \pm \frac{n2}{33} = \frac{40}{87}$ or $33\, n_1 \pm 29\, n_2 = 440$

By trial and error $n1 = 23$ and $n2 = 11$ with minus sign.

That is, $33 \times 23 - 29 \times 11 = 440$

$\therefore$ Indexing equation will be: 23/29 - 11/33 = 40/ 87

That is, movement of crank by 23 holes in 29 hole circle forwards and movement of crank and index plate both by 11 holes in 33 hole circle backwards.

Note. The method of compound indexing is little used to-day, as it has been replaced by differential indexing.

3.20.4 Differential Indexing

Differential indexing in reality is an automatic method of doing compound indexing. It is achieved in a single step as compared to two stages needed in compound indexing. In differential indexing, the index plate is connected to the head stock spindle by means of a gear train. Fig. 4.40 shows one such design where *z1, z2, z3* and *z4* are interchangeable gears. During indexing, the index plate rotates in relation to the crank movement. For this, the locking pin which kept the index plate locked while doing simple indexing, is disengaged. As the index crank is turned for indexing, rotating the spindle through worm and worm gear, the index plate will receive power through the change gears, equal bevel gear and the sleeve, and will rotate slowly. The index plate can be made to rotate either in the same direction or in the opposite direction to the index crank (by gear train design).

Indexing is performed in the same manner as that for simple indexing except that the location of the hole from which the index pin is turned will move slightly during indexing. The required movement of the index plate is calculated and taken care of by the gear train.

Differential indexing is thus more straight forward and so has wider applications as compared to compound indexing.

Procedure

Let z = number of divisions required to be indexed for one complete revolution of the spindle and hence the work-piece

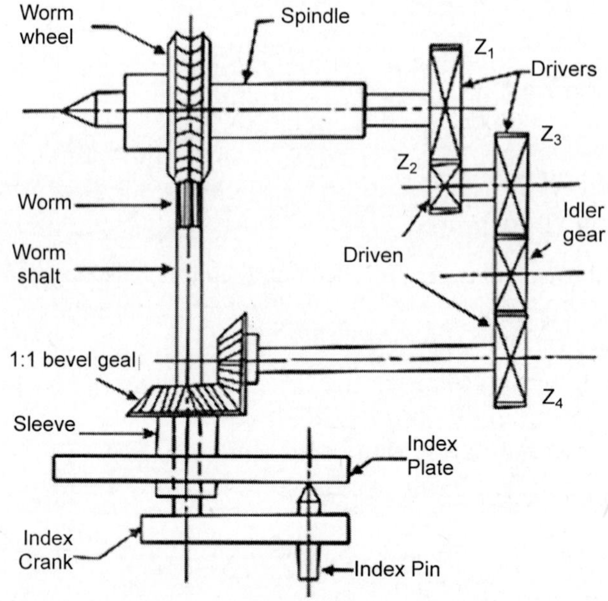

Figure 3.40: Differential indexing

k = A number very nearly equal to z and which can be used in simple indexing method.

∴ Number of crank turns for each simple indexing, $n = 40 / k$

∴ Number of crank turns needed for z indexings,

$$N = \frac{40}{k} \times z$$

But, we know that the crank must make only 40 turns for the spindle (and hence the work) to turn through one complete circle. So,

(i) If $N > 40$, then $(N - 40)$ turns have to be subtracted. This is achieved through the change gears so that while the spindle makes one turn, the index plate makes $(N - 40)$ turns in the opposite direction to that of the crank.

(ii) If $N < 40$, then the index plate should rotate $(40 - N)$ turns in the same direction as that of the crank. The gear ratio will be :

(iii) $I = \frac{40}{k} \times (k - z)$

Thus, the movement of the index handle (crank) operates according to the principle of simple indexing and the gear ratio makes it possible to find gears which take care of residual divisions.

Example. Do differential indexing for 93 divisions.

Solution. z = 93,

∴ Simple indexing = 40 / 93

It is clear from the available index plates, that 93 cannot be simple indexed.

So, let k = 90, which can be simple indexed each indexing $= \frac{40}{90} = \frac{4}{9} = \frac{8}{18}$, that is, 8 holes in an 18 hole circle. ∴ for 93, indexings, $N = \frac{8}{18} x\ 93 = 41\frac{1}{3}$ turns of the crank

Since N > 40, the index plate must rotate 4/ 3 turns backwards, that is, in the opposite direction.

$$i = \frac{40}{k} \text{ x } (k - z) = \frac{40}{90} \text{ x } 3 = \frac{4}{3}$$

In the Brown and Sharpe dividing head, the gears supplied are: 24 (2), 28, 32, 40, 44, 48, 56, 64, 72, 86 and 100 teeth.

$$\therefore \quad i = \frac{4}{3} = \frac{32}{24} = \frac{Drivers}{Driven}$$

It is a simple gear train.

Example. z = 127

Let k = 128

Simple indexing $= \frac{40}{128} = \frac{5}{16}$

$$\therefore \quad N = \frac{5}{16} \text{ x } 127 = 39\frac{11}{16} \text{ turns of the crank.}$$

Since N is < 40, therefore, the index plate must rotate $(40 - 36\frac{11}{16})$, that is, 5/16 turns in the same direction as the crank, as the spindle completes one turn.

$$i = \frac{40}{k} \text{ x } (k - z) = \frac{40}{128} \text{ x } 1 = \frac{5}{16} = \frac{5x1}{8x2} = \frac{40}{64} \text{ X } \frac{24}{48} = \frac{Drivers}{Driven}$$

It is a compound gear train.

In Fig. 4.40, gears Z_1 and Z_3 drivers and gears Z_2 and Z_4 are driven gears.

∴ With this gear train and an indexing of 5 holes in a 16 hole circle, the 127 divisions would be obtained.

Rule of Thumbs:

(i) If (k - z) is positive, the index plate must rotate in the same direction as that of the crank.

(ii) If (k - z) is negative, the rotation of the index plate is in opposite direction to that of the crank.

3.20.5 Angular Indexing

Angular indexing is used when it is necessary to cut grooves or slots subtending a given angle at the centre of the circle upon which they are spaced. We know that 40 turns of the index crank will rotate the head spindle and hence the workpiece through one revolution, that is, 360°.

$\therefore$ 1 turn of the crank = 9° of the spindle

$$\therefore \quad \text{Turns of crank to give any angle} = \frac{\text{angle required}}{9}$$

Example. Do angular indexing for 38°.

$$\text{Indexing} = \frac{38}{9} = 4\frac{2}{9} = 4\frac{4}{18}$$

That is, four complete turns of the crank and 4 holes in a 18 hole circle.

3.21 MILLING CUTTERS

A milling cutter is a multiple-edged rotary cutting tool that has the shape of a solid of rotation with cutting teeth positioned on the perimeter, end face, or both. During the machining procedure, the cutter is usually kept in a fixed (though rotating) location, while the workpiece passes past the cutter.

3.21.1 Tool Signature of Milling Cutter

Tool signature or tool nomenclature is a numerical means of identifying a tool and specifying tool angles by using a defined abbreviated system. It denotes the angles used by a tool during a cut. The features of tool signature for a plain milling cutter are given in Fig. 3.41. Tool signature order varies amongst milling cutters.

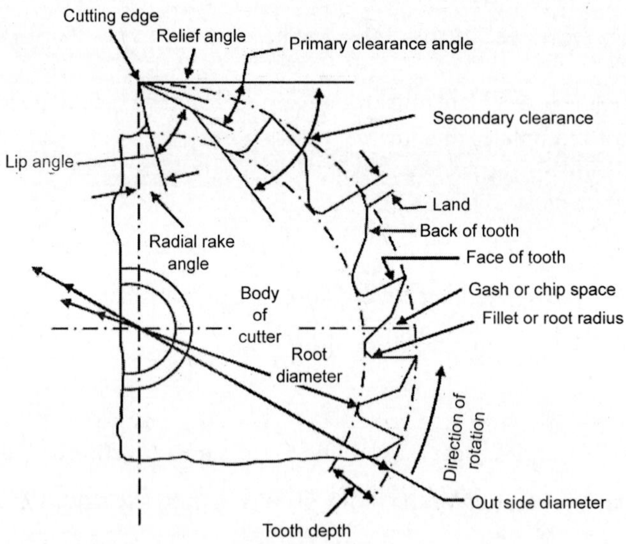

Figure 3.41: Tool signature of a plain milling cutter

The role of different parameters of a milling cutter is defined as given below in Table 3.4.

Table 3.4: Parameters of a milling cutter and their role

Parameters	Roles
Outside diameter	The diameter of a circle passing through the peripheral cutting edges. It is the dimension used in conjunction with the spindle speed to find the cutting speed (SFPM).
Root diameter	This diameter is measured on a circle passing through the bottom of the fillets of the teeth.
Tooth	The tooth is the part of the cutter starting at the body and ending with the peripheral cutting edge. Replaceable teeth are called inserts.
Tooth face	The tooth face is the surface between the fillet and the cutting edge, where the chip slides during its formation.
Land	The area behind the cutting edge on the tooth that is relieved to avoid interference is called the land.
Flute	The flute is the space provided for chip flow between the teeth.
Gash angle	The gash angle is measured between the tooth face and the back of the tooth immediately ahead.
Fillet	The fillet is the radius at the bottom of the flute, provided to allow chip flow and chip curling. The terms defined above apply primarily to milling cutters, particularly to plain milling cutters. In defining the configuration of the teeth on the cutter, the following terms are important.
Peripheral cutting edge	The cutting edge aligned principally in the direction of the cutter axis is called the peripheral cutting edge. In peripheral milling, it is this edge that removes the metal.
Face cutting edge	The face cutting edge is the metal removing edge aligned primarily in a radial direction. In side milling and face milling, this edge actually forms the new surface, although the peripheral cutting edge may still be removing most of the metal. It corresponds to the end cutting edge on single point tools.
Relief angle	This angle is measured between the land and a tangent to the cutting edge at the periphery.
Clearance angle	Is provided to make room for chips, thus forming the flute.
Radial rake angle	The angle between the tooth face and a cutter radius, measured in a plane normal to the cutter axis.
Axial rake angle	Measured between the peripheral cutting edge and the axis of the cutter, when looking radially at the point of intersection.
Blade setting angle	When a slot is provided in the cutter body for a blade, the angle between the base of the slot and the cutter axis is called the blade setting angle.

3.21.2 Milling Cutter Materials

Milling cutters are manufactured of High Speed Steel (HSS), carbide tipped, and many have replaceable or indexable inserts. Arbor-mounted peripheral milling cutters are commonly used to execute a variety of activities.

3.21.3 Types of Milling Cutters

Milling cutters come in a variety of shapes and sizes. Depending on the design, milling cutters might have solid or embedded blades. The latter are equipped with interchangeable, mechanically retained blades that are typically adjustable. Cutters with a diameter more than 75 mm are often built with an inset blade to preserve tool steel. Depending on how the teeth are sharpened, milling cutters are classed as "profile sharpened" or "form relieved." Sharpening most cutters (former) involves polishing a narrow region behind the cutting edges; sharpening form relieved cutters involves grinding only the face of each tooth without changing the shape. As a result, the profile of form-relieved cutters is preserved after re-sharpening for the life of the cutter. This is particularly critical for form cutters.

3.21.3.1 Plain milling cutters

These cutters have cutting teeth just on the periphery (around the exterior) and are cylindrical in shape. They are used to grind flat or plain surfaces. Straight (Fig. 3.34 (a)) or helical (Fig. 3.34 (b)) teeth can be found on a simple milling cutter. When a cutter with straight teeth is used, each tooth enters the cut simultaneously along its entire length. This causes intermittent loads to act on the machine, lowering the quality of the surface produced. Cutters with helical teeth run more smoothly because the teeth enter the cut gradually and the machine load is more homogeneous. When the breadth of the cutter exceeds the width of the workpiece, it is referred to as a "slab cutter" (Fig. 3.34 (c)). When two plain cutters are used side by side to mill a large surface, one has right-hand helix and the other has left-hand helical flutes to offset the axial stresses.

3.21.3.2 Face milling cutters

For machining large, flat surfaces, face milling cutters with teeth on the end face are utilized as shown in Fig. 3.35 (a). The cutter can be positioned on an arbour or tightly fastened to the machine spindle's snout. Face milling cutters are similar to end mills but much larger in diameter. They are intended to machine flat surfaces perpendicular to the spindle's rotational axis. These cutters are used on vertical milling machines, planer milling machines, and bed milling machines. Facing milling is more of a production activity that uses cutters ranging in diameter from 140 mm to 380 mm.

3.21.3.3 Profile milling cutters

Profile or form milling cutters are cutters with a curved tooth outline that is the same shape as the profile of the workpiece as shown in Fig. 3.35 (b). Concave, convex, and corner rounding cutters are among of the most popular shapes. Gear milling cutters are form milling cutters used to machine any conventional gear tooth.

3.21.3.4 End mills

End mills have cutting teeth on both the end and the perimeter. End mills can be built as solid cutters, with the cutter body becoming part of the shank (Fig. 3.35 (c)). They can also be produced as "Shell end mills," with the cutters having a centre hole for mounting on a short arbour. End mills are utilised in tracer-controlled profile milling operations. They are used to create deep grooves in base parts, profile recesses, steps, perpendicular planes, and so on. End mills can be used on horizontal milling machines, although they work best on vertical milling machines. Their sizes range from roughly 3 mm to 50 mm. Shell end mills range in diameter from 30 mm to 150 mm.

3.21.3.5 Side milling cutters

These cutters have teeth on the outside and on one or both sides. Straight teeth surround the outside of plain side milling cutters, which have side teeth on both sides (Fig. 3.35 (d)). These cutters are available in widths ranging from roughly 5 mm to 25 mm and diameters ranging from 50 to 200 mm. "Half-side milling cutters" have teeth just on one side and all the way around the diameter. They are available in both right and left-handed versions as shown in Fig. 3.35 (e).

3.21.3.6 Angular milling cutters

These cutters are available in single-angle (Fig. 3.35(f)) or double-angle (Fig. 3.35(g)) configurations and are used to machine angles other than 90°. The 45° and 60° single angle cutters, as well as the 45°, 60°, and 90° double-angle cutters, are popular. They are most commonly used in tool production for milling chip flutes on various cutting instruments.

3.21.3.7 According to the purpose of the cutters

For milling dovetail guides, T-slot milling cutters, Woodruff key slot milling cutters, and dove tail cutters are available, as shown in Fig. 3.35 (h). These may be chosen based on their use.

3.21.3.8 Metal slitting saws

Metal slitting saws, as shown in Fig. 3.35 (i), are used to cut splines and narrow grooves on workpieces as well as to cut materials. Slitting mills with large diameters (above 120 mm) are commonly referred to as disc saws. These mills can be solid or have inserted teeth composed of H.S.S. or hard metal. The end faces of these mills are alternatively chamfered at a 45° angle to encourage uniform work. Chamfers typically cut 1/5 - 1/3 the length of the cutting edge, so each tooth creates chips that are narrower than the width of the groove. This permits the chips to move freely in the tooth space, making removal easier.

3.21.3.9 According to the method of mounting the cutters

These are of two types as:

(a) ***Arbor type milling cutters.*** These are designed to be installed on a machine arbour. They have a precisely ground centre hole for this. The arbour comes with a choice of collars or spacers that allow for precise placement of cutters on the arbour. To place the cutters as precisely as possible, very tiny shims might be employed. Arbor cutters are used in horizontal milling machines, both plain and universal. A "stub arbour" is a short arbour with the cutter fixed on one end and secured with a nut. The stub arbour is designed for facing work and has no exterior support.

(b) ***Shank type cutters.*** These cutters are held and located by shanks (similar to drills and reamers). The shank can be either straight or tapered. The taper shanks are put into the spindle's taper hole and clamped by a draw bolt that passes through the hollow spindle. A key prevents the cutter from rotating and a screw holds it in place. Adapters are provided for cutters with shanks that do not fit the spindle nose. Larger shank mounted cutters with replaceable shanks are referred to as "Shell-type cutters." These shanks do not have to be made of pricey tool material. Straight shank cutters are clamped with collect holders. Horizontal and vertical spindle milling machines use shank mounted cutters.

(c) ***Facing type cutters.*** When the diameter of a milling cutter, comparable to an end mill, is large enough, arrangements are provided to place such cutters directly on the milling machine spindle nose with bolts; otherwise they may be mounted at the end of a stub arbour or utilised with an adaptor.

3.21.3.10 Hand of milling cutters

Looking at the cutter end of the spindle will reveal the hand of any cutter (that is viewing from the front end as mounted on the spindle). The cutter is right-handed if it revolves counterclockwise; left-handed if it rotates clockwise. Only face mills and end mills can be classed by rotational direction. Other cutters are switched from one hand to the other by flipping their arbour mounting.

3.22 WORK HOLDING DEVICES

There are numerous mechanisms available for holding the workpiece to be machined:

i. The work may be clamped on the table by means of T-bolts, strap clamps and pads.
ii. *Plain vise.* On a milling machine, this is the most typical work holding device. T- bolts can be used to secure it to the table, with the jaws parallel or at right angles to the T- slots.
iii. *Swivel vise.* The vise is made in two parts. The top part can be turned in a complete circle. The base is divided into 360°. The jaws can be set to any angle.
iv. *Universal Vise.* If the vise, apart from being swivelled in the horizontal plane, can also be tilted in the vertical plane, it is called as "Universal Vise". It is used for milling compound angles.
v. *Universal chuck.* It is used to hold round workpieces and is used mostly on the dividing head (discussed ahead).
vi. *Rotary table.* The rotary table is constructed of two pieces and is attached to the machine table via T-bolts. The base is divided into sections that allow the workpiece to rotate in a complete circle. It's used to hold workpieces for precise spacing, splitting, and radius milling.
vii. *Dividing head.* The dividing head is a device that holds and turns the workpiece in order to make a series of evenly spaced divisions or cuts around it. It is made up of a head stock and a tail stock. The work can be kept between centres or in a chuck positioned on the head stock spindle.
viii. Work may also be held in various types of milling fixtures.

UNIT SUMMARY

Welding and milling techniques have been examined in this unit. Welding categories such as, gas welding, and welding flames are discussed. Other welding procedures, such as arc welding, are discussed, as well as the equipment. Shielded metal arc welding applications such as submerged arc welding, TIG/MIG welding, resistance welding, spot welding, seam welding, and projection welding are thoroughly explored. Diagrams are used to explain the most frequent welding flaws, including brazing and soldering processes, as well as their applications. Milling is a critical machining technique. Figures describe the details of milling machine types, including constructional features and specs. Examples are provided to explain various milling operations and differential indexing approaches. Different Milling cutters & their types and Nomenclature of teeth are also explained. Milling cutter Teeth materials, Tool signature of milling cutter and Tool & work holding devices used for milling are presented.

EXERCISES

Multiple Choice Questions:

Questions for self-assessment

1. Projection welding is.......
   (a) Multi-spot welding process
   (b) Continuous spot welding process
   (c) Used to form mesh
   (d) Used to make cantilevers
2. Seam-welding is.........
   (a) Multi-spot welding process
   (b) Continuous spot welding process
   (c) Used to form mesh
   (d) Used for welding cylindrical objects
3. Cross-wire welding is.......
   (a) Multi-spot welding process
   (b) Continuous spot welding process
   (c) Used to form mesh
   (d) Used where additional strength is desired
   (e) None of the above
4. Thermit welding is a form of......
   (a) Resistance welding
   (b) Gas welding
   (c) Fusion welding
   (d) Forge welding
   (e) Arc welding
5. TIG welding is best suited for welding.......
   (a) Mild welding
   (b) Stainless steel
   (c) Carbon steel
   (d) Silver
   (e) Aluminium
6. Submerged arc welding is.......
   (a) A process which uses a mixture of iron oxide and granular aluminium
   (b) Accomplished by maintaining a hot molten metal pool between plates
   (c) A process in which arc is maintained under a blanket of flux
   (d) All of the above
7. The electroslag welding is.......
   (a) A process which uses a mixture of iron oxide and granular aluminium
   (b) Accomplished by maintaining a hot molten metal pool between plates
   (c) A process in which arc is maintained under a blanket of flux
   (d) There is nothing called electroslag
8. Arc-welding uses following electric supply ....
   (a) A.C.
   (b) D.C.
   (c) Both AC and DC
   (d) Spiral waveform
9. The most commonly used flame in gas welding is......
   (a) Neutral
   (b) Oxidising
   (c) Carburising
   (d) All of the above

10. Carbon arc welding is.......
    (a) A process which uses a mixture of iron oxide and granular aluminium
    (b) Accomplished by maintaining a hot molten metal pool between plates
    (c) Used to weld carbon rods
    (d) None of the above
11. In inter gas arc welding following is used for welding alluminium.......
    (a) No-combustible electrode in combination with helium and d.c. current
    (b) Combustible electrodes and argon in combination with a.c. current
    (c) Straight polarity d.c. current
    (d) Carbon dioxide, because of its excellent penetration and high speed
12. Distortion in welding occures due to......
    (a) Use of excessive current
    (b) Improper clamping methods
    (c) Use of wrong electrodes
    (d) Oxidation of weld pool
    (e) Improper composition of parent material
13. In MIG welding, the metal is transferred in the form of.......
    (a) A fine spray of metal
    (b) Molten drops
    (c) Weld pool
    (d) Molecules
    (e) Very fine metal
14. In reverse polarity welding.......
    (a) Electrode holder is connected to the negative and work to positive
    (b) Electrode holder is connected to the positive and work to negative
    (c) Work is positive and holder is earthed
    (d) Holder is positive and work is earthed
    (e) E.Work is negative and holder is earthed
15. Which of the following is strongest for brazing joints.......
    (a) Butt
    (b) Scarf (inclined)
    (c) Lap
    (d) All are equally strong
    (e) Strength depends on other factors
16. Forge welding is best suited for.......
    (a) Stainless steel
    (b) High carbon steel
    (c) Cast iron
    (d) Wrought iron
    (e) All of the above
17. Arc length in arc welding should be equal to......
    (a) Half the diameter of electrode rod
    (b) Rod diameter
    (c) Twice the rod diameter
    (d) 2.5 times the rod diameter
    (e) None of the above
18. The melting point of the filler metal in brazing should be above.......
    (a) 420° C
    (b) 820° C
    (c) 1020° C
    (d) 1200° C
19. Which type of electrode is used in submerged arc welding......
    (a) Bare rods
    (b) Coated electrodes
    (c) Core wires
    (d) Copper electrodes

20. Flash butt welding is.......
    (a) Gas welding
    (b) Arc welding with straight polarity
    (c) Arc welding with reverse polarity
    (d) Resistance welding
21. The phenomeon of weld decay occurs in.......
    (a) Cast iron
    (b) Brass
    (c) Bronze
    (d) Stainless steel
    (e) E.Carbon steel
22. Which of the following defects occur due to flux employed and electrode coating?
    (a) Inclusion of slag
    (b) Inadequate penetration
    (c) Incomplete fusion
    (d) Porosity
23. Which of the following defects occur when weld metal layer fails to fuse together?
    (a) Inclusion of slag
    (b) Inadequate penetration
    (c) Incomplete fusion
    (d) Porosity
24. Which of the following defects occur due to filler material having a different rate of contraction compared to parent metal?
    (a) Undercut
    (b) Spatter
    (c) Cracking in weld metal
    (d) Cold cracking
25. Form cutting can be performed more effectively by ______ milling machine.
    (a) horizontal
    (b) vertical
    (c) can't say anything
    (d) none of the mentioned
26. Slab milling can be performed more effectively by ______ milling machine.
    (a) horizontal
    (b) vertical
    (c) can't say anything
    (d) none of the mentioned
27. Boring can be performed more effectively by ______ milling machine.
    (a) horizontal
    (b) vertical
    (c) can't say anything
    (d) none of the mentioned
28. Dovetailing can be performed more effectively by ______ milling machine.
    (a) horizontal
    (b) vertical
    (c) can't say anything
    (d) none of the mentioned
29. Angular milling can be performed more effectively by ______ milling machine.
    (a) horizontal
    (b) vertical
    (c) can't say anything
    (d) none of the mentioned
30. Which type of milling machine is ideally suitable for boring, pocket milling, profile milling and for keyways in the middle of the shaft?
    (a) Plain milling machine
    (b) Vertical milling machine
    (c) Universal milling machine
    (d) Special type milling machine
31. To what angle must the milling machine table be swiveled to cut a helix having a lead of 450 mm on a workpiece of Dia 40 mm?
    (a) 18° 12'
    (b) 17° 24'
    (c) 16° 18'
    (d) 15° 36'

32. Which among the following statements is NOT correct?
(a) The column is the main supporting frame of a milling machine
(b) The table of a milling machine is provided with 'V' slots for mounting workpiece on it
(c) The saddle of a milling machine moves horizontally to provide cross feed
(d) The table of a milling machine moves the workpiece longitudinally

33. Which milling process the cutting is done on the end of the cutter as well as periphery?
(a) Plain or slab milling
(b) Side milling
(c) Face milling
(d) End milling

34. A slot is to be milled with a 16 mm slot mill cutter. If cutting speed is 20 m / min., the rpm of the machine should be:
(a) (397.90
(b) 198.90
(c) 99.50
(d) 795.77

35. Rotary table is used on milling machine to achieve....
(a) Longitudinal movement
(b) Cross movement
(c) Combination of longitudinal and cross movements
(d) Combination of longitudinal, cross and vertical movements

36. A milling attachment is mounted on a milling machine. Which one of the following is used to transmit spindle motion to the milling attachment?
(a) Chain and wheel
(b) Belt and pulley
(c) Worm and worm wheel
(d) Couplings

37. Which machine is removing material at faster rate in comparison with other machines?
(a) Lathe
(b) Milling machine
(c) Shaping machine
(d) Grinding machines

38. Milling cutters are manufactured generally from two materials to give them the required hardness and toughness. Which one of the following is used for this purpose?
(a) Cast iron and plastic
(b) High speed steel and carbides
(c) Mild steel and stainless steel
(d) Carbon steel and nickel steel

39. What type of cutter having teeth at the end as well as on periphery?
(a) Slitting saw
(b) End mill cutter
(c) Slab milling cutter
(d) Side and face cutter

40. Gang milling operation is usually performed when:
(a) Single piece is to be milled
(b) Duplicate pieces are to be milled in mass production
(c) Repair work is to be done
(d) None of the above

41. Which milling attachment the cross feed is used to move the cutter into the work piece and the longitudinal feed is to index the cutter?
(a) Rack milling attachment
(b) Circular table attachment
(c) Circular table attachment
(d) Universal spiral attachment

42. What is the reason for the breaking of cutter while rough milling?
    (a) Heavy feed
    (b) Low cutting speed
    (c) High cutting speed
    (d) Less depth of cut
43. Which among the following statements is correct if milling cutter has negative rake angle?
    (a) Cutter forces tend to push the work against the work holding device
    (b) Reaction forces tend to pull the cutter into the work
    (c) Reaction forces tend to push the cutter away from the work
    (d) Both 'A' and 'B'
44. While indexing which one of the following is used to give exact location of the indexing movement?
    (a) Index plate
    (b) Index crank
    (c) Selector arm
    (d) Worm shaft
45. Vertical milling operation can be performed by mounting vertical milling attachment on:
    (a) Vertical milling machine
    (b) Plain milling machine
    (c) Bed type milling machine
    (d) Planer type milling machine
46. In a spur gear, if pitch diameter = 40 mm; outside diameter = 48 mm, module = 4 mm, the number of teeth will be:
    (a) 10 teeth
    (b) 20 teeth
    (c) 30 teeth
    (d) 40 teeth
47. Two side and face milling cutters were mounted on a long arbor in a milling machine with arbor support. The arbor nut should be:
    (a) Tightened after the over arm support is in place
    (b) Tightened before the arbor support is in place
    (c) Tightened with extra large leverage
    (d) Allowed to tighten on its own during spindle rotation
48. Which part of the milling machine the feed motor and gear box are accommodated?
    (a) Base
    (b) Knee
    (c) Saddle
    (d) Column
49. Which type of side milling cutters having teeth on both sides?
    (a) Half side milling cutter
    (b) Inter locking side milling cutter
    (c) Plain side and face milling cutter
    (d) Staggered teeth side milling cutter
50. A finish cut is given to improve the surface finish of a rough milled workpiece. What adjustments are needed on the cutting parameters?
    (a) Decrease cutting speed, feed rate and depth of cut
    (b) Increase feed rate, depth of cut and reduce cutting speed
    (c) Increase feed rate, depth of cut and cutting speed
    (d) Increase cutting speed, reduce feed rate and depth of cut

ANSWERS															
1.	(a)	2.	(b)	3.	(c)	4.	(c)	5.	(e)	6.	(c)	7.	(b)	8.	(c)
9.	(a)	10.	(d)	11.	(b)	12.	(b)	13.	(a)	14.	(b)	15.	(c)	16.	(d)
17.	(b)	18.	(a)	19.	(a)	20.	(d)	21.	(d)	22.	(a)	23	(c)	24	(c)

25	(b)	26	(a)	27	(b)	28	(b)	29	(c)	30	(b)	31	(d)	32	(b)
33	(d)	34	(a)	35	(c)	36	(d)	37	(b)	38	(b)	39	(b)	40	(b)
41	(a)	42	(c)	43	(d)	44	(c)	45	(d)	46	(a)	47	(a)	48	(b)
49	(c)	50	(d)												

Short and Long Answer Type Questions

Welding

1. Give the applications of the "welding process".
2. Write the advantages and drawbacks of the "welding process".
3. How the "welding process" may be classified?
4. Sketch the various weld joints.
5. Sketch the various types of welds used in making a joint.
6. Sketch and write on the various edge preparations used for welded joints.
7. Sketch and write on the various "welding positions".
8. Why the cleaning of a joint is important before welding?
9. What is meant by "fluxing"? Why it is done? What are the properties which a good flux should possess?
10. Define: OAW and PGW processes.
11. Sketch and compare the two systems of OAW process.
12. Write on the "Gas welding equipment".
13. Sketch the three types of flames used in OAW process. Give the uses of each.
14. Write the steps in lighting up the OAW flame.
15. Write the closing down procedure of OAW flame.
16. Define power of blow pipe and nozzles.
17. Sketch and compare the two welding techniques used in OAW process.
18. Sketch and explain PGW process.
19. Write on "oxy-acetylene flame cutting". How the cutting tip differs from a welding tip?
20. Define "electric arc welding".
21. List the principal advantages of: (a) Arc welding over gas welding. (b) Gas welding over arc welding. (c) D.C. arc welding over A.C. arc welding.
22. Sketch the two polarities of D.C. supply and compare these for welding process.
23. Write on the different types of electrodes used in arc welding.
24. What is the purpose of coating on an arc welding electrode?
25. Write the constituents of a "coating" and write the function of each.

26. For what commercial applications can the EBW process be economical?
27. What are "flow welding" and "diffusion welding" processes?
28. Distinguish between "welding", "brazing" and "soldering" processes.
29. Which method of resistance welding is used to join dissimilar metals?
30. Distinguish between "brazing" and "braze welding".
31. Write the steps to be taken in brazing process.
32. Write about the various fluxes used in brazing process.
33. Write about the filler materials used in brazing process.
34. Write a note on the various brazing methods.
35. Write the common uses of brazing process.
36. Distinguish between "soft solder" and "hard solder".
37. Write about the various soldering techniques used.
38. Define "weldability".
39. What are the effects of the following elements on weldability? Mn, Si, P, and S.
40. What is the purpose of preheating a part to be welded? How would you select a preheat temperature?

Milling

1. Define the "milling" process.
2. Define a "milling cutter".
3. What type of surfaces can be produced by a milling process?
4. Sketch and explain the two basic types of milling operations.
5. Sketch and contrast the two milling methods of machining flat surfaces.
6. What is the basic type of milling machine?
7. Sketch and explain the working of a plain column and knee type milling machine.
8. What are the three motions on a plain milling machine?
9. What are universal and omniversal horizontal milling machines?
10. What is the difference between a fixed head and a swivelling head vertical milling machine?
11. Describe the difference between a horizontal milling machine and a vertical milling machine.
12. What is feed on a milling machine?
13. How is the size of a column and knee type milling machine given?
14. Sketch and describe a Bed type milling machine.
15. Sketch and describe a Drum type milling machine.
16. Write on the following milling machines: (a) Planer type milling machine. (b) Hand operated millers. (c) Continuous or rotary millers. (d) Tracer controlled production milling machines. (e) Special purpose milling machines.

17. How the milling cutters are classified according to: (i) design. (ii) the way the teeth are sharpened. 18. What is a plain milling cutter?
18. What is a "slab cutter"?
19. Name four types of side-milling cutters.
20. What is the difference between face milling and end milling?
21. What is a "shell end mill"
22. Why is end milling done best on a vertical milling machine?
23. How can sawing be done on a milling machine?
24. Describe the three types of milling cutters according to the method of mounting the cutters.
25. Describe the construction of milling cutters.
26. Write on the materials for milling cutters.
27. What is meant by hand of milling cutters?
28. Describe the various work holding devices used on milling machines.
29. How will you cut the following types of surfaces on milling machines: (a) flat surfaces (b) Slots, grooves and splines (c) Recesses (d) Contoured surface (e) Toothed gears and helical grooves?

PRACTICALS

1. Perform lap joint welding of similar material (Mild steel).
2. Perform butt joint welding of ductile material.
3. Perform brazing operation of brass material.
4. Study and perform milling operation for making spur gear of ductile material.
5. Study the various tool signatures used in a milling cutter.

KNOW MORE

Explore the historical welding work for joining objects like in aluminum, copper, and steel using similar welding/brazing/soldering processes. See milling process as old practices of lassi making by milling like operation. Identify similar milling machines and processes around your locality and try to find how it is evolved with time as one could see the modern welding and milling machines and the operations today. One can observe it carefully.

SUGGESTED RESOURCES FOR FURTHER READING/ LEARNING

Reference books & websites referred

1. Manufacturing technology – P N Rao, Tata McGraw-Hill Publications
2. Elements of workshop Technology (Volume I & II) – S. K. Hajra Chaudary, Bose & Roy, Media Promoters and Publishers Limited.

3. Production Technology (Volume I & II) – O. P. Khanna & Lal, Dhanpat Rai Publications.
4. Fundamental of metal cutting and machine tools– B. L. Juneja, New age internationallimited.
5. Manufacturing Technology, Metal Cutting & Machine tools– P. N. Rao, Tata McGraw- Hill Publications
6. A Text book of Production Technology: Manufacturing processes –P.C. Sharma, S. Chand & Com. Pvt. Ltd., New Delhi
7. Production Technology – R.B. Gupta, Satya Prakashan, New Delhi
8. Fundamentals of Design & Manufacturing- G K Lal, Vijay Gupta, N. V. Readdy, NarosaPub. House, ND

VIDEOS

Welding

https://www.youtube.com/watch?v=TWLWP1u_Xrs
https://www.youtube.com/watch?v=b0EfJaYUfF8
https://www.youtube.com/watch?v=twUAa5LWUvk
https://www.youtube.com/watch?v=H6QGLGJ-BOE

Brazing-soldering

https://www.youtube.com/watch?v=neL4CMdUpjg
https://www.youtube.com/watch?v=cd3vn8GsmzA

Milling machines

https://www.youtube.com/watch?v=YQUeOPxkvVU
https://www.youtube.com/watch?v=Gun5Kr-lmls

4 Gear Making and Press Working

Gear Making: Manufacture of gears - by Casting, Moulding, Stamping, Coining Extruding, Rolling, Machining; Gear generating methods: Gear Shaping with pinion cutter & rack cutter; Gear hobbing; Description of gear hob; Operation of gear hobbing machine; Gear finishing processes;Gear materials and specification; Heat treatment processes applied to gears.

Press working: Types of presses and Specifications, Press working operations - cutting, bending, drawing, punching, blanking, notching, lancing; Die set components-\punch and die shoe, guide pin, bolster plate, stripper, stock guide, feed stock, pilot; Punch and die clearances for blanking and piercing, effect of clearance.

UNIT SPECIFIC / LEARNING OBJECTIVE

Objective of this unit in to talk about following aspects

- To introduce significance of Gear manufacturing and press working function
- To learn about the importance of gear manufacturing methods and press working operations and their principles of working
- To introduce the underlying advantages and applications of gear manufacturing processes and press working operations and types
- To introduce the gear manufacturing and press working operations
- To understand the significance of various types of gear manufacturing methods, and press working methods and their significance
- To learn about gear specification and press working operations & the specification

Additionally, few fundamental questions for self-assessment based on fundamentals are also included in this Unit in form of recall, application, comprehension, analysis and synthesis. There are further suggested readings and reference for reader's assistance.

RATIONALE

Gearing is a specific area of mechanical engineering for power transfers. Gearing encompasses gear design, production, inspection, and implementation, as well as some other supplementary subjects like manufacturing. Gears are generally manufactured by by Casting, Moulding, Stamping, Coining, Extruding, Rolling, and Machining for different applications. Gear profile generating methods involve Gear Shaping with pinion cutter & rack cutter and by an important process called as Gear hobbing. After manufacturing of a gear it requires proper finishing operation on it for smooth working in mesh with other gears. To make the gear hard, it is heat treated according to specific process and material. For commercial usage gears are specified for different machines applications.

Presses are an important part of machining and forming operations like Cutting, bending, drawing, punching, blanking, notching, lancing etc. Mechanical, hydraulic, pneumatic and power presses are very common for sheet metal & other operations. Die set is an integral part of a presses having different components like: punch and die shoe, guide pin, bolster plate, stripper, stock guide, feedstock, and pilot. While performing different operations on sheet metal workpieces, punch-die clearances is very crucial for proper quality of product especially for blanking and piercing operations. A proper press tonnage and die set is need for producing quality products of sheet metal. This chapter covers all such issues for the readers.

PRE-REQUISITES

A course on Basic Mechanical Engineering (MEPC102)

LEARNING OUTCOMES

U4-O1: Ability to choose suitable work-piece for gear manufacturing job under different processes and Press working jobs

U4-O2: Ability to choose suitable method/process for gear manufacturing & Press working with proper machine tools and their operation

U4-O3: Ability to choose suitable operations and proper cutting tools for Gear manufacturing and Press working

U4-O4: choose suitable working conditions and parameters () for Gear manufacturing and Press working operations

U4-O5: Ability to predict the behavior of Gears and its dimensions after gear manufacturing and press working part behaviour in applications

COURSE OBJECTIVES

- To understand the importance of gears and press working machines and the process equipments.
- To study and recognise various types of gear making mathods and press working machines, their parts and operations.
- To be able to select, operate and control the appropriate gear manufacturing and press working operations for specific applications.

Mapping of learning outcomes and Course Objectives

Unit-4 Outcomes	EXPECTED MAPPING WITH COURSE OUTCOMES (1- Weak Correlation; 2- Medium correlation; 3- Strong Correlation)					
	CO-1	CO-2	CO-3	CO-4	CO-5	CO-6
U4-O1	1	2	3			
U4-O2	1	2	3			
U4-O3	1	2	3			
U4-O4	1	2	3			
U4-O5	1	2	3			

4.1 INTRODUCTION TO GEARS

Gears have been in use for over 3000 years, and they are an important element in all machinery used nowadays. Gears are used in most types of machinery, like nuts and bolts. Gears are common machine elements that will be needed from time to time by almost all machine designers. The ongoing need to create machinery that is more affordable, quieter to operate, lighter, and more powerful has led to a regular change in gear designs, which is a highly complex art. The load-carrying capability of gears is currently well understood, and there are numerous challenging gear manufacturing procedures available. All industrialised nations conduct research on gear in academic labs and manufacturing firms. Even less developed nations carry out some study on the mathematics of gears and on interesting uses of gears. Those who are just beginning their study of gears should begin by being familiar with some basic terms that have particular significance in the topic of gears. The many types of gear in use are shown in Figure 4.1.

Figure 4.1: Various gears in usages [9]

There is a huge area of gear work where tooth tension is essentially irrelevant. Punched gears are widely employed in the simplest sort of gear drive, such as those seen in toys. Pinions with a few teeth can be extruded or die-cast. Injection-molded gears and pinions may be employed if loads are light enough and quiet operation is desired. Figure 4.2 displays molded-plastic gears from a toy train.

(a) (b)

Figure 4.2: (a) Plastic Moulded gears[10] (b) gears used in a toy train[11]

In order to transmit little amounts of electricity, devices like calculators, oscillating fans, cameras, cash registers, and movie projectors commonly require quiet-running gears. In these circumstances, molded-plastic gears are frequently employed. It should be noted, however, that the aforementioned devices frequently require precision-cut gears where loads and speeds are noticeable. Small, inexpensive gears are frequently produced by die-casting on metals like zinc alloy, brass, or aluminum. This method is especially preferred when the gear wheel is permanently linked to another component, such as a clutch member, sheave, or cam. Simply by die-casting the item in a precise metal mould, it is possible to finish the gear teeth and the unique curves of whatever it is attached to the gear to close accuracy. If it had been necessary to produce every one of the challenging gear components shown in Fig. 4.1, many of the inexpensive devices currently available on the market would have been far more expensive.

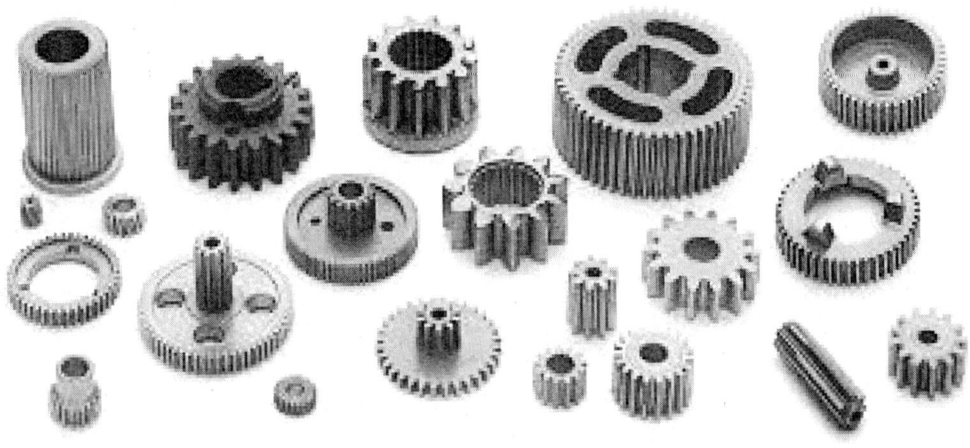

Figure 4.3: Sintered iron gears [12]

Numerous small gears are used in home equipment like fans, food mixers, and washing machines. These gears must be produced for only a few cents each due to competition. However, they must be sufficiently silent to satisfy a picky housewife and durable enough to last for many years with little to no lubrication beyond that provided at the factory. The industry standard used to be medium-carbon steel gears with conventional cutting as the last step. Although cut gears are still widely used, they are frequently cut by high-speed automatic machinery. On such a cutting machine, the operator hardly does anything more than bring up trays of blanks and remove trays of finished pieces. More and more non-cut steel gears are being used in modern products.

Some sintered-iron gears from an automatic washer are shown in Figure 7.3. Sintered iron gears typically wear less than comparable cut gears and are fairly affordable (in big quantities). The porous sintered metal can be impregnated with lubricant due to its porous nature. To increase its tensile strength, it could also be treated with copper. Sintering can totally finish gear teeth as well as intricate gear-blank designs, although the cost of the tools required to create a sintered gear might reach INR 3,50,000. Sintered iron gears (Fig. 4.3) are utilised in automatic washers.

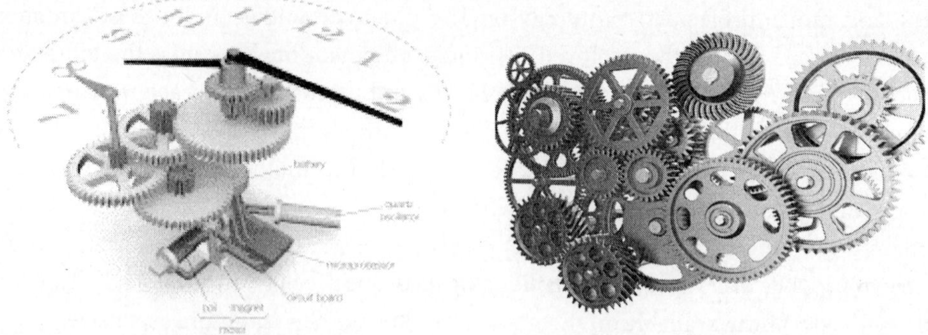

Figure: 4.4: Gears used in small mechanisms [13, 14]

Figure 4.4 (from Winzeler Manufacturing and Tool Co., Chicago, IL, USA) illustrates a variety of gears used in small mechanisms. If 100,000 or more such gears are to be produced on semiautomatic machines, this does not amount to much. Where noise reduction is an issue, laminated gears made of phenolic resins, cloth, or paper have proven to be particularly effective. In general, laminates are far more capable of carrying loads than molded-plastic gears. Cut-tooth nonmetallic gears do not experience tooth inaccuracy to the same extent as metal gears. A laminated phenolic-resin gear tooth will flex around 30 times more than a steel gear tooth under the same strain. It has frequently been able to replace one member of a set of steel gears that was excessively worn due to tooth error effects with a nonmetallic gear and have the set hold up properly.

When high sliding velocity wear is a concern, nylon gear parts have proven to be particularly effective. The nylon substance appears to have some qualities of a solid lubricant. In some processing equipment where the use of a conventional lubricant would taint the material being processed, nylon gearing has been used. Gears are typically described by their kind, such as spur, bevel, or spiral, by the size or dimensions of the material, by the geometry, or by specific features. Before continuing on the trip of gears, it is important for everyone to understand the words in Table 1. The nomenclature of a typical spur gear is shown in Fig. 4.5.

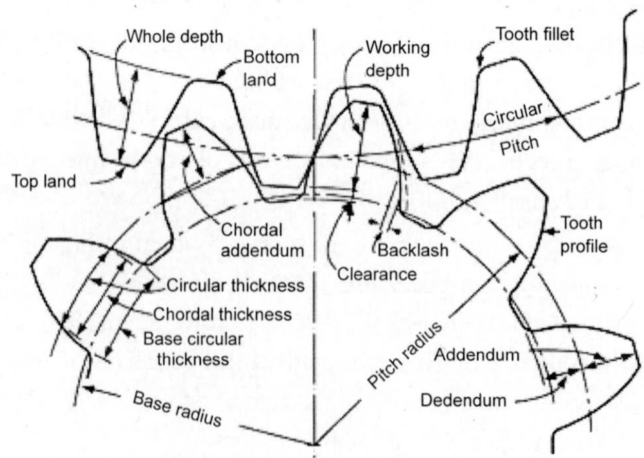

Figure 4.5: Spur gear nomenclature [6]

Table 4.1: Common terms related to gears

Term	Definition
Module	A metric scale for determining tooth size. There are millimeters of pitch diameter in a single tooth. The module also grows as the tooth size does. Typically, modules have a range of 1 to 25.
Gear	A geometric structure with evenly spaced teeth all the way around. A gear's teeth are often designed to interlock with those of another gear.
Pinion	The smaller of two gears that mesh is referred to as the pinion. It is referred to as the gear.
Pitch diameter	It is the diameter of the pitch circle of a gear.
Diametral pitch	A unit used in the English system to measure tooth size. It is the number of teeth per inch of pitch diameter expressed in units. The diametral pitch decreases as tooth size rises. Typically, diametral pitches vary from 25 to 1.
Circular pitch	The circumference measured along the pitch circle between a point on one gear tooth and a similar location on the following tooth. For two gears to mesh, their circular pitches must match. Their circles will be tangent to one another when they interlock.
Ratio	Gear tooth ratio, often known as ratio, is the product of the number of teeth on the gear and the number of teeth on the pinion that it meshes with.
Addendum	It is the radial height of a gear tooth above the pitch circle.
Dedendum	It is the radial height of a gear tooth below the pitch circle.
Whole depth	It is the total radial height of a gear tooth (i.e., Whole depth = addendum + dedendum).
Pressure angle	It is the gear tooth's slope at the pitch-circle position. (If the pressure angle were 0, the tooth would be perpendicular to the gear axis and would actually be a spur-gear tooth.)
Helix angle	It is the longitudinal slant of the tooth. The tooth is actually a spur-gear tooth if the helix angle is 0°, in which case it is parallel to the gear's axis.
Spur gears	It is the gears with teeth straight and parallel to the axis of rotation.
Helical gears	It is the gears with teeth that spiral around the body of the gear.
External gears	It is the gears with teeth on the outside of a cylinder.
Internal gears	It is the internal, hollow cylinder-shaped gears with teeth. (An exterior gear must serve as the mating gear for an interior gear)

4.2 MANUFACTURE OF GEARS

Manufacturing gears requires a variety of methods based on the kind and usage, hence there is no single technique for all gears. Since power transmission is the gear's primary purpose, it requires a number of specific conditions, where gears typically function under very demanding conditions. The first need is that the gears be in flawless condition. Then, they must consistently be trustworthy, have a low level of residual stresses, and have a low to zero likelihood of crack propagation. Naturally, it is very challenging to meet all of these standards. No one can dispute their significance, though. Because of this, the fabrication of gears is a highly specialized industry with very strict tolerances and no opportunity for error. As a result, depending on the type, material, and intended quality of the gears, a number of processing processes must be performed sequentially during the manufacturing process. These steps in the gear manufacturing process might be:

(i) Performing the blank before adding or removing teeth
(ii) If necessary, annealing the blank, as with forged or cast steels
(iii) By using machining, the gear blank is prepared to the necessary proportions.
(iv) Making teeth or using machining to complete already-formed teeth
(v) If necessary, complete or surface hardening of the machined gear's (teeth);
(vi) If necessary, finishing the teeth by shaving, grinding, etc.
(vii) Checking the completed gears.

Gear teeth can be made using a variety of techniques. The gear or pinion's size and geometrical shape must fall within the capabilities of any machine tool. In order to achieve the lowest competitive cost, the gear designer must create the gear in a size, shape, and material that will enable the most cost-effective manufacturing process. The three kinds of gear manufacturing are (i) forming, (ii) casting, and (iii) metal removal via machining as shown in Fig. 4.6. Direct casting, molding, drawing, or extrusion of teeth forms in molten, powdered, or heat-softened materials are examples of form making processes.

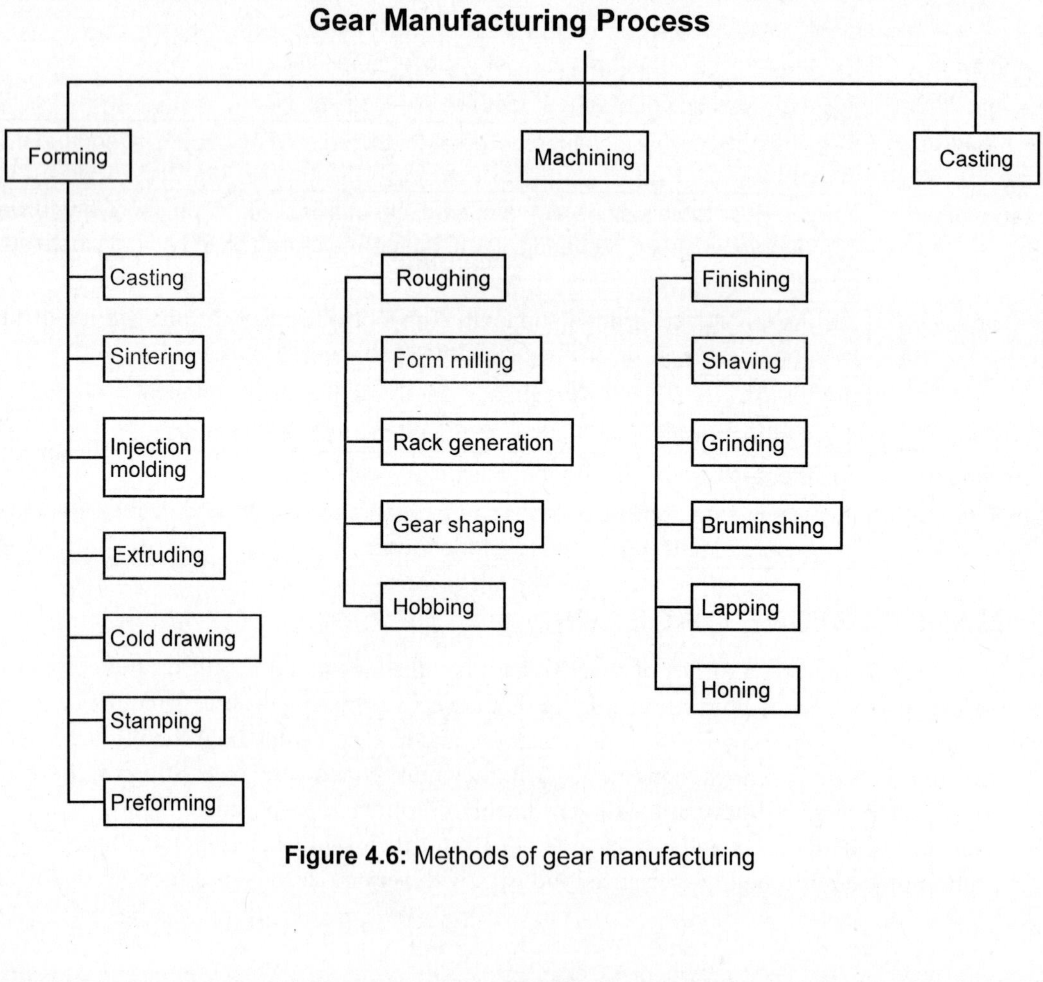

Figure 4.6: Methods of gear manufacturing

4.2.1 Manufacture of Gears by Casting

Gear blanks, which are later machined, and complete gears with cast tooth profiles are both produced through the casting process (Fig. 4.7). When casting gears, tolerances and accuracy are key factors to take into account, and making casting molds requires significant upfront costs. Large production quantities, however, make the expenditure worthwhile after the mold and process parameters are established. While machining is used to produce the teeth of gears, casting is a simpler procedure that is typically employed to prepare blanks or cylinders for gears. However, due to its ability for mass production and relative simplicity, it is a method that may be used to manufacture gears for a variety of applications. However, casting is the most often used production technique in one specific field. Production of really huge gears is possible as shown in Fig. 4.8.

Large dimensions make machining techniques and other gear building techniques less practical. Larger gears are typically almost usually of the spur gear kind. Casting, then, is a very wise choice because of their relative simplicity. The most popular casting techniques for making gear include shell casting, die casting, sand casting, and permanent mold casting. Other approaches have a narrow range of uses. Sand casting, die casting, or investment casting are all options for completing the casting (Fig. 4.7). The method is only applicable to large gears (Fig. 4.8) that are afterwards machined to the necessary accuracy.

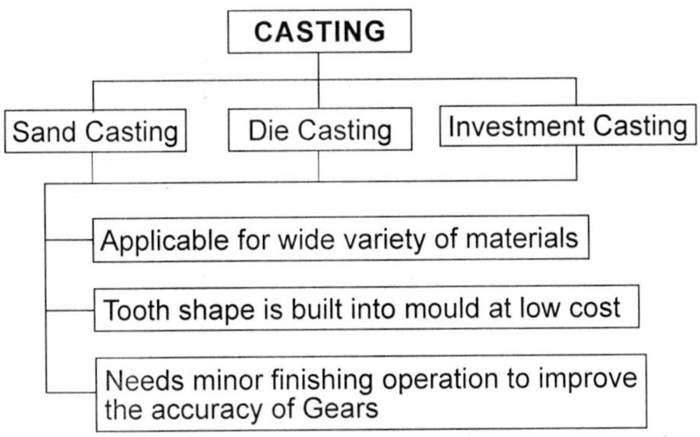

Figure 4.7: Common types of casting for gears

Figure 4.8: Casting large gears [6]

4.2.1.1 Sand casting

Gear blanks for use in other procedures are usually produced by sand casting. Gear casting is used to create fully functional spur, helical worm, cluster, and bevel gears that are found in washing machines, small appliances, hand tools, toys, and cameras. Sand casting is used to create the blanks for big cast iron gears that need to be built in one or more parts. The blank is then made to the correct size, and the cast preform is machined to create the teeth. Direct production of complete gears with teeth is also possible with this type of casting, and they can be used in low-speed machinery like farm equipment and manually operated devices where a high degree of gear accuracy and finish is not necessary.

Major features of cast gears include: (i) their low cost and low quality, but small quantity (ii) their reasonable tooling costs (iii) their poor surface finish and good dimensional accuracy (iv) their noise due to their low precision and high backlash; and (v) their suitability for non-critical applications. These gears are used extensively (without finishing operation) in a variety of industries, including toys, small appliances, cement mixer barrels, the hoist gearbox used in dam gate raising mechanisms, hand-operated cranes, etc. Cast iron, cast steel, bronzes, brass, and ceramics are typically the materials used to make cast gears.

4.2.1.2 Metal mould casting

Medium-sized steel gears with limited accuracy and finish are frequently produced in a single or small number of pieces by metal mold casting. Many agriculture industries employ such unfinished gears. The cast preforms are appropriately machined for both general and precise application. The following are some of the major attributes of such gears: (i) Better surface smoothness and precision (tooth spacing and concentricity) high tooling costs (ii), suitable for mass production (iii). These gears are used in a variety of devices, including lawn mowers, cameras, office equipment, washing machines, gear pumps, and small speed reducers. Zinc, aluminum, and brass are the often utilised materials for metal-molded gears. These gears are often used to tiny size gears and are not used for high speeds or significant tooth loading.

4.2.1.3 Die casting

Die casting is the primary method used for large-scale or mass manufacture of tiny gears made of low melting point alloys of Al, Zn, Cu, Mg, etc. Such reasonably precise gears are employed in toys, instruments, and cameras, among other things, under light loads and moderate speeds.

4.2.1.4 Investment casting or lost wax process (Fig. 4.9)

A single metal object is produced using the lost wax casting process, commonly referred to as "investment casting," from a wax model. It is a very flexible procedure that produces outcomes that are incredibly precise. A mould is constructed around a wax sacrifice model in lost wax casting. The wax is melted off and produces a hollow into which the metal or glass flows after the mould investment has been set. Fine details in both metal and glass can be captured with this casting technique. Since 3000 B.C., this age-old technique has been utilised to artistically record the tales of historic societies and religions. It entails the following 8 steps: Create a wax model (step 1), make a mold (step 2), remove the wax (step 3), choose a metallic alloy (step 4), melt the alloy (step 5), pour into the mould (step 6), release the cast from the mold (step 7), and complete your item (step 8).

Major characteristics of characteristics of such gears are: (i) reasonably accurate gears (ii) Applicable for a variety of materials (iii) Refractory mould material (iv) Allows high melt-temperature materials (v) Accuracy depends on the original master pattern used for the mold. The common materials used for lost wax process are Tool steel, Nitriding steel, Monel, Beryllium copper and the process is used only if no other process is suitable since production cost is high.

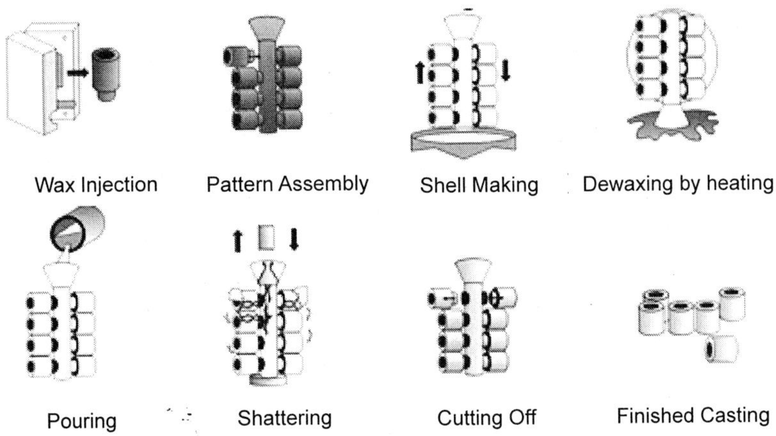

Figure 4.9: Investment casting of gears

4.2.1.5 Shell mold casting

This method is frequently used to create small gears in batches. This method offers quality that is halfway between investment casting and sand casting.

4.2.1.6 Centrifugal casting

Centrifugal casting is preferred for the solid blanks or outer rims (without teeth) of worm wheels composed of cast iron, phosphor bronze, or even steel. The preforms are machined to provide the right size gear blank. The teeth are then created through machining.

4.2.2 Manufacture of Gears by Moulding

Nonmetallic gears are made by injection molding (Fig. 4.10) from a variety of thermoplastics, including nylon and acetal (Fig. 7.10). These tiny, low-precision gears have the advantages of being inexpensive and operating without lubrication under light loads. Cameras, projectors, windscreen wipers, speedometers, lawn sprinklers, and washing machines all use IM gears. Nylon, cellulose acetate, Polystyrene, and Polyimide phenolics are the materials.

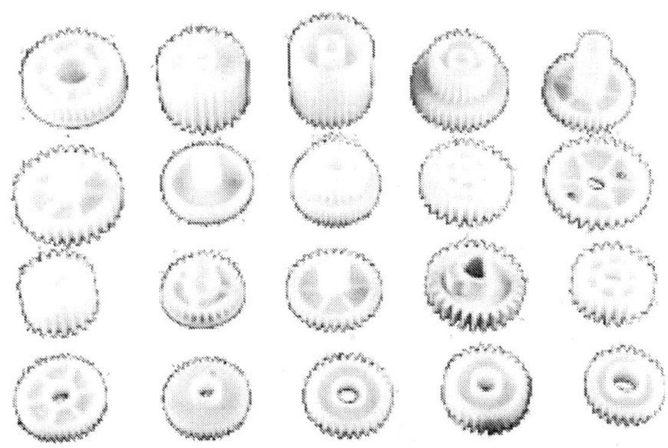

Figure 4.10: Moulding of gears [15]

4.2.3 Manufacture of Gears by Stamping (Fig. 4.11)

In order to create poor precision gears in large quantities at a low cost, sheet metal can be stamped with tooth forms. Poor precision and surface quality. Such gears are frequently used in (i) toys, manually driven machines, slow-moving mechanisms, (ii) precision stampings as gears without burrs, and (iii) precision stampings as dies constructed of greater precision with tight tolerances such as in watch, clock gears, etc.

Figure 4.11: Stamping gears [16]

4.2.4 Manufacture of Gears by Blanking

Extrusion and blanking (Fig. 4.12) are extremely similar processes, although blanking only works in two dimensions. With the aid of numerous dies, this gear forming procedure employs sheet metal to produce the necessary shape. With the blanking technique, various sorts of gears can be produced. The finest results, however, are provided by spur gears. Today, a variety of industries use the gear blanking method for lightweight applications. Typical examples of applications with modest load needs include office equipment, hydraulics, minor medical devices, and others.

Figure 4.12: Blanking of gears [17]

4.2.5 Manufacture of Gears by Coining

In the closed die forging process of gear coining (Fig. 4.13), pressure is applied to the forging's surface to provide tighter tolerances, smoother surfaces, and draught elimination. In a procedure known as "closed die forging," the work piece is forged while sandwiched between two shaped dies. Although it is primarily a cold work process, this process can be carried out in hot working circumstances as well. This method of precision stamping involves applying high stress to the metal work piece in order to cause plastic deformation that conforms to the shape of the die. With the use of a hydraulic press or forging hammer, gears are coined from blanks. This procedure produces gears that either don't require heavy grinding or can be utilised as such.

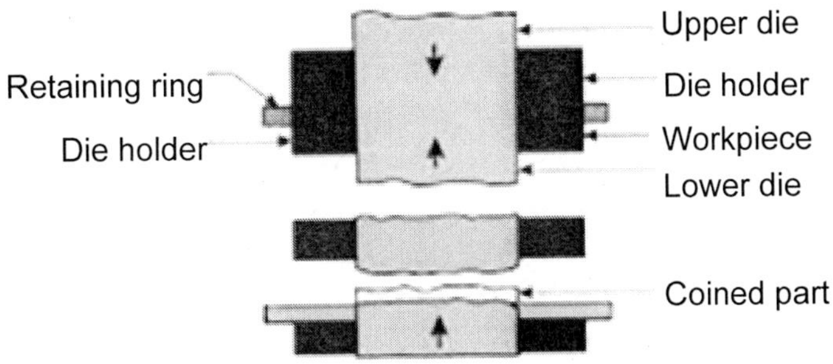

Figure 4.13: Coining of gears [6]

4.2.6 Manufacture of Gears by Extruding

Long rods are formed into gear teeth by extrusion (Fig. 4.14), which are subsequently chopped into manageable lengths and machined for bores and keyways. Steels are rarely extruded, instead, nonferrous materials like aluminum and copper alloys results in a dense, pore-free structure with better strength and a nice surface finish with crisp edges. Other extruded materials include aluminum, copper, architectural bronze, phosphor bronze, brass, and naval brass. Sector gears and splined hollow and solid shafts are also applications of extrusion.

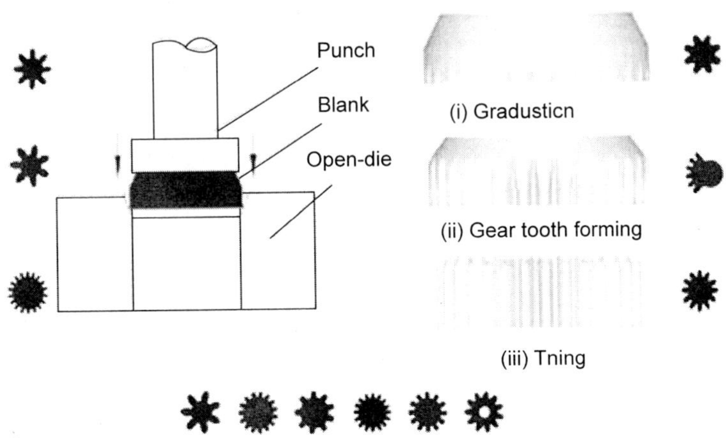

Figure 4.14: Extrusion of gears

4.2.7 Manufacture of Gears by Rolling

One of the earliest forms of formation is rolling. As shown in Fig. 4.15, the gear is created by hot or cold rolling a blank work piece through two or three dies. Rolling is a suitable alternative because there is no chip creation when material savings are a top priority during manufacturing. Before ramping up production, you must take rolling parameters, deformations, and microstructure impacts into account to obtain an efficient process.

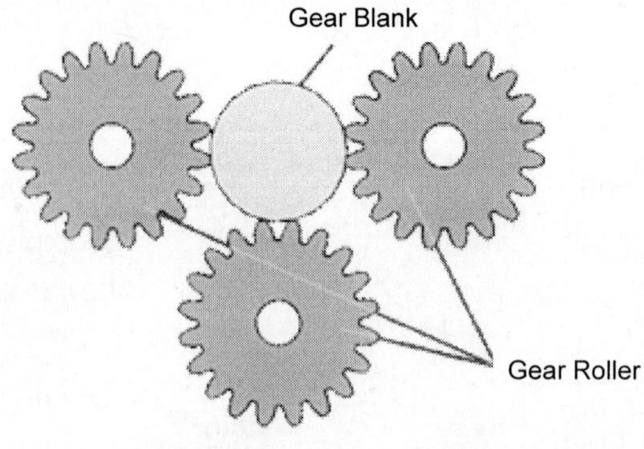

Figure 4.15: Rolled gears [6]

Gear rolling can be done in one of two ways. In the first method, forming tools are flat tools (racks). The flat rolling approach is this. Utilizing circular toothed gears as tools is the second method of rolling gears. The circular rolling approach is what is used in this. Tools used in flat rolling move linearly. Both tools are in touch with the workpiece. The shaping happens in a single motion of the instruments rubbing up against one another. The press load that the tools place on the workpiece as it is moving linearly is what causes the deformation. Figure 4.16 shows the flat rolling process in phases.

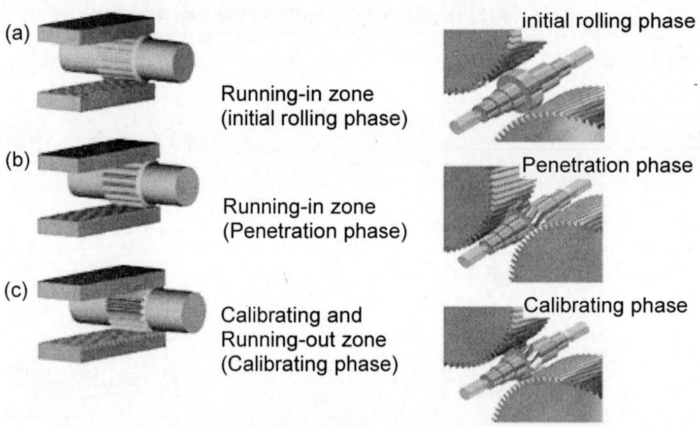

Figure 4.16: Rolling of gears by flat rolling or stepped rolling

As shown in Fig. 7.16, the straight and helical teeth of external steel disc or rod gears with small to medium diameter and module are produced by cold rolling using either flat dies or circular dies. As opposed to cutting, material flow results in the formation of teeth, which have great precision and surface integrity. Despite having somewhat high initial equipment expenditures, gear rolling is a reasonable method for achieving high productivity and quality. Hot rolling is used to create larger gears, which are then finalised by machining.

4.2.8 Manufacture of Gears by Powder Metallurgy

As a cost-effective alternative to traditional, machine-finished steel and cast-iron gears, powder metallurgy (4.17) is a high-precision forming technique. Although this technique is good for producing small, premium spur, bevel, and spiral gears, it is not appropriate for larger gear sizes. Larger gears have less fatigue and impact resistance due to the porosity of the produced material, but a sintering technique can be employed to enhance its mechanical qualities. When gear designs feature holes, depressions, or varied surface levels or projections, powder metallurgy is also extremely advantageous. These gears can be found in household appliances, farm and garden machinery, cars, trucks, and military vehicles and are extremely effective, easy to use, and practical for huge numbers is powder metallurgy. However, the resulting gears have size restrictions and are limited in terms of load capacity. Additionally, the initial investment required for any powder metallurgy setup is rather large, making it unworkable for low-volume production. To create compact, high-quality external or internal spur, bevel, or spiral gears, a powder metallurgical process route is employed (Fig. 7.17) For increased durability and strength, large gears are rolled following briquetting and sintering. Almost no additional finishing work is necessary for gears manufactured via powder metallurgy.

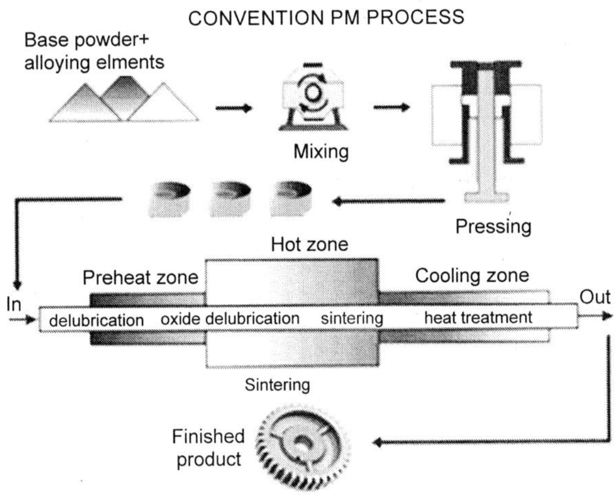

Figure 4.17: Gear manufacturing steps by powder metallurgy

4.2.9 Manufacture of Gears by Forging

Depending on the needs, this is another shaping method that can produce both blanks and ready-to-use gears. When one has reasonably basic gears, forging is a very viable option. Theoretically, forging (Fig. 4.18) is a great method of producing gears for heavy-duty applications for one reason in particular. Heat treatment is necessary during forging, so the finished gear would have improved fatigue characteristics. However, the size and thinness of this technique are constrained by the enormous force needed for forging. Forging typically works effectively for gears with a diameter between 6 and 10 feet. One might or might not need to manufacture the gears in the end, depending on the type of forging, for instance precision forging.

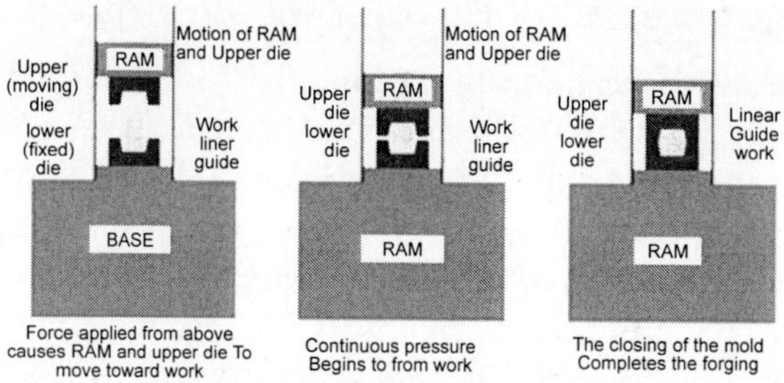

Figure 4.18: Forging of a gear

4.2.10 Manufacture of Gears by Machining

The prefabricated blanks are shaped roughly and have an irregular surface; they are then machined to the necessary dimensions and finishes, and the teeth are often created through machining but occasionally through rolling. Following additional machining and/or grinding, complete gears with teeth are created using a variety of techniques. By using near-net-shape processes, such as rolling, plastic molding, powder metallurgy, etc., accurate gears are manufactured immediately in final form with little to no additional finishing. The most often used technique entails preforming the blank through casting, forging, etc., followed by pre-machining to prepare the gear blank to appropriate dimensions, and finally manufacturing of the teeth through machining and further finishing through grinding if necessary.

Gear teeth are created through machining based on form, where the profile of the teeth is obtained as a copy of the shape of the cutting tool (edge); for example, milling, broaching, etc. Rolling type, tool-work motions, such as hobbing, gear shaping, etc. are used to generate the complex tooth profile, as shown in the following examples:

4.2.10.1 Shaping, planning and slotting

Figure 4.19 illustrates schematically how straight toothed spur gears can have their teeth made in a shaping machine if necessary. This procedure is only utilised, if at all, to make one or a few teeth on one or two pieces of gears as and when necessary for repair and maintenance because both productivity and product quality are very low. Planning and slot machines operate on the same basic tenet. If at all necessary, a planning machine is utilised to create the teeth for large gears, while slotting is typically employed for internal gears.

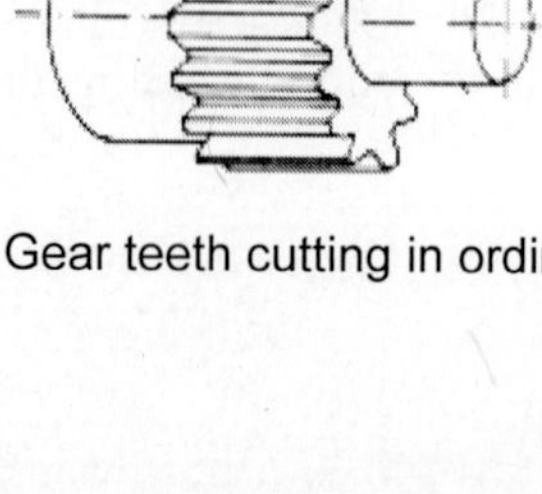

Figure 7.19: Gear teeth cutting in ordinary shaping machine [6]

4.2.10.2 Milling

As shown in Fig. 7.20, milling cutters of the disc and end mill varieties can both be used to create gear teeth. Gear teeth are produced by form milling, which is distinguished by (i) the use of HSS form milling cutters and (ii) the use of standard milling equipment (iii) Slow speed and feed due to ((a) the need for indexing after milling each tooth gap (b) poor production rate) low precision and surface polish (iv) Inventory issue-each module-pressure angle combination requires a set of eight cutters (v) To cut the teeth of big gears and/or modules, end mill type cutters are employed.

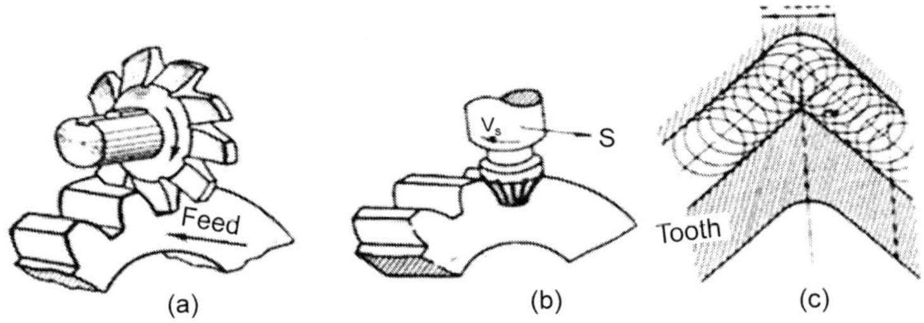

(a) (b) (c)

Figure 4.20: Producing teeth by (a) disc type end mill (b) single helix (c) double helix [6]

4.2.10.3 Fast production of teeth of spur gears

In theory, (i) parallel multiple teeth shaping is identical to conventional shaping; but, as shown in Fig. 4.21 (a), a set of radially in feeding single point form tools are used to concurrently create all of the tooth gaps without the need for indexing. Although this outdated method was extremely effective, it nearly completely lost popularity due to its high upfront and ongoing costs.

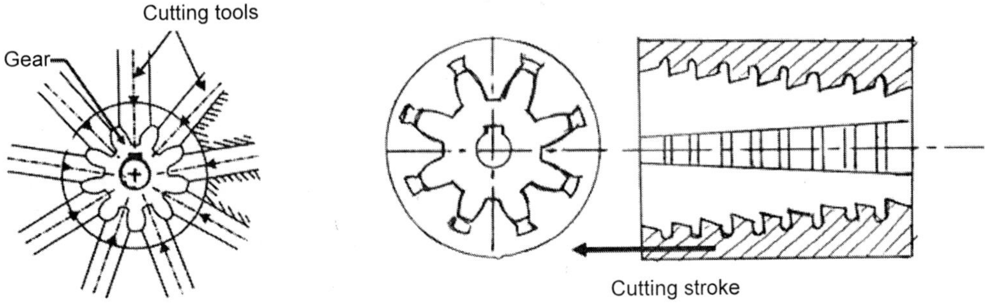

(a) (b)

Figure 4.21: Faster production of teeth on spur gear [6]

(ii) broaching procedure can be used to create a lot of the straight or single-helical teeth for small internal and exterior spur gears made of somewhat softer materials. In one pass, a broaching can produce external teeth, as shown schematically in Fig. 4.21 (b). Although the productivity and quality of this technology are quite good, the cost of the machine and the broach is also very high. (iii) the generation concept is used to produce gear teeth, and this method is characterised by automatic indexing, the ability of a single cutter to cover the whole range of teeth for a particular combination of module and pressure angle, and high productivity and efficiency.

4.2.10.4 Sunderland method using rack type cutter

In order to complete the machining (cutting) action, the rack type HSS cutter, which has rake and clearance angles, reciprocates while rolling type interaction with the gear blank, simulating a pair of rack and pinion. This generating process is schematically shown in Fig. 7.22. The advantages and key uses of this technique (and machine) include: (i) producing moderate-sized straight and helical toothed external spur gears with high accuracy and finish (ii) cutting the teeth of double helical or herringbone gears with a central recess or groove (iii) and producing straight or helical fluted cluster gears. However, although being automatic, this method only requires a few indexing operations.

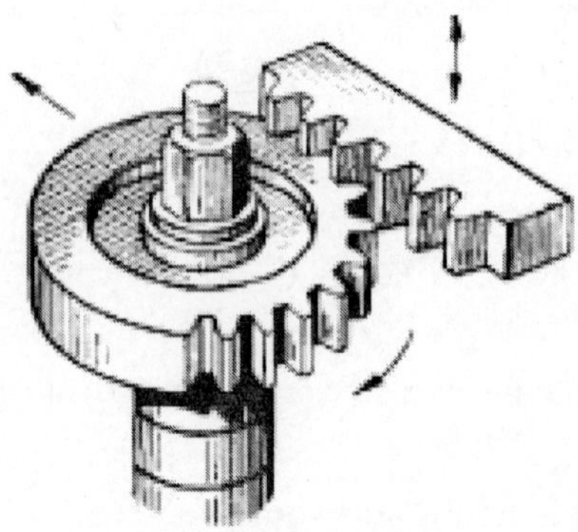

Figure 4.22: External gear teeth generation by rack type cutter (Sunderland method) [6]

4.2.10.5 Gear shaping

In theory, gear shaping is identical to rack type cutting, with the exception that the circular cutter shown in Fig. 4.23, which rotates both the cutter and the blank as a pair of spur gears in addition to the reciprocation of the cutter, replaces the linear type rack cutter used in rack type cutting. The generation method, which has great productivity and economy, is characterised by automatic indexing and the capacity of a single cutter to span the complete range of number of teeth for a given combination of module and pressure angle. The gear type cutter is built of HSS, has the right rake, and has the right clearance angles. Additionally, there are benefits of gear shaping over rack type cutting including: (i) External and internal spur gears can be made with high accuracy and finish with either straight or helical teeth, (ii) negating the need for separate indexing entirely and (iii) Productivity has increased as well.

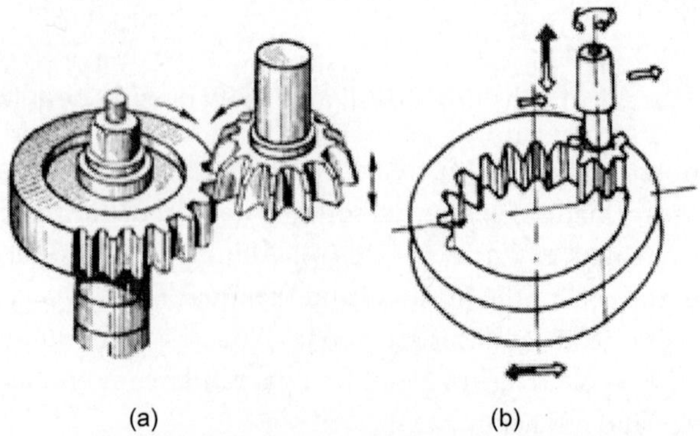

(a) (b)

Figure 4.23: Gear teeth generation by gear shaping (a) external spur (b) internal spur [6]

4.2.10.6 Hobbing

Figure 4.24 depicts the tool-work configuration and motions involved in hobbing. A gear milling cutter-like HSS or carbide cutter and a gear blank appear to cooperate in hobbing like a pair of worm and worm wheel. The hob (cutter) resembles a single or multiple start worm in appearance and behavior. Hobbing machines are far more stiff, sturdy, and productive than gear shaping machines while having fewer tool-work motions, only three than gear shaping machines. However, hobbing only works for cutting straight or helical (single) teeth on external spur gears and worm wheels and offers less accuracy and polish.

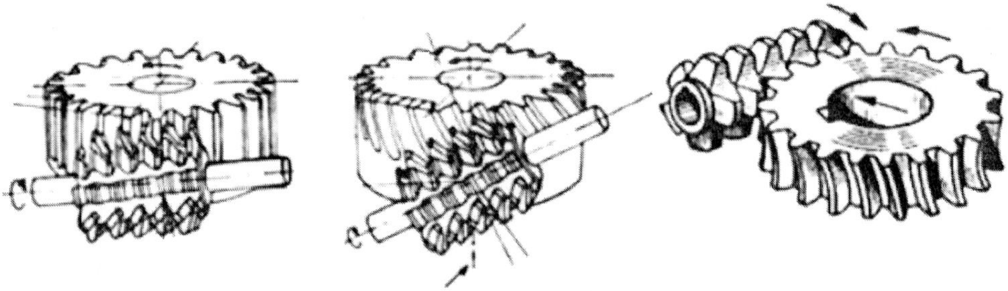

(a) (b) (c)

Figure 4.24: Gear generation by hobbing (a) straight tooth (b) helical tooth (c) worm wheel

The process of making steel screw-like single- or multi-start worms (gears) typically involves machining, such as long thread milling, or cold rolling, such as thread rolling, followed by heat treatment for surface hardening and finishing by grinding. Bevel gears are made by first casting or forging the blanks, which are then turned on lathes or other specialised machinery to the desired proportions. After that, machining is used to create the teeth in the blank. Based on the shape of the teeth and the volume of production, the method of machining and the machine tool are selected as follows:

(i) **Straight-toothed bevel gear.** (a) Forming by milling cutter- poor productivity and quality; used for production needing less volume and accuracy (b) Generation- high accuracy and finish; used for batch to mass production. The method of tooth formation and generation for a straight-toothed bevel gear is depicted graphically in Fig. 4.25. During the generation process, the cutters' straight teeth under rolling action form an involute profile on the inner flanks of two neighboring teeth.

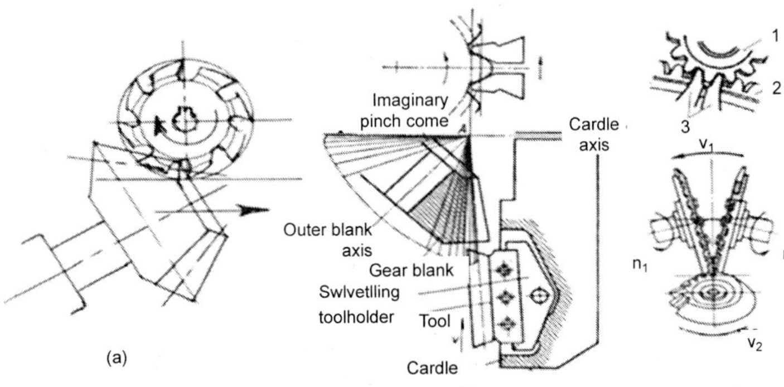

(a) (b)

Figure 4.25: Production of straight toothed spur gear (a) forming (b) generation

(ii) Teeth of spiral and hypoid bevel gears are produced by almost the same generation principle but the cutter resembles face milling cutter as shown in Fig. 4.26.

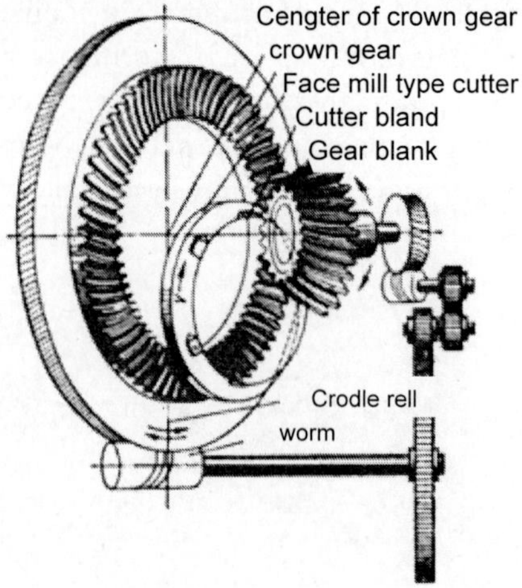

Figure 4.26: Generation of tooth of spiral and hypoid bevel gear [6]

4.2.11 Electrical Discharge Machining (EDM)

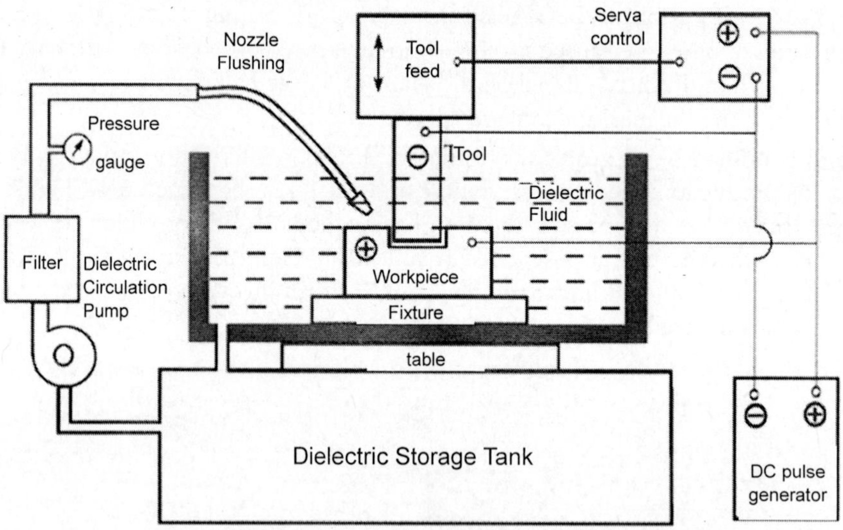

Figure 4.27: Electrical discharge machining (EDM)

A series of current discharges between two electrodes separated by a dielectric bath liquid are used in the industrial process known as electrical discharge machining (Fig. 4.27) to remove material from the workpiece. Despite its strengths in cutting intricate geometries of various sizes, EDM has some drawbacks. Without a strong control and program, it's simple to damage part surfaces, particularly curved tooth profiles, which are notoriously difficult for CNC programs to implement. The smooth EDM motion required to cut curved teeth, however, may be created by high-quality and user-friendly 3D modelling and CAM software, such as Feature CAM, Autodesk Fusion, Master CAM, and others.

Early EDM devices and applications had drawbacks, but they have since improved. This development has reduced surface finish problems, enhanced cutting accuracy, and improved material characteristics (microstructure, mechanical properties, etc). The procedure can produce both small (with a diameter of fractions of an inch) and big gears with tolerances as tight as thousandths of an inch (diameter of over 20 inches). This method is used to cut more durable gears, such as those used in race vehicles, as well as sensitive applications in watches and clocks.

4.2.12 Additive Manufacturing

Additive manufacturing (Fig. 4.28), also referred to as 3D printing, builds a three-dimensional object layer by layer from a CAD 3D model. Because of how the process works, additive machines can create intricate shapes with lattice structures. Mass reduction that is difficult to achieve using conventional techniques can be achieved by modelling these structures. Utilizing generative computer design and 3D topology optimization, this form of geometry is frequently produced.

With additive manufacturing techniques, conventional and non-circular gears can be created, and high-quality 3D printers are widely accessible and reasonably priced. Due to its accessibility, it has taken the lead in mechanical projects and repairs for items like educational toys and other devices that require fully operating gears. In order to add unique shafts, keys, or grooves to the same solid, you may also insert other characteristics and even combine geometry with the gear designs.

Figure 4.28: Gear geometry made using 3D printing

4.3 GEAR GENERATING METHODS

The gear manufacturing process begins with the gear producing procedure. The phrase "generating" in gear cutting refers to the formation of the involute curve by the cutter's straight cutting edges, which results in a number of facets on the blank to create the involute profile. When in working contact, the cutter and blank behave as mated gears. In this procedure, a cutting machine is used to carve the gears from a solid piece of metal. The gears are taken to a grinding machine after being cut out, where their teeth are ground down to the required size. The gears are then run through a polishing machine to provide a smooth surface. The gears are then examined to verify sure they adhere to the manufacturer's standards. There are three common methods of creating gears: gear hobbing, gear shaping with a pinion cutter, and gear shaping with a rack cutter.

4.3.1 Gear Shaper with Pinion

Gear shaping (Fig. 4.29) involves the use of a pinion-type cutter. With a top rake and clearance, the cutter teeth are ground. On a vertical spindle, the cutter is fixed. A cutter's and a blank's axes are parallel. The cutter and the blank are designed to spin in tandem like two meshing gears. The cutter and blank appear to be moving at the same speed. Along the width of the blank, the cutter rotates in a vertical manner. To determine the depth of cut, the pinion cutter is inserted radially into the gear blank. Till all of the teeth are produced on the blank, the cutter and blank gently rotate together. The blank is pulled from the cutter during each return stroke. This is done to avoid cutting the gear teeth and causing damage to the cutting edges. The various movements are described below:

i. Rotational movement of the blank and cutter.
ii. The cutter's vertical reciprocating motion.
iii. The cutter is fed in a radial motion toward the blank.
iv. During the return stroke, the blank is pulled away from the cutter.

This technique for shaping gears is frequently used for other kinds of gears, but because it involves utilising a cutter that reciprocates the gear shape, it has proven helpful for the gear types indicated above because it makes production setup simple. There are also alternative ways to make these kinds of gears, but gear shaping has advantages in terms of speed, setup, and design for mass production. The position of the cutter (on the exterior) and the cut direction, however, make this approach a poor choice for internal gears and worm gears.

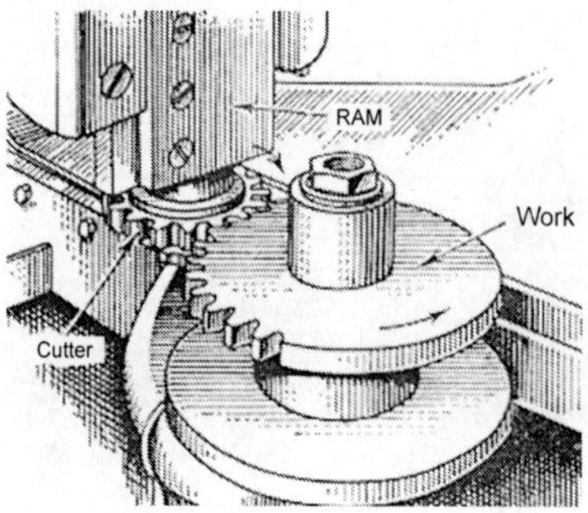

GEAR SHAPING

Figure 4.29: Gear shaper [6]

Frequently, a work tool is entirely encircled by two different cuts. Roughing is done on the first cut, and finishing is done on the second cut, which improves precision and smoothness. In gear shapers, helical gears can also be made. The cutters employed should have helical teeth, and while a cutter reciprocates on a machine, a guiding cam put on it twists the cutter during cutting strokes to force the cutter teeth to follow helical courses.

4.3.2 Gear Shaping with Rack Planning

The cutter in this instance is shaped like an involute rack. The clearance and rake angles are carved into it. The cutter is fixed to a sliding reciprocator. The blank is fixed to an arbour that is vertical. To determine the depth of cut, the cutter is fed radially into the gear. The blank's face is reciprocated across by the rack cutter as shown in (Fig. 4.30).

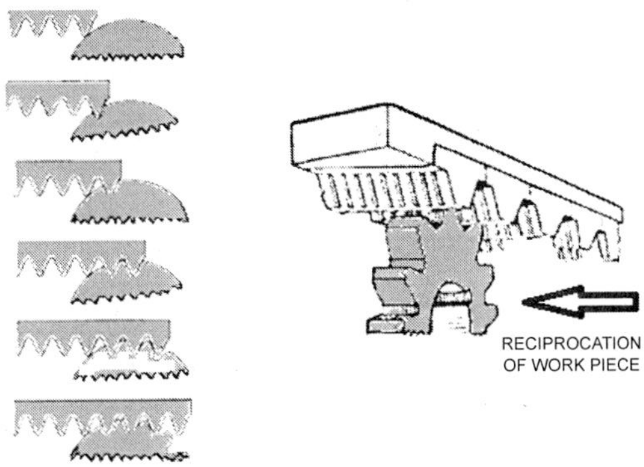

Figure 4.30: Gear cutting in a Planner [6]

The blank spins. The cutter rolls in tandem with the blank as a rack and pinion while reciprocating in order to move longitudinally. One of the main approaches to gear generation use rack type cutters. The technique, which is sometimes referred to as the Sunderland method (Fig. 7.31), uses a rack cutter with rake and clearance angles to design the teeth profile on a gear blank. Similar to a rack and pinion, it uses precise relative motion between the work piece and the cutter throughout the machining process to produce tooth profiles. This is shown in Figure 4.31. The geometry of the teeth profiles is represented by an involute of a circle, which is essentially a spiraling curve traced by the end of a fictitious thread unwinding from that stationary circle or if one traces the point of contact from one tooth to another as illustrated in Fig. 4.31.

A rack-type HSS cutter with rake and clearance angles reciprocates to perform the machining (cutting) action while interacting with the gear blank in a rolling manner, much like a pair of rack and pinion. The advantages and key uses of this technique (and machine) include: I cutting the teeth of double helical or herringbone gears with a central recess (groove), (ii) cutting the teeth of straight or helical fluted cluster gears, and (iii) producing moderate size straight and helical toothed external spur gears with high accuracy and finish. Although automatic, this method only requires a small number of indexing operations.

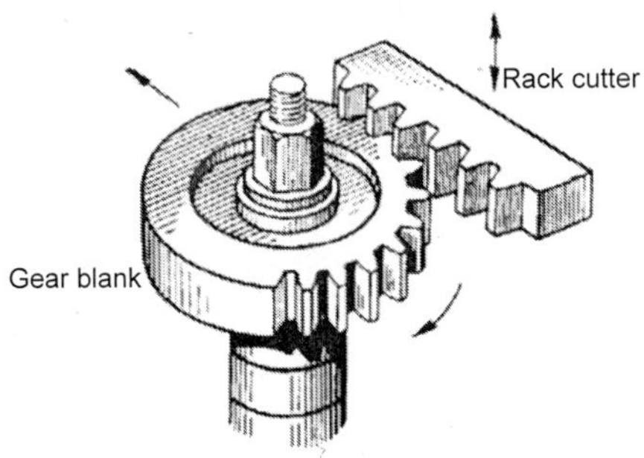

Figure 4.31: Sunderland process [6]

4.3.3 Gear Hobbing

Using a spinning shaped cutter to create gear teeth is known as gear hobbing (Fig. 4.32). This process is used to create the vast majority of involute gears. Although a variety of different gears, including cycloid gears, helical gears, worm gears, ratchets, and sprockets, are all formed by hobbing, spur gears are most frequently manufactured using this technique. The hob must be carefully thought out, especially when cutting complicated geometries. Internal gears often do not respond to this operation.

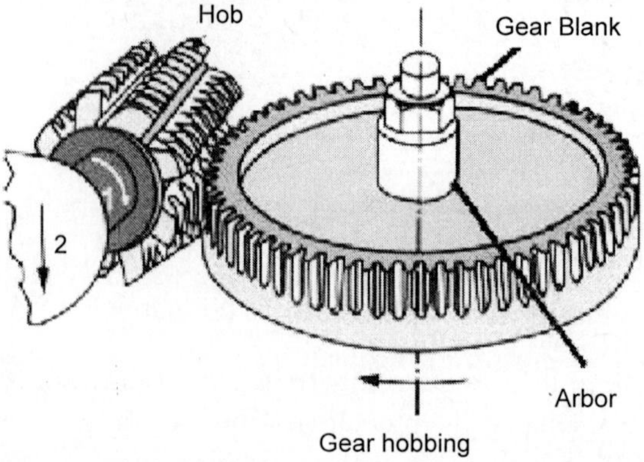

Figure 4.32: Gear hobbing process [6]

Since the hob is cutting the outside of the gear blanks, the procedure, which is similar to gear shaping, provides advantages in the setup but only for exterior cuts. The gear blank is fixed to an arbour that is vertical. A spinning arbour is used to support the hob. To align its teeth with the axis of the gear blank, the hob axis is slanted through the hob lead angle. A cutting-speed rotation of the hob is used. It is fed into the blank of the gear. The hob and gear blank are made to rotate in the proper direction with respect to one another. The gear moves one tooth for every turn of the hob.

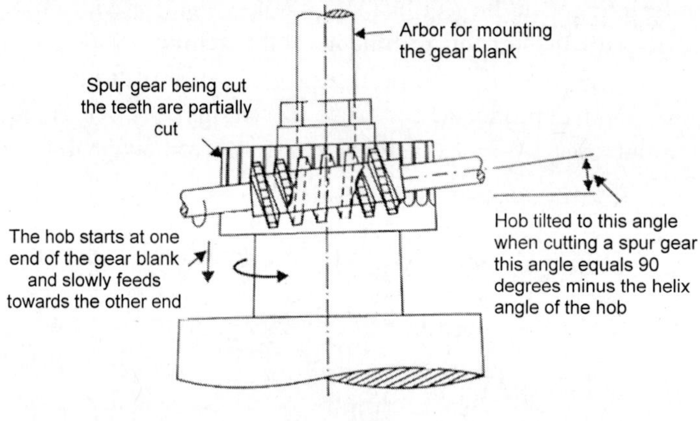

Figure 4.33: Gear Hobbing of helical gear [6]

The main focal points of gear hobbing includes: (i) Hobs can have a single thread or several threads. While a double threaded hob can produce two teeth in a single revolution, a single threaded hob requires one revolution to produce each tooth (ii)The index worm and gear drive the blank at a constant pace. The hob is driven by the bevel gears at the proper ratio of speed, and a feed screw moves the hob across the gear's face (iii) Gear cutting with a hob requires three fundamental motions that all take place at the same time. The hob advances radially in two motions. Indexing and cutting both happen continually (iv) The hob axis is set at an angle that is equal to the thread's helix angle with respect to the gear blank's axis. This aligns the hob's teeth with the blank teeth. This aircraft is known as a generating aircraft. In a single pass over the piece, the cutter completes all of the teeth and (v) the hob must be adjusted over an additional amount equivalent to the helical angle of the gear for cutting helical gears (Fig. 4.33) All kinds of gears made of ferrous, non-ferrous, and non-metallic materials can be hoofed and Hobs with carbide tips can be used in large quantities.

4.3.4 Gear form Cutting

Form cutting is the next important gear manufacturing technique. Due to its drawbacks, including low productivity and subpar product quality, this procedure is not chosen. However, when repair or maintenance is required, the various form cutting processes are practical substitutes.

4.3.5 Gear Shaping, Planning and Slotting

The workpiece is stationary while shaping, and the tool is pushed back and forth across the workpiece by the ram (Fig. 4.34). When planning, the tool is fixed, and the workpiece moves back and forth on the table beneath the tool (Fig. 4.35). When slotting, the workpiece is kept still while the tool on the ram is moved across it in an upward and downward motion (See Figure 4.36).

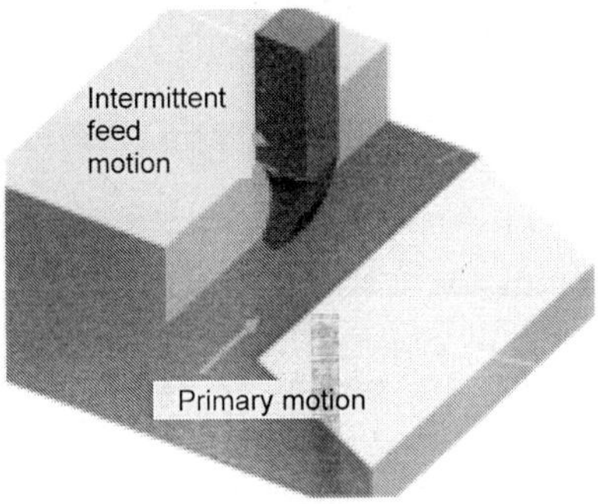

Figure 4.34: Gear form cutting by planning

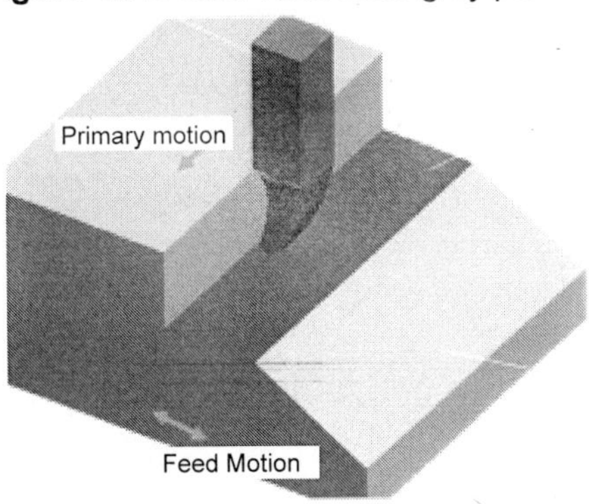

Figure 4.35: Gear form cutting by shaping

Shapers and planers both produces straight cuts. The planer, on the other hand, is designed for larger applications, while the shaper tackles tiny size geometries. Slots, grooves, and keyways can be made with shapers. A vertical shaper that cuts internal gears and grooves is what slotting essentially is.

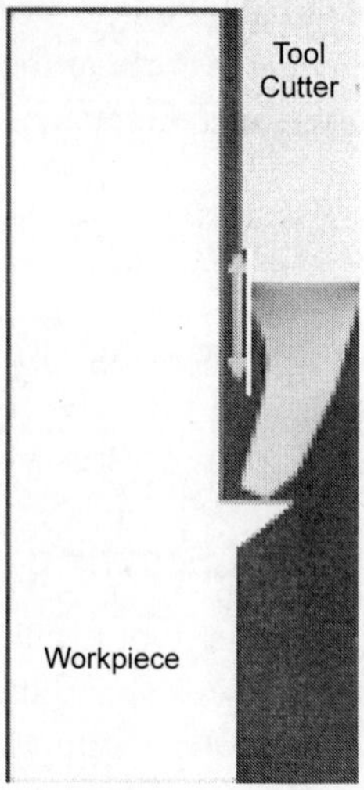

Figure 4.36: Gear form cutting by slotting

4.4 OPERATION OF GEAR HOBBING MACHINE

For large or low volume production of external cylindrical gears, the industry frequently uses the continuous gear creation technique known as hear hobbing. One of the main manufacturing techniques used in the sector is gear hobbing. The requirements for additional gearing of both old and new varieties with a better and higher degree of accuracy are continuously rising in modern engineering practise. The gear hobbling machine's construction is depicted in Fig 4.37.

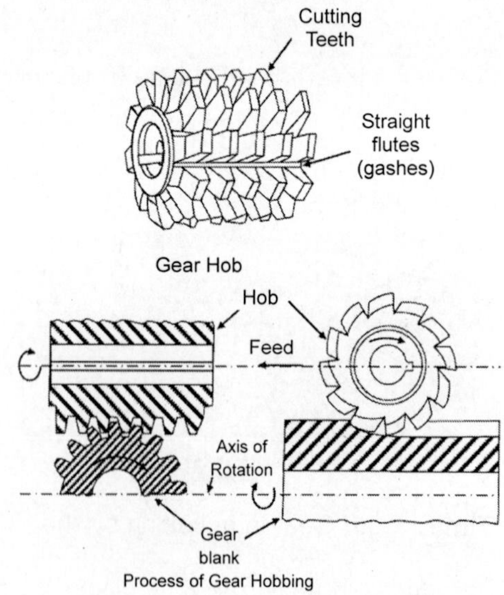

Figure 4.37: Process of Gear Hobbing [6]

Hob: During this procedure, a spinning cutter known as a hob is used to roll the gear blank. A multipoint cutting tool called a gear hob is used to gear hob. It resembles a worm gear with several straight flutes running parallel to its axis all around its circumference. These flutes are fashioned in such a way by being given the correct angles that they serve as cutting edges. In a gear hobbing procedure, the hob is fed to the gear blank while rotating at an appropriate rpm. The gear blank is maintained as rotating as well. Gear blank and gear hob's rpm are coordinated such that for every gear bob revolution, the gear blank spins one pitch distance of the gear hob.

Both the hob and the gear blank move consistently and steadily. Figure 4.37 depicts a gear hob and the gear hobbing operation is demonstrated. The hob teeth have a distinct helix angle and act like screw threads. In order for the hob's cutting blades to stay square with the gear blank during operation, it is tilted at a helix angle. A wide range of gears, including spur gears, helical gears, hearing-bone gears, splines, and gear sprockets, are made by gear hobbing. Figure 4.38 illustrates how the shaving is done.

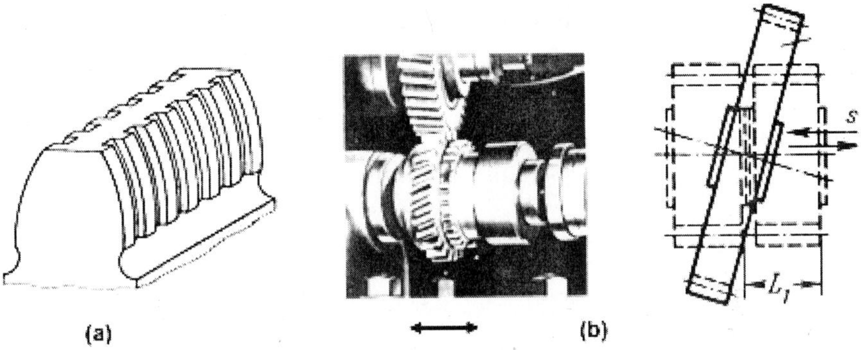

(a) (b)

Figure 4.38: (a) Cutting teeth of gear shaving and (b) action

4.4.1 Working of Gear Hobbing

Important features of hobbing are: (a) Gear hobbing is a technique in which gears are cut using a generating process in which the cutter, known as a hob, and the gear blank are both rotating simultaneously with a set gearing ratio. The gear blank is fed into the rotating hob in this method until the necessary depth is obtained. Until all of the teeth are formed, the hob is fed across the blank's face (b) the hob teeth in a hobbing spur gear are positioned parallel to the blank's axis of rotation. The axis of the hob is placed over an angle to create the proper helix for helical teeth bobbing. While producing worm gears, the hob's axis must be at the proper angle to the gear blank (c) Typically, the hobbing procedure uses two techniques: (i) conventional hobbing (also known as 'traditional hobbing') and (ii) climb hobbing (d) Compared to other gear-generating techniques, the manufacturing rate is fairly high. Spur, helical, worm, sprocket, and spline gears, among other types of gears, can be produced using this method. But cutting up to the shoulder is impossible because of the rotary cutter.

4.4.2 Gear Hobbing Parameters

Indexing movement, feed rate, and the angle between the axis of the gear blank and the gear hobbing tool are three crucial variables that must be under control (gear hob).

4.4.3 Types of Hobbing Process

The process of gear hobbing is classified into different types according to the directions of feeding the hob for gear cutting as: (i) Hobbing with Axial Feed - In this technique, the gear hob is fed against the gear blank while being parallel to its axis and along the blank's face. Gears like spur and helical gears are made using this. (ii) Hobbing with Radial Feed - In this technique, the axes of the gear blanks and the hob are configured to be parallel to one another. In a radial direction or perpendicular to the axis of the gear blank, the rotating hob is fed against the gear blank. This method is used to create the blank and the worm wheels. (iii) Hobbing with Tangential Feed - This technique is also used to shape the worm wheel's teeth. In this instance, the hob is held horizontally with its axis angled at the axis of the blank. The hob is positioned at the whole depth of the tooth and fed axially forward. To the face of the gear blank, the hob is fed tangentially.

4.4.4 Advantages of Gear Hobbing Process

1. When compared to other gear generation techniques, gear hobbing is an economical procedure since it is a quick and continuous operation.
2. Shorter manufacturing cycles, or a higher output rate.
3. In comparison to other gear machining procedures, the process has greater variability in the following senses:
    a. Able to create several different types of gears, including spur gears, helical gears, worms, splines, and sprockets.
    b. The so-named needed indexing process is remarkably straightforward and capable of producing any number of teeth while maintaining the module's precision.
    c. Gear hobbing alone can produce a specific kind of gear known as a herringbone gear.
    d. This procedure can handle a wide range of batch sizes (from tiny to huge volume).
4. It is possible to process multiple gear blanks placed on the same arbour at once.
5. A hob is a multipoint cutting tool with several cutting teeth or edges. Because there are fewer cutting edges operating at once, there is a lot of time for the heat to be dissipated. There isn't a heating or cutting device.

4.4.5 Disadvantages of Gear Hobbing Machine

(a) It is not adopted to generate internal gears.
(b) It is restricted adjacent shoulders larger than the root diameter of the gear.
(c) Splines and serrations are not suitable for hobbing.

4.4.6 Applications of Gear Hobbing

(a) It is widely used to produce spur, helical gears, worms, and worm wheels.
(b) It can also be used for producing internal gears for which the machine should have a facility for fitting a special head.

4.5 GEAR FINISHING PROCESSES

Depending on the method used for gear production, the gears will require some post-processing before they are completely ready. The post-processing can include dimension correction, surface polishing, and heat treatment for better fatigue characteristics. Here are the top five popular methods used in gear manufacturing for surface polishing.

1. **Grinding.** As its name suggests, grinding is a typical surface finishing technique that leaves the surface with a smooth finish. It won't matter if you do it continually or sporadically; the outcomes will remain the same.
2. **Lapping.** This procedure is used for delicate gears where high precision is required. Lapping is a low- to medium-speed process that uses tiny abrasive particles to smooth a surface.
3. **Honing.** Another typical technique for smoothing and polishing the surface. Additionally, you can make a few tiny corrections to the shape of your teeth.
4. **Shaving.** To create a smooth profile, this operation involves removing incredibly thin layers from the surface. Since shaving is typically expensive, it is rarely employed in the manufacture of gear.
5. **Burnishing.** Essentially, burnishing is the process of applying compression to a surface to make it smoother.

Gears need to go through a number of finishing processes after production. Heat treatment and final dimensional and surface finishing are examples of finishing activities. Shaving, grinding, and honing are among finishing techniques. The gears must meet the following requirements for smooth operation, effective performance, and extended service life: (i) exact dimensions and forms (ii) excellent surface finish and (iii) hardness and wear resistance at the sides of the teeth. Which are accomplished by a small amount of gear tooth finishing work following rather precise preforming and machining. Small gears produced by cold rolling frequently don't need additional polishing.

A little finishing by grinding and/or lapping is done after hardening if a rolled gear simply requires additional surface hardening. Gears made by die casting, powder metallurgy, extrusion, blanking, etc. that are nearly net-shape require minimum polishing. However, gear teeth that have been machined and hardened are virtually finished for accuracy and surface finish. Common techniques for polishing gear teeth after preforming and machining, gear teeth are typically completed by: (a) for soft and unhardened gears such as gear shaving and gear rolling or burnishing. (b) for hard and hardened gears such as grinding and lapping (c) for soft but precision gears such as shaving followed by surface hardening and then lapping.

Gear shaving. External spur gears and worm wheels with moderately sized straight or helical teeth composed of soft metals like aluminum alloy, brass, bronze, cast iron, etc. and unhardened steels are typically polished by shaving. Figure 4.39 depicts the various shaving cutter types that, while performing their finishing function, seem to function as a spur gear, rack, or worm in mesh with the corresponding gears that need to be finished.

(a) (b) (c)

Figure 4.39: Gear shaving cutters (a) spur gear type (b) rack and (c) worm type [6]

All of those gear, rack, or worm type shaving cutters are made of hard steel or HSS, and to produce sharp cutting edges, all of their teeth are consistently serrated as illustrated in Fig. 4. 39 (a). The shaving cutter's cutting teeth continue to smooth the mated gear flanks as they interact with the gears by finely milling to a high degree of accuracy and surface finish. As shown in Fig. 4.39 (b), the shaving teeth require an actual or apparent movement relative to the mating teeth throughout their length to perform such minute cutting action.

4.5.1 Gear Teeth Grinding

Although relatively expensive, grinding is a very accurate procedure that is more frequently employed for smoothing out the teeth of various types and sizes of hard-material or hardened surfaces on gears. With the aid of fine machining or abrasive action from the fine abrasives, the properly formed and dressed wheel finishes the sides of the gear teeth. Like gear milling, gear grinding is also done on two principles as (i) Forming (ii) Generation, which is more productive and accurate.

4.5.1.1 Gear teeth grinding on forming principle

As seen in Fig. 4.40, when the grinding wheel is prepared to the precise form needed on the gear, this is quite similar to milling gear teeth using a single disc type form cutter. The method is sluggish and less precise when indexing is required. With changes in the module, pressure angle, and even number of teeth, the wheel or dressing must be altered. Straight or single helical spur gears, straight toothed bevel gears, as well as worm and worm wheels, can all be finished using form grinding.

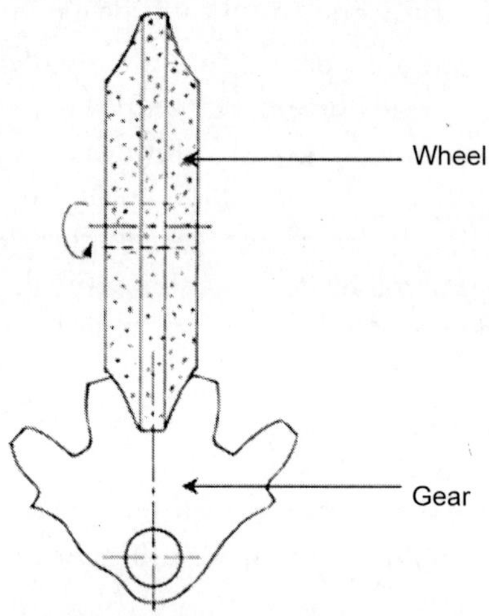

Figure 4.40: Gear teeth finishing by grinding [6]

4.5.1.2 Gear teeth grinding by generation principle

The methods for polishing spur gear teeth by grinding using the generation principle are shown schematically in Figure 4.41. The simplest and most popular technique is quite similar to cutting spur gear teeth with a single or many rack cutter teeth. The gear teeth are reciprocated along by the rotating grinding wheel, which can have one or more ribs, as indicated. As shown in Fig. 4.38b, the other tool-work motions are the same as when gear teeth are generated by a rack type cutter. As shown in Fig.

4.41(c), a pair of thin dish-type grinding wheels are utilised to polish massive gear teeth. In either case, the two flanks of the virtual rack tooth are made to behave as the contacting surfaces of the wheels.

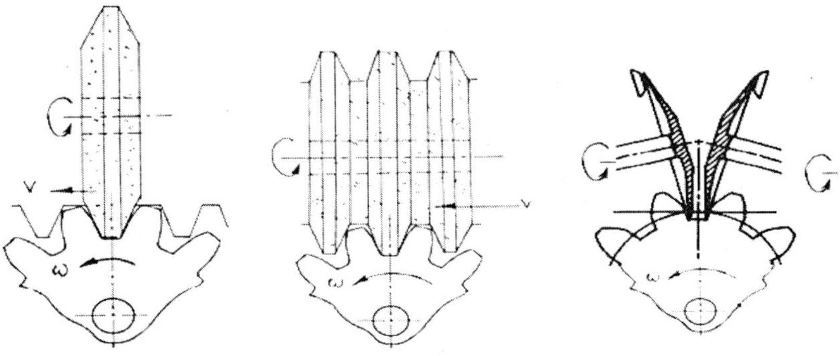

(a) (b) (c)

Figure 4.41: Gear teeth grinding on generation principle [6]

4.5.1.3 Gear teeth finishing by lapping

Only little variations from the ideal gear tooth profiles are corrected by the lapping procedure. The gear that needs to be completed is run in mesh with a gear-shaped lapping tool or another cast iron mating gear after being machined, heated, and even after grinding. They are separated by an abrasive lapping substance. Such lapping significantly increases the gear tooth contact.

4.6 GEAR MATERIALS AND SPECIFICATION

Gears have been made from a wide range of steels, cast irons, bronzes, and phenolic resins. Additionally, new materials like sintered iron, titanium, and nylon have grown in significance in the gear industry. If not for the fact that each of the materials used for gears has been adopted for a reason, designers might get utterly perplexed when presented with such a wide variety of gear materials. Steel gears stand out for having the highest strength per unit volume and the lowest cost per pound. Steel is the only material to take into consideration in many disciplines of gear work. Because of their great machinability, good wear properties, and ease of producing complex shapes using the casting method, cast irons have enjoyed a long history of use.

Due to its capacity to tolerate high sliding velocities and to wear in to suit hardened-steel worms, bronzes play a crucial role in worm gear work. Additionally, they are excellent in areas where corrosion is a problem. Bronze is a good option when producing small gear teeth by stamping or by drawing rods through dies because of how easily it can be manipulated. Despite the material's poor physical strength, diverse combinations of phenolic resins can be employed to create laminated gears with astonishingly good weight carrying capability. These substances are typically 30 times more elastic than steel. Due to their "rubbery" nature, they operate with less shock from tooth faults and can have teeth that can bend enough to make more contact and distribute load than designs made of metal. Several of these materials can withstand sliding at quite high speeds.

4.6.1 Gear Specification

The specification establishes the requirements for the manufacture, inspection, testing, and workmanship. The parameters of a spur gear specification are: Gear Type, Module, Number of teeth and thickness, radius of pitch circle, nominal circle radius, radius of base circle, radius of addendum circle, radius of dedendum circle, pressure angle, fillet radius, material of the gear, heat treatment type, surface finish and circular pitch etc. One of such specification is shown in Table 4.2. There are few more parameters (form of teeth, size of teeth, face width of teeth, design of the hub of the gear, degree of precision required, means of locating the gear on the shaft etc.) that esquires additionally depending on the type of meshing gears.

Table 4.2: Gear specifications

Module, m	4 mm
Number of teeth, Z	14
Radius of Pitch Circle, $R_p = mZ/2$	28 mm
Radius of Base Circle, $R_b = 0.94R_p$	26.33 mm
Radius of Addendum Circle, $R_a = R_p+m$	32 mm
Radius of Dedendum Circle, $R_d = R_p-1.25m$	23 mm
Pressure Angle, α	20 degrees
Fillet Radius, $R_f=0.39m$	1.56 mm
Circular Pitch, $p=\pi D_p/Z$	12.56 mm
Module, m	4 mm
Number of teeth, Z	14
Number of teeth, Z	28 mm
Radius of Base Circle, $R_b = 0.94R_p$	26.33 mm
Radius of Addendum Circle, Ra = Rp+m	

4.7 GEAR HEAT TREATMENT PROCESSES

The qualities of a component can be improved by a procedure called heat treatment to suit application-specific criteria. The performance of each gear in terms of transferring power or carrying motion to other components in an assembly is significantly impacted by heat treatment, which is a crucial and difficult step in the manufacturing of gears. By changing their chemical, metallurgical, and physical characteristics, heat treatments improve the performance and lengthen the lifespan of gears in use. Heat treatment is the process of repeatedly heating and cooling a material to modify its microstructure and, in turn, its mechanical properties.

Both tooth flanks are in sliding and rolling contact as the power is transferred between mated gears. That is to say, the pressure applied to the tooth flank is equivalent to the pressure experienced when a cylinder slides while rolling on a flat surface. The tooth flank must withstand this strain without breaking. However, some hard materials, like ceramic, are fragile and break readily. When the gears begin to turn, the dedendum is commonly subjected to bending force, and impact may result. In order to obtain high durability against external pressures and impact, the material of the gear must be tenacious. Therefore, exactly like a Japanese sword, gears need to be tough on the surface and tough on the inside.

The process used to impart such features is heat treatment. Gears can be heated using three different methods: Carburizing, Induction hardening, and Nitriding.

4.7.1 Carburizing

A common method of treating low-carbon steel gears. As implied by the term, the metal surface is quenched and tempered to harden after being pierced by "carbon." Depending on the gear size, the hardened layer's thickness ranges from 0.2mm to 2mm. Crushed carbon was once applied to metal before it was sealed and heated. High-temperature, molten inorganic salts based on sodium cyanide were used to coat items in Europe, but the toxicity of sodium cyanide presented a challenge. The major method utilised at the moment is gas carburization, which involves heating goods in carbon dioxide gas, methane, propane, and steam. A huge number of materials can be processed efficiently even though gas carburization is expensive due to the vast amount of specialised equipment required. Usually, carburizing takes place after cutting the gear and forming the gear teeth. The tooth surface is then finished by being lapped and ground.

4.7.2 Induction Hardening

A common method of treating gears composed of medium-carbon steel. When the metal gear that is wound with wire is electrified, the eddy current moves through electromagnetic induction. The eddy current's ability to concentrate at the metal surface and heat metal is exploited by induction hardening. The wiring coil that is layered on top of the cut-out gear tooth is subjected to an electric current as part of the standard procedure for induction hardening. Induction hardening is less precise and can handle fewer items at once than other techniques like carburizing. On the other hand, because the gear tooth can be partially hardened, this procedure is appropriate for processing items with integrated gear and axis or big gears.

4.7.3 Nitriding

Most steel gears contain molybdenum or chromium. Aluminum-containing steel, also referred to as "nitride steel," has a particularly potent effect among the numerous types of steel that are appropriate for nitriding. With nitration, gears are heated in nitrogen gas to create an iron nitride layer on the gear surface that ranges in thickness from 0.1 to 1 mm. The layer that is hardened by nitriding is thinner than that produced by other heat treatments, but it can produce harder materials than carburizing and induction hardening. At 500o to 600o Celsius, the temperature required for nitriding is quite low. In contrast, carburizing and induction hardening need items to be heated to 800o Celsius. In contrast to other heat treatments, nitriding does not result in quenching cracks or deformation. Since nitriding doesn't deform and produces high hardness, it is typically done as the final stage in the production of gears.

4.8 INTRODUCTION TO PRESS WORKING

In almost every industry today, presses are employed. Presses have been around for a very long period (Fig. 4.42). It can be used to manipulate a wide range of materials, both hot and cold, and it can perform a number of operations that call for intense pressure, including packing, squeezing, forging, stamping, flush mounting, extrusion, laminating, and stretching. Even if we keep with the functioning of metals, its great variety allows for many different classifications of such presses. Depending on the positioning of the guides in the space (vertical, horizontal, inclined), the motor agent (manuals, gravity, engine), or the drive's active elements (single, double, or triple effect presses), or the methods of implementing the drive's energy (of eccentric lever, friction, screw, etc) (mechanical, hydraulic, pneumatic), the fact shows that there are so many variations on a single theme and that the evolution of the press throughout the narrative does not proceed in a straightforward or linear fashion. On the other hand, it has taken a lot of various methodologies, far-flung theoretical foundations, and multiple individual contributions to get the pressing technology to where it is now.

(a) (b)

Figure 4.42: Press working history (a) Hammer type (b) Nicolas Briot (1626) rocker type [18]

One of the manufacturing techniques that is virtually chip-free is metal shaping. Presses and other press-related equipment are mostly used to carry out these processes including applying pressure or force to metal workpieces to cause them to deform to the required size. Using mechanical pressure or force, the press is a metal-forming device that can cut or shape metal. One of the most popular ways to create parts with complicated shapes and thin walls is with this technique. Press working activities have a number of benefits, including: Material economy, high productivity, part uniformity, and use of fewer labour.

In general, all press working procedures on sheet metal are referred to as press working. Stamped pieces made of sheet metal are moulded or curled through deformation such as shearing, punching, drawing, stretching, bending, coining, etc. High production rates enable completed products to be produced within tolerance without the need for further machining. Work related to mass production is made easier by presses and press tools. Numerous industries, including those that produce office furniture, electric goods, radios, air travel, telephones, and stainless-steel home waves, use press working.

Therefore, a press is a tool for working with sheet metal that has a stationary bed and a powered ram that can be moved in either direction to impart force or the necessary pressure for different metal forming activities. Figure 4.43 (a) shows a manual and 4.43 (b) shows a powered system illustrating a line diagram of such a typical presses. The press's frame construction determines the base and ram's relative placements. In most cases, the punch is held in the punch holder, which is connected to the ram. The press bed is covered with a balster steel plate, and a die is fixed on the plate. There are numerous capacities, power systems, and frame types for presses. The ability of a press to exert the necessary power to finish an operation is the definition of capacity.

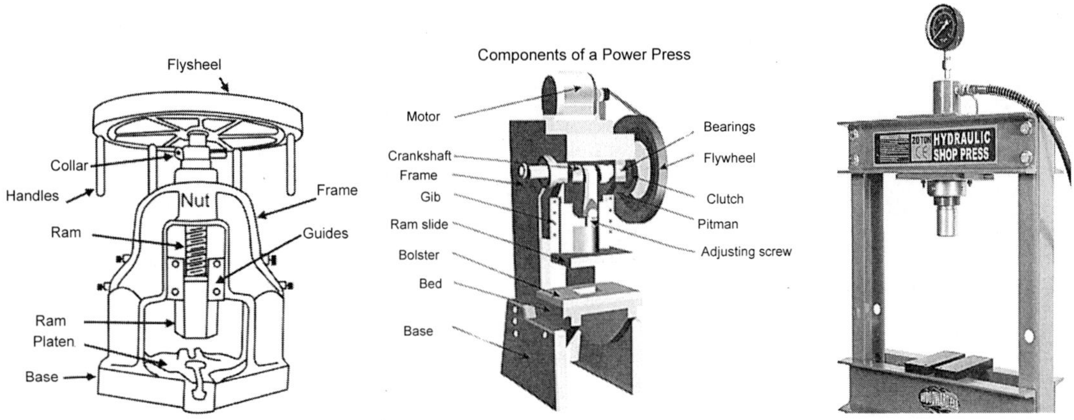

(a) (b) (c)

Figure 4.43: Typical Press of (a) Manual type (b) Power Press (c) Hydraulic press

4.9 CLASSIFICATION OF PRESSES

Many different industries employ press working. Some of the prominent examples are: automotive, aerospace, communications, electrical appliance, and utensil manufacturing industries. Hydraulic presses use a sizable piston and cylinder to drive the ram as their power source. Longer ram strokes can be provided by this technique than by mechanical dries. A constant applied load is provided. It operates somewhat more slowly. These presses can be one- or two-action, among other variations. The amount of independently operating slides determines the number of actions.

There are various drive mechanisms that are employed with mechanical presses. Eccentric, crankshaft, knuckle joint, and other drives are among them. These drives are used to change a motor's rotational motion into a ram's linear motion. Typically, a fly wheel serves as an energy source for forging processes. These presses are advised for blanking and punching operations due to the drives' ability to generate extremely high forces at the end of their strokes.

4.9.1 Presses Classified on the Basis of Source of Power

(i). **Mechanical presses.** These presses utilize flywheel energy which is transferred to the work piece by gears, cranks, eccentrics, or levers. 5 to 100 tons capacity. (Fig. 4.44a)

(ii). **Manual (fly) Presses.** These are either hand or foot operated through levers, screws or gears. A common press of this type is the arbor press used for assembly operations. Capacity ½ to 10 tons.

(iii). **Hydraulic Presses.** These presses provide working force through the application of fluid pressure on a piston by means of pumps, valves, intensifiers, and accumulators. These presses have better performance and reliability than mechanical presses (Fig. 4.44b).

(iv). **Pneumatic/Power Presses.** These presses utilize air cylinders or motor power (Fig. 4.44c) to exert the required force. These are generally smaller in size and capacity than hydraulic or mechanical presses, and therefore find use for light duty operations only.

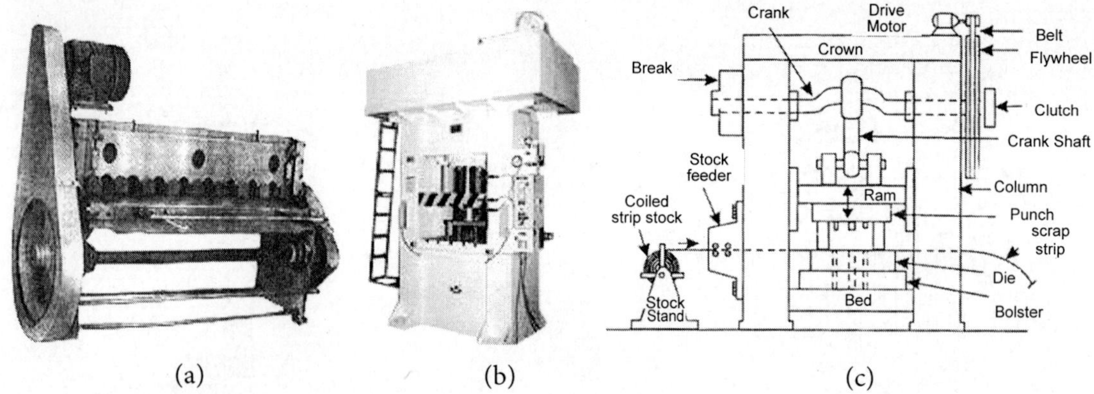

Figure 4.44: Types of Presses (a) mechanical (b) hydraulic (c) power

Presses with power hammers (Fig. 4.44c) are also frequently employed for demanding, hard work. For the necessary blanking, shaping, and drawing processes on sheet metal, mechanical presses are employed extremely frequently. Hydraulic presses are preferable for specific tasks that demand a lot of force, for instance. There are some distinctions between the use of mechanical and hydraulic presses, as given below:

Characteristic	Mechanical Presses	Hydraulic Presses
Force	Depends upon slide position.	Dose not depend upon slide position. Relatively constant.
Stroke length	Short strokes	Long strokes. Even as much as 3 m.
Slide speed	High. Highest at mid- stroke. Can be veriable	Slow. Rapid advance and retraction. Variable speeds uniform throughout stroke.
Capacity'	About 50 MN (maximum)	About 500 MN. or even more.
Control	Full stroke generally required before reversel.	Adjustable, slide reversal possible from any position.
Application	Operations requiring maximum pressure near bottom of strock. cutting operations (blanking, sharing, piercing, forming and drawing to depths of about 100 mm.	Operations requiting steady pressure lhrough-out stoke. Deep drawing. Drawing irregular shaped parts. Straightening. Operations requiring variable forces and 'or strokes.

4.9.2 Presses Classified on the Basis of Number of Slides

(i). **Single Action Presses:** A single action press features a single reciprocating slide that transports the tool used for metal shaping. The bed of the press is fixed. For procedures like blanking, coining, embossing, and drawing, it is the press that is most frequently utilised.

(ii). **Double Action Presses:** A double action press uses two slides that move in unison against a stationary bed. Compared to a single action press, it is better suited for drawing tasks, particularly deep drawing.

(iii). **Triple Action Presses:** There are three moving slides in a triple action press. The third or lower slide moves upward through the fixed bed in a direction opposite to that of the other two slides (the blank holder and the inner slide move in the same way as in a double action press). While both upper actions are residing, this action permits reverse drawing, shaping, or bending operations against the inner slide.

4.9.3 Presses Classified on the Basis of Frame and Construction

(i). **Arch-Frame Presses.** The frames of these presses are shaped like arches (Fig. 4.45).

(ii). **Gap Frame Presses.** The frame of these presses is C-shaped. These are the most adaptable and widely used since they allow free access to the dies from three sides and typically have open backs for the ejection of stamping and/ or trash (Fig. 4.45).

(iii). **Straight Side Presses.** These presses are more durable because the large side frame can support huge weights in a vertical direction, and the alignment of the punch and die is less likely to be impacted by stress. These presses typically have a capacity of more than 10 MN (Fig. 4.45).

(iv). **Horn Presses.** Instead of the typical bed, these presses typically feature a large shaft protruding from the machine frame. This press is mostly used to punch, rivet, emboss, and flange edges on cylindrical items (Fig. 4.45).

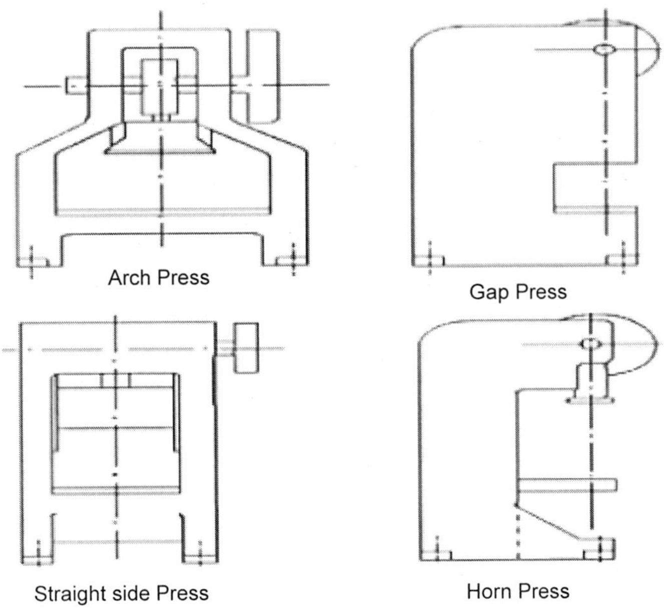

Figure 4.45: Typical frame designs used for power presses [6]

4.9.4 Presses Classified on the Basis of Design of the Frame

(i) Inclined (ii) Straight side (iii) Gap (iv) Horn (v) Arch (vi) Inclinable.

4.9.5 Presses Classified on the Basis of the Drive Mechanism

(i) Crank (ii) Eccentric (iii) Rack and pinion (iv) Screw (v) Toggle drive (vi) Knuckle joint.

4.9.6 Presses Classified on the Basis of the Number of Slides

(i) Single action (ii) Double action (iii) Multiple actions.

4.9.7 Presses Classified on the Basis of the Uses

(i) Shearing (ii) Punching (iii) Coining (iv) Stretching (v) Extruding (vi) Straightening (vii) Bending etc.

4.10 SPECIFICATION OF PRESSES

For practical selection of a press, specification is needed. The specification of a press involves the following parameters:

(i). **Length of stroke.** The length of stroke is defined as the distance between up and down position the ram

(ii). **Shut height.** The shut height is defined as the distance between the top of the bed to the bottom of the ram.

(iii). **Die space.** The die space is defined as the available area for mounting the punch and dies components in the press.

(iv). **Press adjustment.** The press adjustment means the capability of press to adjust the length of stroke as per need, as in the case of rack and pinion-driven presses.

(v). **Number of ram head.** The number of ram heads provided for simultaneous operations i.e. single- acting, double-acting or multiple-acting.

(vi). **Amount force or press.** The size of any press is determined by the maximum force or pressure that can be exerted by the ram on the work piece without any failure.

(vii). **Capacity of working.** The capacity of mechanical press is determined by the shear strength of the crank shaft material multiplied by the area of the crankshaft bearings. The capacity of mechanical presses ranges from 50 tons to 4000 tons. On the other hand, the capacity of a hydraulic press is determined by the piston area multiplied by the pressure of oil in the cylinder. The capacity of a hydraulic press ranges from 100 tons to 40,000 tons.

4.10.1 Mechanical Press Specification

It may be done on basis of *Capacity of press* (kN): 400, Stroke range (mm): 10-70, *Number of stroke* (stroke/min): 72, *Morse diameter* (mm): 35 *Dimensions of table* (mm): 420 x 500, *Hole diameter* of the table (mm): 140, *Distance between table and head* (mm): 450, *Motor power* (kW): 4, *Speed* (rpm): 1400, *Speed of the hammer* (m/s): 0.14 etc.

4.10.2 Hydraulic Press Specification

It may be done on basis of *Maximum load:*150 KN, *Internal fluid pressure:* 3.82 N/m^2, *Tangential stress:* 480×10^6 N/m^2, *Shear stress of flange:* 480 x 10^6 N/m^2, *Maximum bending moment:* 45 KN/m, *Pumping pressure:* 47.16×10^6 N/m^2, *Piston stroke:* 600 mm, *Piston diameter:* 80 mm, *Thickness of cylinder wall:* 17×10^{-3} m, *Core diameter of bolt:* 16×10^{-3} m, *Internal radius of cylinder:* 50×10^{-3} m, *Length of the* *lever:* 0.8 m, *Width of flange:* 22.2 × 10^{-3} m, *Thickness of cylinder wall:* 17 × 10^{4} m, 0-*ring seal dimension:* 4 mm × 3 mm, *Outside diameter of seal:* 134 × 10^{4} m etc.

4.10.3 Power Press Specification

It may be done on basis of *Capacity:* 80 Tones, *Bed Area:* 900 X 600 mm, *Stroke:* 100mm, *Shut Height:*400 mm, *Adjustment:*75 mm, *Speed:*40mm/min, *Motor:* 5.5 Kw, 1800 RPM, *Drive shaft:* RPM 300, *Approx. Weight:* 800Kg, *Approx. Height:* 1.8 M etc.

4.10.4 Application Basis

There are many factors for selection of a Press based on the application :(i) Work piece material, (ii) Work piece size, (iii) Work piece thickness, (iv) Operations to be performed, (v) Operational speed required, (vi) Production rate, (vii) Power required, (viii) Dimensional tolerances and accuracy required for parts, (ix) Die types i.e., single, compound or progressive type etc.

The application of different presses also depends on: (i) Crank or eccentric type presses. Because their small working strokes and high production rates, these types of presses used for punching, blanking and trimming operations (ii) Knuckle joint type Presses. Because of their large force capacities, these presses are used for coining and squeezing operations (iii) Toggle presses. These are used for operations like heading, perforating, upsetting, etc.(iv) Hydraulic presses. Hydraulic presses are best suited for operations require slower speed, like pressing, forming, drawing, etc.

4.11 PRESS WORKING OPERATIONS

Press working operations are same as sheet metal presses operations. This is because different operations are performed on sheets through various press tools to get the required shape. These press working operations are mainly divided into two categories as cutting and forming. There are various sub operations that fall under each of these two categories. The working methods of sheet metal presses will vary depending on specific application requirements.

4.11.1 Sheet Metal Cutting Operations

In this press work process, the sheet metal is subjected to tensile and compressive stresses to break its structure and separate it into different parts. Hence, it is considered an efficient material utilization operation. Sheet metal cutting operations include:

(a) **Punching.** It is a metal fabrication process where enough shearing force is applied on the sheet metal to produce holes and cutouts of different sizes and shapes. Punching is performed by placing the sheet metal between the punch and die. The punch presses drive downward at high speed through the sheet metal to create holes.

(b) **Blanking.** This press working process removes a pre-defined part from the sheet metal. The part is punched out with a single stroke, using one die and punch. This method usually produces a flat shape from a metal sheet. Cutting or shearing of outside contours or shapes from sheet or strip stock. The piece cut out is the useful part.

(c) **Coining.** A squeezing operation, usually performed in a closed die in which the metal is forced to flow and fill the shape and profile of the die. There is a definite change in metal thickness.

(d) **Perforating.** It is the method of punching or stamping slots or holes in a pattern, not specifically in a round shape. The wastage of material here is minimal.

(e) **Shearing.** The sheet metal is separated into two or more pieces by simply cutting a long line. Shearing creates clean cuts with smooth edges. It doesn't produce wastage in the form of chips or debris.

(f) **Trimming.** As the name implies, this process removes the excess metal portions surrounding the formed pre-designed parts.

(g) **Notching.** This process produces desired parts by removing the edges of the metal workpiece. Notching is a manually operated and low-production process.

(h) **Slitting.** Slitting is similar to the shearing process. However, this process cuts a wide coil of sheet metal into various narrow coils using circular knives.

(i) **Piercing.** Practically the same operation as blanking, except it is limited to holes or slots in sheet metal. The piece cut out is the scrap.

(j) **Trimming.** A secondary operation on drawn or formed parts to remove excess metal on the flange or axial length.

4.11.2 Sheet Metal Forming Operations

It is one of the most widely used processes that cause stress below the ultimate strength of the metal, which results in distortion. Sheet metal forming operations include:

(a) **Bending.** A sufficient amount of force is used in this operation to bend the sheet metal into a curved shape. The metal's volume is kept constant while its shape is altered during bending. Different techniques can be used to bend sheet metal. Among the most common varieties are v-bending, offset bending, channel bending, and edge bending.

(b) **Drawing.** With this technique, a workpiece is transformed into hollow components with thin walls or vessel shapes. Deep drawing and shallow drawing are the two types of drawing that are distinguished.

(c) **Squeezing.** It is the most well-liked and frequently applied method of producing ductile metals. The procedures of squeezing include coining, scaling, and riveting. These procedures are used to lessen the metal's overall thickness.

(d) **Curling.** The creation of an edge with a circular cross section around the end of a shell or tube or along a sheet. Sometimes this procedure is referred to as fake wiring.

(e) **Embossing.** A process for producing raised or sunken designs in sheet metal by means of a male and female die.

(f) **Extrusion.** A process in which pressure is applied to a slug of metal causing the metal to flow either up around the punch (toothpaste tubes) or down in the direction of pressure (cartridge cases – Hooker process).

(g) **Ironing.** A process in which the wall thickness of the shell is reduced without changing the O.D. of the shell (cartridge case work for example).

(h) **Necking.** Reducing the diameter of a portion of the length of a cylindrical shell or tube.

(i) **Redrawing,** The second operation after deep-drawing operations, in which the cross section of cups is narrowed and deepened.

4.11.3 Cutting & Forming Operations

A combination of processes, including the following, result in a part having partial cutting and forming as: Slitting. **Slitting** is a sheet metal cutting process with circular knives, which is used to split wide coiled sheet metal into narrower widths or for edge trimming of rolled sheet and **Lancing**. Slitting and forming a pocket shaped opening in sheet metal, without removing metal.

4.11.4 Other Operations

(a) **Crimping.** When a can or shell's open end is crimped, it is squeezed tightly over or around a compatible portion. The majority of this type of employment is restricted to assembly tasks.

(b) **Staking.** An action that permanently joins two or more components together by moving a tiny metal piece over the mating part, which creates compression on the assembled pieces.

(c) **Swaging.** Forming a metal with the swift application of several repeated strikes. When using aviation cable fittings, the fitting is rotated while being struck by press blows.

Table 4.3: Press operations

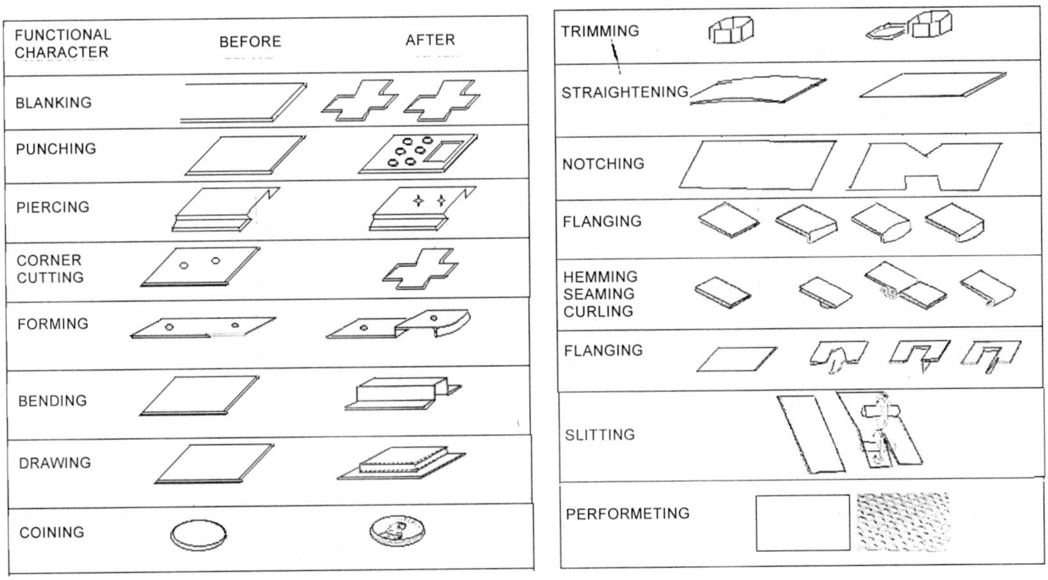

4.12 DIFFERENT TERMINOLOGY USED FOR PRESS WORKING TOOLING

These are:

(a) **Stock Material.** General term used for the material that will be used to produce the piece part.

(b) **Die.** Die has many definitions with reference to tooling. A die normally refers to a complete production tool that can make piece parts accurately and consistently, it may also refer to a female part of a complete die.

(c) **Punch.** A punch can be described as a male component of a complete die that acts in conjunction with the female half of the die to produce a piece part.

(d) **Piece Part.** A piece part is the product a die produces, it may also be a component of a product.

4.13 DIE SET COMPONENTS

A punch, a die, and a few more accessories make up the entire die set (Fig. 4.46), these accessories are discussed in this section later. The key to a successful punch's operation is exact alignment of the punch and die. Accessories for a die set give the system the necessary alignment and rigidity and increase the performance's accuracy. An assortment of dice includes:

4.13.1 Press Tool

Punches and dies are commonly used instruments that are essential elements of press operating (Fig. 4.46). The punch, which is secured to the ram and pushed into the die where the workpiece to be processed is supported, is a crucial component of the system. Die is a work-holding tool created especially for a specific product design. Die is fixed firmly to the press's base. An opening on the die is ideally positioned to match the punch's motion. A die set is a combination of a die and a punch that functions as a single entity. High speed steel is used to make the punch and the die. The section of the die that requires both strength and wear resistance. As a result, satellite or cemented carbide is typically used for the die's working surface. Below is a description of the die set specifics.

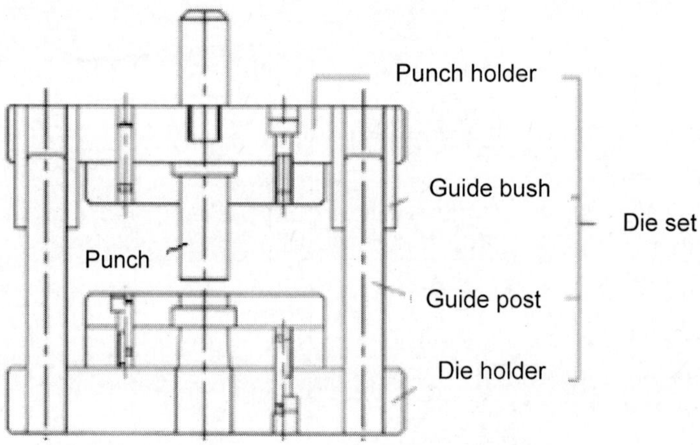

Figure 4.46: Die & punch as a die set [6]

4.13.2 Punch

Punch holder at the ram's lower end is fitted with a punch plate. Punch plates are often constructed of HSS or stainless steel. The punch is held firmly and precisely by the punch plate. Various punch holding positions are illustrated in Fig. 7.47 as follows: (1) Punch may be secured by pressing it on the punch plate; the punch's top end has been flattened to fit in the countersunk recess (2) A set screw can be used to clamp the punch to the punch plate. By making a slot in the punch plate, the correct punch location can be found (3) The punch's top end is flattened to fit into the countersunk recess before the punch's shank is pressed into the punch plate (4) Grub screws can be used to firmly fasten the punch to the punch plate (5) The punch is attached to the punch plate using set screws (6) The punch is fastened using a set screw, which is located during fastening with the help of two dowel pins (7) The punch's flange end is fastened to the punch plate using set screws that are inserted from the punch end.

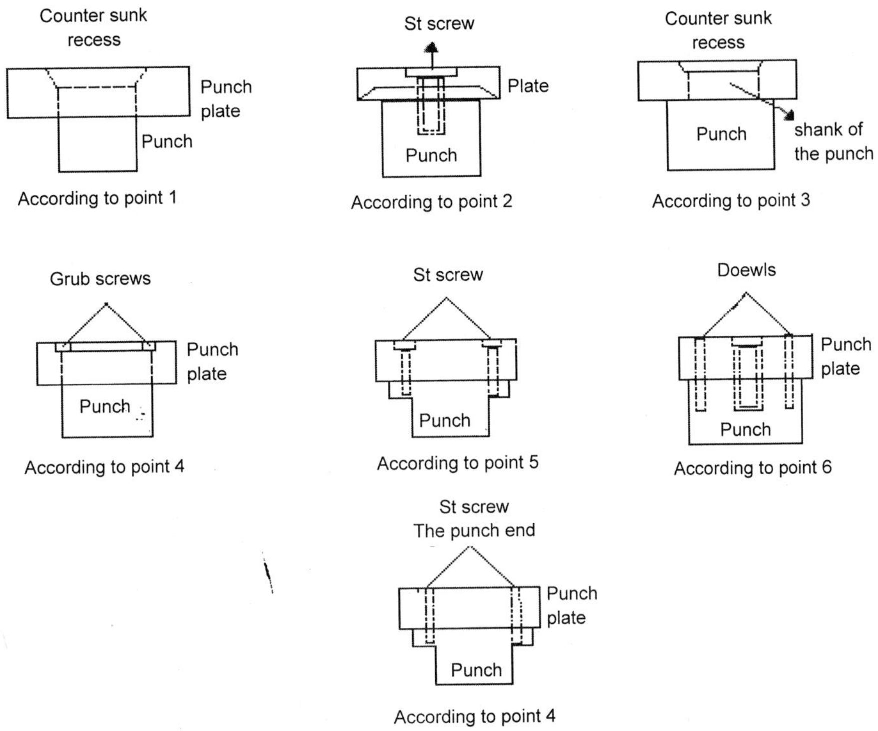

Figure 4.47: Different ways of holding a punch [6]

4.13.3 Accessories of Die Set

Cutting shapes and piercing metal, at the most basic level, is really all the toolmaker is trying to achieve. Like everything, when ONE learns a new skill or topic, it will have a set of principles and terminology that one should become familiar with. It's like learning a new language. Similar to the language of medical jargon, one should learn the following tooling's terminology as the language of the tool making and the accessories. These accessories are the finished parts, removal of waste. The die accessories are shown in Fig. 7.48 with their description as given below:

(a) **Punch Holder.** Other names for it include upper shoe of die set. The press's ram is secured to the punch holder. The punch below it is held by it.

(b) **Punch.** It is the primary die assembly tool that makes direct contact with the workpiece as it is being processed; its specifics have already been covered.

(c) **Die Holder.** Additionally, known as die shoe. It serves as a support for the die block and is firmly secured to the press's base plate.

(d) **Stops.** Stops are used to keep the sheet metal properly spaced when it is fed below the punch to maintain output quality. These, without taking any action, limit the feed of stock (workpiece) to a predetermined length each time. Bottom stop and lever stop are the two common types of stops employed. The bottom stop is a mechanical mechanism tape. After each cut, this device puts a stop to punch motion. A button is positioned so that when fresh stock is fed to die, the impact of the fed stock presses the button, showing genuine stock length being fed. In this manner, the device also serves as a fixture. The system can be made ready for the next cutting activity by pressing a button. Lever Stop, slow acting power presses, and manual presses all employ the button stop. A lever is used to move this device. When fresh stock is fed, the stop mechanism prevents the downward movement of the punch for the subsequent cut after the stock has reached a predetermined length. The punch can move for a cut thanks to the lever as well.

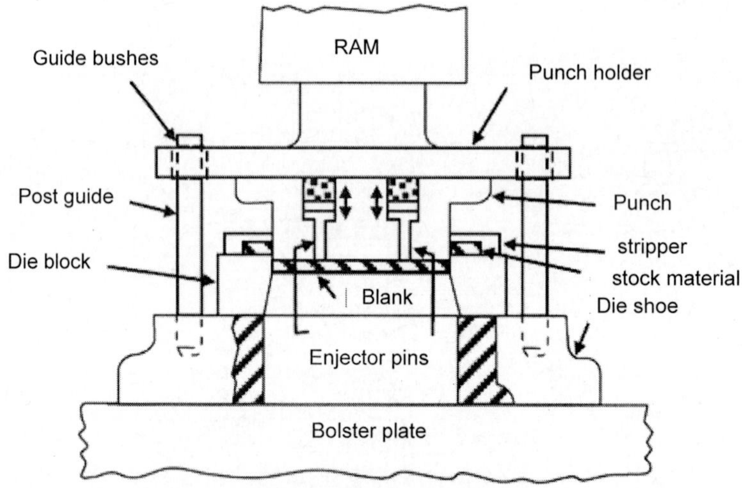

Figure 4.48: Accessories of a die set.

(e) **Pilots.** Pilot is used for correct location of blank when it is fed by mechanical means. The pilot enters into the previously pierced hole and moves the blank to the correct position to be finally spaced by the stops. Normally pilots are fitted to the punch holders.

(f) **Strippers.** After the cutting or forming procedure is finished, the workpiece is removed from the press using a stripper. The blank is separated from the punch's cutting edge after the cutting and is thus prevented from being lifted with the punch when the upward stroke comes next. The stripper carries out this preventative activity.

(g) **Knockouts.** Another kind of stripper called knockout is typically employed with inverted dies. The knockout plate ejects the blank from the cutting edge when the cutting process is finished.

(h) **Pressure Pads.** When the workpiece flows plastically between the punch and the die, pressure pads are plates that firmly hold the workpiece at both ends. This firm gripping prevents the possibility of creasing during the metal-forming process. The same purpose can alternatively be achieved by a plunger that is spring-loaded and acts on the workpiece plate's bottom. The sheet metal workpiece is ironed in a manner by the pressure pads.

(i) **Guide Posts.** The precise alignment of punch action and die opening is crucial. For proper punch and die shoe alignment, guide posts are used.

(j) **Punch Plate.** Punch retainer is another name for punch plate. The punch holder has this fastened to it. Punch plates provide as a reference point for holding the punch in the correct alignment and position. Punch replacement becomes swift and accurate as a result.

(k) **Backing Plate.** A backing plate is utilised to maintain uniform pressure distribution over the entire region and minimise stress build up on any one part of the punch holder. Between the punch and punch holder, this is often formed of hardened steel.

(l) **Die Retainer.** The punch holder, punch plate, and die retainer all serve the same function. To hold the die block in the proper alignment with the movement of the punch, a die retainer is fastened to the press's bed (base). In certain circumstances, the die shoe itself serves as a die retainer.

Typically, the die is held in a die holder that is secured to the base plate mounted on the press's table or base. There are three distinct ways to attach die blocks to the die holder:

(i). Using the four set screws depicted in Fig. 4.48, the die block is fastened to the die holder. Currently, only one screw is visible. By using a dowel pin, the die is placed exactly where it should be.

(ii). The set screws at the bottom of the die holders illustrated in Fig. 4.48 hold the die block in place.

(iii). The wedge in Fig. 4.48, which is attached to the die holder by set screws, holds the die block in place.

4.13.4 Design and Materials for Different Components

This is also equally important to consider following points listed below while designing a good die set.

(a) The life of the die set determines the cost of production; thus, material selection should be done carefully while keeping strength and wear-resistant features in mind.

(b) Since heat treatment is typically used to harden die, design should take all necessary safety measures and provide for heat treatment's negative consequences.

(c) The precision of a die set's production is directly correlated with the precision of the die set's individual parts. Focus should be placed on keeping precise measurements and small tolerances during design.

(d) Block-shaped portions should be used in place of long, thin sections to prevent warpage.

(e) Standardized parts ought to be utilised to the greatest extent practicable.

(f) Reinforcing grips should be employed in accordance with the sections' specifications.

(g) Easy upkeep should be taken into account. Parts replacement ought to be simple.

(h) When choosing the material for the die set's component parts, shock resistance qualities should also be taken into account if the process cannot be made shockproof.

Along with the crucial design factors, one should be aware of the appropriate material choice for a die set's component parts and the many types of tool steel that are suitable for such parts. In order to resist wear and be strong enough to withstand loads, the material or tool steel chosen should be very hard. At the same time, die set components may have very complex shapes and designs, necessitating extremely precise sizing. The majority of them are produced using machining and finishing processes. Tool steel is processed to create these components, which are then hardened using a variety of techniques, including water hardening, oil hardening, air hardening, and hard coatings. The following aspects should be considered when choosing a material for a die set component:

(i). The required lifespan of the die set component.

(ii). Their manufactured mobility and precision level.

(iii). Ability to withstand load, stress, and wear (type of process subjected).

(iv). Their expenses, including their startup and ongoing costs.

4.14 ROLE OF PUNCH AND DIE CLEARANCES FOR BLANKING AND PIERCING

A punching machine for blanking, punching, and piercing operations is shown in Figure 7.49. High rigidity, stability, precision, safe operation, automated production, labor-saving efficiency, slider adjustment mechanism, novel design, and environmental protection are only a few of the qualities of an excellent punching machine.

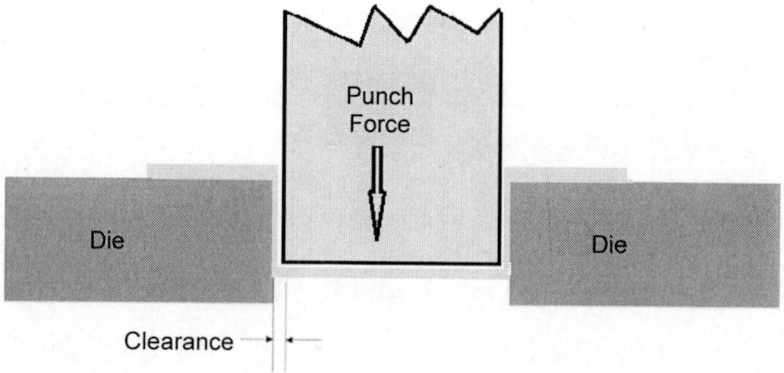

(a) (b)

Figure 7.49: (a) Blanking machine (b) Punching, piercing operations

The following factors provide better practice when choosing the appropriate die clearance for punching and blanking operations on a punching machine. The benefits include: (i) extending the mold's useful life (ii) good material return effect (iii) small generated burr (iv) getting a cleaner and tidy hole (v) reducing the chance of sticking (vi) work piece levelling (vii) more accurate positioning of the hole (viii) needing the least amount of punching force for blanking and (ix) the ideal distance between the punch and die. When the blanking force is balanced, the punching quality is good, and the mould has a long service life, a good clearance can make the shear fracture joint safe. Table 4.2 below lists the recommended punch and die clearance.

Table 4.4: Recommended die clearance

Thickness (mm)	Aluminum (mm)	Mild Steel (mm)	Stainless Steel (mm)
1.00	0.15	0.20	0.20
1.50	0.23	0.30	0.40
2.00	0.30	0.40	0.50
3.00	0.60	0.75	0.90
4.00	0.80	1.00	1.20
5.00	1.00	1.25	1.75
6.35	1.60	2.00	2.22

The consequences of inadequate clearing include: (i) secondary shearing (ii) an increase in punching force and (iii) a reduction in mould life.

4.14.1 Determination of the Punch and Die Clearance Value

Due to experience, it goes without saying that someone who has worked as a stamping die fitter and stamping die designer for a significant amount of time will understand and be familiar with a wide range of products, including their material, size, and appearance accuracy requirements. They will also be knowledgeable about how to design the mould to successfully produce qualified products, how to reduce mould repair, repair times, etc.

The die clearance c, has very important role and there are two methods (i) by experience and by formula as, $c = (t - ho)\tan\beta = t\,(1\text{-}ho/t)\tan\beta$. Where, *ho* – Punch penetration depth; β - The angle between the maximum shear stress direction and the vertical direction, the gap *c* is related to the material thickness *t*, the relative penetration depth *ho/t* and the crack direction β. While *ho* and β are related to the nature of the material, the harder the material, the smaller the *ho/t*.

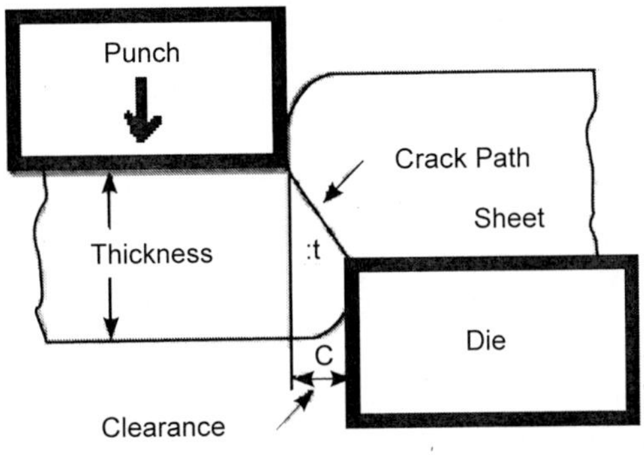

Figure 4.50: The role of die clearance across the crack path.

4.14.2 Determine the Punch and Die Clearance by Experience

The percentage of the die clearance to the material thickness is selected as below:

- Min service life of dies: 15%
- Optimal clearance: 20~25%
- Long service life of dies: 30%
- Heavy duty die clearance: 30%

4.14.3 The Punch and Die Clearance by Formula

The value of c can be calculated according to the following punch and die clearance formula as: $c = (t - ho)\tan\beta = t\,(1\text{-}ho/t)\tan\beta$.

For Soft materials:

- Material thickness $t < 1$ mm, blanking clearance $c = (3\% \sim 4\%)\,t$
- $t = 1 \sim 3$mm, $c = (5\% \sim 8\%)\,t$
- $t = 3 \sim 5$mm, $c = (8\% \sim 10\%)\,t$

For Hard materials:

- $t < 1\text{mm}$, $c = (4\% \sim 5\%)\ t$
- $t = 1 \sim 3\text{mm}$, $c = (6\% \sim 8\%)\ t$
- $t = 3 \sim 8\text{mm}$, $c = (8\% \sim 13\%)\ t$

Material characteristics and material thickness are thus the key determinants of clearance value. The die clearance value increases with the hardness or thickness of the material. In order to determine the proper clearance, consider the following criteria: (i) Correct die clearance (Low tonnage, Small burr, and More to Life); (ii) Tight die clearance (Higher tonnage, Small burr, and Less to Life); and (iii) Excessive die clearance (Low tonnage, Larger burr, Less too life).

When a piece part is produced by blanking, that means the piece part has been made out of a stock strip of material. The distance the stock strip moves through the die is called the advancement. The scrap material left on the stock strip, in between the piece parts, is called the scrap bridge. When a die is used to make a hole or an opening in the piece part, the operation is called piercing. The unwanted material removed by the piercing operation is called the slug. The effect of the tool on the stock material is the same whether it is punching out slugs, in order to produce the desired opening in a piece part, or punching out blanks which are the desired product of the die.

4.15 PRESS CYCLE DURING BLANKING OR PIERCING

When a press is tripped or activated, a clutch will allow engagement with a flywheel. The crankshaft rotates in one full turn. During the first half of the cycle, the ram moves toward the bed of the press, then, during the last half of the cycle, the ram moves back up. The distance travelled by the ram during the first half of the cycle is called the Press Stroke.

4.15.1 Actions of Blanking or Piercing Die

Stripping. Once the punching or piercing operations have taken place and the press moves up, the piece part or slug may remain in the die. The stock material will want to cling to the punch and stick unless another step, known as stripping, is added in the part production. The function of the stripper is to keep the material from travelling with the punch on the return stroke.

4.16 THE REACTION OF THE STOCK MATERIAL

In tool making, there are 3 important stages:

(i). The plastic deformation – The press is tripped and the punch is driven toward the die. The punch exerts a force on the stock material. Plastic deformation takes place once the elastic limits are exceeded.

(ii). Penetration – This is the true shearing stage of the cutting cycle. The punch is forced to penetrate the stock material and the blank or slug is pushed out.

(iii). Fracture – The punching force causes fracturing of the piece part/slug. Then the fractures extend and meet to complete the piece part/slug. This is when the greatest stress or pressure is applied to the cutting edges.

4.16.1 Typical Appearance Characteristics

The radius edge forms as a result of plastic deformation when the piece part is cut under optimal circumstances. The cut band is produced as a result of the shearing operation and is highly burnished. The cutting band's width is roughly equal to the stock material's thickness. The break, which is the outcome of the third step of the cycle, makes up the remaining portion of the cut. The distance between the cutting edges of the punch and the corresponding cutting edges of the die is known as the cutting clearance. The break is close to the piece part's burr side. Nearly no burr should be present. A blank or slug's burr side is always facing the punch, and a punch opening's burr side is always facing the die opening.

4.16.2 Excessive Cutting Clearance

When there is too much clearance, the punch behaves more like a shaping tool than a cutting tool when it comes to the material. The edge radius thus exceeds the tolerance provided for the piece part and does not merge seamlessly into the cut band. The ring that was sliced gets smaller or thins out. The crack starts to look uneven and could even reach the radius of the edge. Large fractures and burrs are produced on the component as a result of the material being forced into the die's clearance gap.

4.16.3 Insufficient Cutting Clearance

Objectionable burrs may appear on the piece part if the cutting clearance is insufficient. When there is insufficient clearance, the burr is caused by compressive forces.

4.16.4 Misalignment of Punch and Die

The piece part will show burring to one side and this information is useful for the toolmaker for detecting the misalignment.

4.16.5 Importance of Cutting Clearance

For the life of the die and the quality part, proper cutting clearance is required. Undesirable piece-part qualities are the result of excessive cutting clearance. Because more punching force is needed, insufficient cutting clearance puts undue strain and wear on the tool's cutting element. The aforementioned rule does not always apply. For instance, circular cutting punches can function properly with less cutting clearance than usual, and decreased cutting clearance can also be employed to defeat slug pulling.

4.16.6 Determining Cutting Clearance

Experience and actual experiments are frequently required to find the ideal clearance. Increasing the cutting clearance is always a fairly straightforward process. A toolmaker always starts with less cutting clearance than he anticipates being required. Always expressed as thickness per side is cutting clearance.

4.16.7 Relationship of Piece-Part and Die Size

The die opening's cutting edge performs the actual cutting of the blank or slug. Therefore, the size of the blank or slug depends on the die opening. The punch determines the size of the punch aperture.

4.16.8 Angular Clearance

In order to relieve the internal pressure of the blank or slug as it goes through the opening, angular clearance is a draught or taper added to the sidewalls of a die opening.

4.16.9 Importance of Angular Clearance

The pressure created inside the die aperture by the blank or the slugs as they are forced through will prevent the blank-through kind of die from operating correctly unless there is a release for the pressure.

4.16.10 Specifying Angular Clearance

Angular clearance should not be expressed as an overall or included angle value, but rather as the amount of clearance per side. The punching and die clearance is what the CNC punching machine and CNC turret punching machine refer to as the distance between the punch and the lower die when the punch is inserted into the lower die, which is often referred to as the overall clearance. The fundamental tenet of choosing the correct blanking die clearance is that the blanking die's punch cross section is often smaller than the die hole. The clearance is the appropriate distance between the punch and the die (Fig. 7.50).

According to the analysis of the blanking deformation process, the upper and lower microcracks created at the edge of the punch and die can coincide with one another when the blanking gap is reasonable. This results in a big brilliant band, a small collapse angle, a small burr, a moderate section taper, and a generally flat part surface for the blanking section. According to the specified regions of Fig. 7.51 below, the quality of blanking parts can produce satisfactory results.

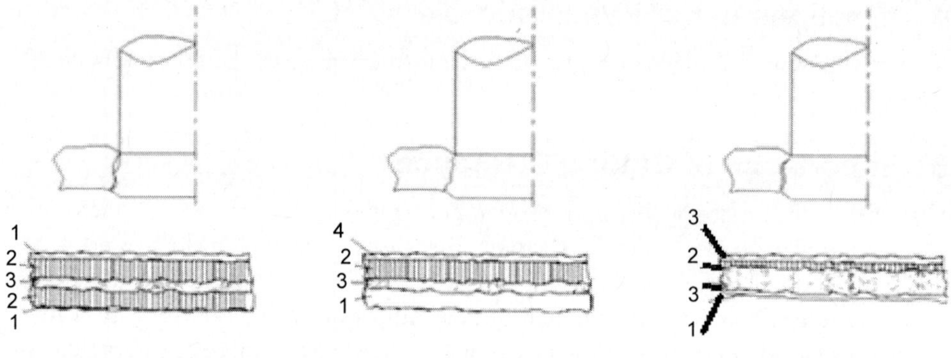

Figure 4.51: The role of die clearance across the edge of punch and die

If the clearance is too tiny during blanking, two bright bands will develop on the blanking part's section, and the burr at the top end is also very large. This is primarily caused by the higher microcrack being located at the punch's edge due to insufficient blanking clearance. To ensure that the upper and lower cracks cannot be heavier than one line, stagger the die edge where the lower microcrack appears by a predetermined amount (see Fig. 7.51). As the punch diminishes, the material wedged between the two cracks will create the second shear, leading in the formation of a second brilliant band and further extension of the burr, which will lower the section quality. The upper microcrack will develop at the punch's edge if the clearance is too large during blanking. The upper and lower cracks cannot be heavier than one line because of the staggered inward location of the lower microcrack near the edge of the die.

With the punch's drop, the material in between the two cracks is extensively stretched before being torn and fractured. On the blanking portion, there is a noticeable fracture zone that reduces the brilliant zone and increases the burr and taper. The section quality declines as the collapse angle rises (see Fig. 7.51).

According to the research above, even if a suitable clearance value is chosen during die design, the uniform distribution of die clearance cannot be ensured because of how the die is processed or put together. The optimal section quality and the side with the smallest gap cannot be attained in the same way. As was already noted, the section feature of a too-small gap will be present, and a too-big gap will be present on the side with a large gap, which is especially noticeable for dies without guide posts. Production must take this into account.

4.17 IMPACT OF CLEARANCE ON OTHER ASPECTS

(1) Influence of blanking clearance on blanking dimensional accuracy. As mentioned earlier, elastic deformation and plastic deformation will occur in metal parts during blanking. This means that there must be elastic deformation when the material is plastic deformation. Because there is elastic deformation in the material during blanking, the elastic deformation of the material will recover after blanking. The recovery of this elastic deformation will cause a certain deviation between the actual size of the blanking part and the edge size of the punch and die. See Fig. 4.52 below.

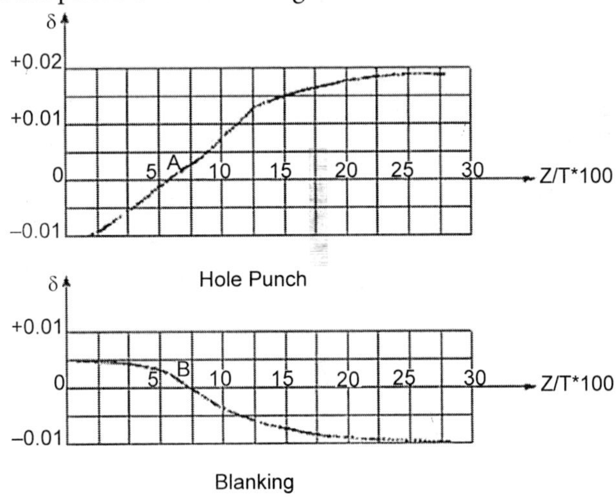

Figure 4.52: The role of die clearance on elastic recovery of blanking [6]

The ordinate in the above Fig. 4.52 is the elastic recovery of the blanking part. The abscissa is the relative clearance of the blanking part. During blanking, we can find from the size change curve of the blanking part that when the blanking clearance gradually increases, the tensile deformation of the deformed metal also increases due to the increase of the tensile stress at the deformed part. After blanking, the compressed metal will recover elastically, so as to reduce the size of blanking parts. This rebound increases with the increase of blanking clearance. When the blanking clearance decreases gradually, the size of the blanking part also decreases. When the clearance is small to a certain extent (point B in Fig. 4.52), the deformation property of the blanking part will also change.

In addition to shear, there is extrusion deformation in the material, which changes the deformation zone from the original tensile state to the compressive state. After blanking, the elasticity of the compressed metal will recover, so that the size of the blanking punch is larger than that of the die edge. During punching, the deformation process and elastic recovery principle are the same as those above, but the measured objects are different. Therefore, the conclusion is opposite to that of blanking parts, that is, the size of punching parts increases with the increase of blanking clearance. When the clearance value is less than a certain value (point A in Fig. 4.52), the punching size will decrease, that is, the size of punching hole is less than that of punch. It is pointed out that the dimensional accuracy of blanking parts mainly depends on the design and machining accuracy of blanking die.

The above analysis is carried out under a certain die manufacturing accuracy, and the influence of clearance on the accuracy is much smaller than that of the die itself.

(2) The impact of blanking clearance on blanking force. The smaller the gap, the greater the compressive stress component in the material deformation zone, the greater the deformation resistance of the material and the greater the blanking force required during blanking. On the contrary, the larger the gap, the greater the tensile stress component in the material deformation area, which reduces the material deformation resistance and the blanking force required during blanking. However, practice has proved that when the gap (single side) gradually increases in the range of 5% ~ 2% of the material thickness, the reduction of blanking force is not obvious.

(3) Influence of blanking clearance on unloading force and pushing force. The smaller the gap, the greater the elastic recovery of the material in the deformation zone, making the punching size smaller and the blanking size larger, so the unloading force and pushing force increase. When the gap increases, due to the elastic recovery of the material, the punching size increases and the blanking size decreases, so it saves labor to unload the material from the punch or push out the parts from the die opening. Generally, when the gap (single side) increases to 10% ~ 20% of the material thickness, the unloading is almost zero.

(4) Influence of blanking clearance on die life. Practice has proved that blanking clearance is the most important factor among many factors affecting die life. In the blanking process, there is fierce friction between the punch and the punched hole, and between the die and the blanking part, and the smaller the gap is, the more serious the friction is, so too small gap is extremely unfavorable to the service life of the die. The larger clearance will reduce the friction between the side of the edge of the punch and the die and the material, and can slow down the adverse impact of the uneven clearance caused by the manufacturing and installation error of the die, so as to improve the service life of the die.

4.18 DETERMINATION OF CLEARANCE VALUE

The so-called reasonable gap means that when this gap is used for blanking, it can obtain satisfactory workpiece section quality, high dimensional accuracy, minimize the blanking force (unloading force and pushing force), and make the die have a long service life. However, it is impossible to meet many of the above requirements at the same time if the numerical requirements of one gap are adopted. Therefore, in production, according to the specific requirements of parts, comprehensively consider the influence of various factors, and appropriately select an appropriate gap range as a reasonable gap. The upper limit is the maximum reasonable gap and the lower limit is the minimum gap, that is, a reasonable gap refers to a range value. In the specific design of the die, it can be selected according to the following principles according to the specific requirements of parts and production.

(i) When there are no special requirements for the cross-section quality of the counter cutting part, in order to improve the service life of the die and reduce the blanking force to obtain greater economic benefits, a larger clearance value can be selected.

(ii) When there are high requirements for the cross-section quality of counter cutting parts, the smaller clearance value shall be selected.

(iii) When designing the cutting-edge size of blanking die, considering the actual situation that the die will be worn in the process of use, which will increase the cutting-edge gap, the cutting-edge size should be calculated according to the minimum gap value.

In the actual work, the die industry has accumulated a large number of empirical values for stamping parts with different thickness of various stamping materials, so the theoretical gap calculation method is only used as a reference.

4.19 PIERCING OPERATION

Punching holes into sheet metal is the process of piercing. Shearing processes include blanking and piercing. When piercing or punching sheet metal, the material that is removed is scrap, and the retained material is the real part. Both metal shearing processes are employed to cut sheet metal. In contrast, when piercing, the punch is made to fit the size of the hole, and room is left in the die. The following are the main variations:

(i) The material section that is cut out of the sheet is what is needed while blanking. In contrast, when piercing, the sheet section that is punched out is scrap.

(ii) The die size determines the blank dimension. The punch's dimension determines the size of the punctured hole.

(iii) As a result, while blanking, the die is created to the part's size and the punch is provided the cutting clearance.

(iv) A sheet is divided into two parts using a mould during the stamping process known as "blanking," which follows a specific contour shape. Blanking, in its simplest form, is the separation of the sheets using a mould (Fig. 4.53).

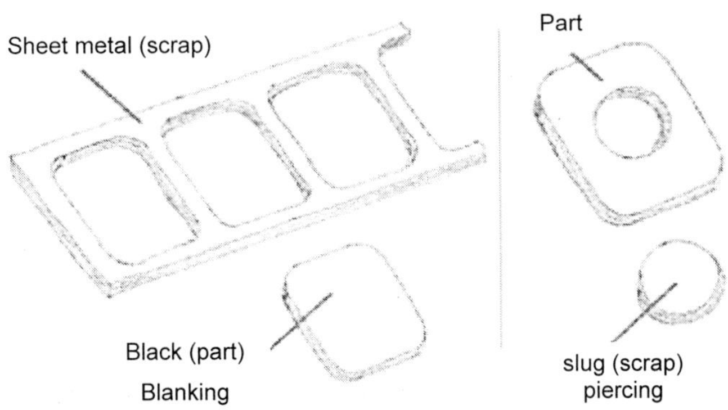

Figure 4.53: Difference between Blanking and Piercing

The sign of the end of the blanking (Fig. 4.54 (a & b)) shows that the punch passes through the sheet into the die. Here the mold for blanking is called as blanking die.

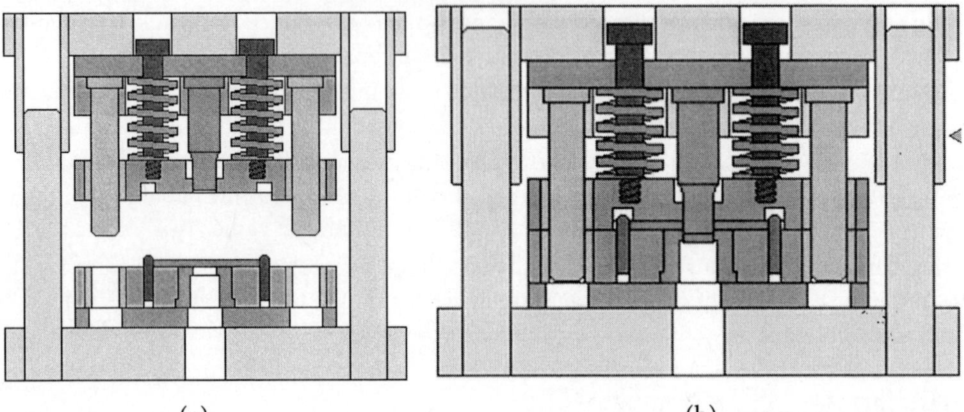

Figure 4.54: Die & mold tooling in Blanking (a) before (b) after the operation

4.20 ANALYSIS OF BLANKING DEFORMATION PROCESS

Figure 4.55 shows force analysis on sheet metal blank during the blanking process. Fig 4.55 (a) shows the moment developed when the mold and the blank begins to contact and Fig 4.55 (b) shows the blank action during the blanking process.

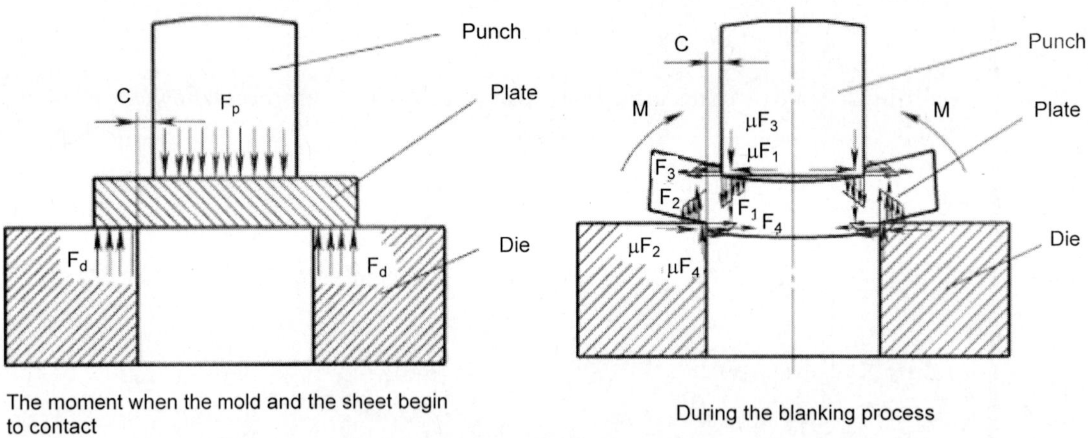

Figure 4.55: Forces in blanking operation in beginning and during the process.

As a result, the punch experiences a sever force variation (Fig. 4.56) due to change in the force of the blanking during punching stroke. When the mold gap is appropriate, the blanking deformation process can be divided into three stages as: Elastic deformation stage, Plastic deformation stage and Fragmentation separation stage.

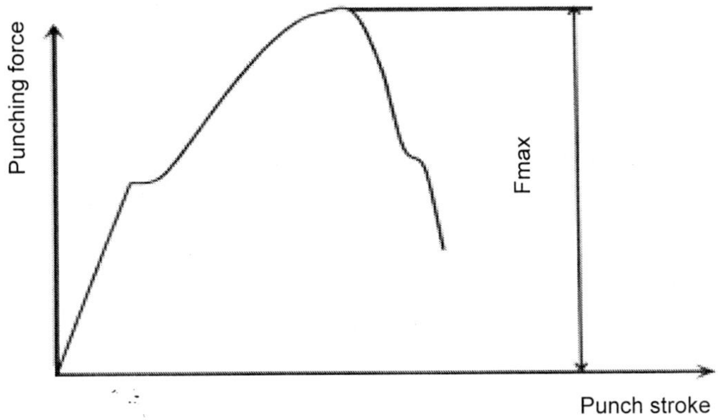

Figure 4.56: Force analysis on blanking operation in beginning and during the process.

4.20.1 Elastic Deformation Stage

At this stage, after the edge of the upper die contacts with the plate, the plate is flattened first, and then the edge of the upper die and the lower die are pressed into the plate respectively. Due to the blanking gap C, the resultant force of the upper die and the resultant force of the lower die are not collinear, so the plate will receive a bending moment Mg', which makes the plate slightly bend under elastic compression. As the upper die continues to descend, the stress on the cutting edge of the material will reach the elastic limit. The stress state of the plate in this process is shown in Fig. 4.57.

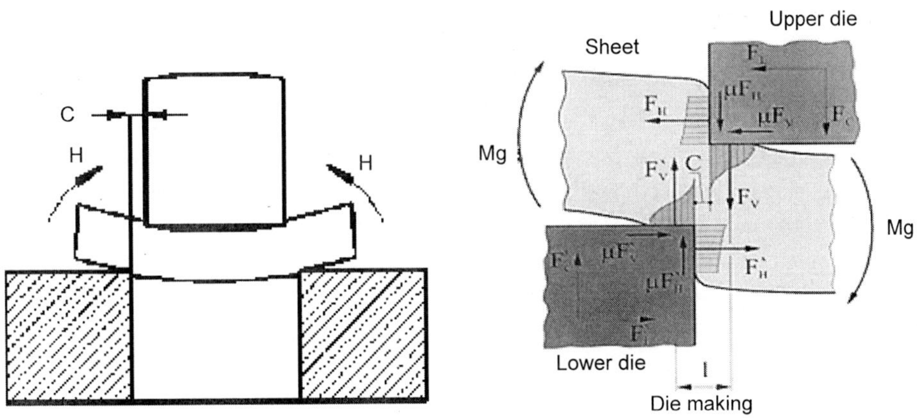

Figure 4.57: Blanking Stress Analysis during elastic stage deformation.

In the figure, F_C is the shear force acting on the upper die, F_C 'is the shear force acting on the lower die, F_L is the transverse force acting on the upper mold, F_L 'is the transverse force acting on the lower die, μ is the friction coefficient, F_H is the horizontal component force received by the plate from the upper die edge, and F_H ' is the horizontal component force received by the plate from the lower die, F_V is the vertical component force received by the plate from the upper die edge, F_V 'is the vertical component force received by the plate from the lower die, M_g is the bending moment of the plate, *I* is the lever arm, and *C* is the blanking clearance.

4.20.2 Plastic Deformation Stage

At this stage, due to the continuous downward movement of the upper die, the stress of the plate increases, and the stress of the material reaches the yield limit, resulting in plastic deformation. With the increase of the degree of plastic deformation, the tensile stress and bending moment in the plate continue to increase, the hardening of the material intensifies, and the material near the edge first reaches the strength limit.

Here four things are common as: larger sag angle, Plastic shearing - bright band, Internal stress reaches the limit and Micro cracks appear near the edge. The stress state of the plate in this process is shown in Fig. 4.58.

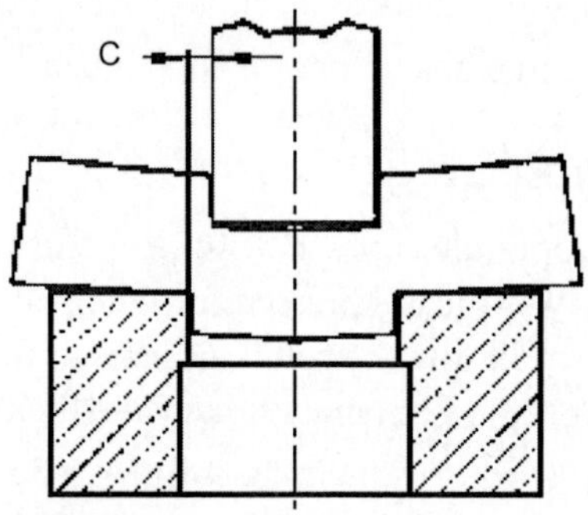

Figure 7.58: Blanking stress analysis during plastic stage deformation

4.20.3 Fragmentation Separation Stage

At the last stage, the pressing depth of the upper die continues to increase, and the cracks first appear on the sides of the upper and lower die edges. At this time, the strain energy stored in the elastic and plastic deformation stage is released, and it extends to the interior of the material along the direction of the maximum shear stress. When the main cracks at the upper and lower die edges coincide, the material is cut off and separated. If the knife edge gap is unreasonable and the two main cracks cannot coincide, a third main crack will appear. This produces a rough and tapered fracture zone and therefore, burr formation occurs. The stress state of the plate in this process is shown in Fig. 4.59.

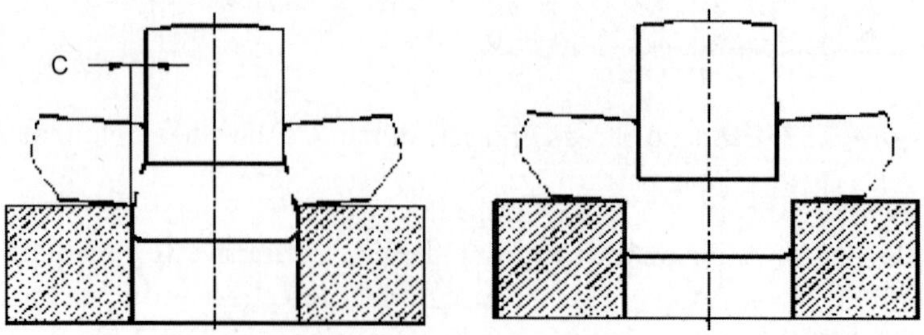

Figure 4.59: Blanking stress analysis during fragmentation stage deformation

Therefore, while considering no elastic spring back, important conclusion (Fig. 7.43) during blanking is drawn as: (i) Blanking part size = die edge size and (ii) Piercing part size = punch edge size. As a result, the punch and die last stage is depicted in Fig. 4.60.

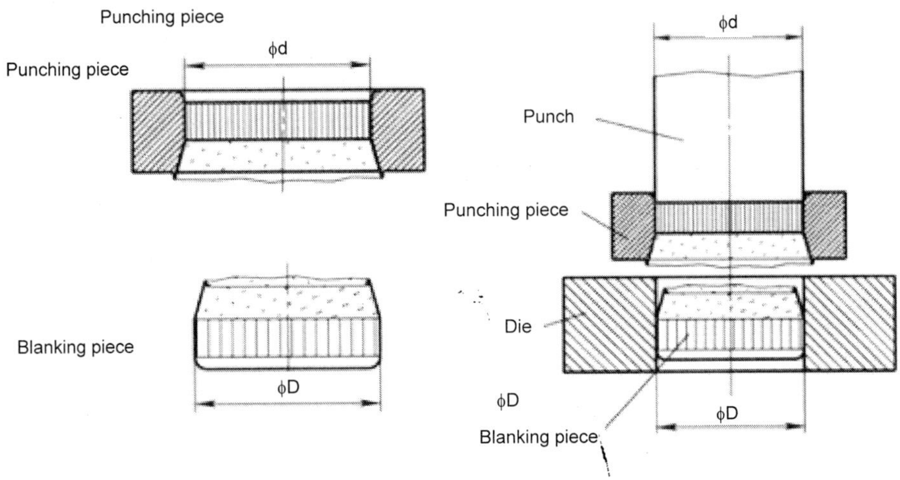

Figure 4.60: Blanking stress analysis during fragmentation stage deformation

The punched deformation zone is generally located in the spindle section of the upper and lower cutting edges as shown in Fig. 4.61.

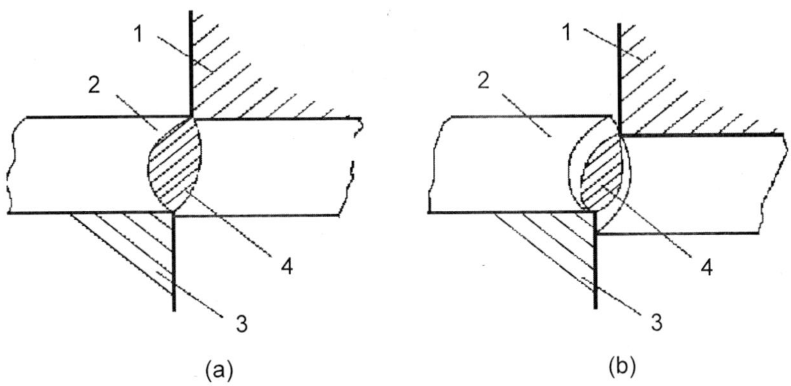

Figure 4.61: Deformation cutting edges location of spindle section (a) the upper and (b) lower

4.20.4 Quality Analysis and Control of Blanking Parts

The quality of blanking parts (Fig. 4.62) refers to: (i) Section quality- vertical, smooth or small burr (ii) Dimensional accuracy- within the tolerances specified in the drawings (iii) Shape error- the shape meets the drawing requirements and (iv) The surface is straight- that is, the arch is small.

The section of the blank part is divided into four component zones under normal clearance (Fig. 4.62 a) as follows: Bright band: plastic shear deformation, which is the area with the best quality. *Collapse zone:* the material near the edge produces bending and tensile deformation. *Fracture zone:* the formation and expansion of cracks. *Burr:* the gap is present, the crack is not generated at the edge of the blade, and the burr is unavoidable. The area where the burr is produced: The crack is a little above the sides of the punch and die, rather than on the blade's tip (Fig. 4.63). The brilliant band is of the highest quality (Fig. 4.62 b).

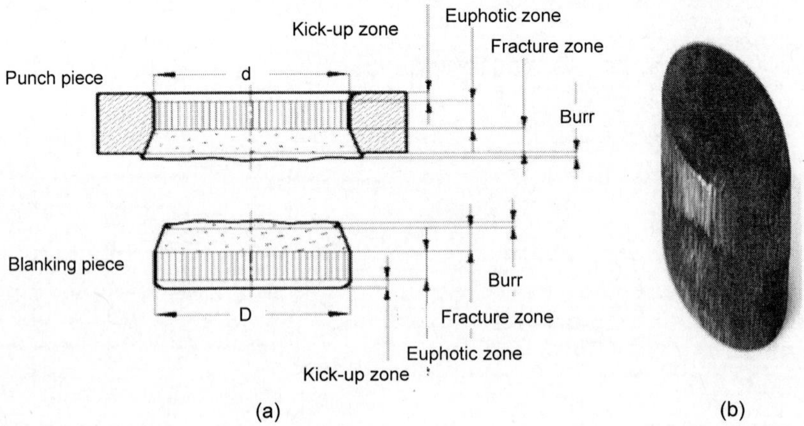

Figure 4.62: Quality of the blanking parts (a) zones and (b) the bright band

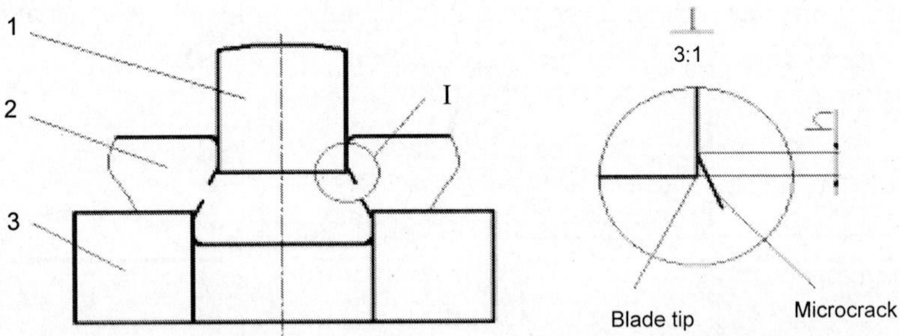

Figure 4.63: Quality of the burr is generated

4.21 OTHER PIERCING TECHNIQUES

These are many piercing techniques. Although technically speaking the cutting procedure is similar, the finished product will differ. These piercing procedures include:

4.21.1 Lancing

Lancing is a partial cutting procedure in which the same punch is used for both bending and piercing. In the example of a rectangular profile, we can state that lancing would be produced by cutting three of the sides and bending the remaining two. Please take note that there is no slug and no material waste during lancing operations.

4.21.2 Shaving

A little quantity of material is removed from a previously pierced hole as part of the finishing process known as shaving. The hole and finish quality are improved by the shaving process. Furthermore, piercing and shaving is the best method for producing precise holes with tight tolerances.

4.21.3 Cut-off

The portion is cut and separated from the sheet metal in this type of piercing procedure. For instance, the cut-off station is frequently the last step in progressive dies, where the stamped result is cut and removed from the strip.

4.21.4 Parting-off

Similar to a cutoff procedure, this. The distinction between parts off and cutting off, however, is that splitting off results in material waste. Depending on how the contour is shaped, there may be a large amount of wastage. However, splitting produced two cut paths that can differ and are therefore helpful in situations when cutting can be done.

4.21.5 Precautions in Sheet Piercing

Cutting clearance is a crucial factor in both blanking and piercing. As you are already aware, the die has a cutting clearance for piercing operations. This implies that the die will be larger and the piercing punch will be created to the desired hole size. The type of material to be punched and the sheet thickness affect how much cutting clearance is required. Typically, 3% to 10% of the sheet thickness per side clearance is used. Less clearance is needed when the material is softer, while more clearance is required when the material is firmer. Correct calculation and provision of the necessary cutting clearance quantity is crucial. This is necessary to prevent slug pulling, jamming, and excessive wear and tear.

4.21.6 Piercing Punch and Die Material

Punch and die materials ought to be ear resistant, compressive strong, and temperature resistant. Along with the characteristics of the sheet metal that needs to be cut and the quantity needed, take into account these tool material parameters. Tool steels high in carbon and high in chromium are typically utilised. To an HRC of 60–62, the punch and die must be hardened and tempered. HSS (high speed steel) is a preferable option for small, quickly breakable punches. Another material that performs well when numerous parts need to be cut is tungsten carbide. This is due to the fact that carbide can resist higher temperatures while still maintaining cutting edges that are sharp for a longer period of time.

These two issues, known as slug stacking and slug pulling, are typically encountered by persons during piercing or pounding.

(a) Slug Stacking or Jamming

Particularly when penetrating soft and thin sheet metals, this is a prevalent issue. The most common causes of slug stacking are excessive lubricant use, an excessive amount of land length in the die, and insufficient cutting clearance between the punch and die. One of the alternatives is to provide the die ample clearance. Use a new, less sticky lubrication or cut back on the amount of cutting oil. One can also attempt to shorten the length of the land so that the slug drops freely without stacking. As counter-bore relief can result in slug tumbling due to the slug sliding at an angle from the edge of counter-bore relief, it is also advised to offer angular relief in the die instead.

(b) Slug Pulling

The situation with slug pulling is more significant. This is the point at which the punched slug clings to the punch and emerges out the die. Slug pulling can occur for a number of reasons, such as high clearance, sticky lubricants, the cut profile's form, etc. However, proper methods for slug pulling include attaching a spring-loaded ejector pin to the punch, using an air blow through punch, and giving a shear angle on the piercing punch, among other things. In addition, one can employ a suction system and slug retainer die bushes to keep the slug inside the die.

UNIT SUMMARY

Metal forming is one of the chips less manufacturing processes. These operations are performed by the press and press tools. Presses can be classified into different categories depending upon their capacity, capabilities and mechanisms used for their operations. Presses can also be categorized depending upon their construction and frame as straight side, adjustable bed type, open end honing press. Method of transmission of power from the place of its generation to the place of its utilization also serve an important criterion for the classification of presses. In general, a press is described by its main parts like base, frame, ram, pitman, driving mechanism, controlling mechanism, flywheel, brakes, balster plate all these parts along with their functions are described here. Die and punch are the integral part of a press tool system. Die and punch are normally fitted to a press tool system. Punch and die can be fitted to a press by different methods as described in the unit. Different types of dies are also described in the unit, which are used for different types of workpieces and operations. Accuracy of the operation largely depends on the accuracy of die and punch. So die and punch should be designed and manufactured very carefully. The important considerations for designing die set and punch for press tool system are described in details.

EXERCISES

Multiple Choice Questions

Questions for self-assessment

1. The rolling action between engaging gear teeth is due to:
   (a) high viscosity lubricants
   (b) points of tangency between teeth
   (c) the involute curve form
   (d) gear rotational synchronization

2. The imaginary rolling circle produced by meshed gears during rotation is called the:
   (a) Pitch Circle (b) Base Circle
   (c) Dedendum Circle (d) Addendum Circle
3. The most common type of gear is the:
   (a) spur gear (b) helical gear
   (c) straight bevel gear (d) hypoid gear
4. A worm gear is an example of a gear type used along:
   (a) a. parallel axes (b) b. non-intersecting, non-parallel axes
   (c) c. connecting axes (d) d. intersecting axes
5. The most common gear manufacturing method is:
   (a) forging (b) machining
   (c) injection molding (d) stamping
6. Hobbing is used to produce only:
   (a) helical gears (b) spur gears
   (c) external gear teeth (d) internal gear teeth
7. Gear form cutting involves the use of:
   (a) hobbing and shaping (b) shaping and milling
   (c) multiple stacked blanks (d) broaching and milling
8. The gear finishing method typically performed prior to heat treatment is:
   (a) honing (b) continuous grinding
   (c) form grinding (d) shaving
9. Which of the following is a gear finishing operation:
   (a) Milling (b) Hobbing
   (c) Shaping (d) Shaping and brushing
10. Gears are best mass produced by:
    (a) Milling (b) Hobbing
    (c) Shaping (d) Forming
11. The gears are used to connect two parallel shafts except
    (a) Spur gear (b) Helical gear
    (c) Double helical gears (d) Bevel gears
12. The gears used to connect non-parallel and non-intersecting shafts is
    (a) Straight bevel gears (b) Spiral bevel gears
    (c) Spiral gears (d) Double helical gears
13. To connect two intersecting shafts, we use
    (a) Spur gear (b) Helical gear
    (c) Worm and wheel (d) Bevel gears
14. The gear used to convert rotary motion into translating motion is
    (a) Worm and wheel (b) Crown gear
    (c) Rack and pinion (d) Spiral Bevel gear

15. Which of the following type of gear has inclined teeth?
    (a) Spur gear (b) Helical gear
    (c) Spiral gear (d) All of the above
16. The point of contact of two pitch circles of mating gears is called
    (a) Pressure point (b) Pitch point
    (c) Module (d) Contact point
17. Thread rolling is restricted to
    (a) ferrous materials (b) ductile materials
    (c) hard materials (d) none of the above
18. Teeth of internal spur gears can be accurately cut in a
    (a) milling machine (b) gear shaping machine
    (c) slotting machine (d) hobbing machine
19. Gear hobbing produces more accurate gears than milling because in hobbing
    (a) there is a continuous indexing operation (b) pressure angle is larger than in milling
    (c) hob and work piece both are rotating (d) a special multi-tooth cutter (hob) is used
20. Internal gear cutting operation can be performed by
    (a) milling (b) shaping with rack cutter
    (c) shaping with pinion cutter (d) hobbing
21. Reaming is primarily used for achieving
    (a) Higher MRR (b) Higher surface finish
    (c) Higher speed of machining (d) None of the above
22. The purpose of heat treatment is
    (a) To change the mechanical property of steel
    (b) To change the internal structure of steel
    (c) To change the appearance of the component
    (d) To change the chemical property of steel
23. Approximately hardness of HSS milling cutter is
    (a) 45 HRC (b) 52 HRC
    (c) 62 HRC (d) 75 HRC
24. Lower critical temperature of high carbon steel while hardening is
    (a) 960°C (b) 900°C
    (c) 723°C (d) 560°C
25. Which one of the following processes is used for hardening the surface of tool steel
    (a) Carburizing (b) Cyaniding
    (c) Induction hardening (d) Hardening
26. The height from the top of the bed to the bottom of the press ram is called?
    (a) Die height (b) Maximum height
    (c) Shut height (d) Center height

27. Which of the following holds the punch in position?
    (a) Bolster plate (b) Punch holder
    (c) Lower shoe (d) Lipper shoe
28. Which die is used for more than one cutting operation per stroke?
    (a) Blanking die (b) Piercing die
    (c) Compound die (d) Progressive die
29. Which die is mostly used to produce the washer?
    (a) Blanking die (b) Piercing die
    (c) Progressive die (d) Compound die
30. By which operation a cup is formed from a flat blank?
    (a) Trimming (b) Drawing
    (c) Forming (d) Bending
31. When a sectional die block is used?
    (a) Die cavity is medium (b) Die cavity is too large
    (c) Die block is too small (d) Die block is too large
32. What is the name of operation for making hole in a work piece with the help of die?
    (a) Trimming (b) Piercing
    (c) Drilling (d) Boring
33. Presses are generally employed in ___ production of ___ components.
    (a) mass, identical (b) mass, dissimilar
    (c) job, identical (d) job, dissimilar
34. Which of the following is power press?
    (a) hand press (b) fly press
    (c) hydraulic press (d) all of the above
35. In press, which of the following mechanism used for applying power to ram.
    (a) Rack and pinion (b) Pneumatic
    (c) Hydraulic (d) All of the above
36. The press can be used for
    (a) Shearing (b) Extruding
    (c) Forging (d) All of the above
37. In fly press, the ram is moved by means of a
    (a) crankshaft (b) screw
    (c) both (a) and (b) (d) none of the above
38. A thick plate fastened to the bed of the press which supports and holds the die assembly, is known as
    (a) supporting plate (b) Bolster plate
    (c) holding plate (d) rigid plate
39. The size of press is expressed in terms of
    (a) Its stroke length (b) The maximum force its ram can exert
    (c) Die space (d) Ram speed

40. The total opening between the ram and the bed when the ram is in its extreme down position
    (a) Stroke length (b) Die space
    (c) Shut height (d) Press adjustment
41. Ram speed is calculated as
    (a) Meters/minutes (b) Rounds per minute
    (c) Strokes per minute (d) None of the above
42. Which of the following acts as a support for the die block?
    (a) Punch holder (b) Punch
    (c) Die shoe (d) Stops
43. Which of the following help in obtaining correct alignment of the punch holder with the die shoe?
    (a) Guide posts (b) Stops
    (c) Pilot (d) None of the above
44. The following helps in freeing the punch from the scrap in the return stroke?
    (a) Knock out pins (b) Stripper
    (c) Pilot (d) Punch plate
45. Following is a multi-operation die.
    (a) Cutting die (b) Forming die
    (c) Compound die (d) All of the above
46. The following die is used for two or more cutting operations in single stroke of the ram?
    (a) Forming die (b) Compound die
    (c) Combination die (d) All of the above
47. In which of the following type of die, a combination of cutting and some other operation can be performed at a single station?
    (a) Cutting die (b) Forming die
    (c) Compound die (d) Combination die
48. ___ Clearance is that value of the clearance which is just sufficient to enable production of a blank with a clean edge.
    (a) Minimum (b) Maximum
    (c) Optimum (d) Average
49. Following is not a shearing operation.
    (a) Blanking (b) Piercing
    (c) Punching (d) Forming
50. Which of the following is a drawing operation?
    (a) Embossing (b) Curling
    (c) Trimming (d) All of the above

ANSWERS															
1.	(c)	2.	(a)	3.	(a)	4.	(b)	5.	(b)	6.	(c)	7.	(d)	8.	(d)
9.	(d)	10.	(b)	11.	(d)	12.	(c)	13.	(d)	14.	(c)	15.	(b)	16.	(b)

17.	(b)	18.	(b)	19.	(a)	20.	(b)	21.	(b)	22.	(a)	23.	(c)	24.	(c)
25.	(c)	26.	(c)	27.	(b)	28.	(c)	29.	(d)	30.	(b)	31.	(d)	32.	(b)
33.	(a)	34.	(c)	35.	(d)	36.	(d)	37.	(b)	38.	(b)	39.	(b)	40.	(c)
41.	(c)	42.	(c)	43.	(a)	44.	(b)	45.	(c)	46.	(b)	47.	(d)	48.	(c)
49.	(d)	50.	(a)												

Short and Long Answer Type Questions

Gear Making

1. What is a gear generating?
2. What are stepped gears?
3. What are the gear forming methods?
4. What are the differences between gear shaping and gear hobbing?
5. What are the differences between gear milling and gear hobbing?
6. What is the list of some methods under the gear forming and the gear generation methods?
7. What is the Fellows gear cutting method?
8. Which gear manufacturing method is mostly preferred in industry?
9. Is it true that the reverse gear is weaker than the other gears?
10. What are the methods for maintaining the gear motor?
11. What are the differences between gear cutting and gear shaping in points?
12. What are compare and contrast (as referred to gear making), gear forming and machining (with examples), form cutting and generation (with necessary diagrams), and gear hobbing and generation?
13. What is gear and mechanism?
14. Which methods are used to enhance the performance of gears?
15. What is the difference between gear grinding and gear shaving?

Press working

1. How is sheet cutting operation carried out?
2. List out the various sheet cutting operations.
3. Mention the three different ways of working sheet metal in presses.
4. Classify sheet metal operations
5. State the advantages of press working operations.
6. What are the applications of press working operations?
7. Name some types of sheet forming operations.

8. List out the press working terminology.
9. When will be hydraulically driven presses used?
10. How will you select the proper material for press tools?
11. What factors are considered for selecting an appropriate press for a given job?
12. List down the material used for press working operations.
13. What is a progressive die? When should a progressive die be used?
14. Explain the function of bolster plate in press tool.
15. What are the methods of holding pilots?
16. What are the types of stock stop?
17. State the function of a knockout.
18. What is the purpose of pilot?
19. List down the various methods of arranging guide pins in the die set.
20. What are the types of die set?

PRACTICALS

1. Study various gear manufacturing processes.
2. Study various gear generating processes.
3. Perform gear teeth finishing using lapping.
4. Study various presses used based on the number of slides.
5. Study the punch and die clearance concept for blanking and piercing.

KNOW MORE

Explore the historical gear making work in aluminum, copper, and steel using different methods & processes. See press working process as an old practices of squeezing action or similar operation in your near vicinity. Identify similar gear making and press working machines and processes around your locality and try to find how it is evolved with time as one could see the modern gear hobbing and hydraulic press working operations today. One should observe it carefully.

SUGGESTED RESOURCES FOR FURTHER READING/ LEARNING

Reference books & websites referred

1. Manufacturing technology – P N Rao, Tata McGraw-Hill Publications
2. Elements of workshop Technology (Volume I & II) – S. K. Hajra Chaudary, Bose & Roy, Media Promoters and Publishers Limited.
3. Production Technology (Volume I & II) – O. P. Khanna & Lal, Dhanpat Rai Publications.

4. Fundamental of metal cutting and machine tools– B. L. Juneja, New age international limited.
5. Manufacturing Technology, Metal Cutting & Machine tools– P. N. Rao, Tata McGraw- Hill Publications
6. A Text book of Production Technology: Manufacturing processes –P.C. Sharma, S. Chand & Com. Pvt. Ltd., New Delhi
7. Production Technology – R.B. Gupta, Satya Prakashan, New Delhi
8. Fundamentals of Design & Manufacturing- G K Lal, Vijay Gupta, N. V. Readdy, NarosaPub. House, ND.
9. https://engineeringlearn.com/wp-content/uploads/2021/02/Types-of-Reduction-Gear-1.jpg
10. https://tse4.mm.bing.net/th?id=OIP.RBfCXaE1rLNDVWa1tGGQFQHaFI&pid=Api&P=0
11. https://m.media-amazon.com/images/I/71T+cX5mRsL._AC_SL1500_.jpg
12. https://tse3.mm.bing.net/th?id=OIP.utVDezXmGKaLNydQqafmRQHaDC&pid=Api&P=0
13. https://cdn.britannica.com/00/99000-050-6F49C304/components-quartz-watch.jpg
14. https://img2.cgtrader.com/items/713496/8056cf37b7/large/gear-mechanism-set-3d-model-max-obj-mtl-3ds-fbx-c4d-lwo-lw-lws.jpg
15. https://tse3.mm.bing.net/th?id=OIP.yACWYN5ZMyFcB3ewQDZ8qgHaE7&pid=Api&P=0
16. http://www.scrapfx.com.au/store/images/cogs-stamp.jpg
17. https://image.made-in-china.com/2f0j00sKpErcNhZYqB/Fine-Blanking-Gears.jpg
18. https://tse2.mm.bing.net/th?id=OIP.BD3S6GTGU9WF3ty5GHT1BgAAAA&pid=Api&P=0

VIDEOS

Gear making

https://www.youtube.com/watch?v=B0XSsa79Y1w
https://www.youtube.com/watch?v=XZgsV0AZJJ0

Press working

https://www.youtube.com/watch?v=J_d8IRT9r7E
https://www.youtube.com/watch?v=eWHv3Bexg5I
https://www.youtube.com/watch?v=bIKCuE3Me5c

5 Grinding and Finishing Processes

Grinding and finishing processes: Principles of metal removal by Grinding; Abrasives – Natural & Artificial; Bonds and binding processes: Vitrified, silicate, shellac, rubber, bakelite; Factors affecting the selection of grind wheels: size and shape of wheel, kind of abrasive, grain size, grade and strength of bond, structure of grain, spacing, kinds of bind material; Standard marking systems: Meaning of letters & numbers sequence of marking, Grades of letters; Grinding machines classification: Cylindrical, Surface, Tool & Cutter grinding machines; Construction details; Principle of centreless grinding; Advantages & limitations of centreless grinding;

Finishing Processes: by grinding: Honing, Lapping, Super finishing; Electroplating: Basic principles, Plating metals, applications; hot dipping: Galvanizing, Tin coating, Parkerising, Anodizing; Metal spraying: wire process, powder process and applications; Organic coatings: Oil base Paint, Lacquer base, Enamels, Bituminous paints, rubber base coating; finishing specifications.

UNIT SPECIFIC / LEARNING OBJECTIVE

Objective of this Unit in to Talk About Following Aspects

- To introduce significance of Grinding Process and various finishing process function
- To learning about the importance of grinding methods and finishing operations and their principles
- To introduce the underlying advantages and applications of Grinding processes and finishing operations and their types
- To introduce various grinding and finishing operations
- To understand the significance of various types of Grinding methods, and metal finishing working methods and their significance
- To learn about grinding machines & their specification and metal finishing operations & their applications

Additionally, few fundamental questions for self-assessment based on fundamentals are also included in this Unit in form of recall, application, comprehension, analysis and synthesis. There are further suggested readings and reference for reader's assistance.

RATIONALE

Grinding is an old art of metal machining at micro level. The grinding quality varies with different grinding wheel abrasives used and their working conditions affecting the surface finish of products. Principles of metal removal by grinding is quite different as compared to conventional machining operations that depends on the grind wheel grain size and shape, kind of abrasive used, grade and strength of bond, structure of grain, spacing and kinds of binding material used. Various grinding machines are Cylindrical, Surface, Tool & Cutter grinding etc. Centreless grinding is unique process of fine finishing. Finishing of metal surfaces are also done with Honing, Lapping and super finishing operations. Electroplating and hot dipping by Galvanizing, Tin coating, Parkerising, Anodizing is also used as industrial methods of finishing. Metal spraying using wire and metal powder process used for hard facing of metal surfaces. Organic coatings such as Oil-based Paint, Lacquer base, Enamels, Bituminous paints, rubber base coating are also very common for Finishing of metallic surfaces. In this section all such topics are discussed in details.

PRE-REQUISITES

A course on Basic Mechanical Engineering (MEPC102)

LEARNING OUTCOMES

U5-O1: Ability to choose suitable work-piece for grinding job under different processes and their finishing process jobs.

U5-O2: Ability to choose suitable grinding method/process for fine grinding of metallic surfaces & fine metal finishing with proper process and machine tools and their operation.

U5-O3: Ability to choose suitable grinding operations and proper grinding wheels for grinding & finishing of components .

U5-O4: choose suitable working conditions and parameters for grinding and finishing operations.

U5-O5: Ability to predict the behavior of grinding quality and its dimensions after grinding and finishing of components for various applications.

COURSE OBJECTIVES

- To understand the importance of grinding and finishing processes and equipments.
- To study and recognise various types of grinding methods and finishing methods and machines, their parts and operations.
- To be able to select, operate and control the appropriate grinding and finishing manufacturing operations for specific applications.

Mapping of learning outcomes and course objectives

Unit-5 Outcomes	EXPECTED MAPPING WITH COURSE OUTCOMES (1- Weak Correlation; 2- Medium correlation; 3- Strong Correlation)					
	CO-1	CO-2	CO-3	CO-4	CO-5	CO-6
U5-O1	1	2	3			
U5-O2	1	2	3			
U5-O3	1	2	3			
U5-O4	1	2	3			
U5-O5	1	2	3			

5.1 INTRODUCTION TO GRINDING PROCESSES

To grind means to abrade, to wear away by friction, or to sharpen something. In manufacturing it refers to the removal of metal by a rotating abrasive wheel. Wheel action is similar to a milling cutter. The cutting wheel is composed of many small grains bonded together, each one acting as a miniature cutting point. Therefore, grinding operation is a method of machining workpieces by the use of a rotary abrasive tool, called "grinding wheel" as shown in Figure 5.1. Grinding is a unit operation that reduces solid matter into smaller particles.

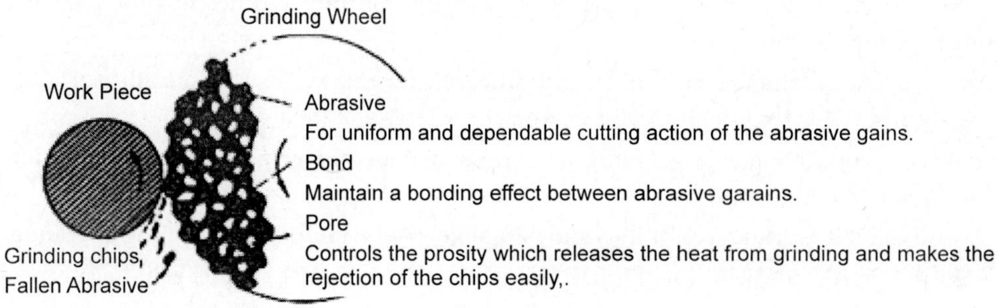

Figure 5.1: Grinding Process

People have been using grinding since the dawn of time, according to ancient technologies. Grinding stone tools were utilized as this technology in the Paleolithic epoch. The advancement of grinding technology was afterwards aided by the introduction of metal equipment. It is yet contemporary, nevertheless, to create a true grinding machine. Early in the 19th century, individuals continued to grind by turning a natural grindstone and allowing it to come into touch with the thing to be processed. In the United States, the first grinder was created in 1864. This was a tool used to mount a grinding wheel automatically on a lathe's slide tool holder. Twelve years later, in the United States, Mr. Brown created a universal grinder that is similar to modern grinders.

Artificial grinding stones became necessary with the invention of grinding wheels (1892). Humanity has long wished to find a way to create grinding stones that are more wear-resistant than natural ones. An American named Mr. Acheson created silicon carbide, a synthetic grinding stone commonly known as C abrasive, in 1892 with great success using coke and sand. Due to this success, grinding machines are being employed more frequently. The accuracy of the grinding machine is increasing in the future due to the continued development of the bearings and guide rails, and it is moving in a professional direction.

The fine grains of abrasive materials used to make the grinding wheels (Fig. 5.1) are held together by a binding substance known as a "bond." Each distinct grain, which has an uneven shape, serves as a cutting element (a single point cutting tool). The type of grinding might be either rough or finishing (precision grinding). A typical technique for eliminating superfluous material from castings, forgings, and weldments is rough grinding. It is also used to remove or snag thin fins, sharp edges, burrs, and other undesirable projections from a variety of types of workpieces. When it comes to generating surfaces on objects with higher dimensional accuracy and a finer surface finish than is possible with other traditional equipment, precision grinding is the primary way.

Since the grits' cutting edges are so thin, it is able to refine surfaces with a significantly higher degree of polish and dimension precision than with conventional machining techniques. Abrasive material, grit size, bonding material, wheel structure, which refers to the relative spacing of grains, and wheel grade, which refers to the wheel's ability to hold on to abrasive grains, are the parameters of grinding.

5.1.1 Structure of Grinding Wheel

The quantitative relationship and arrangement of the grains, bonds, and voids (pores) in a wheel define its structure (or, more simply, the spacing of the grains). The voids or spaces give cutting fluid and chips access to enter and exit cuts, respectively. More grains will fit into the surface unit and there will be fewer pores in a structure that is denser. The tool has more pores and a wider spacing between the abrasive grains in an open structure. A grinding wheel is harder and more durable the denser its structure is. However, when chopped chips accumulate on the wheel face, the wheel becomes increasingly "clogged" or "laden."

The open design improves cutting efficiency by preventing cut chips from loading or fouling the wheel face. The percentage of the bond to the overall wheel volume might range from 10% to 30%, giving rise to either very close or open abrasive spacing. The structure of the grinding wheels is predetermined. According to the amount of abrasive grains in the wheel, the structures are designated by numbers ranging from 0 to 12 as follows: (i) Dense structure: 0, 1, 2, 3 (ii) Medium structure: 4, 5, 6, 7, 8 (iii) Open structure: 9, 10, 11, 12. Lapping, final grinding, and polishing are the major uses for dense structures with plenty of grain and small pores. When a high standard of surface finish is required, medium structures 4 and 5 are used in the grinding of hard and brittle materials. Structures 7 and 8 are utilised for soft material surface grinding, while Structure 6 is used for cylindrical grinding. Although activities can be carried out more productively with open structures, wheel durability is reduced. They are applied to high-speed grinding.

Abrasive gain is marked according to the mesh size of the abrasive or grit, for example, grain sizes (μm). For instance, D126 stands for Diamond grain of 126 μm, and B46 represents Cubic Boron Nitride of 46 um. Table 5.1 lists many grain varieties, along with their characteristics and potential uses. Some of the toughest abrasives utilised in grinding operations are depicted in Fig. 5.2.

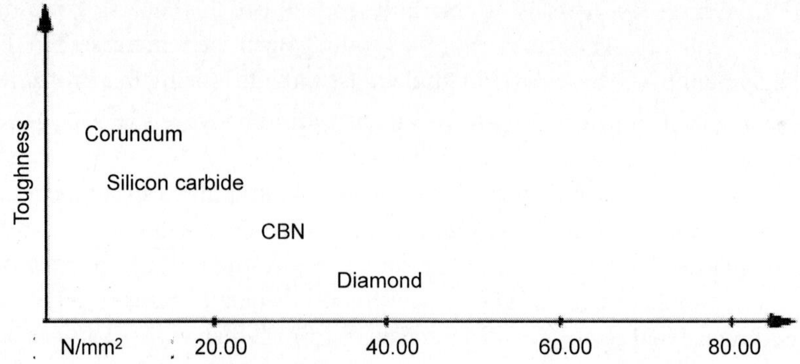

Figure 5.2: Hardness of some of the hardest abrasives

The majority of the time, bonds are used to hold together the fine abrasive material grains that make up wheels. Each distinct grain, which has an uneven shape, serves as a cutting element (a single point cutting tool). The type of grinding might be either rough or finishing (precision grinding). A typical technique for eliminating superfluous material from castings, forgings, and weldments is rough grinding. It is also used to remove or snag thin fins, sharp edges, burrs, and other undesirable projections from a variety of types of workpieces.

In contrast to other manufacturing techniques, precision grinding is one of the main production methods for cutting materials that are too tough to be machined by other conventional tools or for generating surfaces on products with higher dimensional accuracy and a finer surface quality. Since the grits' cutting edges are so thin, it is able to refine surfaces with a significantly higher degree of polish and dimension precision than with conventional machining techniques.

5.1.2 Grinding Ratio

The volume of material removed from the job per unit volume of wheel wear is referred to as the grinding ratio. It is a very helpful term to characterize a material's "grindability." Utilizing a set of particular boundary conditions, this ratio is experimentally calculated. The ratio will therefore change depending on the type of operation, the type of grinding wheel, the type of grinding fluid, speeds and feeds, and other factors for a given material.

Table 5.1: Grain types and their properties

Grain type	Proportion	Profiteroles	Area Application
NK Normal corundum	95.97% Al_2O_3	high durability	Low allow steel, in particular for high materid removal performance when rough grinding
EK Precious white corundum	99.9% Al_2O_3	vary hard and brittle	Board of uses for precious grinding such tool, Round and flat grinding
HK Normal corundum with Precious corundum	98% Al_2O_3	high durability very hard and brittle	Well suited for grinding unharded and low alloy steel all precision grinding also.

Grain type	Proportion	Profiteroles	Area Application
HKs Melted semi-precious corundum	98% Al_2O_3	high durability than precious corundum	Main application are as are precious and tool grinding
EKd Precious pink corundum	over 99% Al_2O_3	vary hard higher grain durability than precious corundum	Outstandingly suitable for flat profile during and saw-blade sharpening.
FF Ruby Corundum	98% Al_2O_3	vary hard, high residence to wear	Used for HSS steel grinding alloy steel
EKa Single-crystal corundum	99.2% Cr_20_3	very high grain durability	For Grinding HSS steel and for tod grinding.
EKT Chrome- titanium oxide	99.33% Al_2O_3 0.25% TiO_3	more durable than precious corundum, less hard	Machine leaming for alloy and thermally sensitive steel
Alloyed corundum NAXOS-KSB	Micro-crystalline 96% Al_2O_3	extremely durable, 15% harder than precious corundum	Used for almost all grinding process if the machine is designed appropriately (rigidity)
SB Sintered bauxite	NK or NK + ZrO_3	extremely durable	Exclusively for highly compacted grinding wheel for high pressure grinding of austenitic steels.
SCg Silicon carbide green	98% SiC	extremely hard and brittle	Used for hard brittle and metallic material cast iron (to some extent) and austenitic steels
SC Silicon carbide	97% SiC	hard and britle	For rough grinding of cast materials
CNB Boron nitride	100% BN	high hardness, resistance to wear and breakage	Grinding of hard alloy's containing carbide tool steels, special steel HSS, etc.
D Diamond	100% C	High hardness and durability	Grinding of amorphous, extremely hard materials hard metals concrete natural stone

5.2 PRINCIPLES OF METAL REMOVAL BY GRINDING

The mechanics of metal removal regulate the removal of metal via grinding. Let's look at Fig. 5.3 to better grasp the theory of grinding. A grinding wheel (width W, lenghth lw) is used to grind a metal workpiece at n rpm (velocity V) and fd feed. It is expected that (i) the work piece is fed into contact with the abrasive wheel as it rotates. (ii) Material is removed as a result of friction between the abrasive particles and the workpiece.

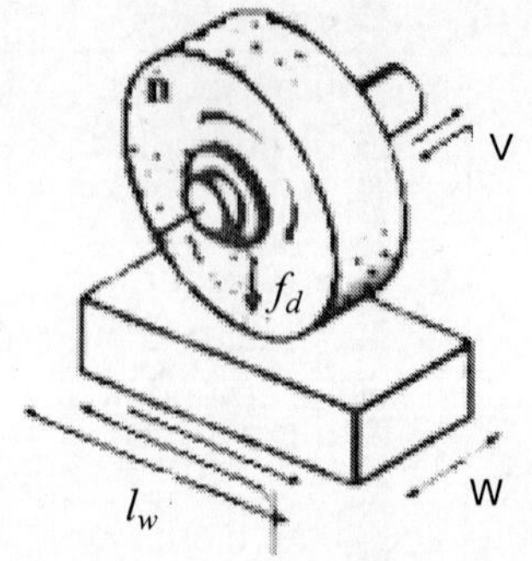

Figure 5.3: Grinding wheel and workpiece interaction

5.2.1 Chip Geometry

Let us consider the Grinding chip formation geometry as shown in Fig. 5.4 (a). As with rolling contact length, the chip length can be defined as: $l = \sqrt{D.d}.$ Where, D is grinding wheel diameter and d is the depth of cut as shown.

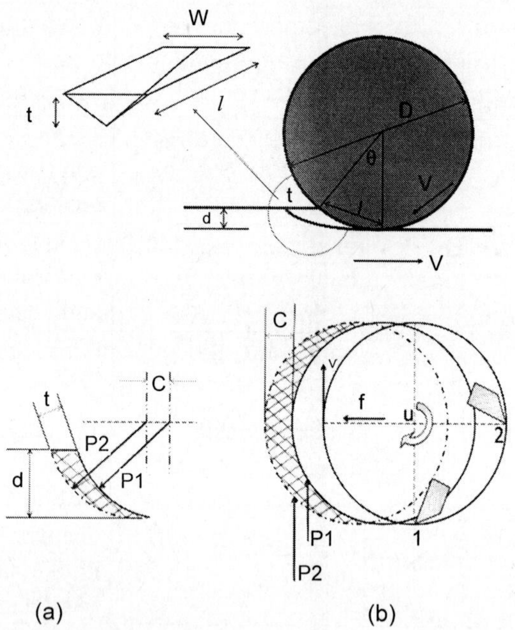

Figure 5.4: (a) Grinding chip formation geometry and (b) one chip geomet

5.2.2 Material Removal Rate (MRR)

If v is the workpiece velocity, d is depth of cut and b is width of cut, the material removal rate (MRR), can be obtained as:

$$\text{MRR} = v\,d\,b$$

As shown in Fig. 5.4 (a & b) (enlarged view in circle), the chips have a triangular cross-section, and ratio (r) of chip thickness (t) to chip width (w) can be found as:

$$r = \frac{w}{t} \approx 10 \text{ to } 20$$

Therefore, the average volume per chip can be evaluated as:

$$Vol_{chip} = \frac{1}{2} - w\frac{1}{2}tl = +\frac{1}{4}wtl$$

Let us refer the Fig. 5.4 (b) for one chip geometry. The number of chips removed per unit time n can be found as:

$$n = Vbc$$

Where c = number of cutting edges (grains) per unit area (typically, 0.1 to 10 per mm^2), and V is the peripheral wheel velocity.

Combining the above, MRR can be obtained as:
MRR = $vdb = n$ Vol_{chip}, i.e.

$$vdb = Vbc\frac{1}{4}wtl$$

Since, $l = \sqrt{D.d}$. and w = r t

$$vdb = Vbc\frac{1}{4}rtt\sqrt{D.d}$$

Therefore,
$$t^2 = \frac{4vd}{Vcr\sqrt{Dd}}$$

And so, the Chip thickness (t) is evaluated as:

$$t = \sqrt{\frac{4v}{Vcr}\sqrt{\frac{d}{D}}}$$

5.2.3 Specific Grinding Energy

The specific grinding energy, u, consist of chip formation, plowing, and sliding. Therefore,

$$u = u_{chip} + u_{uplowing} + u_{chsliding}$$

Total grinding force. This force is important for grinding and it can be evaluated. For this one may get the total grinding force from power calculation as:

$$\text{Power} = u \times \text{MRR}$$

Therefore,
$$F_{grinding}\, V = u \times vdb$$

Thus total grinding force,
$$F_{grinding} = u \times \frac{v.d.b}{V}$$

Since, from empirical results, as t decreases, the friction component of u increases, i.e.

$$u \;\alpha\; \frac{1}{t} \text{ or } u = K_1.\frac{1}{t}$$

Where K_1 is temperature constant, thus substituting

$$F_{grinding} = K_1.\frac{1}{t}.\frac{v.d.b}{V}$$

Total grinding force after substituting for *t*,

$$F_{grinding} = K_1.\frac{1}{\sqrt{\frac{4v}{Vcr}\sqrt{\frac{d}{D}}}}.\frac{v.d.b}{V}$$

Rearranging the same,

The Total grinding force $$F_{grinding} = K_1.b.\sqrt{\frac{d.c.r.v}{4V}\sqrt{Dd}}$$

5.2.4 Force on a Grain

The force per grain can be calculated as:

$$F_{grain} = u \times \text{Area}$$

$$F_{grain} = u \times \frac{1}{2} wt$$

Since, $w = rt, \ u = K_t.\frac{1}{t}$

Therefor,

$$F_{grain} = K_1.\frac{1}{t} \times \frac{1}{2}.r.tt$$

Substituting for t, and rearranging, the Force on a grain, F_{grain} becomes,

$$F_{grain} = \frac{K_1}{2}.r.\sqrt{\frac{4V}{V.c.r}\sqrt{\frac{d}{D}}}$$

$$F_{grain} = K_1.\sqrt{\frac{v.r.}{V.c}\sqrt{\frac{d}{D}}}$$

Grinding temperature. If K_2 be the room temperature, the grinding temperature rise () goes with energy delivered per unit area. i.e.

$$\Delta T = K_2.\frac{Energyinput}{arer}$$

$$\Delta T = K_2.\frac{u \times b.l.d}{b.l} = K_2.K_1.\frac{1}{t}.d$$

$$\Delta T = K_1.K_2.d.\frac{1}{\sqrt{\frac{4v}{vcr}\sqrt{\frac{d}{D}}}}$$

Rearranging the above, the grinding Temperature rise (ΔT) can be written as:

$$\Delta T = K_1 K_2 d^{\frac{3}{4}} \sqrt{\frac{Vcr}{vc4vr}} \sqrt{D}$$

Generally, the grinding temperatures can go up to 1600°C for a short period of time.

5.2.5 Demonstration

Let us take an examples to demonstrate this.

Example 1. If one is grinding a steel, which has a specific grinding energy (u) of 35 W-s/mm³. The grinding wheel rotates at 3600 rpm, has a diameter (D) of 150 mm, thickness (b) of 25 mm, and (c) 5 grains per mm². The motor has a power of 2 kW. The work piece moves (v) at 1.5 m/min. The chip thickness ratio (r) is 10. Determine the grinding force and force per grain? Determine the temperature (the value of K_2 is 0.2°K-mm/N and room temperature is 20°C.

Solutions:

First we need to calculate the depth of cut, d. We can have this from the power, i.e.

$$\text{Power} = u \times MRR = u.v.d.b$$

$$2000W = 35\frac{W-s}{mm^3}.1.5\frac{m}{min}.d.25mm \times 10^6\frac{mm^2}{m^2} \times \frac{min}{60\,\text{sec}}$$

i.e. $d = 91.4 \times 10^{-6}$ m

Now for the total grinding force,

$$F_{grinding} = u \times \frac{v.d.b}{V}$$

$$F_{grinding} = 35 \times \frac{W-s}{mm^3}.\frac{1500\frac{mm}{min}91.4\times10^{-3}.mm.25mm}{3600\frac{rev}{min}.150\eth\frac{mm}{rev}.\frac{m}{1000mm}}$$

i.e. $F_{grinding} = 70.7\text{N}$

Next, the force per grain can be evaluated as:

$$F_{grain} = u.1/2 \text{ wt a and } w = rt$$

Therefore, one need t as:

$$t = \sqrt{\frac{4\text{v}}{\text{V.c.r}}\sqrt{\frac{\text{d}}{\text{D}}}}$$

$$= \sqrt{\frac{4.1500\frac{\text{mm}}{\text{min}}}{3600.150\pi.\frac{\text{mm}}{\text{min}}.5\frac{\text{grains}}{\text{mm}_2}.10}\frac{91.4\times10^{-3}mm}{150\text{mm}}}$$

$$=1.32\times10^{-3}\text{ mm}$$

Substituting,

$$F_{grain} = u \times \frac{1}{2} r.t.t = 35.\frac{1}{2}.10.(1.32 \times 10^{-3})^2$$

$$F_{grain} = 3.05 \times 10^{-4} \text{ J|mm}$$

For the temperature, we need K_1 and K_2. Since, K_2 is given, so we need to calculate K_1.

$$3.05 \times 10^{-4} \text{ N} = K_1.\frac{1}{2}.10.1.32 \times 10^{-6} \text{ m}$$

$$K_1 = 46.2 \times 10^3 \text{ N/m}$$

Substituting, K_1

$$\Delta T = K_2.K_1.\frac{1}{t}.d$$

Therefore,

$$\Delta T = 0.2 \text{ Km/N}.46.2 \text{ N/m} \frac{1}{1.33 \times 10^{-6} \text{m}}.91.4 \times 10^{-6} \text{ m} = 640°\text{K}$$

$$T = T_{initial} + \Delta T = 20 + 640 = 660°\text{C}$$

The above exercise shows the role of temperature in grinding.

5.3 ABRASIVES

Abrasives are finely crushed materials that can be found as fine grains and powders made from crushed synthetic or natural materials. Grain size and form, hardness, toughness, resistance to attrition, and friability are the major attributes of abrasive materials. A grain must be friable after attrition in order to shatter into pieces and create fresh, sharp edges. Abrasives come in two varieties: synthetic and artificial, or artificial and natural.

Natural abrasives. Sandstone or solid quartz, emery (50 to 60% crystalline Al_2O_3 + Iron oxide), corundum (75 to 90% crystalline Al_2O_3 + Iron oxide), and natural diamond are the natural abrasive minerals. The "borts," or abrasive grains, that make up natural diamonds are created by crushing undesirable gem stones to the proper particle size. Due to the cutting faces' propensity for dulling and glazing, their use is restricted. Natural abrasives have mainly been supplanted by manufactured abrasives because they lack the consistency of characteristics and dependability.

Artificial abrasives. Aluminum oxide, silicon carbide, diamond (which is a form of pure carbon), boron carbide, and cubic boron nitride are some of artificial abrasives. The hardness, toughness, and type of structure of the manufactured abrasives are well defined and under strict control. These abrasives are given below.

5.3.1 Aluminium Oxide

Al_2O_3, or aluminium oxide, is marketed under the names "Alundum" and "Aloxite." Crystalline aluminium oxide makes up the majority of the aluminium oxide abrasive. In an electric furnace, it is produced by melting minerals high in this oxide (bauxite ore, which mostly contains aluminium hydroxide). Impurities are combined with and removed using coke and iron chips. A "pig" is the huge lump of refined aluminium oxide that is produced when it exits the furnace. It undergoes crushing and rolling into tiny grains, magnetic treatment to remove ferrous impurities, and washing. Silicon carbide is harder than aluminium oxide. It is therefore strong and does not fracture readily. As a result, it is frequently used for grinding materials with high tensile strengths, including most steels, H.S.S., ferrous alloys, and non-ferrous cast iron.

5.3.2 White Aluminium Oxide

It has a very high concentration of Al_2O_3, making it the most polished form. For cool and precise grinding, where heat must be kept at a low temperature, this cutting tool material is advised. Particularly for jobs in the tool room, it is advised. For surface grinding as well as tool and cutter grinding, this material is very ideal.

5.3.3 Silicon Carbide

The chemical combination of silicon and carbon is known as silicon carbide. Quartz sand and coke powder are fused together in an electric furnace to create it. The mixture also includes salt and sawdust. Silicon carbide is created when carbon from coke and sand mix at a temperature of about 2300°C. Sawdust burns and develops pores that allow gases to escape. Impurities are removed by the salt. The furnace is cooled after the procedure is complete. Individual grains are separated from the centre of the loosely linked silicon carbide crystals. There are two varieties of silicon carbide: pure silicon carbide in the green variety and black or grey. Since green silicon carbide is harder and hence more brittle and friable, it is generally a better material. Compared to synthetic Al_2O_3, silicon carbide of both forms is harder. SiC is not suggested for grinding hard materials because of its severe brittleness. Cast irons, non-metallic materials, and non-ferrous metals can all be ground using silicon carbide wheels.

5.3.4 Green Silicon Carbide

Tungsten Carbide tools are ground using this type of SiC catting tool material. The only effective abrasive for tools with carbide tips is this material, which is specially developed for this kind of operation.

5.3.5 Diamond

In order to sharpen carbide tools, truing and dressing other grinding wheels, and processing glass, ceramics, and stone, synthetic diamonds (a type of pure carbon) are frequently employed.

5.3.6 Boron Carbide

The compound boron carbide is composed of boron and carbon (B4C). It is produced as a grayish-black powder with a grain size of no more than 120 m. Sharp faces and a greater capacity for abrasion are characteristics of the grains. Grinding and lapping extremely hard metals, hard alloys, glass, and gems are the major uses for boron carbide (ruby, topaz).

5.3.7 Cubic Boron Nitride

Boron and nitrogen are combined to form cubic boron nitride. It is employed for grinding workpieces made of hard high alloy steels and a variety of hard tool and die steels.

5.4 BONDS AND BONDING MATERIALS

Abrasive grains are sustained or held together by a bond in a grinding wheel. To withstand the strains of the high-speed rotating grinding wheel, all bonds must be suitably robust. They must be able to firmly hold the abrasive grains while not being too dense to obstruct the cutting operation. The abrasive tool's operational parameters, including grinding speed, pressure on the tool, heat production in the grinding zone, and cooling conditions, determine the bond to use. Non-organic and organic bonds are different types of bonds. Non-organic bonding include metallic, vitrified, and silicate bonds. Organic bonds include those in retinoid, rubber, shellac, and oxychloride. Followings are the discussion of these bonds.

Vitrified bond. The vitrified connection is the most prevalent. Refractory clay, feldspar, and quartz are the main ingredients. When heated, it becomes more like glass (the word "vitrified" literally means "to be transformed into glass by the action of heat"). The benefits of vitrified bond include its strength, high porosity, heat resistance, excellent chemical stability (unaffected by water, oils, or acids), high cutting capability, and effective heat removal. Wheels made of vitrified-bonded material can be employed at speeds up to 35 m/s. The brittleness of vitrified-bonded wheels is a drawback. Bonds made of vitrified material are the toughest and strongest.

Silicate bond. This bond is made of zinc oxide, lime, and various fillers combined with water glass ($NaSiO_3$). When heated to roughly 260°C, it becomes harder. Because self-dressing (crumbling out of dull grains) occurs more frequently, the relationship is not as strong as the vitrified bond. When exposed to dampness, the wheels become brittle. The softest wheel is one made of silicate. Silicate bond is utilised for face grinding when a significant portion of the wheel is in touch with the workpiece as well as for grinding heat-sensitive goods like cutters and precision tools.

Bakelite or resinoid bond. A synthetic resin or plastic is used to bond bakelite or resinoids. The porosity of resinoid-bonded grinding wheels is smaller than that of vitrified-bonded wheels, yet they are nevertheless exceedingly strong, springy, and highly stable under varying loads. Due to growing demands for higher quality and longevity, bakelite bonded grinding wheels are quickly taking over as the preferred option for grinding and finishing processes in the automotive, aerospace, and other specialised domains of industry. Surface roughness is reduced by the polishing action of resinoid. Resinoid-bonded wheels are utilised for high speed activities like cutting off or fettling and operate at a surface speed of 35 to 40 m/s. It provides an extremely quick stock removal rate. These wheels' drawbacks include a loss of hardness at temperatures between 200 and 250 °C and a lack of adequate resistance to alkaline coolants (it becomes soaked). To boost their flexural strength, these wheels can easily be strengthened with steel rings, fibreglass, or other fibres.

Rubber bond. With vulcanizing additives and fillers, synthetic rubber makes up the majority of it. The abrasive material is combined with rubber during the creation of the wheels, and then sulphur and other ingredients are added. When heated to 150°C, rubber hardens while maintaining its suppleness, and is then pushed into heated moulds. The resulting grinding wheels may rotate at higher rotational rates and are stronger. These wheels, which are just slightly elastic and are less than 8 mm thick, are utilised for finishing grinding as well as slitting and cutting-off operations. They are resistant to water and are not softened by alkaline cooling drinks. However, the wheel gets soft (dull) at temperatures above 150° and needs cooling and dressing. These wheels are also used as control wheels for centerless grinding.

Shellac bond. Like resin and rubber, this relationship is likewise organic. In a heated solution, the abrasive substance is combined with shellac. After that, it is rolled and compressed into the desired forms. At roughly 150°C, baking is done for several hours. With the help of this connection, robust, flexible wheels can be created. These wheels are used to grind parts like mill rolls and camshafts because they create a high surface polish. These wheels are occasionally used to slice wheels that are thicker than 0.80 mm.

Oxy-chloride bond. For disc grinding wheels in particular, this organic connection is utilised. Compared to vitrified-bond wheels, these wheels are less brittle and less susceptible to side loads. Additionally, other than the silicate bond, the temperature during grinding is lower than with other bonds. These wheels' shortcomings include being vulnerable to acidic solutions, moisture, and abrupt temperature fluctuations. With prolonged storage, these wheels' strength is also reduced.

Metallic bond. The cubic boron nitride and diamond grains are joined by metallic bonds. As bonding materials, copper, tin, aluminium, and their alloys are employed.

5.5 TYPES OF GRINDING WHEEL

The Grinding wheels are available in different shapes and sizes to suit with the different machine operation as shown in the Fig. 5.5 below.

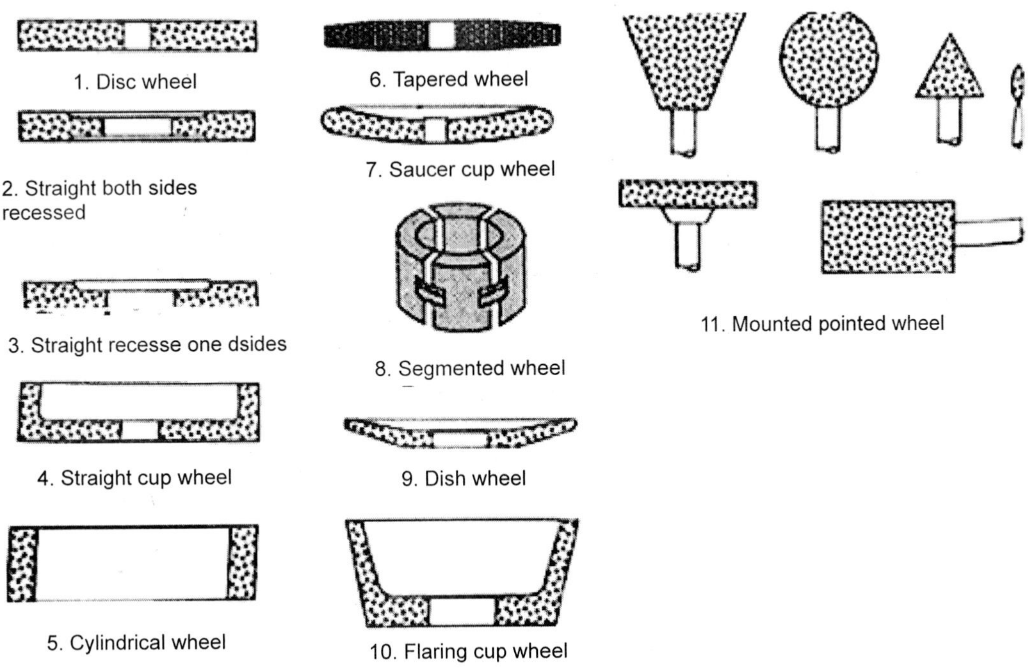

Figure 5.5: Types of grinding wheels [6]

Straight side grinding wheels. These are used for the cylindrical, center-less, and surface grinding operation like Straight Disc wheel, Straight both side recessed, Straight one side recessed and Straight cup wheel

Cylindrical wheel. Used for producing a flat surface

Tapered wheel. Used for grinding thread, gear teeth, etc.

Saucer wheel. Used for sharpening of circular and band saws

Segmented wheel. Used for the vertical spindle, rotary, and reciprocating table surface grinders

Dish wheel. This is used for tool room work

Flaring cup wheel. This is used for tool and cutter grinding and

Mounted pointed wheel. These are used for grinding the special contours and Sharpening saws.

5.6 FACTORS AFFECTING THE SELECTION OF GRIND WHEELS

The selection of a grinding wheel is based on the following factors:

Size and shape of wheel. The mean abrasive grain diameter and the screen or sieve number are roughly connected as follows: The average abrasive grain diameter is 15/mm of grit size. The size of the grains can be broadly categorised as follows: coarse-sized grains (up to 24) are typically employed for roughing, which entails the removal of heavy materials. For finishing procedures where there is less material to be removed, finer grits (70 to 180) are utilised. For example, when grinding threads, grain sizes between 220 and 600 and even finer (up to 1000) are employed to produce very high surface finishes. When stock removal and finish are required, such as during routine grinding and tool grinding, medium large grains (30 to 60) are utilised.

Kind of abrasive. Natural (Al_2O_3, SiC and diamond) or artificial (Alundum, Aloxite, CBN, art. diamond)

Grain size of abrasive particles. The standard grain sizes are: (i) Coarse: 10, 12, 14, 16, 20, 24 (ii) Medium: 30, 36, 46, 54, 60 (iii) Fine: 70, 80, 90, 100, 120, 150, 180 (iv) Very fine: 220, 240, 280, 320, 400, 500, 600, 700, 800, 900, 1000.

Grade of bond. The grade describes the force or tightness with which the bond secures the grinding wheel's abrasive grains in place. The English alphabet from A to Z denotes the Grade. A stands for Sofest, and Z for Hardest Grade. A, B, C, D, E, F, G, H, I, J, K, L, M, N, O, P, and Z are examples of soft grades. Q, R, S, T, U, V, W, X, Y, and Z are examples of hard grades.

Structure. The structure describes how far apart the grinding wheel's abrasive grains are spaced. The number of cutting edges per unit area of the wheel face and the size of the void spaces between the grains serve as indicators. The structure is known as a Dense structure (1,2,3,4,5,6,7,8) if it has many cutting edges per unit area rather than an Open structure (9,10,11,12,13,14,15).

Kind of bond material- V-Vertified, B-Resionid, R-Rubber, E-Shellac, S-Silicon, O- Oxychloride

Function of grinding wheel. The primary purpose of a grinding wheel is to remove material from the surface in the form of tiny chips and to make it as smooth as possible. A surface finishing tool, a grinding machine uses grinding wheels as the tool to polish the surface. Even grinding wheels come in a variety of designs and are used for a variety of workpieces.

Other factors. wheel speed, work speed, materials to be ground and general condition of the machine

The general guide lines for selection of grinding wheel, are given as below:

(a) The best abrasive for grinding steel - both hardened and unhardened- malleable iron, and soft bronzes is aluminium oxide. Cast iron, bronze, aluminium, and cemented carbides can all be ground most effectively with black silicon carbide abrasive. Sharpening carbide-tipped cutting tools involves the use of green silicon carbide.

(b) The wheel should be softer the harder the metal being ground, and vice versa, as the harder the metal being ground, the more quickly the wheel's grains will wear out and break off, exposing fresh, sharp grains. A hard-grade wheel should be used for soft materials and a soft-grade wheel for hard materials.Coarser wheels (a large grit abrasive) are used in grinding ductile and soft metals to avoid rapid loading of the wheel; fine-grained wheels are used for brittle and hard metals.

(c) The wheel's grain should be coarser the more surface area it will have in touch with the work. In other words, select a coarse grit for maximal metal removal and a fine grit for optimum finish.

(d) Harder wheels should be more coarse-grained to prevent breaking down since, under similar circumstances, the stress placed on the grain of a coarse-grained wheel is greater than that of a fine-grained wheel. The longer the arc of contact with the work, the less the grain depth of cut, and the greater the tendency to load the wheel and overheat the surface being ground. Therefore, the longer the arc of contact, the softer the wheel should be.

(e) With regard to the wheel's construction: For finish and form grinding, choose wheels with a dense structure since they hold their shape effectively. For grinding hardened steel parts, honing cutting tools, cylindrical, centerless, and internal grinding, as well as surface grinding with the wheel's periphery, use wheels with a medium-density construction. When surface grinding soft and ductile metals with the face of a cup, cylinder, or segmental wheel, wheels with an open structure are utilised.

(f) Select a vitrified bond for the highest rate of metal removal and a resinoid, rubber, or shellac bond for a good finish.

Table 5.2: Surface speeds of grinding wheels

Type of bond	*Surface Speed m/s*
1. **Vitrified or Silicate**	
Soft	23 – 28
Medium	25 – 30
Hard	28 – 33
2. **Organic**	
Soft	23 – 33
Medium	35 – 40
Hard	38 – 50

5.7 STANDARD MARKING SYSTEMS

Every grinding wheel has a mark. On the flat surface of the wheel, markings in the shape of conventional designations are painted with an indelible paint. The labelling gives information about the producer, the abrasive substance, its grade, structure, bond type, etc. Below is a common wheel marking style:

51 - A - 36 - L - 5 - V - 23

Where figures stand for:

51 - Manufacturer's symbol indicating exact kind of abrasive, (use optional),

A - Abrasive type: A for Al_2O_3, C for SiC and D for diamond, **36** - Grain size, **L** - Grade, **5** - Structure,

V - Bond type (V: Vitrified, S: Silicate, R: Rubber, B: Resinoid, E: Shellac, O: Oxychloride, BF: Reinforced resinoid, RF: Rubber reinforced) and **23** - Private marking to identify wheel (use optional).

5.8 GRINDING METHODS

There are several distinct grinding techniques, including creep feed grinding, centerless grinding, centred grinding, surface grinding, and vertical grinding. Each one must be chosen based on the application and level of surface finish required.

Method of Grinding	Representative figures
Horizontal grinding: A spindle is for grinding with an axis parallel to the table. The grinding wheel spins slowly constantly or sporadically. The workpiece's radial feed is accomplished during the horizontal feed movement until the grinding achieves the required size. The smooth surface is created when the wheel's periphery (flat edge) comes into contact with the workpiece.	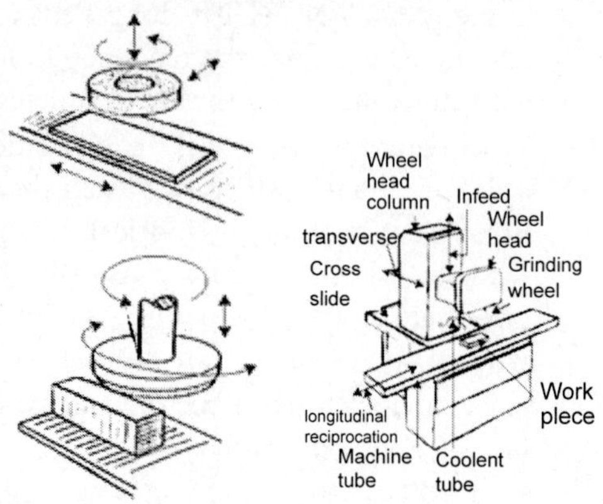
Vertical grinding: The work piece is supported by a rotary table machine with continuous or indexed rotation, or a reciprocating table that can be adjusted depending on the task. An axis of the grinding spindle in this instance is perpendicular to the table. On a flat surface, a wheel's face, whether it be a cup, cylinder, disc, or segmented wheel—is used. Wheel-face grinding is frequently used to quickly remove material, however some machines are capable of performing highly precise work.	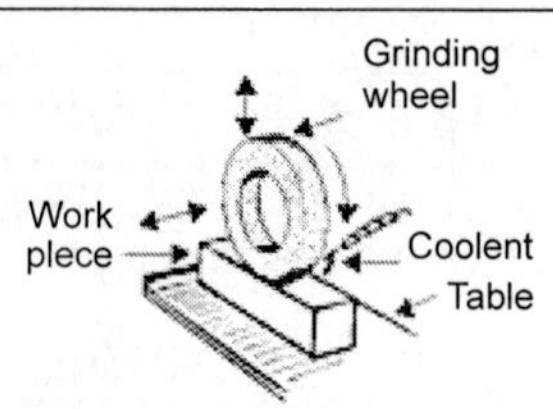 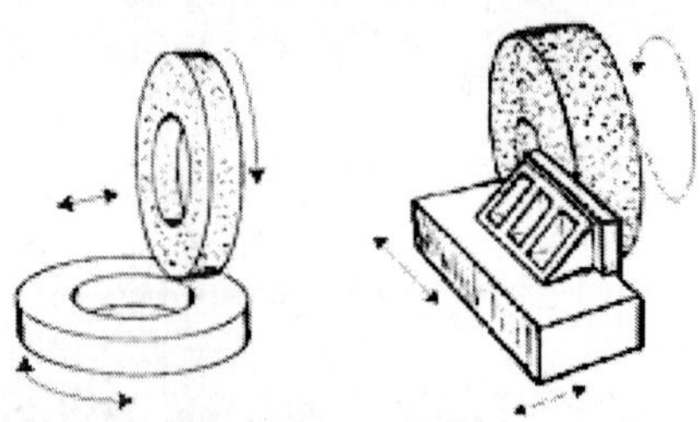
Surface grinding: Surface grinding employs a square table or a circular table, a straight type wheel or a cup type wheel, and either a vertical axis grinding or a horizontal axis grinding for grinding. To execute grinding, the workpiece is mounted to a table and the wheel is turned quickly. The most typical grinding technique, surface grinding, is utilised in a variety of industries.	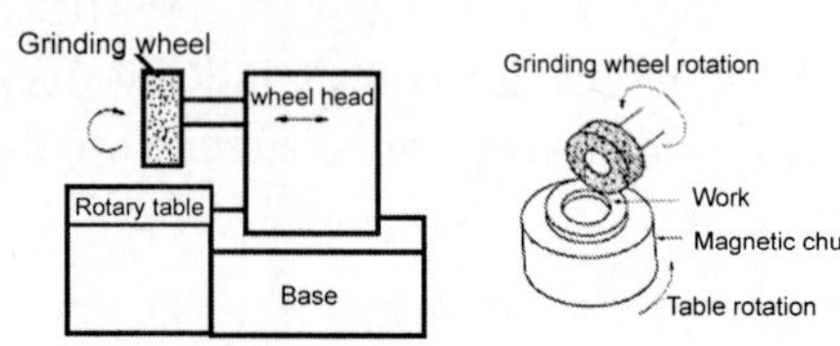 Horizontal spindale rotary table surface grinder

<table>
<tr><th>Method of Grinding</th><th>Representative figures</th></tr>
<tr><td>Cylindrical grinding: Either a universal grinding machine or a cylindrical grinding machine is employed. The cylindrical workpiece is rotated together with the wheel, and its outer rim is machined. Straight cylindrical, taper, end face, and complete shape grinding are a few of the several ways of grinding. It is a generic grinding technique that is popular and similar to surface grinding.</td><td>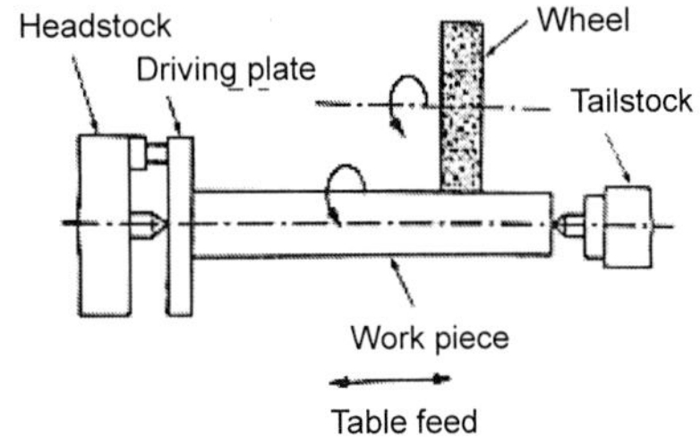
</td></tr>
<tr><td>Internal grinding: The inner surface of the fixed workpiece is machined using the rotating axle wheel. Taper and end face grinding are part of the grinding process. An internal grinding machine, cylindrical grinding equipment, or internal grinding equipment connected to a universal grinding machine are used to complete the task.</td><td>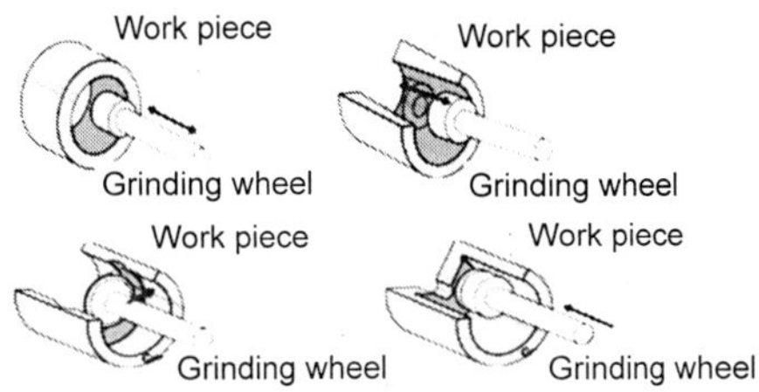
</td></tr>
<tr><td>Centered grinding: Between the centres, the workpiece is secured. The spinning grinding wheel is used to machine the workpiece's exterior. A cylindrical grinding machine or a universal grinding machine is used to complete the task.</td><td>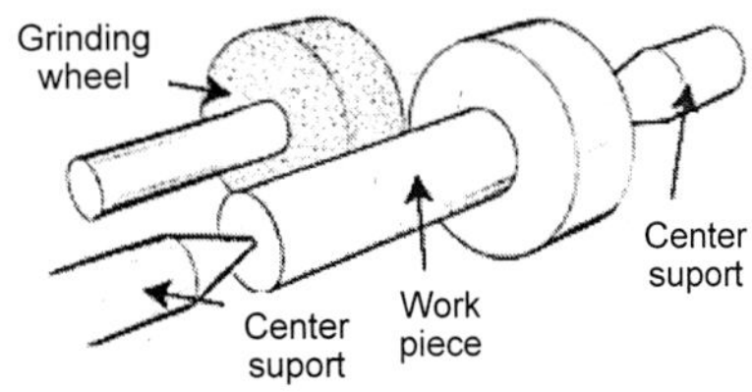
</td></tr>
<tr><td>Centreless grinding: In this instance, the workpiece is held between two grinding wheels that are revolving at various speeds in the same direction. In order to apply downward force to the workpiece, one grinding wheel spins around a fixed axis.</td><td>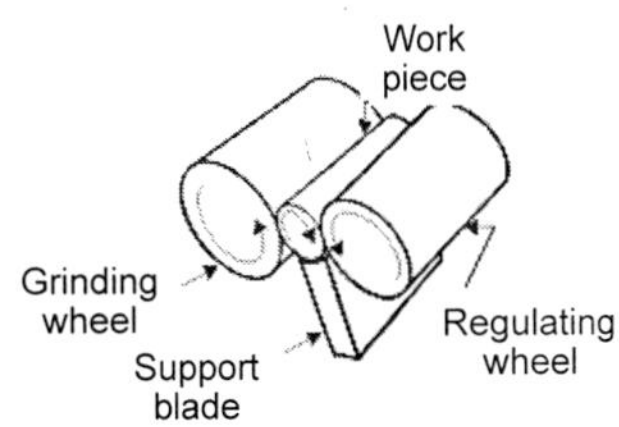

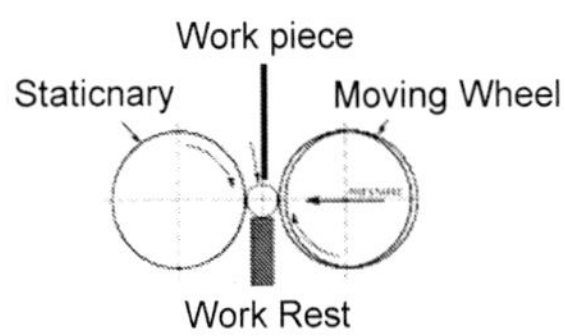
</td></tr>
</table>

Method of Grinding	Representative figures
Creep feed grinding: When compared to reciprocating or pendulum grinding, creep feed grinding is characterized by lower workpiece speeds and deeper depths of cut, resulting in a longer arc length of contact between the grinding wheel and workpiece.	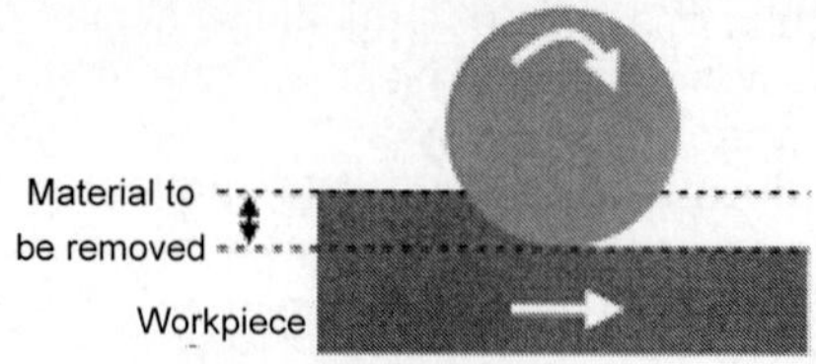

5.9 GRINDING MACHINES AND THEIR CLASSIFICATION

An abrasive wheel-equipped machine tool known as a grinding machine is used to produce fine finishes or make slight cuts in metals and other materials. Machines for industrial grinding come in many different varieties. There are five different types of grinding machines: cylindrical, internal, centerless, surface, and special.

5.9.1 Cylindrical Grinding Machines

The broad category of grinding machines that use centres to mount the workpiece to be ground is referred to as "cylindrical." The most popular external cylindrical grinding machine is the plain grinder, a multipurpose production tool for grinding axles, shafts, splines, and other components. Figure 5.6 shows a simple grinding device. On the base, which also houses the drive mechanisms and the hydraulic drive, are all the machine's components. The hydraulic drive reciprocates the sliding or traversing table (lower table) to get the longitudinal feed at a speed ranging from 0.08 to 10 m/min, or it can be manually moved by a hand wheel through a gearing system. The worktable or the swivel table (upper table) with T slots for securing the head stock and tailstock is mounted on the sliding table.

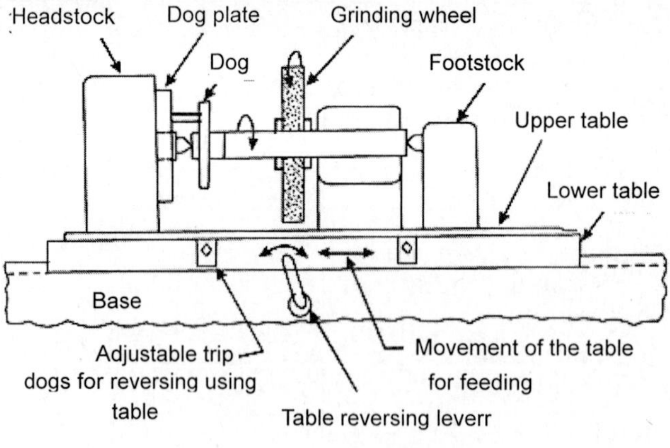

Figure 5.6: External cylindrical grinding machine [6]

The workpiece is mounted and driven by the headstock while being held either between centres or in a chuck. An electric motor housed in the headstock's upper section powers the work spindle. The workpiece held between centres is rotated similarly to how a centre lathe works. The tail stock serves as support for the back of work that is mounted between centres. It has an advance/retract spindle. Commonly, a spring device is used to advance and clamp the tailstock spindle with the centre. The tail stock can be moved along the worktable's slots to accommodate different workpiece lengths, and it can be held in place using bolts or an eccentric clamp. On the spindle of the wheel head, which moves crosswise at the back of the base, the grinding wheel is mounted and clamped. A motor located at the top of the helmet propels the wheel at up to 1500 revolutions per minute.

Trip dogs that can be adjusted are set up to reverse the sliding table at the conclusion of the stroke by clamping them into longitudinal holes that are provided at the side of the table. One can manually or hydraulically shift the wheel head in a transverse direction to feed the wheel after each stroke of the table. Chucking type cylindrical grinders are manufacturing tools used for quick grinding of relatively short items, including ball-bearing races. Cylindrical grinding is done using a variety of techniques. Plunge-cut grinding, full-depth grinding, and traverse grinding are the three that are most frequently utilised as given below.

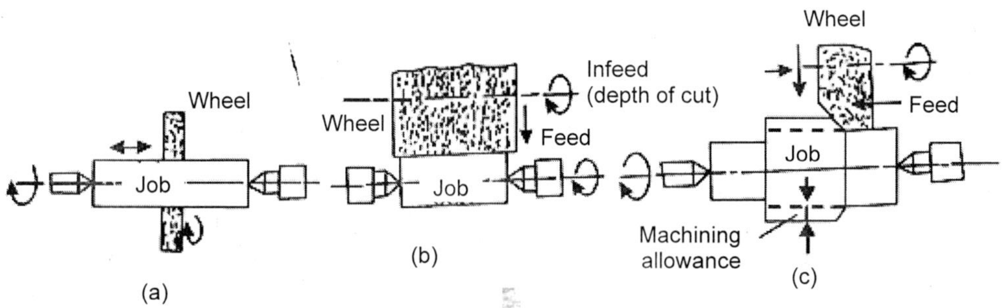

Figure 5.7: Methods of cylindrical grinding [6]

Traverse grinding. In traverse grinding or infeed grinding (Fig. 5.7 (a)), the grinding wheel is moved into the work. The desired surface is then produced by traversing the workpiece across the wheel on vice-versa. This method is used to grind workpieces of considerable length.

Plunge cut grinding. In the plunge-cut grinding (Fig. 5.7 (b)), the grinding wheel is radially supplied into the work while the latter circles around centres. It is comparable to lathe form cutting. The technique is applied on brief workpieces where the wheel's width overlaps the length that needs to be ground. By using this technique, short, stiff workpieces can be ground.

Full depth grinding. In the full depthe grinding (Fig. 5.7 (c)), the entire allowance is ground off in one or two lengthwise passes after the wheel is trued to create an entry taper or step. The technique is typically used on relatively short surfaces of workpieces with inflexible shafts. Center type cylindrical grinders are effective for grinding tapers. By rotating the worktable to the desired angle with regard to the axis of the grinding wheel, adjustments of up to 10 degrees can be performed.

As required, the complete grinding process can be carried out manually, semi-automatically, or automatically. The tiniest pieces can be handled by plain grinders up to 0.9 m in diameter by 4.8 m in length, with the lengths being proportionate to each machine's swing capacity. In very large grinders, the wheel is reciprocated across the workpiece held and rotated between centres, because of the massiveness of the work.

Universal cylindrical grinders. These grinders include a swivelling headstock and a swivelling wheel head in addition to the advantages supplied by conventional grinders. This makes it feasible to grind taper at any angle, which is far more than is achievable with conventional grinders. There are machines that can handle items that need swings up to 450 mm and an 1800 mm centre distance.

5.9.2 Internal Cylindrical Grinding Machines

When other, more productive ways of finishing correct holes, such as precision drilling, honing, etc., cannot be used, internal grinding is primarily used to complete accurate holes in hardened objects. Internal grinding can be done in one of two ways: (i) with a revolving workpiece, or (ii) with the workpiece held still. The first technique is used to grind holes in relatively tiny workpieces, primarily bodies of rotation, such as the inner surfaces of ball bearing rings and gear bores. The workpiece is rotated in the same way as a lathe by being held in a chuck or other appropriate fixture (Fig. 5.8 (a)). A straight-type grinding wheel is rotated while receiving two feeds: intermittent cross feed (radial feed) at the end of each pass, which controls the depth of cut, and longitudinal feed along the wheel axis, which reciprocates back and forth over the length of the hole. A grinding head holds the grinding wheel. In a different machine design, the workpiece is slowly rotated and moved back and forth while the grinding wheel rotates in a fixed location.

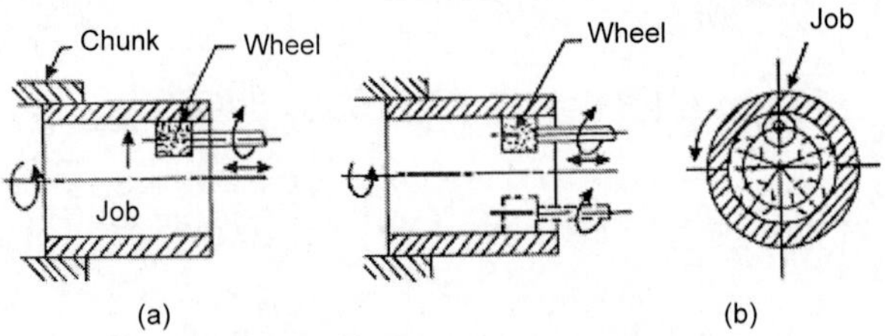

Figure 5.8: Internal grinding [6]

When grinding tiny holes, the wheel's peripheral speed is 10 m/s or less. The speed rises as the hole's diameter increases, reaching 30 m/s for sizes greater than 30 mm. The wheel spindle's comparatively low stiffness places a restriction on the depth of cut (infeed per stroke). For rough grinding steel and cast iron, infeeds range from 0.005 to 0.02 mm, and for final grinding, they range from 0.002 to 0.01 mm per stroke. For holes with a large length-to-diameter ratio and holes with a diameter less than 40 mm, lower infeed rates are used. Internal grinding calls for an over-travel at each end of the stroke that is equivalent to 1/3 of the wheel width. For grinding holes in large, bulky workpieces (housing-type parts) that are difficult or impossible to clamp in a grinder's chuck, employ the second method of internal grinding. They are set up on the planetary grinding machine's table (see Fig. 5.8 (b)). The wheel spindle of this kind of machine revolves not only about its axis but also in a planetary motion about the axis of the hole being ground. The longitudinal feed is produced by the wheel's axial motion.

Internal grinding is fundamentally different from cylindrical (external) grinding in that it is carried out using a wheel that is significantly smaller, often 0.7 to 0.9 of the hole diameter. The life of internal grinding wheels is naturally lower than for other types of grinding because of their small diameters. Since the angle of contact with the surface being ground is much larger and the workpiece may be heated to a high temperature during grinding, wheels of a lower grade (softer wheels) should be chosen for internal grinding than for identical conditions in cylindrical (external) grinding.

5.9.3 Centreless Grinding

On workpieces that lack centres or cannot have centres, such as pistons, valves, rings, tubes, balls, wrist pins, drills, bushings, drill rods, shafts, and balls and rollers for bearings, etc., centerless grinding is used. Internal and external surfaces can both be ground without a centre.

5.9.3.1 External centreless grinding

There are three methods as (i) through feed, (ii) infeed and (iii) end feed methods for External centreless grinding.

(i) *Through Feed Grinding.* Fig. 5.9 (a) provides an illustration of the through feed centerless grinding principle. The workpiece travels between the grinding wheel and the regulating wheel while resting on the workpiece rest blade. By moving axially past the grinding wheel, the workpiece extends the grinding operation throughout its entire length. The regulating wheel gives the workpiece its traverse motion. The controlling wheel is made of rubber-bonded abrasive and rotates the work at its own rotational speed thanks to its frictional properties. The controllable speed of this wheel ranges from 0.6 to 1.0 m/s. By tilting the regulating wheel downward at the feeding end, at a 45-degree angle, the work is moved axially past the grinding wheel. This tilt causes the regulating wheel's peripheral speed to be divided into two components: (i) the rate of longitudinal feed (f_{lg}=V_{rw} $\mu sina$) and (ii) the speed of work rotation (V_{wk}=V_{rw} $cosa$) , where μ is the co-efficient (μ= 0.94 to 0.98) that takes into consideration the work slipping in relation to the grinding wheel. The angle *a* is typically measured between 1 and 5 degrees; the larger the angle *a*, the faster the rate of feed, and vice versa. The grinding wheel removes a layer of metal in one pass, reducing the workpiece's diameter by 0.02 to 0.3 mm.

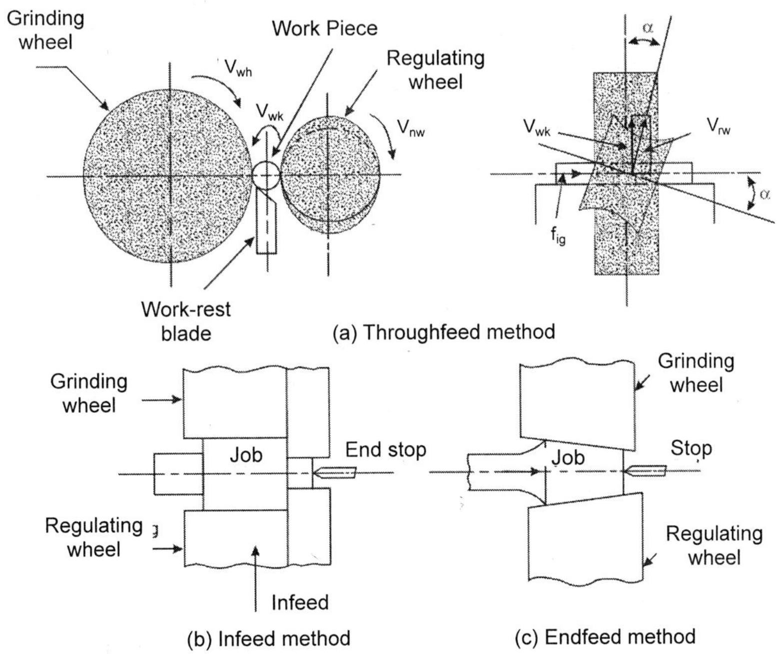

Figure 5.9: External centreless grinding[6]

To increase contact between the regulating wheel and the work, its perimeter is somewhat concave rather than cylindrical. The work rest blade features a 30° angled top face to retain work against the regulating wheel face for the same purpose. This approach is utilised for uninterrupted parallel work of any length. A magazine feeding system can be installed to automate the grinder.

According to Fig. 5.9 (a), the centre of the workpiece is typically held above the line joining the centres of the grinding and regulating wheels. This will guarantee that the piece has a correct cylindrical surface. This distance is equal to 0.125 to 0.25 times the diameter of the workpiece. The ground surface might not be circular if it is too small, but instead resemble an equilateral triangle with arcs for sides. Vibrations and chatter will happen if it is too big. No more than 10 to 12 mm should be present.

(ii) *Infeed Grinding.* In case of Fig. 5.9 (b), infeed centerless grinding is used when the workpiece has a stepped or uneven profile and cannot be moved between the wheels. Here, the regulating wheel is retracted before the workpiece is set on the workrest blade. The workpiece is then fed toward the grinding wheel as the regulating wheel is then moved closer to it. The regulating wheel is pulled back out after the grinding is finished, and the final workpiece is expelled. The axes of the grinding and regulating wheels are strictly horizontal because there is no requirement for longitudinal feed of the workpiece in this approach.

(iii) *End Feed Grinding.* This process (Fig. 5.9) produces tapered workpieces because both the grinding and the regulating wheels are tapered. Up until it encounters the stop, the workpiece is fed from one side. With this approach, the taper and size are precise.

5.9.3.2 Advantages of centreless grinding

i. Its high productivity, which is far higher than cylindrical grinding between centres, is the key benefit.
ii. The operator must possess less expertise.
iii. There is no noise or deflection of the work, and it is firmly supported.
iv. The work's size is reasonably manageable.
v. Less grinding stock is needed since a real floating state obtains during the grinding process.

5.9.3.3 Disadvantage of centreless grinding

i. Keyways and work with flats cannot be ground.
ii. Work with various diameters is difficult to handle.
iii. There is no guarantee that the exterior diameter and internal diameter of hollow work will be concentric.
iv. Changing over a centerless grinder to grind different diameters takes a lot of time. As a result, it may be used to large lot production more quickly.

5.9.3.4 Internal centreless grinding

Internal centerless grinding machines can be used to mill the holes in ring-type parts (Fig. 5.10). The work-piece 1 is loaded into the grinding zone and is held between three steel rollers installed in housing 5: support roll 2, pressure roll 3, and regulating roll 4. The workpiece is held against the support and regulating rolls by the lever-mounted pressure roll 3, which applies a predetermined force. The workpiece is rotated by the regulating roll, which is connected to the workdrive, at a speed that ranges from 0.7 to

1.0 m/s. The regulating wheel axis's approximate 1/2° inclination causes an axial force to apply on the workpiece, holding it axially with one end face up against a roller stop.

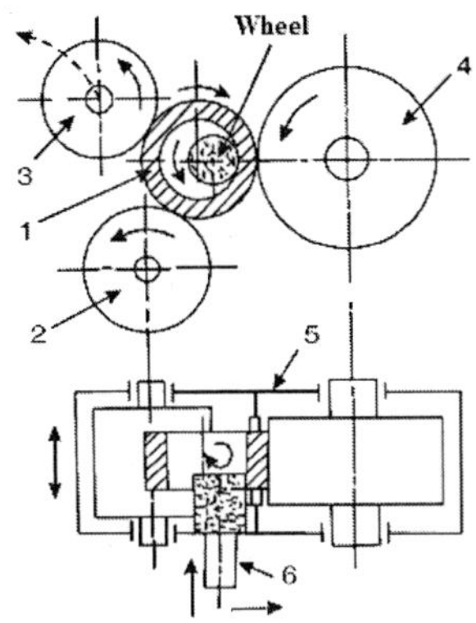

Figure 5.10: Internal centreless grinding[6]

A wheel positioned on spindle 6 is used to grind the hole. The friction force between the grinding work and the regulating roll causes the grinding work to rotate. The pressure roll is rolled outward to load and unload the workpiece. Centerless grinding allows for the maintenance of extremely high precision. On centreless machines, internal tapered surfaces are ground by rotating the housing and the workpiece to the taper angle.

5.9.4 Surface Grinding

Surface grinding machines are used to grind flat surfaces. Heavy workpieces are held in fixtures or secured to the table using pads, strap clamps, and other tools. A magnetic chuck typically holds little pieces of work. The surface grinders come with either a reciprocating table or rotating table, as well as either a horizontal spindle or a vertical spindle.

The perimeter of a straight wheel is used to grind in horizontal-spindle reciprocating table grinders (Fig. 5.11 (a)), and at each full stroke of the table, in addition to its rotating motion, the grinding wheel also undergoes a crossfeed action (back and forth). The infeed of the wheel, in which it is fed to the depth of cut, is the other motion. The edges of the grinding wheel are likewise used by horizontal-spindle rotary-table grinders (Fig. 5.11 (b)), but the workpieces are held, often by a magnetic chuck, on a rotating table. The wheel has rotation, a cross feed that is parallel to the surface being ground, and infeed here, same like before.

Wheels made in cups, cylinders, or segments are used by vertical-spindle machines. They might be either the rotary table (Fig. 5.11 (d)) or the reciprocating table (Fig. 5.11 (c)). The work moves in grinding with the wheel's end face are identical to those in grinding with the wheel's perimeter. The vertical feed of the wheel along its axis provides the depth of cut while wheel revolution about its vertical axis provides the principal rotational action. Typically, trued form wheels are used to grind contoured surfaces. The main purpose of reciprocating grinders is to create long, straight surfaces that can be flat or have shaped sections. The main application of rotary-table machines is the quick fabrication of flat surfaces on tiny and medium-sized items, either singly or constantly. Vertical machines can handle work up to 2400 mm in diameter and segmented wheels up to 1050 mm in diameter when equipped with a 1500 mm magnetic rotary table chuck. Multiple-spindle types of vertical-spindle rotary table machines are also available for rough, semi finish, and finish grinding in a single pass with automatic size, wheel advance, and gauging.

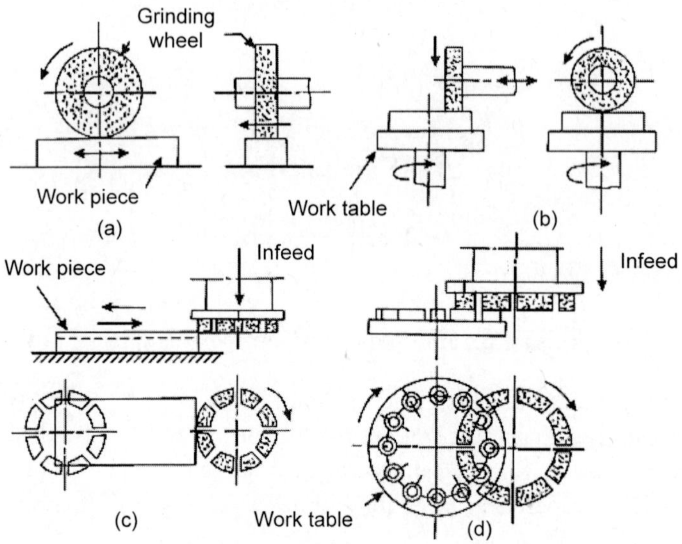

Figure 5.11: Surface grinding methods [6]

5.9.5 Special Grinding Machines

The cylindrical kind of grinders also includes form grinders, tool and cutter grinders for sharpening tools, cam grinders, gear grinders, thread grinders, grinders for rolling mill rolls, tool post grinders, and so on.

5.9.5.1 Form grinders

Depending on the type of workpiece to be machined, formed surfaces are polished on cylindrical or surface grinding machines. The grinding of bed ways with intricate cross-sections is another job in this category (Fig. 5.12).

5.9.5.2 Gear teeth grinding

On gear grinding machines, the teeth of gears are ground either through the generating process or by a forming process that employs formed wheels. The two saucer-shaped grinding wheels used in the producing grinding method are shown in Fig. 5.13 (a), and they are positioned so that their active sides (on the spindle side) are in planes tangent to the involute curvatures of two gear teeth. To do this, truing the wheels at an angle equal to the pressure angle of the gear being ground is necessary. The gear generates a complicated rolling motion when it is grinding. When grinding gears with formed wheels, as shown in Fig. 5.13 (b), the contour of the wheel is trued by a specific fixture so that it matches the profile of the tooth gaps on the gear. The adjacent flanks of two teeth are ground simultaneously.

5.9.5.3 Thread grinding

Machines for thread grinding are used. The only way these machines differ from traditional cylindrical grinding machines is in the type of grinding wheel, which might have one or more ribs. The piece is fixed in place between centres and rotated at a set speed. A separate drive rotates the ribbed grinding wheel, which is positioned on the wheel head spindle. The wheel also has a longitudinal (axial) movement that corresponds to one thread pitch every work rotation (Fig. 5.13).

5.9.5.4 Cam grinders

Fig. 5.14 depicts an arrangement for grinding a camshaft's cams. The grinding wheel is set up to move radially in conjunction with the rotation of the workpiece, either toward or away from it. A master cam gives the workpiece the appropriate radial movement in relation to the grinding wheel. Throughout operation, the grinding wheel is continuously in contact with the cam surface. For a smooth surface finish, the camshaft simultaneously oscillates and rotates while also moving axially.

5.9.5.5 Tool post grinder

On a lathe, a tool post grinder is employed for various small grinding tasks. The grinding wheel is supported by the tool post and fed across the job using either a normal or compound rest feed. The truing of lathe centres is a typical use for tool post grinders.

5.9.5.6 Tool and cutter grinders

Tools and cutters are ground in specialised tool grinding fixtures equipped with diamond and abrasive wheels of the proper sizes and shapes.

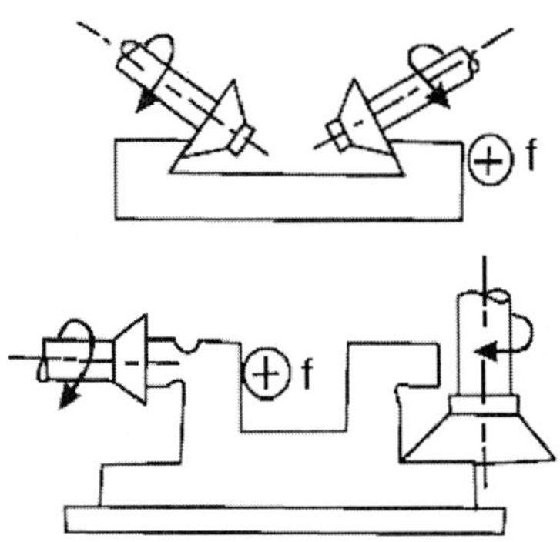

Figure 5.12: Form grinding

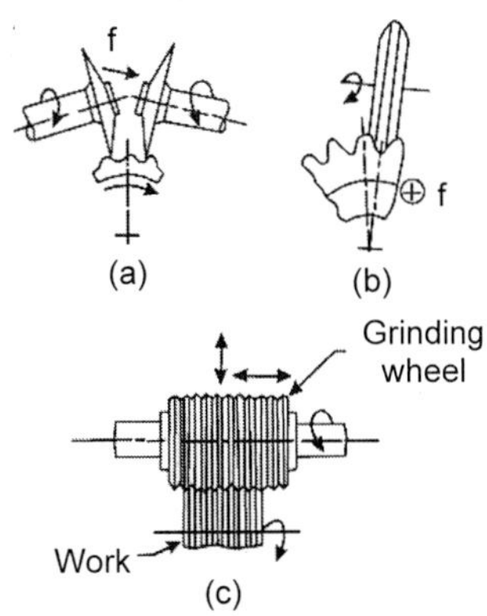

Figure 5.13: Grinding of gear teeth

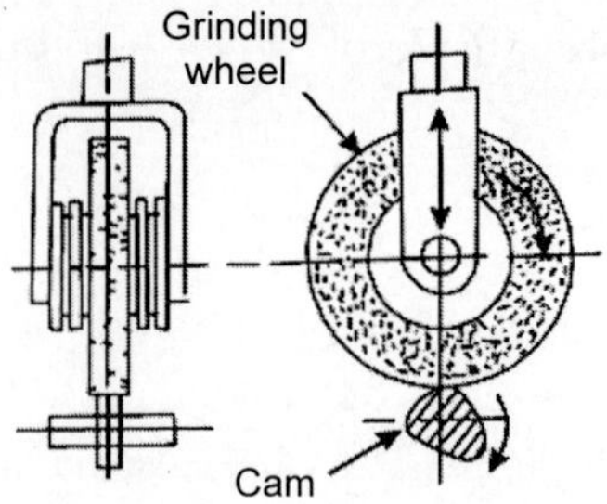

Figure 5.14: Cam grinding

5.9.5.6.1 Types of tool grinding machines

There are three types of tool grinding machines like 1. standard 2. General; 3. Machines that are specialised (for instance, drill sharpeners). Ordinary equipment is used to perform basic sharpening operations on basic instruments, such as emery sharpeners with a tool rest. A wide range of cutting tools, including counterborers, reamers, milling cutters, specialty drills, and specialty cutters, are sharpened using the universal machines. Fig. 5.15 depicts a universal tool and cutter grinder. The machine features a substantial box-type base that gives it stiffness and stability. The base's top is directly supported by the saddle. On the bottom table, which slides longitudinally on the saddle, the upper table (work table) can be rotated. The saddle provides cross movement and is moved by ball bearings on hardened ways. The work table contains "T" slots for attaching various accessories and work holding devices (vice, head stock, tail stock, and so on). The work (for instance, arbour type cutters) is held between the centres by the head stock and tail stock, which are positioned on either side of the table. On the machine's base at the back is fixed the column that supports the wheel head. For different arrangements, it can be rotated to either side of the column and moved up and down.

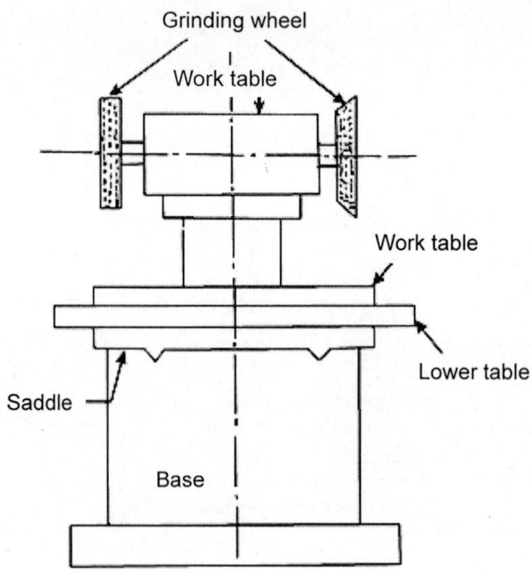

Figure 5.15: Universal tool and cutter grinder[6]

5.9.5.7 Rolls

are hefty, large-diameter workpieces used in rolling mills. For grinding them, specialised cylindrical grinding machines are used. When installed on a solid basis, such workpieces can rotate more rigidly. These huge workpieces may be turned in bearings that fit previously machined cylindrical surfaces rather than supported between centres. By moving the grinding wheel and its stand back and forth along the length of the roll, the cylindrical surface of the roll is ground.

5.9.5.8 Disk grinders

The crucial equipment among the production surface grinders is the disc grinder. They come in single or opposing spindle horizontal-spindle variants. The available single vertical spindle machines are mostly utilised for flat area surfacing without preserving certain specifications. Horizontal single or opposing spindle machines with large, solid abrasive discs or cylinder wheels can produce parts with parallel, flat faces using oscillating, reciprocating, rotary, or through feeds. On several versions, automatic work sizers are offered, and operation is frequently completely automatic. In opposing wheel grinders with wheels up to 750 mm in diameter, work pieces up to 350 mm in length can be ground.

5.10 COATED ABRASIVES

The coated abrasives typically comprise of flexible backing materials like paper or cloth and abrasive granules. They have been applied to low-speed surface finishing. However, "Coated belts" have developed into significant production tools as a result of the development of stronger adhesives and backings. They work with high metal removal rates (usually 200 cm3/min.cm width) and operate at high speeds (up to 60 m/s). In large-scale manufacturing, abrasive belt grinding has replaced turning, planing, and milling (for example, in machining the gasket surfaces of engine blocks and cylinder heads).

In addition to polishing surfaces of rotation, abrasive belt grinding is also used to finish flat and curved complicated shaped surfaces, such as those found on turbine blades, crankshaft journals, and other metal and non-metal parts. By placing grains on an adhesive layer that has been placed to a backing consisting of cloth (for instance, twill), abrasive belts can be created. This is known as "making coat." A second layer keeps the grains in place (size coat). In order to avoid stripping of brand-new grains while enabling release of worn grains, bond strength is adjusted. Electrostatic alignment of grains with sharp edges and elongated forms produces cutting edges with low negative rake angles that are positioned roughly ten times further apart than in grinding wheels. The glue could be hide glue, for example. Steel, malleable iron, and bronze are ground using aluminium oxide abrasive grains, whereas grey cast iron, brass, and aluminium alloys are ground with silicon carbide.

Due to manufacturing challenges and high cost, multi-layer coated abrasive belts are rarely used. Normally, the belt's thickness doesn't go above 2 mm (including the layer of abrasives). The belt's width is chosen based on the length of the surface to be ground. As an illustration, the belt width and shaft length are equivalent when grinding surfaces of rotation (shafts). The size of the workpiece and the specifications specified for the grinding operation's output also affect the length of the abrasive belt. The more grains that participate in the cutting process during one belt revolution, the longer the belt is (for the given belt width). In actual use, coated abrasive belts range in width from 10 to 3000 mm and in length from 500 to 7000 mm.

The ways that the belt is forced on the surface to be crushed vary among abrasive belt grinding techniques. Various techniques are shown in Fig. 5.16. The surface can be ground using either the portion of the belt that is not supported, with a portion supported by the driving contact wheel, or with a portion supported by an intermediate contact roller whose shape the belt follows. The abrasive belt's unsupported section, which has a larger area of contact and covers the majority of the workpiece surface, has the maximum production capacity when used for grinding. All types of surfaces can now be ground, with the exception of cylindrical and curved surfaces with a tiny radius of curvature.

To achieve the same output when grinding with a portion of the belt supported by a contact wheel, a substantially higher pressure is needed. In this scenario, the output is inversely proportional to the contact wheel's diameter. However, using wheels with a diameter of less than 150 mm is not advised. Occasionally, two supports placed at the workpiece's two sides will be more effective than a contact wheel. They widen the region of contact and, as a result, the angle of contact with the workpiece. Idlers can change the tension of an abrasive belt. For steel and cast iron, the contact pressure between the abrasive belt and the surface to be ground should ideally be between 0.05 and 0.2 N/mm2, and > 0.04 for non-ferrous alloys and aluminium. Cutting rates vary depending on the material of the workpiece, the type of operation being done (roughing or finishing), and other elements.

The recommended cutting speed is 25 to 30 m/s for rough abrasive belt grinding of external surfaces of rotation on workpieces made of steel with a tensile strength of less than or equal to 800 N/mm^2, 15 to 20 m/s for cast iron and bronze workpieces, and 45 to 50 m/s for grinding aluminium. In abrasive belt grinding operations, cutting fluids include mineral oils, kerosene, emulsions, and fatty oil pastes.

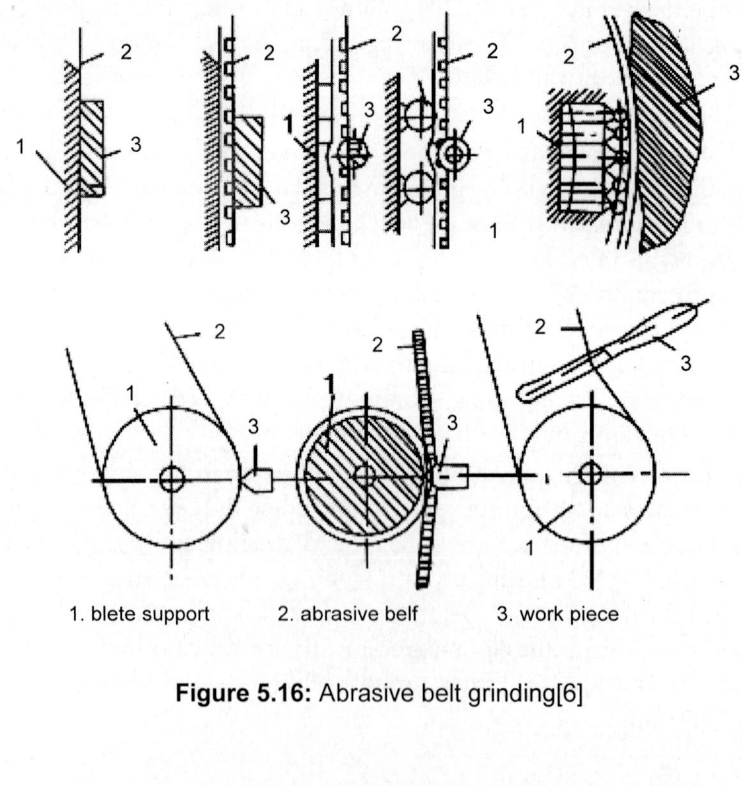

Figure 5.16: Abrasive belt grinding[6]

5.10.1 Advantages of Coated Abrasive Belt

1. The abrasive belt's working area is significantly larger than the grinding wheel's, which encourages heat dissipation during grinding. This increases belt life and virtually eliminates workpiece deformation.
2. The belt's surface is more uniform when compared to a grinding wheel because the electrostatic field approach evenly distributes the abrasive grains so that they are vertically orientated and embedded in the glue-coated backing.
3. More abrasive grains per unit area than on the grinding wheel, which increases grinding capacity and output.
4. Lack of vibration and impact loads guarantees a higher class of surface finish.
5. The machine and tool are cheap and of simple manufacture.
6. 6. The belt's cutting power may be altered by choosing a contact roller with the right hardness and geometry.
7. Quick and simple abrasive belt replacement.
8. Operational safety.

5.10.2 Grinding Points

While grinding wheels are not appropriate, grinding tips [Fig. 5.17] are used for internal grinding and to clean up difficult-to-reach areas when manufacturing moulds and dies. These tips are glued to a unique stem and lack through holes. The diameter of grinding tips varies from 3 to 40 mm.

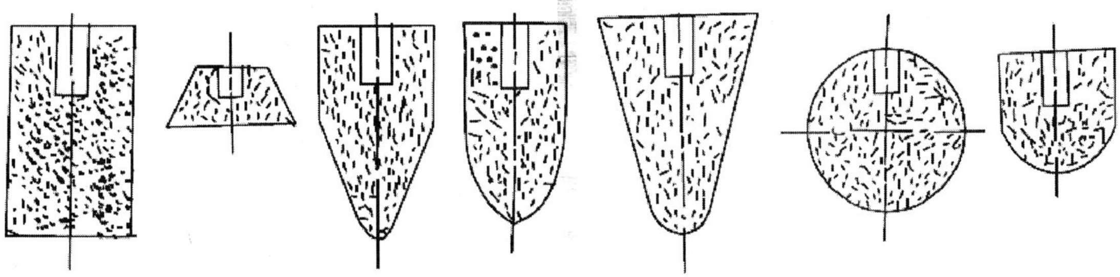

Figure 5.17: Grinding points [6]

5.10.3 Grinding Segments

The several abrasive segments that make up a segmental grinding wheel are held in some way in a chuck. The length of the segments ranges from 125 to 300 mm. Fig. 5.18 depicts some of the shapes of the grinding segments. Wheels with segments are used for surface grinding. A segmental wheel's key benefit is that a damaged segment may be easily replaced without having to toss the entire wheel. The gaps between the segments make it easier to dispose of chips and worn-out wheel fragments as well as to deliver cutting fluid to the grinding zone. The workpiece gets heated less when grinding with a segmental wheel because of the reduced area of contact with the wheel.

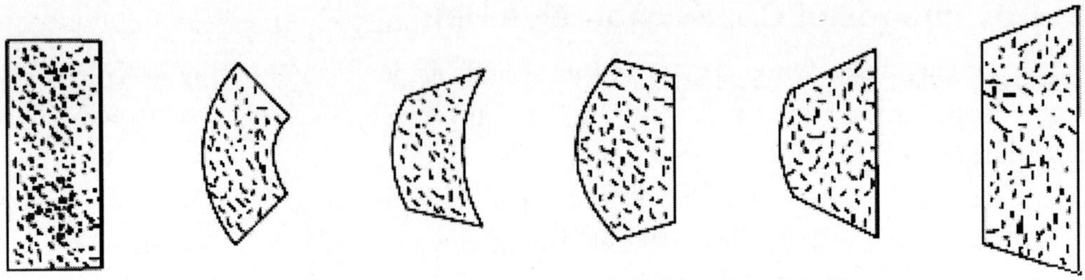

Figure 5.18: Shapes of grinding segments[6]

5.10.4 Abrasive Sticks

For hand fitting tasks as well as honing and super-finishing tasks carried out in specialised equipment for micro-finishing, abrasive sticks are employed. Fig. 5.19 depicts the various designs of the abrasive sticks. Sticks with square (first), flat (second), and special flat (last) honing forms that are mounted in specific heads are used for honing and super-finishing.

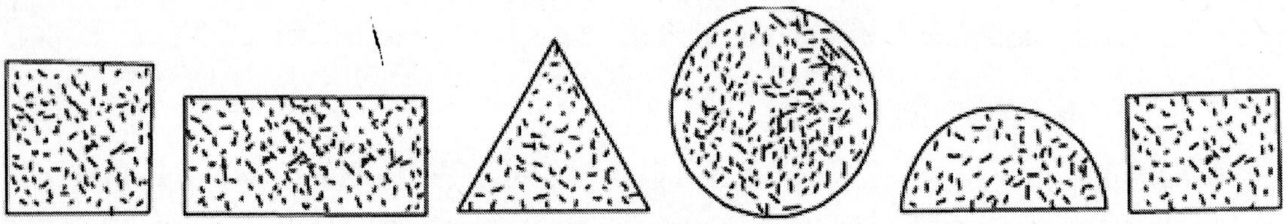

Figure 5.19: Abrasive sticks

5.11 GRINDING PROCESS VARIABLES

There are many process variable like speed, stock removal rate etc.[6]

Wheel Speeds. When employing appropriate grinding-wheel speeds, which have been fairly well established, the majority of machines can be changed to reach the desired cutting efficiency. Since it was difficult to achieve the proper peripheral wheel speeds in the past, internal grinding presented significant challenges. However, high-cycle, direction-driven wheel heads are quickly displacing older varieties of wheel heads today. Effective peripheral wheel speeds are typically as follows, in accordance with manufacturers' specified maximum speeds for certain wheels: Internal grinding (10.0 - 30.0 m/s speed), Surface grinding (20.0 - 25.0m/s speed), Diamond wheels (25.0 - 32.5m/s speed), Resinoid (27.5 - 60.0 m/s speed), Vitrified (27.5 - 32.5 m/s speed), and Cylindrical grinding (30.0 - 50.0 m/s speed).

Work speeds. To obtain the desired finish and the maximum stock removal compatible with long wheel life, certain work rates are necessary. Except for internal centerless grinding, the work and abrasive wheel move in opposite directions when they pass the cutting line. The material being ground at this point should decide the work speed. This range includes soft steel (0.15- 0.25 m/s speed), hard steel (0.35- 0.50 m/s speed), cast iron (1.00- 2.00 m/s speed), and aluminium (0.50 m/s speed), with the low end utilised for rough cuts and the high end for finishing.

Stock removal. The most efficient way to remove stock is with coarse-grit wheels, which also allow for the maintenance of commercially acceptable dimensional accuracy despite a substantially coarser surface quality. Therefore, choosing a surface finish carefully is essential for maximising manufacturing efficiency. Comparative rates for stock removal per pass are shown for the following grinding operations: rough grinding (0.05 to 0.50 mm), semi-finish grinding (0.025 to 0.25 mm), and finishing. However, these rates will vary significantly depending on the type of material being ground (0.0125 – 0.125 mm).

5.12 BALANCING OF GRINDING WHEELS

A mounting technique for a grinding wheel is shown in Fig. 5.20. Two flanges, one on either side, hold it firmly against the spindle. Thick compressible washers (0.5 to 3 mm thick), made of cardboard, rubber, leather, etc., should be positioned between the flanges and the wheel.

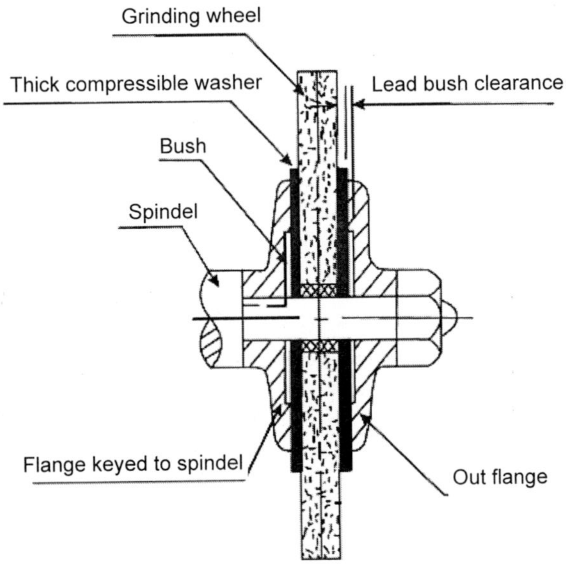

Figure 5.20: Mounting of grinding wheel[6]

High speeds are used to revolve the grinding wheels. Any wheel that is out of true and out of balance will therefore generate significant imbalanced forces and cause excessive vibrations. Poor workpiece surface polish and shorter wheel life will result from this. Each wheel with its sleeve should therefore be balanced before installing on the grinding wheel spindle. Once the wheel face has been trued up, the test should be conducted. The wheel is fixed in the middle of an arbour that is exactly round and straight. The assembly is subsequently supported by the balancing machine's roller rests or straight knife-edged ways, as shown in Fig. 5.21. A wheel that is not balanced properly will not stay still. The heavy side will be underneath when it finally comes to rest. By removing some lead from the bush's heavy side, the wheel is balanced.

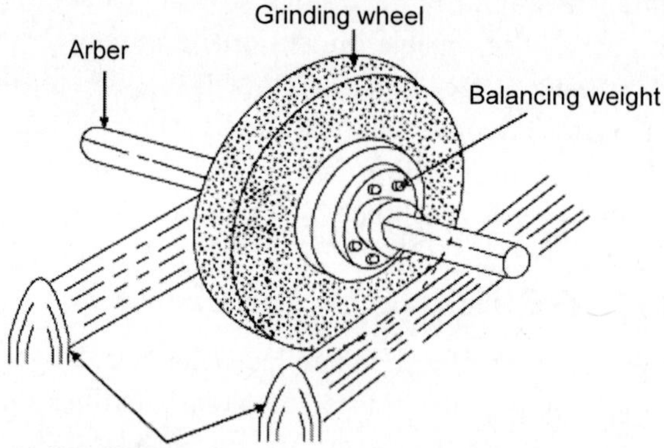

Figure 5.21: Static balancing device[6]

Moving three evenly distributed weights into the wheel sleeve's annular groove is another way to balance the wheel (or mounting flange). By tightening the screws, these movable parts can be fixed around a circle at any location.

5.13 HIGH SPEED GRINDING

Traditional grinding is essentially a finishing technique. It is used to attain high geometric and dimensional accuracy in order to produce a smooth surface. As a result, compared to turning and milling operations, the metal removal rate (MRR) in typical grinding processes is quite low. High speed grinding can boost MRR to levels comparable to turning and milling processes while also producing precision and surface polish on par with conventional grinding. High speed grinding, also known as high efficiency grinding, varies from conventional grinding in that the grinding wheel speeds are significantly higher (often 60 m/s and more, up to 80 m/s), as opposed to roughly 30 m/s for traditional grinding. Since there is less force on the work, the work speeds and rates are really comparable higher (from the power, force, and velocity relationship).

On conventional grinding machines, increasing the wheel speed is not enough to achieve high speed grinding. Wheel speed, work speed, and infeed rate must be compatible with operating factors such machine condition, wheel structure, coolant application, necessary surface quality, and work material hardness. The grinding equipment used for high speed grinding needs to be sturdy (i.e., have vibration-free structures), have increased machine and spindle stiffness, strong wheel and work drives, and suitable and effective safety guards.

Al_2O_3 is the abrasive utilised to create high-speed grinding wheels, and either a unique, high-strength vitrified bond or a polyurethane bond is used for the bond. The wheel construction must be relatively open due to the higher rate of metal loss. Wheel loading is less of an issue with an open structure. With an open construction, coolant feeding is also more effective. A high pressure coolant system with a specific nozzle is employed to guarantee proper cooling of the contact. Also, using oil coolant in place of an emulsion will considerably boost the metal removal rate. To present a full layer of material for each rotation, the infeed rate must be increased correspondingly with the wheel speed in order to increase the metal-removal rate.

It is evident from the information above that high speed grinding causes (i) a reduction in the thickness of the chip removed by each abrasive grain, resulting in a reduction in grinding forces, (ii) an increase in MRR, (iii) increased grinding ratio and (iv) better surface polish.

5.14 ABRASIVE MACHINING

As a finishing procedure, ordinary grinding has a very low rate of metal removal. Such grinding processes are categorised as "abrasive machining" when metal removal rate is the primary factor and surface quality and accuracy are secondary. It covers all processes where choosing between grinding and other machining techniques is mostly based on cost. Increased process variables (feed and/or depth of cut) can be used to increase the metal removal rate. The method compares favourably to other machining techniques like milling, turning, and broaching, among others. The surface quality and geometric tolerances attained are on par with those attained by these machining procedures.

However, abrasive machining consumes about three times as much electricity per unit MRR as milling does. However, it is far less than the standard grinding process. Abrasive machining is currently competitive with other machining processes, nonetheless, for the reasons listed below:

(a) Work surface conditions do not negatively affect the procedure, according to this statement.

(b) Both rough and finishing cuts can be completed in a single step.

(c) Handling costs are significantly decreased since there is no need to alter the machine setup for rough and finish cuts.

(d) Work-holding devices and fixtures can be reduced or deleted in comparison to other machining techniques like milling.

(e) Abrasive machining requires less machining allowance than other machining techniques. Thus, there is a start-up saving (in material).

The above procedure can be used to machine any material, including metals, ceramics, refractory alloys, and superalloys.

5.15 DRESSING / CONDITIONING

The term "conditioning" can be used to describe any technique that aids in the production or regeneration of the grinding capabilities of grinding tools. Profiling, sharpening, and cleaning are subordinate chores that are part of conditioning. In other words, conditioning is done when the grinding wheel's shape, measurements, profile, concentricity, and axial runout are no longer accurate enough. The grinding tool has a tendency to pinch and uses more power if the surface topography of the grinding wheel is in an unfavourable working range as a result of abrasive wear. On the surface of the grinding tool, material from the work piece welds. In this situation, it is also necessary to condition or dress the grinding tool. Dressing must always be done in a controlled environment to provide a reproducible outcome. There is a distinction between "rotary" and "stationary" dressing tools. The following are some of the stationary dressing tools: Plate dressers, Disc wheel dressers, Single-grain dressers, Multi-grain dressers, Dressing sticks, and Diamond dressing rollers and drum dressers are rotary dressing tools.

5.16 COOLING LUBRICANT FOR GRINDING

The cooling lubricant's job is to dissipate heat in order to lower process temperatures. The grinding wheel's surface is also cleaned and freed of any clinging chips at the same time. The two main categories of cooling lubricants are emulsions and grinding oils, respectively.

5.16.1 Grinding Oils

Even after very good lubrication, it is frequently discovered that they have subpar cooling abilities. Grinding oil is typically utilised in these circumstances with materials that are less sensitive to heating up. Emulsions are made up of 94–98% water and 2–6% oil. Ultra-fine oil particles are spread throughout the water. Emulsions have a limited ability to lubricate but very good cooling qualities. They are consequently mostly employed when cutting materials that are susceptible to heat. The design of the process parameters is always based on the cooling lubricant being utilised. The process parameters completely change when switching from oil to emulsion and vice versa. In order to get the cooling lubricant into the chipping zone, the supply of the lubricant is crucial. The nozzle should be pointed tangentially toward the surface, and the outlet speed of the cooling lubricant should be set to the grinding wheel's peripheral speed. This occurs when the grinding wheel partially engulfs the cooling lubricant jet. A significantly worse cooling effect is produced by cooling lubricant speeds that are either low or too high.

5.17 MANUFACTURING OF GRINDING WHEEL

A grinding wheel is made using a skilled procedure, as shown in Fig. 5.22, which calls for raw material grains, a bonding agent, and a wetting agents.

5.18 COMMON PROCESS ERRORS

Grinding process mistakes cause surfaces to be of poor quality. There are three main type mistakes as follows:

5.18.1 Burning and Grinding Cracks

Burning causes the ground surface to become discoloured in this sort of error, and subsequent grinding causes the ground surface to develop cracks with incredibly fine lines. Possible reasons of this inaccuracy include: I excessive heat buildup during the grinding operation; (ii) blunt grinding wheels; and (iii) blunt dressing tools. The following are some potential fixes: I lower peripheral speed; (ii) speed up the workpiece; (iii) change dressing parameters; (iv) optimise cooling lubricant supply (e.g., nozzle); and (v) use a grinding wheel with a slightly coarser grade.

5.18.2 Surface Irregular and Uneven

Errors of this kind are caused by irregular surfaces and fluctuations in dimensions and evenness. It could be caused by I an inaccurate machine and (ii) dirt in the coolant and the clamping region for the work piece. The following are some potential fixes: I inspect the machine and make any necessary adjustments (ii) reduce the grinding depth (iii) dress more frequently (iv) adjust the wheel to be a little softer and more open.

5.18.3 Wheel Wear too Great / Loss of Profile

This type of error occurs when the grinding wheel loses too much contour and profile, which affects the work piece's dimensions and profile. It could be caused by a grinding wheel that is too soft. The following are potential remedies: (i) Increase the observe maximum permissible working speed (ii) Choose a tougher wheel with a denser structure (pores) and a finer grade (iii) Reduce feeding speed and grinding depth.

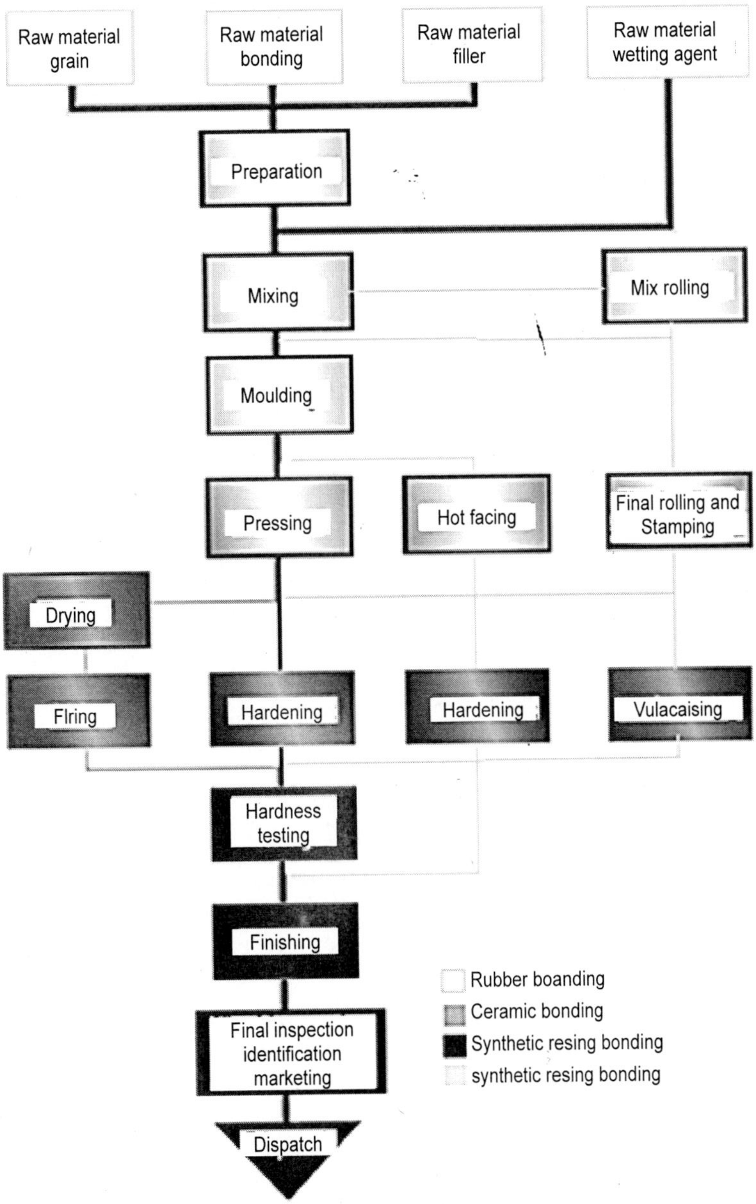

Figure 5.22: Process diagram showing manufacturing of a grinding wheel

5.19 INTRODUCTION TO FINISHING PROCESSES

Whatever the manufacturing technique, it is impossible to produce a surface that is completely flat and smooth. The machine parts or components still have surface flaws from the manufacturing process. The outside border of a part is its surface, and the surface irregularities are the innumerable tiny valleys and wedges that depart from the surface's hypothetical nominal surface (Fig. 5.23, shows a surface on a highly magnified scale).

The appearance of a surface and its suitability for a component's intended application are greatly influenced by these imperfections. The phrases surface finish, surface roughness, surface texture, or surface quality are typically used to describe these surface abnormalities. The surfaces of heat exchanger tubes conduct heat more effectively when they are slightly rough as opposed to well finished. Surface roughness of some kind is best for clutch plates, brake drums, etc. The surface irregularities must be small enough (smooth surface) so that they do not penetrate the oil film under the harshest operating circumstances, yet, if a film of lubrication must be maintained between two moving parts.

Such examples include seal surfaces, machine ways, helical and worm gears, bushings, cylinder bores, piston pins, and bushings. To ensure quiet operations, gears also need smooth surfaces. Sharp irregularities operate as stress raisers for components that experience load reversals, making them the biggest potential source of fatigue cracks. Because of this, exceptionally smooth finishes are applied to the surfaces of components that are subjected to significant stresses and load reversals.

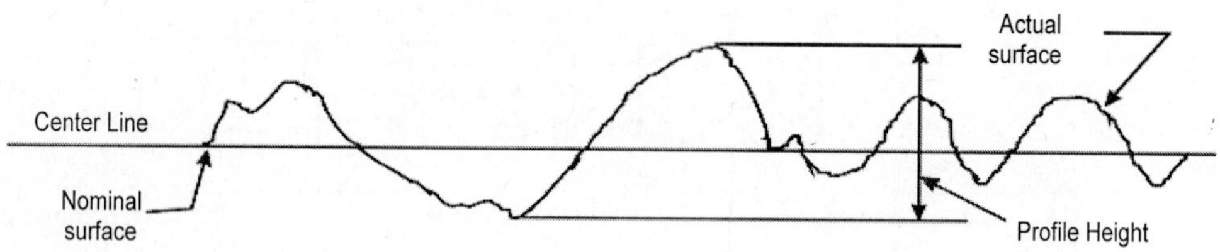

Figure 5.23: Profile of surface irregularities

5.19.1 Evaluation of Surface Roughness

The B.I.S. (Bureau of Indian Standards) classifies it as Ra after calculating its Center Line Average (CLA) or Arithmetic Average (AA). The average value of the ordinates from the centre line (the centre line AB is positioned such that the sum of the areas above the line is equal to the sum of the areas below the line) is referred to as the arithmetic average or the centre line average. The algebraic sign of the ordinates is not taken into account, so,

$$AA = CLA = Ra = \frac{1}{L}\int_{0}^{L} y(x)\,dx$$

Where L is Roughness width cutoff or the sampling length. This is the maximum width of surface irregularities that is included in the measurement of roughness height.

Approximately, $R_a = \frac{\sum_1^n |Yi|}{n}$, where n = number of vertical ordinates

i.e. $$R_a = y_1 + y_2 + y_3 + ... + y_n/n = A_1 + A_2 + A_3 + ... + A_n/L = \frac{\Sigma A}{L}$$

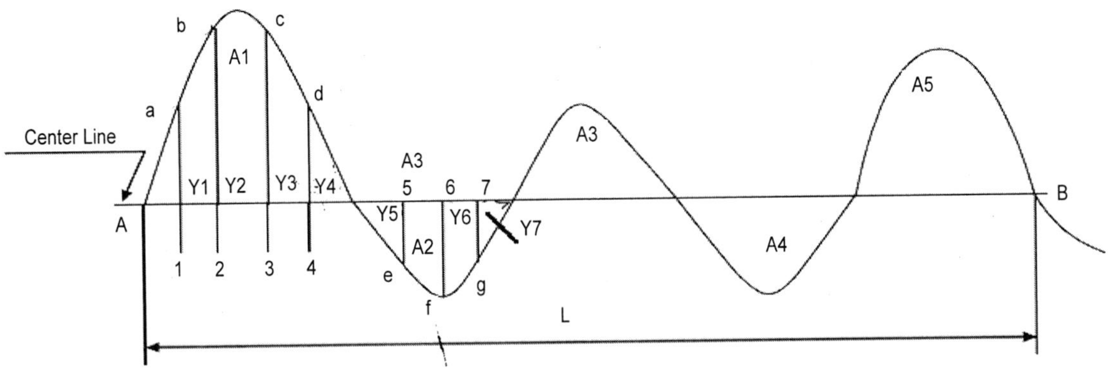

Figure 5.24: Surface roughness

5.19.2 Units of Surface Roughness

Microns or micrometres are used to quantify surface roughness or finish; 1 micron is equal to 10-3 mm or 10-6 metres. The traditional metal machining techniques used in secondary manufacturing are all finishing operations. Table 5.3 lists the variety of surface finishes that can be created using these techniques for typical applications. Other surface finishing techniques, like lapping, honing, buffing, and super finishing, are used to provide higher surface finishes. This chapter will cover these procedures. Table 5.3 lists the usual surface finish ranges that can be obtained using these techniques.

Table 5.3: Typical range of surface finish, Ra value in μm

Process	Average applications
Turning, Boring	0.4 to 6.3
Reaming	0.8 to 3.2
Shaping, Planing	1.6 to 12.5
Drilling	1.6 to 6.3
Milling	0.8 to 6.3
Broaching	0.8 to 3.2
Grinding	0.1 to 1.6
Roller burnishing	0.2 to 0.8
Lapping	0.05 to 0.4
Honing	0.1 to 0.8
Buffing	0.05 to 0.5
Super finishing	0.05 to 0.2

5.20 FINISHING BY GRINDING

Diamond turning, grinding, Honing, Lapping, Super finishing etc. are various methods used for finishing the surfaces of a parts.

5.20.1 Diamond Turning and Boring

Light alloys, bronzes, and tin alloys with metal are frequently turned or bored using diamond tools with geometric controls of approximately 0.0125 mm or below and with surface roughness measurements of between 0.075 and 0.125 m when the application calls for it (AA). Fine finishing using diamond tools is largely limited to materials that cut cleanly with a distinct chip and don't include any hard or abrasive particles that would chip or harm the stone. The cutting edge is quickly lost to materials that come away as an abrasive powder, which increases the cost and unpredictability of using diamond tools. The equipment used for precision turning and drilling must clearly be in excellent condition, with all ways, guides, bearings, and spindles operating flawlessly with the least amount of clearance and no vibration.

5.20.2 Grinding

The most common method of finishing steel is grinding, but it takes a high level of competence to repeatedly produce a limited grade of surface finish to precise geometric tolerances. Finishes in the range of 0.2 to 0.3 m (AA) are frequently produced in operations involving the production of hardened components with tolerances of between 0.05 mm and 0.025 mm, but it should be noted that producing finishes finer than the aforementioned values significantly increases the risk of surface burning and cracking. The machinery used for fine gridding needs to be in excellent condition, with all ways and guides straight and true, and special care needs to be given to wheel balancing.

The preparation of the wheel surface is crucial. It has been discovered that the cleanliness of the coolant has a direct impact on the quality of the surface created, hence it is crucial to have an adequate flow of chip- and granule-free coolant. The material being cut and the desired finish will influence the choice of wheel grit, speeds, and coolants. Although grinding is practical and reasonably cost-effective for generating fine surfaces, it has a number of drawbacks.

An unavoidable side effect of grinding is the formation of an incredibly thin layer of decarburized material due to the high temperature created at the work and wheel contact line. This material has a significant impact on the initial effectiveness of a surface as a bearing and must frequently be removed before truly satisfactory bearing conditions are attained. High temperatures also cause the surface to burn and can cause grinding cracks to emerge that are large enough to reduce a component's fatigue strength. On cylindrical components that have been ground, especially those that have been centerless ground, chatter is also noticeable.

5.20.3 Lapping

Lapping is a surface-finishing technique used on cylinder-shaped or flat surfaces (mainly external). Lapping is the process of abrading a surface using a lap that is charged with tiny abrasive particles and is made of a softer substance than the surface being lapped. The fine abrasive particles become buried in the softer lap when they are pushed against each other between the lap and the work surface. After that, it serves as a holder for the tough abrasive. The hard particles on the surface of the charged lap remove minute amounts of materials from the harder surface when it is rubbed against it. Because the abrasive particles embed themselves in the surface of the soft lap rather than moving over it, it is the abrasive that actually cuts and the soft lap is not worn away. When lapping, the abrasive is typically transported in a vehicle between the lap and the work.

The cutting action is somewhat controlled by the vehicle or lubrication, which also prevents scoring the work and abrasive caking. Kerosene combined with a tiny amount of machine oil, greases, fine sperm oil for fine work, olive oil, lard oil, spindle oil, and soapy water are a few of the vehicles used. The laps are cleaned with naphtha. Almost any substance that is soft enough to hold the abrasive grains in place can be used to create laps. They could be made of wood, leather, soft steel, brass, copper, lead, or soft cast iron. Cast iron with fine grain is the most typical lap. Copper is a common material for lapping diamonds and is used rather frequently. Cloth laps are used to lap hardened metals for metrolographic inspection.

Artificial corrundum is used as an abrasive for preliminary lapping and once more in a finished state for finishing on steel surfaces. Cast iron and alumina both respond well to silicon carbide when used for fine lapping. Diamond dust or boron carbide with the smallest grain sizes work well for lapping tiny components. Other abrasives used include crocus powder, green rough (chromium oxide Cr2O3), and rough (ferric oxide, Fe2O3). From 120 grit to the smallest powdered grains, the abrasive particles range in size. A paraffin lubricant is employed in almost all circumstances. The use of soluble oil or water lubricants while working with soft materials is the exception. The average amount of material removed during lapping is less than 0.025 mm, while harsh lapping can remove as little as 0.0025 mm of material.

Parts can be produced by commercial lap operations with a maximum tolerance of 0.000625 mm. Because it removes metal so slowly, it is only used to remove scuff marks from honing or grinding, or to create extremely flat or smooth surfaces for gauge blocks or liquid-tight seals in applications involving high pressures. It is possible to lap materials of practically any hardness. However, as the abrasives have a propensity to become entrenched, lapping soft materials is challenging. Thus, lapping is done to (i) to produce geometrically true surface (ii) to correct minor imperfections is shape (iii) to obtain fine dimensional accuracy to provide a very close fit between the contact surfaces and (iv) to secure a fine surface finish.

Lapping may be done by hand or mechanically with the help of special lapping machines by the following methods.

5.20.3.1 Hand lapping for flat work

The lap in this instance is flat, like a surface plate. In order to gather extraneous abrasive and chips, grooves are typically carved over the surface of a lap. With one hand holding either the lap or the workpiece while the other performs an erratic rotational motion, the two surfaces in contact can be abraded to complete the work surface. The work is often turned in order to achieve homogeneous cutting activity. Press work dies, dies and metallic moulds for castings, surface plates, engine valves and valve seats, gauge blocks, and piston rings, among other items, are lapped using this technique. By hand lapping, piston rings are often produced parallel and with extreme precision. The final level of dimensional accuracy and parallelism for gauge blocks, with a finish of 0.025 to 0.050 m and a tolerance of 0.000025mm, is achieved by manual lapping.

5.20.3.2 Hand lapping for external cylindrical work (ring lapping)

Fig. 5.25 depicts an exterior lap for external workpieces (round). It has a saw-cut split in it, and one or more screws can be tightened to close it up. The hole is naturally bored before the saw cut is performed, and its diameter is the same as that of the piece to be lapped. Expanding internal laps are designed. Over the surface of the work piece, the ring lap is repeated. The technique is typically applied to gauges that are produced in limited quantities or with stepped plugs.

5.20.3.3 Machine Lapping

Mechanical lapping is a high production technique that, for example, removes 0.05 to 0.075 mm of material from gudgeon pins that are 25 mm in diameter and 75 mm in length, with an accuracy limit of roundness, straightness, and size within 0.025 mm. The work holder is positioned on the lower table of mechanical lappers, which are vertically constructed and oscillate. While the lower lap rotates at around 60 rev/min, the upper lap is still and floating. For lapping rounded surfaces, additional types of lapping machines are available. Small parts like ball bearing races, piston pins, and other components are created to be lapped using a particular kind of centerless lapping machine. Fig. 5.26 depicts a general-purpose machine for lapping both cylindrical and flat surfaces.

Between the top and lower laps, a number of workpieces with previously flattened surfaces are positioned. The axes X-X of the workpieces are positioned in slots in a work holder so that they are not perfectly radial. The workpieces' shape will determine the slots' shape. The work holder is described as oscillating with an amplitude of approximately 25 mm while the two laps are rotated. Workpieces are gradually lapped to size by feeding a stream of vehicle into the centre of the laps and letting it flow outward while carrying fine abrasive flour suspended in it. A pressure of 0.007 to 0.02 N/mm2 for soft materials and up to 0.07 N/mm2 for tougher materials is sufficient for machine lapping. Lapping can be done with mechanical lapping machines: (i) External cylindrical surfaces, and (ii) Flat surfaces.

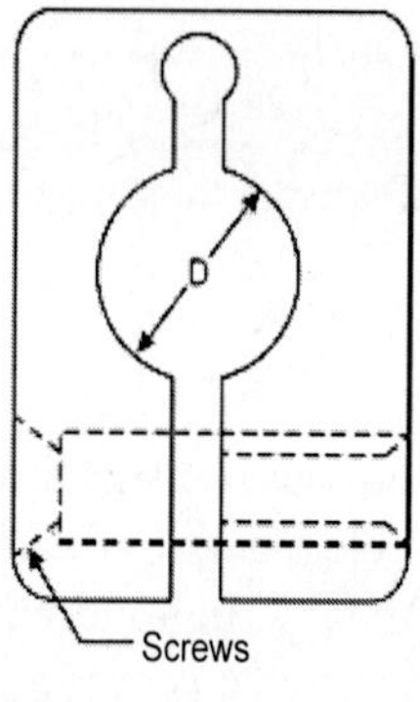

Figure 5.25: External lap

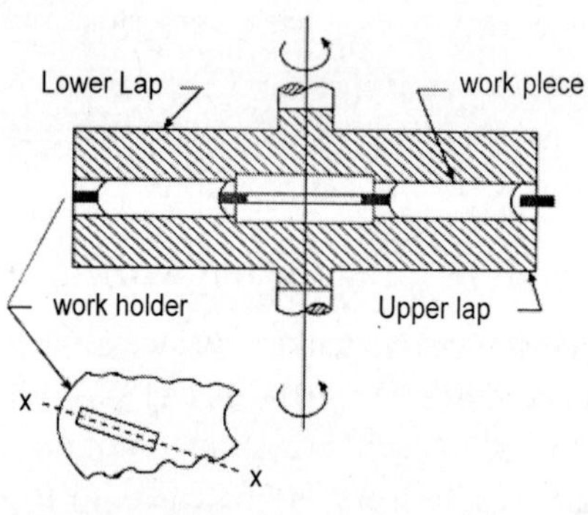

Figure 5.26: Machine lapping

Lapping is used to manufacture a variety of components, including: aircraft piston pins, automotive wrist pins, diesel engine injector-pump parts and spray nozzles, plug gauges, specific dies and moulds, gauge blocks, refrigerator-compressor parts, oil-burner parts, micro-meter spindles, roller bearings, taper rollers, worm and worm gears, crankshafts, camshafts, ball bearing raceways, etc.

When considering the lapping process's specialty, it has developed into a typical manufacturing method due to the necessity for hardened surfaces with only a few micrometres of surface finish. However, because it removes metal at such a slow rate, it is unavoidably expensive and is not economically viable unless working conditions make such surface finishes absolutely necessary. Lapping and polishing are different in that polishing is intended to produce a shining surface, but a lapped surface typically lacks a visibly dazzling sheen. Lapping obviously eliminates metal from the surface it is applied to, although polishing typically does not remove much metal. Lapping, as opposed to polishing, enhances the body's geometrical contour. While polishing entails creating a sort of plastic flow of the surface crystals so that the high places are made to cover the low spots, lapping is really a cutting procedure. Lapping is typically used for exterior surfaces, as stated above. But it can also be applied to inside surfaces.

5.20.4 Honing

A method of abrading or grinding is honing. There is very little material removed from it. This procedure is generally used to eliminate tool or grinding marks that have been left on the surface from earlier operations. Abrasive sticks (made of silicon carbide or aluminium oxide) set on a mandrel or fixture provide the cutting action. There is a floating action between the tool and the job, causing any pressure applied to the tool to be applied and transferred equally on all sides. Honing rates range from 15 to 60 mpm as a result of giving the honing tool a slow reciprocating motion while it turns. By quickly removing the stock, this motion also creates a surface that is straight and round.

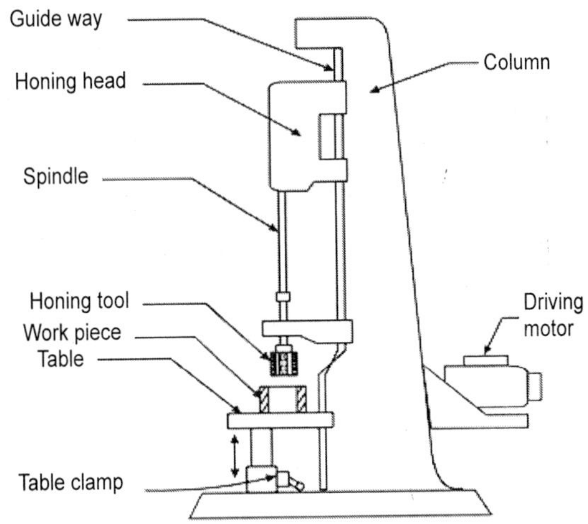

Figure 5.27: Vertical spindle Honing Machine

This procedure can fix flaws left behind from earlier operations such a tiny eccentricity, a wavy surface, or a tiny taper. Only 0.025 mm or less of material is removed while honing parts for the finish. However, values up to 0.50 mm reflect standard procedure when certain mistakes need to be addressed. To maintain temperatures consistent and flush out tiny chips, coolants are crucial to the operation of this process. Most often, lard oil blended with kerosene or sulphurized mineral base is utilised. Additionally, paraffin is employed. The majority of honing is done on interior surfaces or holes, such those in car cylinders. External surfaces can be honed in a few different ways. The surface must be cylindrical, but the parts might be of any shape. It is possible to hone almost any material. Due to the application of bonded abrasive, soft materials that cannot be lapped can be honed. You can hone cast iron, both hard and soft, steel, carbides, bronze, aluminium, brass, and silver, as well as glass, ceramics, and some plastics.

In general design, honing machines resemble vertical drilling machines. Fig. 5.27, however typically hydraulic means are used to reciprocate the spindle. A hydraulic motor or gearing may be responsible for the rotating motion. The work finish is influenced by the speed ratio of two motions, which can vary throughout the process or for various materials. For cast iron, the rotational and reciprocating speeds vary from 60 to 150 mpm and 15 to 21 mpm, respectively. For steel, the equivalent rotational and reciprocating speeds are 45 to 60 mpm and 12 mpm, respectively. The sticks' whole length is worn evenly by the reciprocating motion, which also keeps the bore cylindrical. Automobile cylinder bore finishing is done using vertical-type semi-automatic honing equipment. For this operation, both single- and multi-spindle machines are employed. The honing tool has the abrasive stones installed on it. The conical wedge is adjusted in relation to the honing tool in order to stretch the abrasive stones outward to fit the hole that needs to be polished.

Fig. 5.28 depicts the general layout of a vertical honing machine. If honing is necessary, the abrasive sticks (up to 8 in number) are enlarged using micrometer-controlled mechanical or hydraulic methods. The honing tool or fixture must be free to float since it will follow the axis of the original hole. To do this, universal joints are used, as seen in the picture. As a result, it is no longer essential to properly align the hole and sharpen the axes since the honing tool becomes self-centring. Up to 500 mm diameter work can be done on vertical machines.

Large, long gun barrels and related tasks are the only things that are honed using horizontal honing machines. The tool is rotated and reciprocated by the head on the machine's right end of the bed while the workpiece is kept in place on the left. These machines can produce hone holes up to 1 m in diameter and have stroke lengths of up to 22.5 m.

A clean finish with a distinctive cross hatch appearance results from all honing. The use of different pressures, speeds, and types of abrasives can alter the depth of these hone marks. The use of automatic size-controlled tools in conjunction with honing can preserve precise dimensions. Honing is frequently used to finish rifle barrels, ring gauges, piston pins, and automotive engine cylinders, flange faces and shafts. For primary honing and secondary honing, abrasive sticks are made of material with a grit size of 80 to 180 and 300 to 500, respectively. Honing can produce a surface polish on the order of 0.05 μm R.

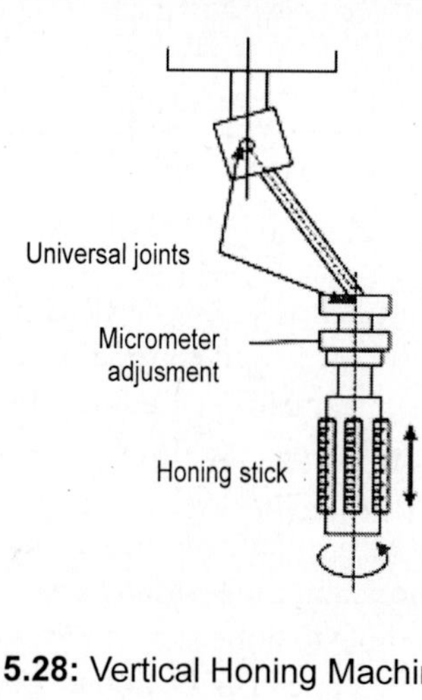

Figure 5.28: Vertical Honing Machine

5.20.5 Buffing

A rotating cloth buffing wheel that is often loaded with a very fine abrasive is used to buff the workpiece as part of the polishing process. Fig. 5.29. When a polishing medium like "rouge" is employed, the cloth buffing wheel turns into a carrying vehicle for the fine abrasives, which is very similar to the polishing process in lapping. The abrasive removes some metal from the workpiece during this motion, erasing the scratch lines and creating an extremely smooth surface. There is some indication that a small amount of metal flow may occur when softer metals are polished, especially without the use of an abrasive, which helps to eliminate the high spots and provide a high polish.

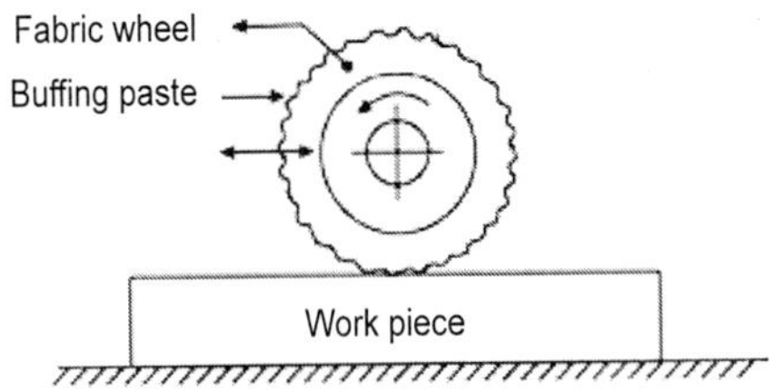

Figure 5.29: Buffing

Fabric discs such as linen, cotton, broadcloth, and canvas are used to make buffing wheels. The quantity of stitches used to bind the layers of material together determines how solid they are. There may be no stitching on buffing wheels used for very gentle polishing or for polishing into interior corners since the centrifugal force created by the wheel's spin will hold the layers of cloth in place. The speeds of buffing wheels range from 32.5 to 40 m/s. There are numerous varieties of buffing rouges. The majority of them contain a soft form of binder and predominantly ferric oxide.

Only extremely small scratches, oxide, or other similar coatings that may be present on the work surface should be removed with buffing. Usually, the job is done by hand while being held against the rotating wheel. Because of the cost of labour, this operation is likely to be somewhat expensive. There are semi-automatic buffing machines on the market that feature a number of independently operated buffing wheels that can be positioned to buff various areas of the workpiece. The workpieces are secured in fixtures and moved past the buffing wheels on a spinning circular worktable. Such equipment can produce extremely excellent results and inexpensive buffing costs if the workpieces are not too complex in shape.

The following goods are examples of products that use the buffing technique to produce a mirror-like finish: items used on mobile homes, cars, motorcycles, boats, bicycles, sporting equipment, tools, retail fixtures, business and residential hardware, and domestic utensils and appliances.

5.20.6 Barrel Tumbling

The procedure of barrel tumbling involves rotating a workpiece in a barrel with abrasive and water in order to produce a high shine or to remove burrs. A standard tumbling barrel has eight sides, is coated with wood, measures 1.2 metres in diameter and 1.8 metres long. It spins at roughly 24 rpm. There could be one to six sections in the barrel. Depending on the task, the time commitment could range from 1 to 4 hours. The barrel or drum is almost completely filled with parts before being loaded with slugs, stars, jacks, or other abrasives like sand, granite chips, or aluminium oxide pallets. After that, the barrel is turned. A fine cutting motion is produced by the movement of the components as they roll and tumble over one another and the associated impingement of the slug or abrasive against the pieces, as shown in Fig. 5.30. Delicate pieces must not move about during tumbling, and in some circumstances, they must be fastened to racks inside the barrel to prevent them from colliding.

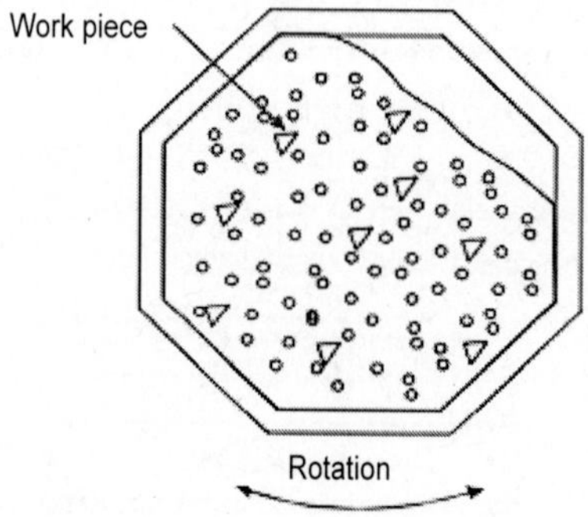

Figure 5.30: Barrel tumbling

A cheap cleaning technique is tumbling. Slug materials can come in a variety of forms. Since forms must be provided that will reach into all areas and corners that need to be cleaned, multiple shapes may be combined in one load. Although it occasionally happens, tumbling is typically done dry. Any one of the following uses for tumbling is possible: Deburring, cleaning, improving micrometre finish, finishing high precision work to a high shine, finishing gears and threaded parts without causing damage, finishing parts free of fins, flashes, and scales, and removing paint or plating are all examples of deburring. To avoid corrosion, the parts must be properly cleaned after tumbling, dried using sawdust or infrared lamps, and then oiled.

5.20.7 Barrel Rolling

Similar to tumbling, barrel rolling uses an appropriate cutting abrasive to reduce the surfaces rather than cleaning them (Fig. 5.31). The barrel is only around 40 to 60% full while barrel rolling. Either open slanted barrels or small horizontal barrels are used for rolling.

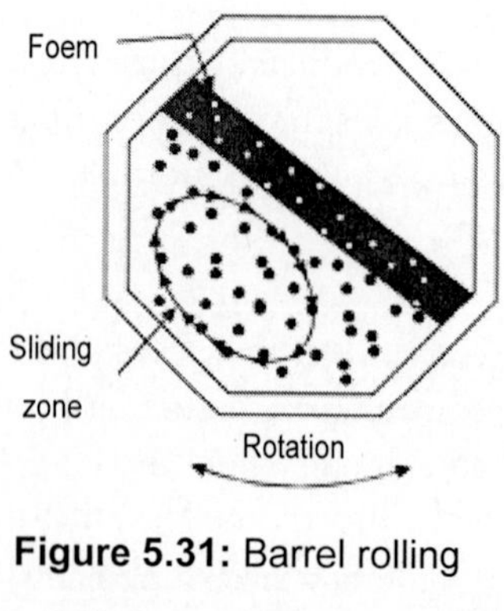

Figure 5.31: Barrel rolling

The barrel is filled with the workpieces, abrasive, water, or diluted acid solutions so that as the barrel rotates, the mass will be carried about 3/4 of the way up the side before rolling over and falling to the bottom. Slag, cinders, sharp sand, granite chips, broken glass chips, and carborundum are the most often used abrasives. The abrasives range in size from roughly 5 mm to 25 mm and vary in shape from round to triangular. Since no cutting action will take place unless the abrasive's sharp edges travel over the surfaces to be polished, the rolling action needs to be such that there is relative motion between the work and the abrasive particles.

Rolling is typically done while wet because it produces a faster cutting action. However, dry rolling is also used to polish small parts, typically using an abrasive and sawdust mixture. A variety of finishes can be achieved by employing the right abrasive. For non-ferrous items, rolling takes 10 minutes; for steel, it takes 2 or 3 hours. It is easy and very cost-effective because it is typically done in batches. Although the finished surface is very consistent, rolling must first be used to remove deep scratches.

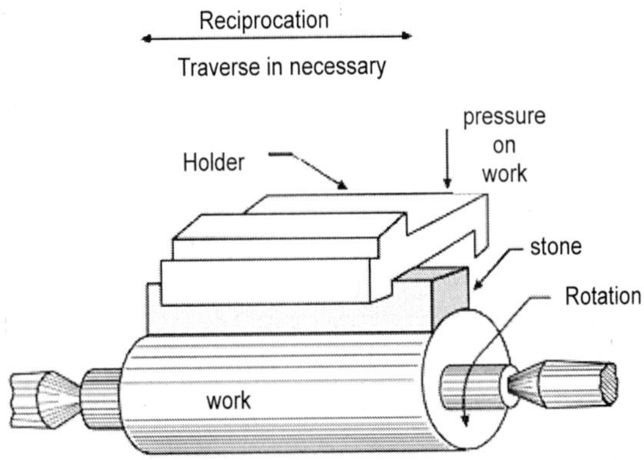

Figure 5.32: Supper finishing

5.21 SUPER-FINISHING PROCESSES

A regulated surface condition on items is produced by the micro finishing technique known as "super-finishing," which is not possible with any other technique. Scrubbing a stone against a surface to generate a fine quality metal finish is an activity known as "microstoning." The procedure entails cleaning chatter marks, broken, or smear metal from a dimensionally finished part's surface. Some manufacturing applications allow for the efficient removal of up to 0.03 to 0.05 mm of stock, although the procedure is most cost-effective when the metal removal is kept to less than 0.005 mm.

The technique involves pushing a soft-bonded fine grit stone against a rotating round workpiece while rapidly reciprocating it, as shown in Fig. 5.32. The stone swiftly ages and takes on the shape of the workpiece. A cutting fluid is flooded onto the workpiece and tool to remove heat, metal shavings, and abrasives. In about 15 to 50 seconds, parts can be super-finished to a smoothness of 0.075 um. However, it can take two or three minutes longer to achieve a superior finish. Automobile cylinders, brake drums, sewing machine parts, computer memory drums, bearings, piston rods and pins, axles, shafts, clutch plates, tappet bodies, guide pins, and automotive brake drums are few examples of products that use super-finishing.

5.21.1 Burnishing

By rubbing and contacting the surface of a hard tool (such as a punch and/or die, rollers, or balls), the burnishing procedure produces a smooth and shining surface. It is a procedure of strengthening and finishing. In essence, burnishing is a sort of cold surface plastic deformation. Cold working surfaces increases surface polish and creates surface compressive residual stresses, which extends component fatigue life.

Figure 5.33 depicts the sizing operation using a punch or mandrel and a die to burnish the bush's inside and outside surfaces. The bush's internal surface is burnished when the mandrel is driven through it, and the bush's exterior surface is polished when the bush is forced through the die. Burnishing also enhances the surface polish of the gear's two components. The tooth surfaces are subjected to a surface rolling action by means of a specific hardened gear-shaped burnishing die. With this technique, burnishing gear that has been precisely shaped and hardened rolls the gear under pressure. Añy high spots on the tooth surface are plastically bent during this cold working procedure to provide an exact and final tooth profile. The two key burnishing techniques are now explained in the following sections.

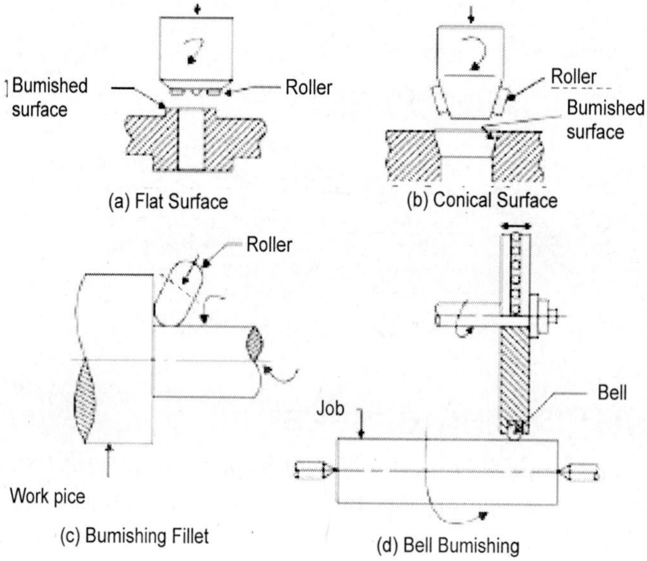

Figure 5.33: Roller burnishing

5.21.1.1 Barrel burnishing

Barrell burnishing frequently yields results that are almost identical to those attained by buffing. Similar to barrel rolling, but with medium balls, shots, or round pins placed to the work in the barrel instead of an abrasive medium. Burnishing does not involve cutting. As opposed to this, the slug material produces peening and rubbing action on the rough work surface, dispersing the tiny surface irregularities to an even surface. Burnishing will typically provide a smooth, uniform surface and reduce the porosity in surfaces that are to be or have been plated, but it won't typically remove obvious scratches or pits. Typically, parts that will be barrel burnished first need to be rolled with a fine abrasive. Typically, barrel burnishing is done wet with water that has cleaning or lubricating chemicals like soap added. No more than half of the barrel should be filled with work and shot. There should be around two volumes of shots to one volume of components since the rubbing action between the work and the shot material is crucial.

It is important that the ratio prevent the workpieces from rubbing against one another. To prevent the workpieces from being thrown out of the mass as they reach the top position and roll down the sloped surface, the barrel's rotational speed should be regulated. To ensure that the material can contact inside corners and other recesses that need to be rubbed, it is typically required to employ a variety of sizes and forms of shot material. Commonly used objects include balls with a diameter of 3 mm to 6 mm, pins, jacks, and ball cones. By attaching them in racks inside the barrel, parts that cannot be permitted to brush against one another can be polished satisfactorily. After that, the shot material is added, and burnishing is done as usual. Barrell burnishing is affordable and creates surfaces suited for further painting or plating when the right conditions have been met.

5.21.1.2 Roller/ ball burnishing

Figure 5.33 shows how to burnish flat, cylindrical, or conical surfaces (internally or externally) using hardened steel or cemented carbide rollers or steel balls set in a holder. By using rollers with a radius edge, fillets and grooves are burnished (Fig. 5.33(c)). The burnishing pressure should be raised when strengthening is the treatment's goal. The machining accuracy is, however, a little less due to this circumstance. Multi roller tools are used to burnish holes on drill presses, automatic lathes, turret lathes, horizontal borers, unit constructed machines, and lathes. The surface becomes 20 to 50% harder and 1.5 to 2 times more resistant to wear after burnishing. Ballizing, also known as "ball burnishing," is the practise of using balls to polish internal surfaces. In order to push smooth balls or mandrels through the length of the hole, they must be somewhat larger than the bore diameter (see Fig. 5.33(d)). Hydraulic system components, seals, valves, spindles, and shaft fillets are a few examples of products that commonly use roller burnishing (Fig. 5.33 (d)).

5.21.2 Powder Coating

In powder coating, the surface to be coated is covered with an appropriate plastic formulation in the form of finely ground powder. The surface is then heated after that. The powder undergoes a plasticization process that enables it to flow and bond into a continuous, uniform coating. For coating, both thermo-setting and thermo-plastic resins are utilised. Other plastics used include nylon, PVC, and thermo-plastic polyester in addition to the aforementioned thermo-plastic resins. The thermo-setting resins category comprises acrylic, polyester, and epoxy. Thermo-plastic resins enable the creation of thicker coatings. The major applications for thermo-setting resins are thin paint-like surface coats. For epoxy resin, the baking temperature should be between 120°C and 135°C, and the baking period should be between 20 and 30 minutes. Both for this film's ornamental coating and for thick coating (functional end applications), it is used. "Fluidized bed" technology is employed for thermo-plastic resins. Here, a heated component is submerged in a bed of fhuidized powder. The temperature of the heated component and the length of time it spends submerged in the powder bed will determine the coating's thickness.

The "Electrostatic fluidized bed" process is another frequently used coating technique. Above the powder bed, a cloud of charged powder particles is produced. The cloud has a covering over the elements (hot or cold). Powder is deposited on the components' surface as a result of an electrical field of attraction that forms between the powder particles and the components. Epoxy, polyester, acrylic, polyethylene, and polypropylene are some of the resins utilised in this process. "Electrostatic spraying" is the technique for powder coating that is most frequently utilised. A powder feed unit, powder sprayers, a spray booth, an electrostatic voltage source, and a powder recovery unit are among the equipment.

5.21.3 Polishing

A part is polished to provide a smooth and shiny surface finish. An abrasive (Al2O3 or diamond) paste is applied on soft/resilient polishing wheels made of felt, cloth, wood, or coarse calico, etc., and these wheels are used to polish surfaces. The method is based on the concurrent activity of the instrument (polishing wheel) and the pastes' surface-active ingredients. Surface roughness is decreased to 0.032-0.012 m Ra. Polishing, unlike lapping, does not increase machining accuracy.

There are three types of polishing operations: roughing, dry fining, and finishing. Dry wheels are used for roughing and dry fining processes, with the abrasive grain sizes being 20 to 80 for roughing and 90 to 120 for dry fining. In finish polishing, the grain size is fine (150), and pastes are made from oil, tallow, or beeswax. It produces a lovely finish. It is challenging to polish parts with irregular shapes, pointed corners, deep depths, and sharp projections.

5.22 ELECTROPLATING

The process of electroplating (Fig. 5.34) involves running an electric current through a solution to deposit a desired metallic coating over a surface (or substance). A chemical mixture containing the metal's ionic form, an anode (positively charged), which may be the metal itself (a soluble anode) or an insoluble anode (typically carbon, platinum, titanium, lead, or steel), and finally a cathode (negatively charged), where electrons are supplied to create a film of non-ionic metal.

An important industrial process known as electroplating is used to restore worn-out parts or improperly machined components as well as to impart functional properties like corrosion resistance, wear and abrasion resistance, tarnish resistance, heat resistance, electrical conductivity, bearing surface, and solderability. It is a very popular technology with a wide range of applications. The coating could be made of a single metal, an alloy, or even a metal-polymer or metal-ceramic composite.

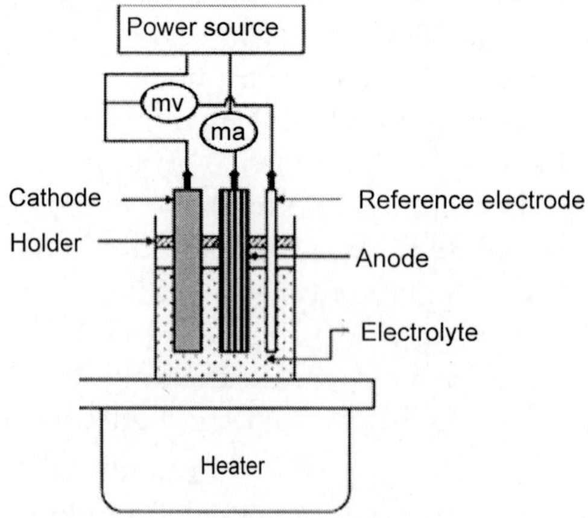

Figure 5.34: Electroplating process

Electroplating is the electrochemical technique of depositing a thin protective layer, often metallic, onto a prepared metal surface. Pee-treatment (cleaning, degreasing, and other preparation processes), plating, rinsing, passivating, and drying are all steps in the procedure. Depending on the metal surface to be plated, the cleaning and preparation processes employ a variety of solvents (typically chlorinated hydrocarbons, whose use is forbidden), surfaces tripping agents, including caustic soda, and a range of strong acids. Since there are water-based solutions available, it is not essential to degrease with halogenated hydrocarbons. The item to be plated is often employed as the cathode in an electrolytic bath during the plating process. Acidic or alkaline plating solutions may also contain complexing agents like cyanides.

Let's use an illustration of a copper plating to help you comprehend the idea more clearly (Fig. 5.35). In this case, metallic jewelry is to have a layer of copper electrodeposited on it to improve its beauty. Typically, the copper plating is attached to the circuit's anode (the electrode that is positively charged), while the jewelry is kept at the cathode (-ve charged electrode). Both are maintained submerged in an advanced electrolytic bat (solution). At this point, the copper ions are oxidized and dissolved into the solution by the anode receiving a DC current.

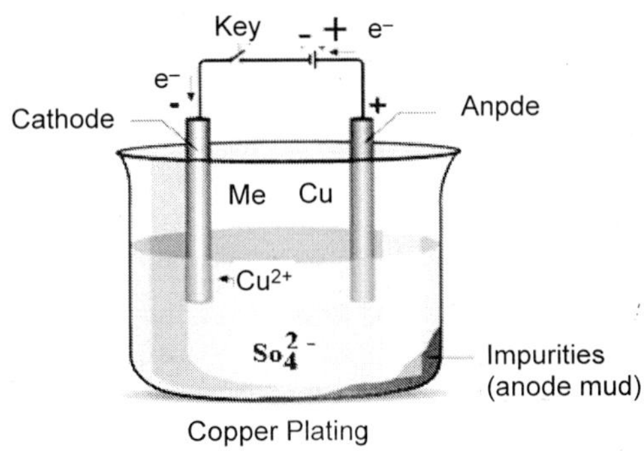

Figure 5.35: Electroplating of copper

Copper dissolved ions are reduced at the cathode and applied to the jewelry as plating. However, a number of important elements affect the final plating. These comprise: the voltage and current levels, the bath's temperature and chemical makeup, the distance between the cathode and the anode and the duration of the current. A single metal or a mix of metals can be electroplated onto an object. To increase strength and conductivity, many manufacturers prefer to layer metals, such as copper and nickel. Brass, Cadmium, Chromium, Copper, Gold, Iron, Nickel, Silver, Titanium, and Zinc are materials that are frequently used in electroplating. Nearly any material, including plastic, stainless steel, and other metals, can be used to create substrates. Both soft fabric ribbons and organic objects like flowers have been electroplated by artists. It's crucial to remember that before being electroplated, non-conductive substrates like plastic, wood, or glass must first be converted into conductivity. A layer of conductive paint or spray can be applied to a non-conductive substrate to achieve this.

In terms of applications of electroplating, besides improving the substrate's aesthetics, there are many more uses for it. The primary use is to maximise a material's corrosion resistance. The fact that the plated layer frequently acts as a sacrificial coating shows that it degrades before the basic material The following are some additional frequent uses of electroplating: (i) Increasing wear resistance; (ii) Increasing metal surface thickness; (iii) Increasing electrical conductivity, such as by plating a copper layer on an electrical component; (iv) Reducing Friction; and (v) Improving surface uniformity. Therefore, electroplating is a procedure that is added on to assist an item or accessory last longer. Although the object is coated to shield it from dirt or the elements, electroplating various objects has a variety of other purposes as well. Here are only a few of them such as: to reduce friction, increase electrical conductivity, protect against radiation, improve aesthetics, and prevent corrosion. Thus, electroplating has advantages and disadvantages of its own.

5.22.1 Benefits of Electroplating

Numerous advantages of electroplating include improved strength, longevity, and conductivity of parts. These advantages are utilised by engineers, producers, and artists in various ways. Electroplating is a common technique used by engineers to improve the durability and strength of various designs. Different parts can have their tensile strength increased by having metal coatings like copper and nickel applied to them. For outdoor or corrosive applications, one can cover parts with a metallic skin to increase their resilience to external conditions including chemical exposure and UV light. Electroplating is frequently used by artists to maintain the natural. An efficient method for adding decorative metal finishes to consumer goods, sculptures, figurines, and works of art is electroplating. Electroplating can be used to improve performance on electrical parts, antennas, and other items.

5.22.2 Limitations of Electroplating

Although electroplating has many advantages, it is constrained by how difficult and dangerous the process is. If suitable safeguards aren't taken, electroplating workers may become exposed to hexavalent chromium. A properly ventilated office is crucial for employees. Self-electroplating resin parts is possible, however inexperienced users may encounter difficulties. The fundamental explanation is competence and quality. DIY electroplating techniques typically result in lesser laminate adhesion strength than services provided by a professional plating company. It is very challenging to reliably do structural plating, which calls for lengthy plate duration, numerous baths, and compatibility between metals.

5.22.3 Types of Metals for Plating

Some of the common metals that can be electroplated with their benefits and limitations are listed in Table 5.4.

Table 5.4: Common metals for electroplating

Copper plating	Copper coatings are both excellent electrical conductors and highly aesthetically pleasing. Hardness can range between 90 HV and more than 200 HV depending on the additives. A copper layer is frequently coated by another metallic layer in functional applications.
Advantages, disadvantages & Limitations	Excellent heat and electrical conductivity can be found in copper layers. By altering the deposition circumstances, an extremely broad range of characteristics can be obtained. Copper plating is a crucial stage in the creation of printed circuit boards and is easily accomplished on a wide variety of metals and polymers. A metallic or organic top layer is required because copper can tarnish in the presence of air or when touched.

Nickel plating	Nickel layers are resistant to corrosion and wear in addition to being attractive. The deposit can have hardness values between 150 and 500 HV, depending of the organic additives. The internal stress and ductility of the metal layer might vary. Bright nickel is frequently covered with a top layer made of chrome or gold since it tarnishes fast and appears yellowish in the sunlight.
Advantages, disadvantages & Limitations	Ornamental layer that looks nice, wear- and corrosion-resistant Applications for different bath mixes can be very different. Widely applicable to a range of substrate materials, a suitable base layer for additional surface finishes, Use of a top layer is required due to the discoloration of nickel in air; for electronics, a final gold coat may be required. Allergies to nickel may result in cutaneous responses.
Tin plating	Tin is very helpful in the production of many different electrical parts since it has a high level of conductivity. It is also extensively employed in the food manufacturing sector.
Advantages, disadvantages & Limitations	Resistant to wear from adhesive and corrosion favourable solderability. After tin is deposited, resistance welding is possible, solid electrical characteristics, used with approval in the food industry (FDA-approved), Hydrogen embrittlement is susceptible to high-strength steel. Heat treatment is required for some substrates to prevent brittleness, in certain circumstances, the tin layer may start to produce whiskers, which could lead to electrical contact short circuits.
Gold plating	Due to their superior corrosion resistance, low electrical contact resistance, and outstanding electrical and heat conductivity, gold layers have a wide range of technical uses. With the use of an intermediary copper or nickel layer, gold coatings can be applied to a wide range of substrates, including metals, polymers, ceramics, and natural materials (such as leather and wood).
Advantages, disadvantages & Limitations	Outstanding heat conductivity, good solderability, good chemical and corrosion resistance, excellent electrical conductivity, High price, which varies throughout the year, Unalloyed metal's malleability.
Silver plating	Silver is frequently utilised in electrical and electronic applications because of its excellent electrical conductivity.
Advantages, disadvantages & Limitations	Excellent electrical and thermal conductivity, tarnishes easily in air under certain circumstances and when sulfur-containing compounds are present.
Palladium plating	Palladium works effectively for plating tasks when it's important to avoid oxide development. It is less expensive (per ounce troy) than gold and has a higher melting point of 1554°C. Palladium is a superb gold alternative in the majority of ordinary electronics applications.
Advantages, disadvantages & Limitations	Plating that is reasonably priced compared to other precious metals, It has a natural resistance to oxidation and is roughly as resistant to corrosion as gold. It is harder than gold while being regarded as a softer metal, which helps it resist impact and denting. Palladium is a great coating for copper objects because it is diffusion-resistant; copper diffuses quickly through gold but not palladium. Excellent solderability, decrease in thermal resistance; Due to its lower melting point than gold, palladium is more prone to deformation in extremely hot conditions. not acid-resistant; Palladium can only be employed in a limited number of applications due to its sensitivity to strong acids. More prone to breaking; due to its hardness, palladium is more likely than gold to crack when put under stress.

5.22.4 Inspection of Electroplated Parts

To ensure high plating quality, finished electroplating items are put through a series of testing. Typical examples of these tests include: (i) Adhesion: Using tape, bake, or twist (ii) Appearance: both microscopic and visual (to the level of magnification contractually agreed on) Solderability (iii) and Bondability (iv) For instance, ultrasonic wire bonding (v) Porosity: Techniques like nitric acid immersion or vaporisation, electrolysis, gas, and (vi) Thickness: Microsection or X-ray Fluorescence (XRF).

5.23 HOT DIPPING

The hot dipping method involves coating steel with a protective layer of zinc to boost steel's endurance, which is essential for shielding steel from all types of corrosion and called as Galvanizing.

5.23.1 Galvanizing

The galvanization method involves coating steel with a protective layer of zinc which is essential for shielding steel from all types of corrosion. This is essentially the technique for galvanising steel that is most frequently employed. The base metal in this case, steel, is immersed in a bath of molten zinc during this operation. Since the procedure involves completely submerging steel in molten zinc, both the inside and the outside must be completely covered. As a result, the protection is full even if the steel to be galvanised is hollow. Preparing the surface of the steel to be galvanised is the most crucial step in the hot dip galvanization process. The steel that will be hot-dip galvanised must be entirely clean in order for the molten zinc to develop a strong and full metallurgical bond with the steel, which is of the utmost importance. The steps that are stated below make up the entire procedure for cleaning and preparing the surface of steel.

- **Pickling.** In this stage, hydrochloric acid at the proper temperature is used to remove scale and rust off the steel's surface. This procedure is essential for removing scale and rust from the surface of the steel that will be hot-dip galvanised.
- **Rinsing.** Following the completion of the chemical cleaning procedure, the steel that will be galvanised is thoroughly rinsed in water to minimise the transmission of acid residues to the subsequent steps of galvanization.Fluxing.
- **Fluxing.** Flexing is the final step in the preparation of the steel surface for the hot dip galvanising process. Fluxing eliminates all oxides and prevents their further production, which is essential for promoting the strongest bond between the zinc coating and the steel.

After the entire process of steel's surface preparation is finished, it is immersed in a bath of molten zinc that is around 830o Fahrenheit in temperature and contains about 98 percent pure zinc. Following the removal of the coated steel and thorough cooling, the hot-dip galvanised steel is then suitably prepared for usage. Other coatings techniques that can be utilised to further enhance the surface characteristics include:

5.23.2 Caustic Cleaning

The stage of caustic cleaning is the first in the process of steel surface preparation. As implied by the step's name, it entails using a hot alkali solution to remove a variety of organic impurities from the surface of the steel, including dirt, grease, and oil. Mechanical methods are used to remove all other undesirable substances like asphalt vinyl, epoxies, or welding slag.

5.23.3 Titanium Nitride (TiN) Coating

This coating is friction-reducing, inert, and resistant to wear. Use it to extend tool life two to ten times or more over uncoated tools on cutting tools, punches, dies, and injection mould components. TiN coating is used by producers of medical devices to prevent galling between sliding parts, keep surgical instruments' edges sharp, and set their products apart from the competitors. Coating your equipment with titanium nitride is a fantastic place to start if you're serious about optimising your production processes. Tool steels can simply have their TiN coating removed. This makes TiN a perfect covering for processes involving pricey tooling, such injection moulding and shaping.

5.23.4 Parkerising

Parkerizing provides further corrosion protection for ferrous metals including wrought iron, cast iron, steel, and alloy steel. Non-ferrous metals including copper, brass, aluminium, and plastic products are not appropriate for this technique. By applying a surface coating, it can also be utilised to increase the wear resistance of materials. This method is utilised in the business world to increase surface roughness, corrosion resistance, wear resistance, and protection against dents and scratches. Other names for the procedure include "phosphating," "phosphatizing," "bonderizing," and "phosphate coating."

Three tanks make up the equipment utilised in the parkerizing procedure. They are totally distinct from one another since they each contain unique elements that should never be combined. A solvent solution that has been created for a particular substance with impurities is kept in the first tank. This is used to clean the work piece's surface of any contaminants. A phosphoric solution, also called the parkerizing solution, is included in the second tank. The solution is heated in this tank as well using a heating element, which operates at a constant high temperature. The only component in the third tank that is rotating and flowing normally is clean water. In order to finish the procedure, the work item is cleaned of the parkerizing solution using this tank. The following is a thorough explanation of the parkerizing procedure:

1. First clean the surface of metallic parts that need to be coated through the parkerizing method. Cleaning is required to remove dirt, grease, oil and other contaminants from the material surface. Usually this preparation process is done by using a soft brush which removes all contaminants from the material surface.
2. The Parkerizing procedure begins with the work piece being submerged in hot water for three to five minutes. The metallic components are then taken out of the hot water rinse and dipped into the parkerizing solution. At a constant operating temperature of between 190o F and 195o F, this is done for 3–10 minutes. By soaking once again for 5 to 10 minutes at a temperature set between 68o and 92o F, this procedure can be improved even more.
3. Lean the parkerized components by completely cleaning them with a sharp brush and the running water from a rinse tank, which also stops the parkerizing process on the surface. To allow extra solution to flow back into the tank once the part has been taken from it, it is left hanging on a rack above the tank. Remove it off the rack once this task is finished, inspect it, and then begin packing and storing it. Parkerizing has several distinct uses, some of them are as follows:

i. The parkerizing process, which adds additional protection against corrosion and normal wear and tear, is arguably best known for usage with guns products.
ii. It is also applied to car parts to prevent rust or corrosion on unfinished metal components.
iii. This kind of procedure is typically employed to safeguard ferrous metals, particularly those utilised in the production of military weapons.
iv. The Marine Corps extensively use the process of parkerizing to shield various pieces of equipment from corrosion.
v. The process of parkerizing is frequently used to give sections of aircraft and spacecraft improved resistance to wear and rust.

5.23.5 Anodizing

An important process in producing aluminium CNC machined parts is anodizing. Anodizing is an electrochemical technique that adds an oxide surface layer to a metal object to give it better durability and a more appealing appearance. Although anodizing is most frequently done on aluminium, it is also possible to do it on titanium and magnesium substrates. Anodizing guarantees that a part can withstand corrosion, long-term use wear and tear, and environmental abrasion while maintaining its aesthetic appeal. Similar to when you need heat treatment, tempering, or electroplating, manufacturers frequently send components to third-party service providers who specialise in anodizing. Type I (Chromic Acid Anodize), Type II (Sulfuric Acid Anodize), and Type III, often known as Hardcoat, are the three most popular methods of anodizing. Every method of anodizing has particular manufacturing requirements and is best for particular materials. Despite the unique benefits and downsides of each type, they all function largely in the same way.

An electrical component's positive terminal, also known as an anode, must be connected in order to anodize a part, which must then be immersed in an acidic electrolyte bath solution. Chemical elements in this solution, including sodium phosphate, flood the bath with positive and negative ions. Apply the negative end of the circuit, or cathode, to a metal electrode in the bath once the component has been immersed and fastened to a hanger so it won't move. When one send voltage through the circuit, the negative electrode attracts positive ions (cations) from the part, and the aluminum part attracts negative O2 ions (anions) from the solution. When positive aluminum ions leave the part's surface, it becomes porous, reacting with the negative O2 ions to grow a layer of aluminum oxide.

The steps in the anodizing process are as follows: I apply a positive charge to the part, making it an anode; (ii) apply a negative charge to the metal plates, making them the cathode; (iii) immerse both in an acidic bath; (iv) apply voltage; (v) remove aluminium ions from the part, causing pores; (vi) attract oxygen ions to the part's surface; and (vii) the reaction creates

Time, Voltage, Electrolyte Composition, Current Density, Temperature, Anodizing Regime, and Pre-treatment are the parameters and characteristics of the anodizing process. The following material attributes can be altered by anodizing after these parameters are set: hardness, colour, porosity, thickness, corrosion resistance, and biocompatibility (e.g. for medical implants). The more time components spend in the acidic solution, the thicker their aluminium oxide layer becomes and the deeper their pores get. Anodized coatings have a thickness range of 8–16 μm or, when hardcoated, up to 35–50 μm. It should be noted that anodizing uses the same general principles as many other finishing techniques.

In actuality, one should proceed as follows: prepare the surface, Anodize, wash the components, Colorize while sealing the pores. For instance, submerge the part in a solution of metallic salts to give it a bronze or black finish. These interact with the surface to fill the pores with a chemical substance that is either black or bronze. It is known as electrolytic colouring.

5.24 DIP COLOURING

Which fills the pores with a dye solution, might be used if someone wants a different colour. Place the component in warm DI water after dipping it in the dye to stop any additional reactions. Dip colouring is the least resilient of the colouring techniques described here since the colour may deteriorate over time if exposed to UV light. The tiny pores on the part's surface must then be sealed in order to stop future corrosion and enhance performance. Anodized parts may feel tacky to the touch if the pores are not sealed. Additionally, dirt, pollutants, and stains can gather in open pores. These three methods are frequently used to close pores:

(i) **Hot DI sealing.** With this technique, you submerge the component in deionized water that has been heated to nearly boiling. Boehmite, or hydrated aluminum oxide, is created when the water reacts with the component. Compared to aluminum oxide, boehmite fills the pores and takes up more space. It is straightforward to standardise this procedure. It can, however, result in dye bleed and colour leakage on dyed materials and has a significant energy cost.

(ii) **Mid-temperature sealing.** This technique, which uses metal salts in solution like salts of nickel, magnesium, or cobalt to react with the surface and fill the pores, requires less energy than heat sealing. This technique lessens sealing smut or surface mineral deposits and is preferable for coloured components. However, it's more challenging to control and challenging to repeat with the same accuracy.

(iii) **Cold or room temperature sealing.** Cold sealing chemistries frequently use nickel-fluoride formulations that interact with the porous aluminum oxide layer to generate a sealed fluoro-aluminate layer that is then deposited on the surface. The surface is etchered during this process to improve performance and adherence.

5.25 METAL SPRAYING

A procedure known as metal spraying or metallizing involves applying molten metal or softened particles to a prepared surface (substrate) with spray equipment to improve its qualities (hardness, anti-corrosion, wear, dielectric, restoring dimensions etc.). The technique has a wide range of modifications. Additionally, it is applied on corroded machine parts, tools, and structural steel frames. In order to offer softer metals additional resistance to wear and strain, it is also used to hard-face them. Cobalt, nickel with a small quantity of chromium, and manganese chrome are some of the common hard-facing compounds used in metal spraying.

In comparison to other coating methods like electroplating, physical and chemical vapour deposition, thermal spraying can produce thick coatings (approximate thickness range is 20 micrometres to several millimetres, depending on the process and feedstock). Metals, alloys, ceramics, polymers, and composites are among the coating materials that can be thermal sprayed. There are many benefits to metal spraying, including higher tensile strength, altered electrical characteristics, improved or worsened corrosion protection, improved or worsened friction, improved wear resistance, and additional defence for materials that have been injured.

5.25.1 Flame Powder Spraying

This type of spraying involves feeding a powder material into a spray cannon through a powder pump, where it melts and forms a coating after being heated in a high-temperature flame. There are primarily three ways to feed powder into spray guns: by connecting the powder pump directly to the sprayer, by utilising a separate powder pump, and by employing an inert gas (e.g., nitrogen).

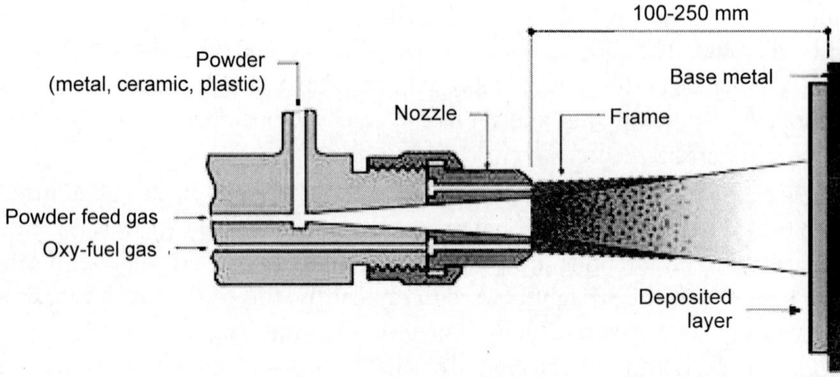

Figure 5.36: Flame powders spraying diagram

A wide range of materials, including metals, alloys, polymers, and ceramics, are available for use in the process. Excellent adhesive strength is provided by materials with a long melting time in a flame (90% efficiency for self-fluxing alloys). very quiet surroundings accelerates and cools particles using compressed gases. Manual spraying is possible with a light spray pistol.

5.25.2 Flame wire Spraying

In the common gas spraying technique known as "flame wire spraying," wires are successively fed into a gas flame, such as one made of oxy-acetylene or oxy-propane, where they melt and are then sprayed with compressed air to create coatings.

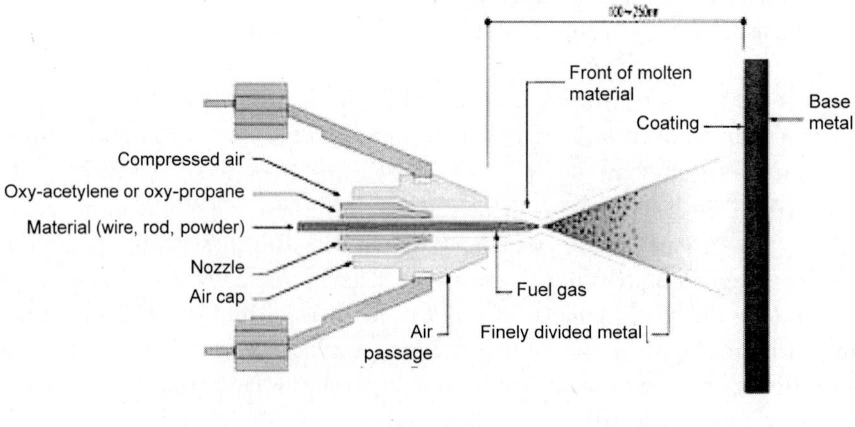

Figure 5.37: Flame wire spraying diagram

The process's characteristics are as follows:

(i) using tools that are portable and appropriate for on-site building

(ii) base metals undergo little to no thermal deformation

(iii) range of thickness adjustment (0.1–10 micrometres)

(iv) a large selection of materials and

(v) high coating wear resistance. Zinc, aluminium, carbon steel, stainless steel, and molybdenum are just a few of the metals that can be used in this spraying process to create wires having a wide range in thickness, from 0.1 to 10 micrometres.

5.25.3 Flame Rod Spraying

This technique uses an oxide ceramic rod as the coating material and operates on the same principles as flame wire spraying. An oxy-acetylene flame is used to heat and melt the ceramic rod, which is then finely split by compressed air and solidified to produce a coating on a base metal. Since it makes use of ceramics, this technique is appropriate for spraying on corrosion prevention or wear management, which increases heat resistance near hot places.

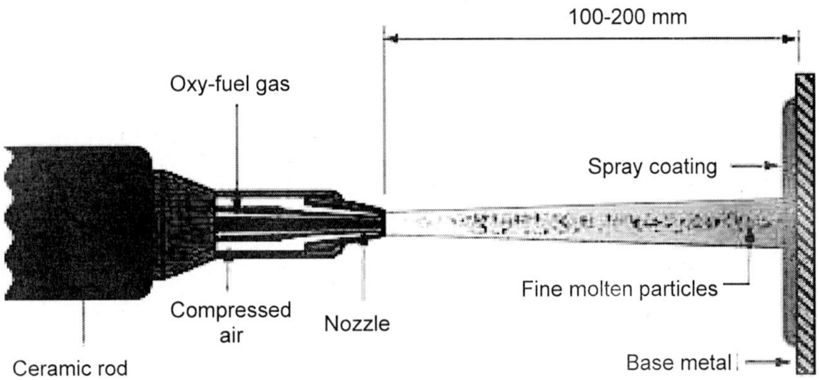

Figure 5.38: Flame rod spraying

Only totally molten particles are sprayed when the method is used that provides superior particle binding and creates very cohesive coatings. The speed of powder spraying is three to four times faster for heat resistant compared to plasma spraying. However there are fewer options for covering materials (limited to oxide ceramics).

5.25.4 High Velocity Oxy-Fuel (HVOF) Flames Spraying

This process creates coatings by applying a powerful spray impact caused by a faster spray rate. It is separated into HVOF (High Velocity Oxy-Fuel), which uses a fuel and oxygen mixture, and HVAF, which uses a fuel and air mixture, and uses the same fuel gas as flame spraying. It operates on the premise that combustion takes place inside a tube. Through a nozzle, a combustible gas is sprayed at a high rate of speed. A coating is created when powder is heated until it becomes molten and then sprayed at a high rate of speed.

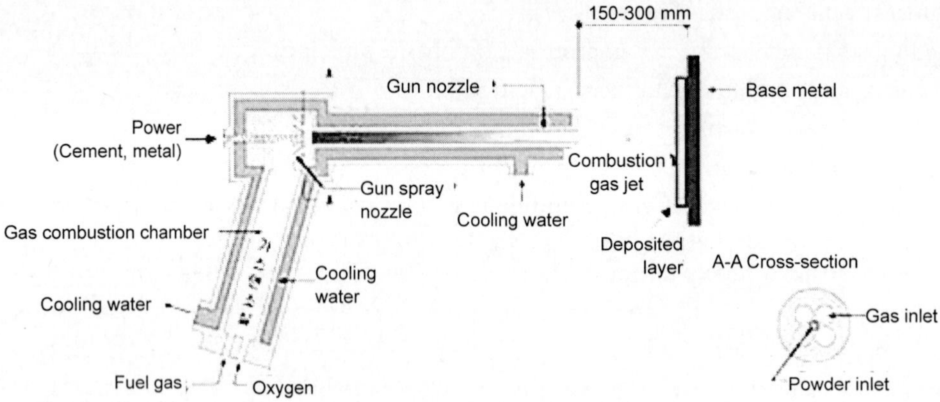

Figure 5.39: HVOF flame spraying diagram

Two or four times faster spraying is one of the characteristics of the method. It can produce fine coatings. Less oxidation takes place in the process. It calls for finer particles. It can lead to spray gun blockage. The process is ultrasonography done and it must be completed in a solitary and in soundproof space.

5.25.5 Arc Spraying

In this common form of electric spraying, two metal wires produce an electrical arc discharge, melt, and are supplied at a rate that matches the melting velocity. The melted metals are then successively moulded onto a base metal, creating a coating, after being finely separated by compressed air. It performs far better than approaches that use flame spraying. A coating material has exceptional adherence to a base material because it can be totally melted at high temperatures. However, only electrically conductive materials can be used as coatings.

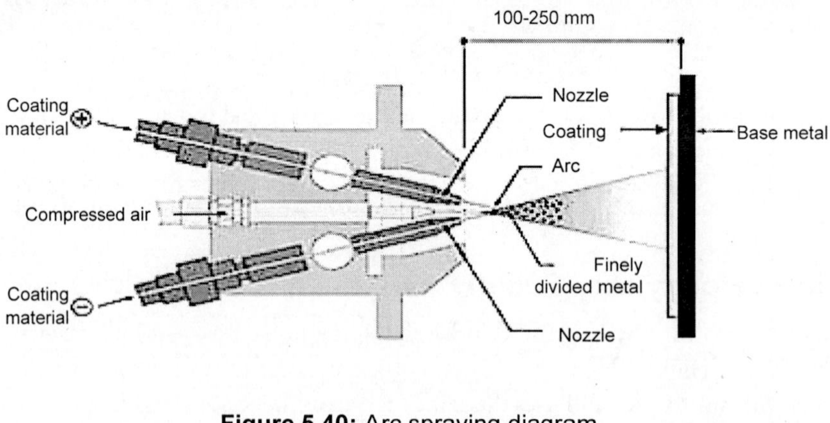

Figure 5.40: Arc spraying diagram

The Characteristics of the process are: (i) fast spraying (two to four times faster than flame spraying) (ii) high adhesive strength and coating strength (iii) using different types of materials, can form alloy coatings and (iv) low operating costs.

5.25.6 Detonation Thermal Spraying Process

Essentially, the detonation gun is a long, water-cooled barrel with powder and gas inlet valves. The barrel is fed with oxygen, fuel (acetylene is most common), and a charge of powder. The gas mixture is ignited with a spark, and the ensuing detonation warms and accelerates the powder down the barrel to supersonic speed. After each explosion, the barrel is purged with a pulse of nitrogen. Many times every second, this process is repeated. When heated powder particles collide with a substrate, their great kinetic energy causes an extremely dense and durable coating to form.

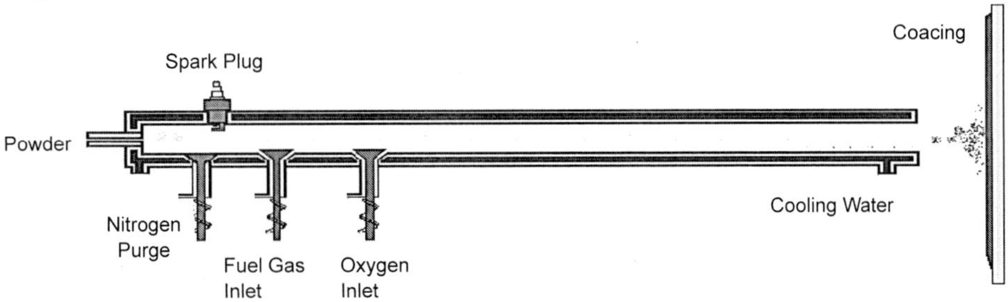

Figure 5.41: Schematic diagram of the detonation thermal spray process

5.25.7 Uses of Metal Spray Coating

These include wear resistance, dimensional restoration, corrosion resistance, thermal barriers, abradables, abrasives media, dielectrics, conduction, RFI/EMI shielding, medical implants, and undercoat for paints and powder coatings are just a few of the uses for metal spray coating.

5.26 ORGANIC COATINGS

In general, organic coatings are additive-style finishes that are applied to practically all kinds of materials. These can be two or more layers thick or monolithic, consisting of just one layer or coat. Coating systems' overall thickness varies greatly. Some are thinner than 1 mil. Others may reach a thickness of 10 or 15 mils. More than 10 mil thick coatings are typically referred to as linings, films, or mastics. Organic coatings' potential to serve as a barrier against corrosion and oxidation is mostly dependent on their chemical inertness and impermeability. However, some coatings also offer protection by using inhibitory pigments that passivate surfaces, especially metal surfaces. Additionally, some coatings include metallic pigments that protect metals electrochemically.

Brush, spray, dip, roller, flow coat, knife, tumble, silk screen, and electrostatic processes are frequently used to apply organic coatings. The slowest of these is brush application; all the others are production techniques. One or more of the following processes can cause an organic coating to dry or cure: (1) solvent evaporation or loss, (2) oxidation, and (3) polymerization. After application of the coating, the volatile ingredients, which are almost always present in at least a small amount, evaporate. Some finishes, like lacquers, cure completely as the solvents evaporate.

Coatings that do completely dry through evaporation remain semifluid after evaporation and need to undergo oxidation, polymerization, or a mix of the two processes in order to take on their ultimate form. The most time-consuming of the three techniques is drying by oxidation, which is typically carried out at room temperature. Both normal and increased temperatures can be used for polymerization, which involves a polymer chain building mechanism. Heat is used to accelerate polymerization. Production uses for radiation curing, which uses an electron beam to quickly polymerize the coating, have been discovered.

5.26.1 Coating Types and Systems, Coating Composition

A carrier and a pigment make up the two main parts of an organic coating. The car is constantly present. It includes the substances necessary for the coating to change from a mobile liquid to a solid film. Additionally, it serves as the pigment's transporter and suspending agent. The colouring agents are pigments, which may or may not be present. Pigments also provide a number of other crucial qualities.

Based on the types and combinations of vehicle and pigment employed in their composition, organic coatings are frequently categorised into around a dozen major categories. They are dispersion coatings, emulsion coatings, latex coatings, varnishes, lacquers, enamels, and paints. However, due to the intricacy of contemporary formulations, it might be challenging to distinguish between the many varieties. Organic finish systems often consist of multiple layers or coats, and these layers are frequently divided into three categories: primers, intermediate coats, and finish coats.

5.26.1.1 Primers

These are the initial surface coatings that have been applied (except for fillers, in some cases). Primer coatings may frequently be unnecessary where chemical pretreatments are utilised. There are two sorts of primers for industrial or production finishing: baking-types and air-dry types. The air-dry varieties are typically referred to as paints and have drying oil vehicle bases. They might or might not have resin modifications. They aren't as often used as baking-type primers, which have varnish or resin vehicle bases and mostly dry by polymerization. Some primers, referred to as flash primers, are applied by spraying and dry within 10 minutes as a result of solvent evaporation. The pigments in almost all primers give the primer the majority of its anti-corrosion qualities and, combined with the vehicle, decide how well the primer adheres to the base metal.

5.26.1.2 Intermediate coats

These include surfacers, fillers, and sealants. They can be used before or after the primer, but they're frequently used after it and occasionally after the surfacer layer. Their purpose is to cover up significant surface abnormalities or little flaws. They typically resemble putty and are made of various materials. Their primary requirements are that they: I harden with the least amount of shrinkage; (ii) have strong adhesion; (iii) have good sanding properties; and (iv) function readily and smoothly.

Surfacers frequently resemble primers and have the same chemical makeup as the priming coat with the exception of the presence of additional pigment. After the priming coat, surfacers are used to smooth out any small surface imperfections. Typically, sealers are applied either on top of fillers or surfacers. The main purpose of sealers is to stop the finish coats from "striking in" by filling up the pores of the undercoat. The entire coating system tends to become stronger as a result of this filling-in of the porous surfacer or sealer. The sealers are often made with the same kind of pigment and vehicle as the final layer when applied over surfacers.

5.26.1.3 Finish coats

Typically, the aesthetic or practical component of a paint system is the finish or top coat. But they frequently also serve a defensive purpose. Although the pigments used in primers are enough for preventing corrosion of the metal, they are typically insufficient as top coats, therefore the primer coats may need to be protected against service conditions. Their physical durability or colour retention after weathering may be subpar. There are one-coat treatments as well, where the finish coats are placed directly to the surface of the base material and serve as the only protective layer.

5.26.2 Vehicles

Vehicles are made of film-forming components as well as a variety of additional ingredients, such as thinners (volatile solvents), which regulate viscosity, flow, and film thickness, and driers, which simplify application and enhance drying properties. The primary area of concern is the vehicle's film-forming component, as it is this component that largely dictates the nature and quality of an organic finish. It establishes the potential methods for applying the finish, how the "wet" finish will cure to a hard film, allows for adherence to the metal surface, and typically affects the finish's longevity.

Oil, resin, and varnish are the three basic categories into which automobiles can be divided. The straight drying oil types of cars are the most basic and among the oldest. Resins as a class can be utilised to create varnish-like vehicles or as standalone vehicles when combined with drying oils. Resins, drying or nondrying oils, as well as the necessary amounts of thinners and driers, make up varnish vehicles. They are frequently utilised by themselves as a complete organic finish.

5.26.2.1 Drying oils

In industrial finishes, oil-only vehicles are mainly utilised in small amounts. The most popular oil is undoubtedly linseed oil. There are numerous types that vary in drying speed as well as features like water resistance, colour, and hardness.

5.26.2.2 Tung oil or china wood oil

When property treated, excels all other drying oils in speed of drying, hardening, and water resistance. Oiticica oil is similar to tung oil in many of its properties. Dehydrated castor oil dries better than linseed oil, but slower than tung oil. Some of its advantages are good color and color retention, and flexibility. The oils from some fish are also used as drying oils. If processed properly, they dry reasonably well and have little odor. They are often used in combination with other oils. Perilla oil is quite similar in properties to fast-drying linseed oil. Its use is largely dependent upon its price and availability. Soybean oil is the slowest drying in the drying oil classes, and is usually used in combination with some faster-drying oil such as linseed oil.

5.26.3 Resins

Although both natural and synthetic resins can serve as organic coating vehicles, today the natural types, such as rosin, have been largely replaced by plastic resins. Nearly all the plastic and resins both thermosets and thermoplastics as well as many elastomers can be used as film formers, and frequently two or more kinds are combined to give the set of properties desired. Typical thermoplastics used in vehicles are acrylics, acetates, butyrates, and vinyls. Commonly used thermosets for vehicles include phenolics, alkyds, melamines, ureas, and epoxies.

5.26.4 Pigments

Pigments are the second of the two principal components that make up most organic finishes. They contribute a number of important characteristics to a coating. They, first of all, serve a decorative function. The choice of color and shades of color by use of one or combinations of pigments is practically unlimited. Closely associated with color is the hiding power function or their ability to obscure the surface of the material being finished. In many primers the principal function of pigments is to prevent corrosion of the base metal. In other cases they may be added to counteract the destructive action of ultraviolet light rays. Pigments also help give body and good flow characteristics to the finish. And, finally, some pigments may give to organic coatings what is termed package stability; that is, they keep the coating material in usable condition in the container until ready for use.

Pigments can be conveniently divided into three classes as follows: (i) white hiding pigments, (ii) colored pigments, and (iii) extender or inert pigments. White pigments are used not only in white paints and enamels, but also in making white bases for the tinted and light shades. Colored pigments furnish the finish with both opacity and color. They may be used by themselves to form solid colors, or in combination with whites to produce tints, and often provide rust-inhibitive properties. For example, red lead, certain lead chromates, zinc chro-mates, and blue lead are used in iron and steel primers as rust inhibiters. There are two general classes of colored pigments (a) earth colors, which are very stable and are not readily affected by acids and alkalies, heat, light, and moisture, and (b) chemical colors, which are produced under controlled conditions by chemical reaction.

The metallic pigments can also be included within this class. Aluminum powder is perhaps the best known. The chief functions of extender pigments are to help control consistency, gloss, smoothness, and filling qualities, and leveling and check resistance. Thus, particle size and shape, oil absorption, and flatting power are important selection considerations. Extender pigments are for the most part chemically inactive. They usually have little or no hiding power.

5.26.5 Enamels

Enamels are a close-knit dispersion of pigments in a varnish, resin, or a mix of the two. Enamels can either dry by polymerizing at low or high temperatures, or by oxidising at ambient temperature. They come in many hues and tones and differ greatly in composition, colour and appearance, and characteristics. Even though they often have a high-gloss surface, some of them can also have a semi-gloss, eggshell, or flat finish. As a group, enamels are strong and durable and provide good mar and abrasion resistance. They can be designed to withstand the majority of chemical agents and corrosive environments.

Enamels are likely the most utilised organic covering in industry due to their extensive range of beneficial qualities. Coating home goods like washing machines, stoves, kitchen cabinets, and the like is one of their main uses. For instance, artificial baking enamels are used to finish a significant number of refrigerators. Since these appliance enamels are often white, they must retain their colour and gloss to a high degree when exposed to heat and light. Automobile products, railroad equipment, office supplies, toys and sporting goods, industrial equipment, and novelty items are some more items coated with enamels.

5.26.6 Lacquers

The raw material for lacquer is lac resin, which serves as the foundation for ordinary shellac. One of the first lacquers used for centuries was lac resin soaked in alcohol. Spirit lacquer is the name given to shellac in modern times. It is just one of several different types of lacquers; all of them, with the exception of spirit lacquer, are named after the main component that forms the film. The most popular ones are cellulose acetate, cellulose acetate butyrate, ethyl cellulose, vinyl, and nitrocellulose. The fact that lacquers dry through the evaporation of the solvents or thinners in which the vehicle is dissolved makes them distinct from other coatings. Contrast this with oils, varnishes, or resin-based finishes, which mostly undergo oxidation or polymerization to produce a hard film. The difference between lacquer and synthetic-type varnishes is smaller as time goes on due to the high resin content in many modern lacquers, until one reaches modified synthetic air-drying varnishes. They may primarily dry through polymerization or oxidation.

At room temperature, lacquers typically take just a few minutes to harden and become dust-free. The practise of forced drying is common in assembly line operations. Therefore, a multicoat project can be completed without losing time between coats. Lacquers are typically not applied by brush due to the speed at which they dry as well as the fact that they are always soluble in the solvents used for application. Common applications involve spraying or dipping.

Lacquers come in an almost infinite variety of colours and can be either pigmented or clear and transparent. Lacquers naturally have good colour retention, although occasionally the use of pigments, altering resins, and plasticizers can have a negative impact on this quality. They resist marring and are tough. They don't naturally adhere well on metal, but contemporary lacquer formulations have greatly enhanced their adhesive capabilities. A wide range of substances, including water and moisture, alcohol, gasoline, vegetable, animal, and mineral oils, as well as mild acids and alkalis, can be manufactured to be resistant to lacquers. The volatile solvents in lacquers make them combustible both in storage and when applied, which can occasionally restrict their use.

Lacquers are frequently used to protect and decorate items that can be dipped, sprayed, roller-coated, or flow-coated due to their quick drying times. They are particularly useful for coating toys, metal hardware and fixtures, and other items that must quickly dry hard enough to handle and transport due to volume production. When repainting cars and commercial vehicles, lacquers are frequently utilised since they dry quickly without the need for baking equipment. For coating metal stampings and castings, particularly die castings, lacquers compete with enamels.

5.26.7 Varnishes

The components of varnishes are drying or nondrying oils and thermosetting resins. They can be used alone as a coating because they are transparent and unpigmented. However, their primary function in industrial finishing is as a carrier for pigments, which creates various kinds of organic coatings. Varnishes all have the same fundamental drying mechanisms. Depending on the nature of the resin and oil, any volatile solvents that are present first evaporate, followed by drying by oxidation and/or polymerization. Naturally, polymerization is more likely at high temperatures. Therefore, varnishes can be designed for either air drying or baking drying. Varnishes can be applied using a brush or any of the available production techniques.

It is clear that varnishes have a wide range of features and characteristics due to the wide diversity of raw ingredients available and the infinite number of combinations that are feasible. They are translucent and lack any discernible amount of opacity. Their colours range from an almost clear white to a deep gold. Japan is an outlier, a hard-baked, dark-looking varnish. Because there is carbon and carbonaceous particles present, it is opaque.

Oil-modified alkyd varnishes have some different characteristics from the other varieties. Alkyds that have been treated with oil typically have superior gloss, colour retention, and weather resistance. They dry quicker and generate a tougher, more durable film. However, they are less resistant to alkali than the other varnishes. There is no obvious distinction between adhesion and rust inhibitiveness, for example. Food storage containers, bottle caps, and other types of bandings are the main uses of varnishes as coatings in and of themselves. A clear finish coat applied over lithographic coatings is another significant application.

5.26.8 Paints

Sometimes, the term "paints" is used to refer generally to all forms of organic coatings. However, a paint is a dispersion of a pigment or pigments in a drying oil vehicle by definition. As industrial finishes, they are hardly used today. Primer use is their main application. At normal temperature, paint dries by oxidation. They dry more slowly than enamels and lacquers, are relatively brittle, and have a propensity to chalk with time.

5.27 OTHER ORGANIC COATINGS

These include:

5.27.1 Dispersion and Emulsion Coatings

Because many of these coatings are primarily made of finely chopped components, such as plastic resins, fillers, and pigments, suspended in water, they have recently earned the name "water-base paints" or "coatings." There could also be an organic media component. Water-base coatings come in three different varieties. Emulsions are aqueous dispersions of high-molecular-weight resins, often known as latexes. In a strict sense, emulsion coatings are suspensions of an oil phase in water, whereas latex coatings are dispersions of resins in water.

Emulsion and latex coatings offer low gloss, high resistance to weathering, and strong impact resistance. They are clear to milky in appearance. Composition affects the resistance to chemicals and stains. Ultrafine, fine, insoluble resin particles dispersed colloidally in an aqueous solution make up dispersion coatings. They are crystal clear, or nearly so. The gloss, durability, and weathering characteristics are comparable to those of traditional solvent paints. Clear finishes that are water-soluble and contain low-molecular-weight resins can be designed to have high gloss, fair to good chemical and weathering resistance, and high toughness. They behave and flow the most like traditional solvent coatings of the three varieties.

5.27.2 Plastic Powder Coatings

Several methods for applying plastic powder coatings have been developed. The most common method involves preheating fluidized bed parts before immersing them in a tank of finely divided plastic powders that are held suspended by a rising current of air. When the powder particles come into contact with the heated part, they fuse and adhere to form a continuous, uniform coating. Electrostatic spraying is another process that works on the principle that oppositely charged materials attract each other. Powder is fed into a gun, where an electrostatic charge is applied in the opposite direction to the part to be coated. When the charged particles exit the gun, they are drawn to the part and cling to it until they fuse together as a plastic coating.

Although the aforementioned methods can be used to apply many different plastic powders, vinyl, epoxy, and nylon are most frequently employed. Epoxy and vinyl both offer good electrical insulation and good weather and corrosion protection. The main reason nylon is chosen is due to its exceptional wear and abrasion resistance. Other plastics that are widely used in powder coating are fluorocarbons, cellulosics, polycarbonate, acetal, chlorinated polyether, and polycarbonate.

5.27.3 Hot Melt Coatings

These are made of thermoplastic materials, which after melting on the metal surface, harden. Either the plastic is sprayed on or flow coated while still molten, or it is first deposited in solid form before being melted and applied to the surface. Thick single coatings are achievable because there isn't any solvent involved. Hot melt processes are also frequently used to apply bituminous coatings.

5.27.4 Lining and Sheeting

To provide corrosion and abrasion resistance, different plastics and elastomers are employed as sheet, film, and tapes that are glued to material shapes and components. Typically, thicknesses fall between 3.2 and 12.7 mm. Neoprene, polyethylene butadiene-styrene rubber, and polyvinyl chloride are the materials that are utilised the most frequently.

5.27.5 Specialty Finishes

There are practically countless speciality or novelty finishes to choose from. The majority of them are actually lacquers or enamels to which unique additives or processing techniques have been added to create the desired results.

5.27.6 Most Common Types

Those that have a roughened or wrinkled appearance; this effect is produced by utilising high concentrations of driers, which cause wrinkles when the finish is baked. Crystalline effects are produced by yet another class of specialised finishes. By keeping the combustion byproducts in the oven while the coating cures, these are enamels in which contaminants are consciously added throughout the baking process. Instrument panels, office equipment, and a range of other industrial and consumer devices frequently have the wrinkling and crystalline finishes. In order to give lacquers a stringy or "veiled" appearance when sprayed by spraying, certain additives are added to create other odd finishes. Unique finishes with colourful effects have also been produced by using the silk-screen method to polish metals organically.

UNIT SUMMARY

In this unit, Grinding and finishing processes have been presented. The principles of metal removal by Grinding including Natural & Artificial abrasives, the Bonds and binding processes of grinding wheels are discussed. There are several Factors affecting the selection of grind wheels including size and shape of wheel, kind of abrasive used, grain size, grade and strength of bond used, structure of grain, spacing and kinds of binding materials are also explained in details. Standard marking systems of grinding wheels is explained. There are different types of grinding machines as Cylindrical, Surface, Tool & Cutter grinding machines are all presented with their constructional details. Special process of Centreless grinding is explained with the Advantages & limitations of it. Surface Finishing methods by Honing, Lapping, Super finishing processes such as Electroplating of metals, Hot dipping such as Galvanizing, Tin coating and Parkerising, alongwith Anodizing processes like Metal spraying by covering wire process, powder process and their applications are explained. Important surface coating processes like Organic coatings including Oil base Paint, Lacquer base, Enamels, Bituminous paints and rubber base coating as finishing process is also discussed in details. Various Finishing specifications are also explained.

EXERCISES

Multiple Choice Questions

Questions for self-assessment

1. Grinding wheel is specified as "A 46 K 5 B 17". Grain size of a wheel will be
   (a) Coarse (b) Medium
   (c) Fine (d) Very Fine
2. Grinding wheel is specified as "C 8 K 5 B 17". Grain size of a wheel will be
   (a) Coarse (b) Medium
   (c) Fine (d) Very Fine
3. Grinding wheel is specified as "A 600 K 5 B 17". Grain size of a wheel will be
   (a) Coarse (b) Medium
   (c) Fine (d) Very Fine
4. Which of the following grinding wheel will have fine grain size?
   (a) A 46 K 5 B 17 (b) C 600 K 5 B 17
   (c) C 8 K 5 B 17 (d) A 80 K 5 B 17
5. Which of the following grinding wheel will have fine grain size?
   (a) A 46 K 5 B 17 (b) C 600 K 5 B 17
   (c) C 8 K 5 B 17 (d) A 80 K 5 B 17
6. Which of the following specified grinding wheel will have Aluminum oxide abrasive?
   (a) Z 46 K 5 B 17 (b) C 600 K 5 B 17
   (c) C 8 K 5 B 17 (d) A 80 K 5 B 17

7. Which of the following specified grinding wheel will have Zirconia abrasive?
   (a) Z 46 K 5 B 17
   (b) C 600 K 5 B 17
   (c) C 8 K 5 B 17
   (d) A 80 K 5 B 17
8. Which of the following specified grinding wheel will have Silicon carbide abrasive?
   (a) Z 46 K 5 B 17
   (b) C 600 K 5 B 17
   (c) A 8 K 5 B 17
   (d) A 80 K 5 B 17
9. Operation done to make periphery of grinding wheel concentric with its axis to recover its lost shape is known as
   (a) Loading
   (b) Glazing
   (c) Dressing
   (d) Trueing
10. Removing dull grains in order to make grinding wheel sharp is known as
   (a) Loading
   (b) Glazing
   (c) Dressing
   (d) Trueing
11. Grain number of grinding wheel is ____ to grain size.
   (a) Directly proportional
   (b) Inversely proportional
   (c) Does not depend
   (d) None of the mentioned
12. Which of the following is a correct range for grain number of the grinding wheel for coarse grains?
   (a) 220-600
   (b) 80-180
   (c) 30-60
   (d) 10-24
13. Which of the following is the correct range for grain number of the grinding wheel for medium grains?
   (a) 220-600
   (b) 80-180
   (c) 30-60
   (d) 10-24
14. Which of the following is a correct range for grain number of the grinding wheel for fine grains?
   (a) 220-600
   (b) 80-180
   (c) 30-60
   (d) 10-24
15. Which of the following is the correct range for grain number of the grinding wheel for very fine grains?
   (a) 220-600
   (b) 80-180
   (c) 30-60
   (d) 10-24
16. Which of the following grinding machine will give a better result for rough machining?
   (a) Fine grain
   (b) Very fine grain
   (c) Coarse grain
   (d) None of the mentioned
17. Which of the following grinding machine will give a better result for finish machining operation?
   (a) Fine grain
   (b) Medium grain
   (c) Coarse grain
   (d) None of the mentioned
18. Which of the following symbol's range of alphabet represent soft grain in grinding wheel?
   (a) A – H
   (b) I – P
   (c) Q – T
   (d) T – Z

19. Which of the following symbol's range of alphabet represent medium hardness grain in grinding wheel?
    (a) A – H
    (b) I – P
    (c) Q – T
    (d) T – Z
20. Which of the following symbol's range of alphabet represent hard grain in grinding wheel?
    (a) D – H
    (b) I – P
    (c) A – D
    (d) Q – Z
21. What type of natural abrasive contains aluminum oxide and other impurities?
    (a) Emery
    (b) Diamond
    (c) Sand stone
    (d) Corundum
22. What type of surface is produced by external cylindrical grinding?
    (a) Flat
    (b) Holes
    (c) Round
    (d) Formed
23. As per Indian Standards the grain size '46' comes under the group
    (a) Coarse
    (b) Medium
    (c) Fine
    (d) Very Fine
24. What denotes by 8 in the (A46H5V8) mentioned marking system of a grinding wheel?
    (a) Grade
    (b) Grain size
    (c) Type of bond
    (d) Manufacturer's code
25. Which terms decides the size of abrasive partials?
    (a) Grade
    (b) Grite
    (c) Bond
    (d) Abrasive
26. Which part of the surface grinding machine mounted on the column and it can be moved vertically up and down?
    (a) Base
    (b) Table
    (c) Saddle
    (d) Wheel head
27. Which natural abrasive is used to make lapping compound?
    (a) Emery
    (b) Diamond
    (c) Corundum
    (d) Sand stone
28. Which one of the following features, refers to vitrified bond wheel?
    (a) Used for longer period due to dense structure
    (b) Used for longer period due to an elastic structure
    (c) Not sensitive to shocks and pressure
    (d) Suitable for wet and dry grinding
29. The depth of infeed per pass in dressing a grinding wheel should be not more than
    (a) 0.25 mm
    (b) 0.025 mm
    (c) 0.0025 mm
    (d) 0.00025 mm
30. As per Indian Standards the 'M' grade of grinding wheel comes under the group
    (a) Soft
    (b) Medium
    (c) Hard
    (d) Very Hard

31. Which one of the following cutting fluids is used during grinding mild steel?
    (a) Mineral oil
    (b) Non-synthetic cutting oil
    (c) Soluble oil
    (d) Paraffin
32. Which part of surface grinding machine carriers the table in its crosswise movement?
    (a) Base
    (b) Table
    (c) Saddle
    (d) Wheel head
33. What type of abrasives is used for grinding of tough materials?
    (a) Brown aluminum oxide
    (b) Green silicon oxide
    (c) Aluminum oxide
    (d) Silicon carbide
34. Calculate the spindle speed (RPM) if the diameter of the wheel is 300 mm and the surface speed is 25 m /sec?
    (a) 1259
    (b) 1459
    (c) 1529
    (d) 1592
35. A grinding wheel is marked: 51 A 46 L 5 V -23. Here what do 5 denote?
    (a) Kind of bond
    (b) Structure
    (c) Kind of abrasive
    (d) Grain size
36. The precision surface finishing operations, employed for producing extremely high surface finish, are called
    (a) Macro finishing operations
    (b) Micro finishing operations
    (c) Precise finishing operations
    (d) All of the above
37. Lapping is used for
    (a) Heat treated parts
    (b) Non heat treated parts
    (c) Both (a) and (b)
    (d) None of the above
38. Lapping is not suitable for
    (a) Tungsten
    (b) Lead
    (c) Brass
    (d) Copper
39. The following is preferred for lapping soft ferrous and non-ferrous metals.
    (a) Silicon carbide
    (b) Natural corundum
    (c) Aluminium oxide
    (d) All of the above
40. In lapping, the lubricant used to hold or retain the abrasive grains during operation is known as
    (a) Vehicle
    (b) Holder
    (c) Absorber
    (d) Retainer
41. The recommended range of lapping allowance to be left on the surface, for general lapping work, is
    (a) 0.0025 mm to 0.0050 mm
    (b) 0.0050 mm to 0.0075 mm
    (c) 0.0075 mm to 0.0125 mm
    (d) 0.0125 mm to 0.0250 mm
42. The following are the lapping operations
    (a) Equalising lapping
    (b) Form lapping
    (c) Both (a) and (b)
    (d) None of the above

43. Machine lapping is performed on
    (a) Roller bearings (b) Crankshafts
    (c) Pistons (d) All of the above
44. Honing is used for finishing
    (a) External cylindrical surface (b) Internal cylindrical surface
    (c) Both (a) and (b) (d) None of the above
45. The usual amount of stock left for removal by honing is from
    (a) 0.1 mm to 0.25 mm (b) 0.75 mm to 0.90 mm
    (c) 0.90 mm to 1.05 mm (d) 1.05 mm to 1.25 mm
46. Apart from honing machine, the honing operation can be carried out on
    (a) Lathe machine (b) Drilling machine
    (c) Both (a) and (b) (d) None of the above
47. The abrasive used in Super finishing is a
    (a) Bonded abrasive (b) Coated abrasive
    (c) Both (a) and (b) (d) None of the above
48. By super finishing operation upto _____ mm can be removed.
    (a) 0.025 (b) 0.050
    (c) 0.075 (d) 0.090
49. In Super finishing operation
    (a) The work rotates, the abrasive block reciprocates
    (b) The abrasive block rotates, the work reciprocates
    (c) Both abrasive block and work rotates
    (d) Both abrasive block and work reciprocates
50. Super finishing is largely used for
    (a) Internal surfaces (b) External surfaces
    (c) Both (a) and (b) (d) Flat surfaces
51. The wheels used in Polishing are disc shaped and termed as
    (a) Pops (b) Bobs
    (c) Tops (d) Lops
52. The following operation is performed after polishing.
    (a) Buffing (b) Superfinishing
    (c) Tumbling (d) Burnishing
53. In which of the following processes, highly polished steel ball are used instead of abrasive
    (a) Honing (b) Lapping
    (c) Polishing (d) Burnishing
54. Scale and sharp edges are removed in
    (a) Honing (b) Lapping
    (c) Tumbling (d) Burnishing

55. Largest amount of material is used in
    (a) Buffing (b) Lapping
    (c) Honing (d) Superfinishin
56. Lapping is not suitable for.
    (a) Tungsten (b) Lead
    (c) Brass (d) Copper
57. Lapping is used for
    (a) Heat treated parts (b) Non heat treated parts
    (c) Both a and b (d) None of the above
58. The Precision surface finishing operation, employed for producing extremely high surface finished, are called.
    (a) Macro finishing operation (b) Micro processing operation.
    (c) Precis finishing operation (d) All of the above
59. The following is preferred for lapping soft ferrous and non ferrous metal.
    (a) Silicon carbide (b) Natural corundum
    (c) Aluminum oxide (d) All of the above
60. In lapping, the lubricant used to hold or retain the abrasive grains during operation is known as.
    (a) Vehicle (b) Holder
    (c) Absorber (d) Retainer
61. The recommended range of lapping allowance to be left on the surface, for general lapping work. Is.
    (a) 0.0025mm to 0.005mm (b) 0.0050mm to 0.0075mm
    (c) 0.0075mm to 0.0125mm (d) 0.0125mm to 0.0250mm
62. The following are the lapping operation
    (a) Equalising lapping (b) from laughing
    (c) both A and B (d) none of the above
63. Machine lapping it perform on
    (a) roller bearing. (b) Crankshafts
    (c) Pistons (d) All of the above
64. Honing is used for finishing
    (a) External cylindrical surface (b) Internals in cylindrical surface
    (c) Both A and B (d) None of the above
65. The usual amount of stock left for removal by horning is form
    (a) 0.1 mm to 0.25 mm (b) 0.75 mm to 0.90 mm.
    (c) 0.90 mm to 1.05 mm (d) 1.5 mm to 1.25 mm.
66. Apart from honing machine the following operation can be carried out on
    (a) lathe machine (b) drilling machine
    (c) both A and B (d) none of the above
67. The abrasive used in surface finishing is a
    (a) Bonded abrasive (b) Coated abrasive
    (c) Both a and b (d) None of the above

68. By super finishing operation uo to __________mm can be removed.
    (a) 0.025 (b) 0.050
    (c) 0.075 (d) 0.090

69. In super finishing is operation
    (a) The work rotates, the abrasive block reciprocates
    (b) The abrasive block rotate, the work reciprocates
    (c) Both abrasive block and work rotate
    (d) Both a basic block and work reciprocates

70. Super finishing islargely used for
    (a) Internal surface (b) External surface
    (c) Both of A and B (d) Flat surface.

71. The wheels used in Polishing are disc shaped and turned as
    (a) Pops (b) Bobs
    (c) Tops (d) Laps.

72. The following operation is performed after polishing
    (a) Buffing (b) Super finishing
    (c) Tambling (d) Burnishing

73. In which of the following process highly polished steel ball are used instead of abrasive.
    (a) Honing (b) Lapping
    (c) Polishing (d) Burnishing

74. Scale and sharp edges are removed in
    (a) Honing (b) Lapping
    (c) Tumbling (d) Burnishing

75. Largest amount of material is used in
    (a) Buffing (b) Lapping
    (c) Honing (d) Super finishing

ANSWERS															
1.	(b)	2.	(d)	3.	(d)	4.	(d)	5.	(c)	6.	(d)	7.	(a)	8.	(b)
9.	(d)	10.	(c)	11.	(b)	12.	(d)	13.	(c)	14.	(b)	15.	(a)	16.	(c)
17.	(c)	18.	(a)	19.	(b)	20.	(a)	21.	(a)	22.	(c)	23	(b)	24	(d)
25	(b)	26	(d)	27	(b)	28	(d)	29	(b)	30	(b)	31	(c)	32	(c)
33	(a)	34	(d)	35	(b)	36	(b)	37	(c)	38	(a)	39	(c)	40	(a)
41	(c)	42	(c)	43	(d)	44	(b)	45	(a)	46	(c)	47	(a)	48	(a)
49	(a)	50	(b)	51	(b)	52	(a)	53	(d)	54	(c)	55	(c)	56	(a)
57	(c)	58	(b)	59	(c)	60	(a)	61	(c)	62	(c)	63	(a)	64	(b)
65	(a)	66	(c)	67	(a)	68	(a)	69	(a)	70	(b)	71	(b)	72	(a)
73	(d)	74	(c)	75	(c)										

Short and Long Answer Type Questions

Grinding

1. Define grinding operation.
2. Why is grinding so important in modern production?
3. What is the difference between `rough' grinding and `precision' grinding?
4. Why the natural abrasives are not suitable for making grinding wheels?
5. How silicon carbide is abrasive produced? Write its field of application.
6. How aluminium oxide is abrasive produced? Write its field of application.
7. Under what conditions are diamond, boron carbide and cubic boron nitride used as abrasive materials for making grinding wheels?
8. Discuss the various types of bonding materials used for making grinding wheels?
9. What is meant by 'grain size' of an abrasive material?
10. Discuss the various methods of making grinding wheels.
11. Sketch the various shapes of grinding wheels and write their fields of application.
12. What is meant by "grade" and "structure" of a grinding wheel?
13. What is meant by standard marking of grinding wheels?
14. How the grinding wheel is selected for a particular job?
15. What is meant by dressing and truing of grinding wheels?
16. Define "grinding ratio".
17. Sketch and explain the working of an external cylindrical grinding machine.
18. Sketch and explain the three methods of cylindrical grinding.
19. What is the difference between plain and universal cylindrical grinders?
20. Describe in detail how an internal grinder operates.
21. Sketch and explain the three methods of external cylindrical centreless grinding.
22. What are the advantages and disadvantages of centreless grinding?
23. Sketch and explain internal centre less grinding process.
24. Sketch and explain the various methods of surface grinding.
25. How the jobs are held during surface grinding operation?
26. Sketch and explain the following grinding processes: Form grinding, Gear tooth grinding,
27. Thread grinding and cam grinding.
28. What is a tool post grinder?
29. What kind of grinding can be done on the lathe?
30. What are disk grinders?
31. What are coated abrasives?
32. Explain abrasive belt grinding.

33. Write the drawbacks of abrasive belt grinding.
34. Discuss the various grinding process variables.
35. Write a short note on: High speed grinding.

Finishing

1. What do you understand by surface irregularities?
2. How is surface roughness evaluated?
3. What are the units of surface roughness?
4. Write on the following surface finishing processes: (a) Diamond turning and boring (b) Grinding.
5. Define Lapping process.
6. How is lapping done?
7. Name the abrasives used in lapping process.
8. List the functions of lapping process.
9. With the help of a neat diagram, explain the process of Mechanical lapping.
10. Define honing process.
11. With the help of a neat diagram, explain the honing process.
12. Define Buffing operation.
13. With the help of neat diagrams, discuss:– (a) Barrel tumbling process. (b) Barrel rolling process.
14. Define Burnishing process.
15. Write briefly on Barrel burnishing process.
16. With the help of neat diagrams, explain the Roller/Ball burnishing processes.
17. List the product applications of roller burnishing process.
18. Write a short note on: Powder Coating.
19. What is "Electrostatic Fluidised Bed" process of powder coating?
20. What is "Electrostatic Spraying"?
21. What is "Polishing" operation?
22. How is the polishing operation classified?
23. Give the limitations of polishing operations.
24. What is the level of surface roughness achieved after polishing operation?
25. Does polishing improve machining accuracy?

PRACTICALS

1. Observe the surface finish obtained in grinding operation for my Steel.
2. Observe the surface finish obtained in grinding operation for brittle material (cost iron)
3. Perform the lapping operation.

4. Perform the honing operation.
5. Perform the Buffing operation

KNOW MORE

Explore the historical grinding processes work in aluminum, copper, and steel using different methods. See finishing and superfinishing processes as an old practices of grinding and polishing action or similar operation in your near vicinity. Identify similar grinder making and finishing machines and processes around your locality and try to find how it is evolved with time as one could see the modern grinding and finishing operations today. One should observe it carefully.

SUGGESTED RESOURCES FOR FURTHER READING/ LEARNING

Reference books & websites referred

1. Manufacturing technology – P N Rao, Tata McGraw-Hill Publications
2. Elements of workshop Technology (Volume I & II) – S. K. Hajra Chaudary, Bose & Roy, Media Promoters and Publishers Limited.
3. Production Technology (Volume I & II) – O. P. Khanna & Lal, Dhanpat Rai Publications.
4. Fundamental of metal cutting and machine tools– B. L. Juneja, New age international limited.
5. Manufacturing Technology, Metal Cutting & Machine tools– P. N. Rao, Tata McGraw- Hill Publications
6. A Text book of Production Technology: Manufacturing processes –P.C. Sharma, S. Chand & Com. Pvt. Ltd., New Delhi
7. Production Technology – R.B. Gupta, Satya Prakashan, New Delhi
8. Fundamentals of Design & Manufacturing- G K Lal, Vijay Gupta, N. V. Readdy, NarosaPub. House, ND

VIDEOS

Grinding

https://www.youtube.com/watch?v=szCsHgI6qp0
https://www.youtube.com/watch?v=gcWj4OcteTk
https://www.youtube.com/shorts/IepSk3Ji2qM
https://www.youtube.com/watch?v=IXYZLxNd-a8
https://www.youtube.com/watch?v=PTU90sAR8xM

Polishing & finishing

https://www.youtube.com/watch?v=MRmlWUDPBvs
https://www.youtube.com/watch?v=F3zLabmwJQk
https://www.youtube.com/watch?v=LI-2FZSZTB0
https://www.youtube.com/watch?v=X0-_OwjQBgI
https://www.youtube.com/shorts/vqFb_MUY8w8
https://www.youtube.com/watch?v=-l-T08cZqb4
https://www.youtube.com/watch?v=dZxVqHmNtKY
https://www.youtube.com/watch?v=d86g0svbIG8
https://www.youtube.com/watch?v=0zCiO_WFvLE

Spraying

https://www.youtube.com/watch?v=xw-v9vnhd7Q
https://www.youtube.com/watch?v=pilpa2hHefQ
https://www.youtube.com/watch?v=iUeUZPkEFTg
https://www.youtube.com/watch?v=xw-v9vnhd7Q

INDEX